KU-736-616

FIRE AND FURY

The Allied Bombing
of Germany and Japan

RANDALL HANSEN

FABER & FABER

First published in the UK in 2020
by Faber & Faber Ltd
Bloomsbury House
74–77 Great Russell Street
London WC1B 3DA

Typeset by Faber & Faber Ltd
Printed and bound by CPI Group (UK) Ltd, Croydon,CR0 4YY

A CIP record for this book
is available from the British Library

ISBN 978-0-571-28868-7

FSC
www.fsc.org
MIX
Paper from
responsible sources
FSC® C020471

10 9 7 6 5 4 3 2 1

CONTENTS

No matter how you slice it, you're going to kill an awful lot of civilians. Thousands and thousands. But if you don't destroy Japanese industry, we're going to have to invade Japan. And how many Americans will be killed in an invasion of Japan? Five hundred thousand seems to be the lowest estimate. Some say a million . . . Do you want to kill Japanese, or would you rather have Americans killed?

Curtis LeMay

[The aim of RAF bombing] is the destruction of German cities; the killing of German workers; and the disruption of civilised life throughout Germany. It should be emphasised that the destruction of houses, public utilities, transport, and lives; the creation of a refugee problem on an unprecedented scale; and the breakdown of morale both at home and at the battle fronts by fear of extended and intensified bombing, are accepted and intended aims of our bombing policy.

Sir Arthur T. Harris

In order to win a war, should you kill 100,000 people in one night? . . . Proportionality should be a guideline of war. Killing 50–90 per cent of the people of 67 Japanese cities and then bombing them with two nuclear bombs is not proportional – in the minds of some people – to the objectives we were trying to achieve . . . LeMay said if we'd lost the war we'd all have been prosecuted as war criminals. And I think he's right! He and I'd say we were behaving as war criminals. LeMay recognised that what he was doing would be thought immoral if his side had lost. But what makes it immoral if you lose and not immoral if you win?

Robert S. McNamara

PREFACE

This book is a study of British and American bombing campaigns during the Second World War.[1] The first edition came out over a decade ago, in 2008. I am grateful to Faber & Faber for the opportunity to revisit and revise my work.

Although the absence of a British book contract was a matter of disappointment to me at that time, I am glad in retrospect that the first edition did not come out in the UK then. The elapsed time allowed me to gather feedback on the first version, to benefit from scholarship that has appeared since 2008, and, not least, to refine my views. I researched and wrote the first version of this book in my thirties, and I did so with the moral certainty of what passes in academic circles as youth. I hope this version, completed in my forties, reflects the maturity and balance that comes with middle age. I will let others judge.

This is not to say that I have fundamentally altered my conclusions. My overall view of the British bombing war remains as it was: with a few important exceptions, notably the Battle of the Ruhr, the Royal Air Force's *area* bombing campaign was a waste of lives, material, and centuries of beauty and culture. Moreover, the evidence leading to this conclusion was available arguably by 1943 and certainly by 1944. I was not alone in making the first argument; the second was, I think, somewhat more novel. For decades, Bomber Command and Arthur Harris came under criticism regarding the morality and effectiveness of the RAF bombing war over Germany. But that war also had its defenders. A large body of popular history, which is of course much more widely read than academic studies published by university presses, continued (and continues) to defend the bombing war, and the renowned military historian Richard Overy stood as something of a lonely academic defender of Bomber Command's military effectiveness. One never knows how academic debates will develop: witness Christopher Clark's 2012 *Sleepwalkers*, which argued for Germany's relative lack of responsibility for the start of the First World War, a thesis that had died with Fritz Fischer's 1961 *Germany's Aims in the First World War* and, in a more complicated way, Barbara W. Tuchman's 1962 *The Guns of August*. But it is reasonable to say that there is a broad scholarly consensus about the ineffectiveness of bombing, and above all area bombing, during the Second World War. Overy himself, without noting that he was in large measure criticising his own work, has reversed his position.

With this in mind, I have adjusted the portions of the book – particularly in the conclusion – that might appear, a decade on, to be tilting at windmills. But the changes go deeper than this, particularly as they concern the US campaign. They are very much a response to constructive criticism, mostly from other academics but also from general readers. In an age in which internet trolls are depressingly common and active, I felt reassured to find that many – indeed most – Amazon reviews of the book were considered and helpful. A reasonable criticism of the first edition was that the book's contrast between American and British bombing campaigns only worked because the first version largely overlooked the American air war against Japan. My initial response was that the book was about Germany, not Japan. But this is feeble: the American air war over Japan featured the same strategy – area bombing designed to destroy as much of a city as possible – as the British bombardment of Germany. This version thus includes three new chapters devoted to the American conventional bombing of Japan and its effects on the course of the war. The book's conclusion has also been revised accordingly.

I have also incorporated new literature on the bombing war and on National Socialism. On the former, Richard Overy published a magisterial 850-page monograph on the European bombing war. On the latter, German scholars have continued to revise our view of Albert Speer, which in turn led me to revise portions of this book. In the preface to the US publication of this book, I wrote that one source worth commenting on was the memoirs of Albert Speer.

Speer was the last man standing: all other senior Nazis killed themselves, were hanged at Nuremberg, or went into hiding. As such, he was able to tell his story without having to worry that those who had been in the room with him would challenge his version of events. His memoirs were, as all memoirs are, an effort in self-justification. They should be treated with caution, but they remain a reliable source. This is partly because they were vetted by the German historian and journalist Joachim Fest. Fest has, however, also attracted much criticism, and he admitted later that Speer had on some issues led him astray. The controversies surrounding Speer are nonetheless specific: they concern his knowledge of the Holocaust, his use of forced labour, and his claims to sympathy with the German resistance. This book does not rely on Speer's memoirs on any of these. Where it does use Speer is in his estimation of the bombing war's effects on German war production. It does so because I find Speer more reliable on this topic (he had little to gain in the late 1960s by commenting on it one way or the other), but also because defenders of area bombing quote Speer frequently – one is tempted to say *ad nauseam*. Given this, I thought it important to provide a fuller picture of Speer's views on area and precision bombing.

This is no longer tenable. Recent scholarship, and above all Magnus Brechtken's *Albert Speer: A German Life*, shows conclusively that Speer lied not only about the Holocaust and his (non-existent) relationship to the resistance. He lied about much else. Improvements in German productivity and armaments production after Speer became Armaments Minister were real enough. However, as was the case in his (also real) efforts to resist Hitler's late-war scorched earth orders, he hugely and shamelessly exaggerated his role and claimed credit that properly belonged to others.[2] Like other unreliable sources written by pivotal actors, Speer's writings cannot be entirely avoided, but they have to be approached with the greatest caution.

I have also incorporated more of Adam Tooze's exhaustive analysis of the German war economy, *Wages of Destruction*. Tooze's work in particular helped me to expand, following a suggestion by military historian Gerhard Weinberg, the chapter on the Ruhr.

Although this book is avowedly comparative and integrative, some readers may be unhappy with the balance. There is somewhat more attention given to RAF Bomber Command than to the American Army Air Forces, and the discussion of Europe is more extensive than that of Japan. The former reflects the fact that much of the moral and strategic debate focuses on the UK rather than the US; the latter that I am a Europeanist who reads German but not Japanese. Lacking language skills has not stopped many scholars, but I hesitated to go too far outside my intellectual comfort zone and draw conclusions about a country whose language I do not speak and that, endlessly fascinating though I find it, I know far less well than the United States, the United Kingdom, or the

Federal Republic of Germany. The conclusions I do draw are, I believe, well supported by secondary literature based on Japanese sources and facts that are themselves beyond dispute. I address the issue of Japanese sources at greater length in the conclusion.

I have many people to thank for their help in the writing of this book. My first debt is to my agent, Andrew Lownie, for backing this book and for providing many invaluable comments along the way. Thanks also to John Pearce and Bruce Westwood of Westwood Creative Artists, to Martha Kanya-Forstner of Doubleday, and to Julian Loose, formerly of Faber & Faber, for taking this book on. I am also grateful to Walter Donohue for his close reading and excellent comments.

I am also immensely thankful to the dozens of individuals – American, British, and German; soldier and civilian – whom I interviewed or who wrote to tell me of their experiences during the war. Inevitably, I could only include explicitly a fraction of these harrowing and often moving accounts, but all were immensely helpful to me. In this vein, I am particularly grateful to Sidney 'Tom' Wingham, whom I interviewed and who invited me to a reunion dinner for 102 Squadron, Bomber Command in July 2003; to Oktavia Christ of the Volksbund Deutsche Kriegsgräberfürsorge in Hamburg, who arranged the interviews that form the core of the first chapter; and to Heinrich Weppert of Würzburg, who allowed me to speak and solicit witnesses at one of his seniors association's meetings. Adrian Fort, author of the highly regarded biography of Frederick Alexander Lindemann (Viscount Cherwell), very kindly discussed with me Cherwell's role in the air war. Thanks also go to Jack Pragnell, who had me to his house for lunch, and for hours of fascinating conversation about his time in Bomber Command. I also owe a debt to the owner of Springfield (Arthur Harris's Wycombe home), who very kindly showed me around the house.

I owe a great debt to the archivists at the UK National Archives, Kew; the Royal Air Force Museum, London; the Bundesarchiv, Koblenz and Berlin; the Library of Congress, Washington, DC; and city archives of Hamburg, Lübeck, Würzburg, and Cologne.

My thanks also to the librarians and staff at Nuffield College and Christ Church, Oxford, for providing access to, respectively, the papers of Cherwell and Sir Charles Portal. The head porter at Christ Church was kind enough to show me Portal's and Cherwell's former rooms at my old college, and, to my juvenile delight, I learned that the room I had occupied as a research fellow had been Cherwell's drawing room. That day, Jonathan Wright (my former tutor and, later, colleague) and Paul Kent met me to talk of Cherwell's time at Christ Church, and Mr Kent sent me information afterwards. My thanks go to both of them.

For research assistance, I am grateful to Guy Tourlamain, Jonas Nahm, Nicholas Fraser, André Ghione, Patricia Greve, Margaret Haderer, Frederik Hayward, Asako Masubuchi, Farzin Yousefian, Aleksander Jeremic, and Joseph Hawker. Dr Janet Hyer, Dr Richard G. Davis, one of the world's greatest experts on the history of air power, Aleksander Jeremic, Farzin Yousefian, and Frederik Hayward, all read the complete manuscript, and I am immensely grateful for their many comments. Joseph Hawker once again proved his skills as an outstanding editor, and I am extremely greateful for his commitment and support. Asako Masubuchi helped me translate some key Japanese sources; the chapter on Japan's surrender could not have been written without her translations of Emperor Hirohito's words in August 1945. Takashi Fujitani and Andre Schmid provided comments on the Japanese chapters, and I am very grateful to them as well as to the Munk School's Asian Institute for their support.

For financial support, my thanks go to the British Academy, Merton College, Oxford, Queen Elizabeth House, Oxford, the

University of Newcastle upon Tyne, the Centre for European, Russian and Eurasian Studies (CERES) at the University of Toronto's Munk School, CERES's Joint Initiative in German and European Studies, and the Social Sciences and Humanities Research Council. The Munk School of Global Affairs and Public Policy itself is an ideal working environment and a word of thanks goes out to its engaged and helpful staff.

Many other people have taken time to discuss the arguments put forward in this book: Michal Bodemann, Timothy Cashion, Robert Falkner, Simon Green, Atina Grossmann, Jeffrey Kopstein, Timothy Garton Ash, Desmond King, Mark Manger, Rainer Ohliger, Clifford Orwin, Derek Penslar, Rebecca Wittmann, Peter Pulzer, and Robert Austin. Margaret MacMillan very kindly read and commented on the proposal for the book and met with me several times to discuss its content.

Finally, my thanks go to Katja, to whom I dedicate this book.

SUMMER 1943

I

THE DAY HAMBURG DIED

27 July 1943

At 16:30, a young boy, Ernst-Günther Haberland, was playing in a bleak courtyard.[1] His mother came to fetch him; they were going to the air-raid shelter. Following police instructions, she collected the family's most important documents, dressed herself and her son in as many clothes as they could wear, and put a rucksack on his back.[2] Her husband was at work, and she could not get word to him. They left their flat at Gotenstrasse 55 at 17:00 and headed to the Berliner Tor (the Berlin Gate), just a few blocks north.

Their neighbourhood was Hammerbrook, a working-class district about two miles southeast of the city centre. The architecture was characteristic of turn-of-the-century Germany. Most buildings were blocks of four- or five-storey houses. The apartments at the front of these houses (Ernst-Günther's family occupied one) were populated by the relatively affluent. The flats at the back were dark and small. They housed the poor. Some eighteen families lived in each house. The streets between the houses were narrow, and it was one of the most densely populated parts of Hamburg: 427,637 people – a quarter of the city's population – lived in Hammerbrook and surrounding neighbourhoods.[3] Between 1928 and 1932, unemployment in the neighbourhood more than quadrupled.

Ernst-Günther and his mother needed to get to the air-raid shelter at the Berliner Tor, some two blocks away. The building, called a *Winkel* (tower shelter), had been built in the late 1930s. It was a multi-storey bunker with curved outer walls and a peaked, oval roof. Many air-raid shelters were made of solid concrete and looked like massive rectangle blocks, but the one at the Berliner Tor was covered in brick. It was almost attractive, resembling a windmill without the sails. There were two large main doors made of steel, with steps leading up to them. The outer walls were just over three feet thick at the base (and about half that near the apex); the roof was nine feet thick. Inside, the shelter's services – heating and electricity, toilets, running drinking water, and ventilation – were all contained in a central, column-like structure. Between the column and the outer walls were rows of wide, backless benches just a few feet apart. A spiral staircase led down to a deep basement and the floors below. In all, some six hundred people could fit into the bunker, but during an air raid it was always far too full.

Ernst-Günther and his mother took their places. The majority of people there were women, children, and old men. Each shelter had an air-raid warden, often Wehrmacht soldiers or Hitler Youth. Most of the other young men were away fighting at the front. Soon, all the benches were taken, and the aisles were full of people standing. Sometime after 20:00, there were around one thousand people inside, and the massive steel door was closed and sealed. Latecomers hoping to enter were left standing on the steps.

Inside, it was horribly uncomfortable. People had barely any room to move. They made stilted conversation. The atmosphere was hot and stale, and everyone was overdressed. They were allowed only one bag in the shelter, so they wore layers of garments. Those who had not drunk enough liquid soon felt desperately thirsty; those who had drunk too much were in need of the toilet. Only the brave or foolhardy gave up their seat, for it would likely not be there when they returned.

* * *

As Ernst-Günther and his mother made their way to the bunker, a
thirteen-year-old girl, Elfriede Bock, was at home with her family.[4]
Like Ernst-Günther, Elfriede was a native of Hammerbrook. She
was raised by a harsh mother and a distant father, who made it
clear to her that he had wanted a son. 'I had no idea,' she said sixty
years later, 'that women could have any value.' The Nazis told her
they could, and did: as mothers, they were Germany's future.

Elfriede's father came home at 17:00, earlier than expected.
He ordered his wife and daughter to pack their things and get
ready to go to the shelter. Elfriede's mother looked startled, and
in her strong Hamburg accent she said, 'Why? It sounds like we
will never come back to this apartment again.' Elfriede's father
barked, 'Just do what I say and be quick about it.'

Elfriede and her mother left the apartment at 20:00, stepped
out onto the Süderstrasse, turned right towards the Berliner Tor,
and followed the path taken by Ernst-Günther and his mother a
few hours earlier. Elfriede was lightly clothed and carried a car-
digan. Everything else was in her suitcase in the basement of the
house. At Heidenkampsweg, the street showed the scars of stray
bombs that had fallen during an earlier raid. City workers were
clearing the sidewalks and climbing ladders to inspect the roofs
for damage. The air was dusty, dry, hot, and stifling; it was 32
degrees Celsius, an unusually high temperature for Hamburg.[5]

Once inside the shelter, Elfriede hoped that she would secure
a good spot, but all of the benches were taken. People were pushing past them looking for a place to sit. Elfriede heard a group
of women nearby frantically chatting. They spoke of a raid on
Hamburg a few days earlier, of a thousand planes over the city,
fifteen hundred bodies, and tens of thousands fleeing the city.

Elfriede viewed such reports as nonsense, though she wondered about the fifteen hundred bodies. She thought, *It must have been horrible to be trapped in a cellar for three hours. But so many aeroplanes? Almost a thousand? Impossible. The Allies couldn't have so many. No fear! . . . If only these women would shut up.*

They would. At 00:41, the first alarm rang out over the city, followed by a second at 00:50. Elfriede heard the bombers fly over, seemingly towards Berlin to the southeast. The aeroplanes soon turned, though, and the roar grew louder. The wishful belief that the city would be spared lasted only a few seconds. The bombers turned southwest towards Hamburg.[6]

At 20:00, as Elfriede was leaving her apartment for the bunker, a boy from an even poorer background, Werner Wendland,[7] was finishing a swim with three friends in the canal. It was close to the river and a favourite spot for working-class boys from the neighbourhood. The streets were hot and dusty, and the three of them walked back, behaving, one imagines, as boys at that age do – laughing, shoving each other and thinking about dinner. Back on his street, Stresowstrasse, Werner saw people with backpacks heading towards the bunker, pushing bicycles overloaded with belongings. He asked them what they were doing. 'There will be a huge air raid tonight,' came the response. The boys laughed it off. Until then, every large attack had been followed by a period of calm or nothing more than nuisance raids.

Werner returned home and told his parents the story. They decided to wait and see how the night would unfold. When the first air-raid warning rang out over the city at 23:40, his father told Werner to go to the shelter, promising to join him afterwards.[8] Ten minutes later, Werner, his mother, and his sister joined a neighbour and her daughter. They guessed that the Berliner Tor shelter would be full and went instead to a smaller shelter down the street. An hour later, Werner's father had still not arrived. Following a tip given by his neighbours, Werner went to the nearby air-raid bunker. It was so full that there was no chance of pushing past the crowds to reach his father. Just then, the roar of planes above became louder, and he saw the marker flares gliding down against the night sky. Werner thought, *If this gets worse, my mother and sister will need my help more than my father.* He headed back to the shelter.

He had barely arrived when the first bombs exploded. The floor of the cellar heaved and then fell. The walls cracked. Dust filled the air. Water spurted out of cracked pipes. People moaned and sometimes cried out. Others prayed. Werner thought about his father.

28 July

01:00: Berliner Tor

The bombing began. When the first high explosives landed in Hammerbrook, everyone in the bunker fell silent. Through the thick concrete walls, the distant explosions sounded like dull thuds. But they gradually became louder and closer. For half an hour, a carpet of bombs hammered the city. There were a few minutes of calm, then a massive explosion. The bunker heaved, then sank. People were thrown from benches and landed on top of each other.

For some time, the light had been flickering in the bunker. Then it went out. The electricity had gone, and with it the pump supplying fresh air. Soldiers forced the few men, at gunpoint, to operate the hand pumps. They got just enough air in to keep everyone alive.

01:00: Stresowstrasse

Werner and his family cowered in the cellar. As the fires caused by the incendiary bombs lit up the neighbourhood, the temperature in the cellar began to rise. They could either wait there or take their chances in the street. If they stayed, they risked asphyxiation, incineration, or being crushed. If they left, there were the dangers of the open street: bombs (old, unexploded ones as well as new ones), bomb craters, falling debris, and more fire. One of the men looked through the keyhole in the cellar's steel door to see what was happening. The roof and walls of the passageway were in flames. They had to get out of there.

Werner and some of the men pushed against the door, but it refused to budge. Debris had fallen against it, trapping them. The air grew thinner. Desperate, they searched the walls with a flashlight. They found an opening in the wall that had been constructed to provide a second escape route to the neighbouring house. Werner took a sledgehammer and smashed their way through.[9] He saw stairs leading up to an exit that, despite the pounding the house was taking, somehow remained passable. They dashed through a burning stairwell and into the neighbouring courtyard.

Holding his sister and mother by the hand, Werner pulled them out into the street. He wanted to get to what he thought would be the relative safety of the banks of the Elbe river, three streets away.

When he had left his street less than an hour before, it had looked like any other in the neighbourhood. Now it was an inferno, having been hit by some of the first bombs. The high explosives tore off roofs, and left wood, coal, and plaster exposed. They were followed by wave upon wave of incendiaries, creating multiple pockets of fire that spread across the floors – consuming the furniture, curtains, clothes, and books – climbed the walls, and travelled through the staircases. Air rushed in through the open roofs and smashed windows, and the fires grew more intense, pushing out more windows as the flames shot into the sky and jumped across to adjacent buildings. The flames sucked in more oxygen and pushed against Werner, his mother, and his sister with such force that they retreated into the next cellar, one house away. Werner later recounted:

It was already overflowing with people, tightly packed together. The air was awful and getting worse. It was so bad that some – mostly children – fell from the chairs and benches, and clung to the feet of those standing. People began to scream 'We have to get out of here!' A few courageous men forced the reluctant air-raid warden to open the door.

The flames had grown more intense, and a wall of fire stood between Werner and the street. His mother and sister were mad with fear. Someone yelled, 'To the middle of the street!' He took each by the hand and pulled them through the flames. They ran west, past Lindlcystrasse, across the hot cobblestones. 'It was a terrifying sight,' Werner later recalled. 'St Thomas's Church in flames, mannequins burning in the window of the C. & L. Meyer clothing store, trees blown over, and the tram cables snapped and dangling.' When they reached the relative safety of the Elbe, Werner left his mother and sister and made one last effort to find his father in the bunker back on the Stresowstrasse.

When he arrived at the bunker, the door was open. The entranceway that had been packed was empty. It was dark and very smoky. Werner could not see anything. He took a few steps into the darkness and heard something: the moans of the dying. Horrified, he fled.

By 01:20, the Stresowstrasse and the rest of the neighbourhood was an inferno. Fire leaped from windows on both sides of the streets, joining in the centre.[10] The cellars were death traps. Those huddled in the cellars of the neighbouring streets – the Wendenstrasse, the Sorbenstrasse, and the Süderstrasse – had a few minutes to make a decision that would save their lives: to leave.[11]

Residents ran for the safety of the canals. Those who tried to cross the main north–south road, the Heidenkampsweg, were stopped by the melting asphalt (asphalt melts at approximately 120 degrees Celsius). Their feet sank. Their trousers and dresses caught fire, and the flames climbed up them. They screamed loudly at first, then grew quiet, gurgled, and died.[12]

Some followed Heidenkampsweg north or south, past the burning buildings and falling debris. Those who were not crushed by falling buildings made for canals running parallel to the east–west streets. They jumped in and were cooked to death.[13] The water was boiling.

The fires in buildings on either side of the street merged into one and began moving in search of oxygen.[14] The entire neighbourhood was in flames. The bombing that night was unusually concentrated.[15] The pathfinders (lead aircraft that used flares to indicate the target) marked the neighbourhood with uncommon precision, and there was little 'creepback' (which occurs when bombers drop their bombs before they reach the aiming point – the point at which they are to release their bomb load). The weather was atypically hot by Hamburg's standards (the city's weather is roughly similar to that of England) and had been so for weeks.[16] It was 32 degrees Celsius in the early evening and humidity was extremely low. The city was a tinderbox.

It did not, however, go down without a fight. Relative to other German cities, Hamburg was well prepared, with an ample supply of fire engines, hoses, and men.[17] The city had over nine thousand air-raid protection police (*Luftschutzpolizei*, a civilian wing of the SS's *Ordnungspolizei*), backed up by Nazi party fire brigades (*Partei-Feuerwehren*), Hitler Youth fire brigades (*Hitlerjugend Feuerwehren*), and factory fire brigades (*Werkfeuerwehren*).[18] The Nazi party created its fire protection agencies in the summer of 1942, both as a means of shifting blame for the bombing war from the air force to civilian fire defences and to claim, with typical arrogance, that the party would take matters in hand.[19]

Hamburg had experienced one of the largest raids of the war three nights earlier, and the city's Gauleiter (regional Nazi party head) had ordered the firefighters to concentrate all of their efforts on putting out the fires. The headquarters of the fire brigade was located at the Berliner Tor, but it had dispatched the fire trucks to other parts of the city. As a result, they were on the wrong side of Hamburg when the bombing began and had to fight their way back through bomb craters, abandoned cars, and rubble. When they finally arrived in Hammerbrook, it was too late.[20] They could only combat fires on the neighbourhood's periphery, and most of their efforts were directed towards helping the victims. Firefighters in the neighbourhood had lost contact with the rest of the city, and the extent and intensity of the flames left them completely overwhelmed.[21]

Somewhere in the middle of Hammerbrook, the flames converged with unimaginable force. As they did so, a chain reaction began: the intense heat led the fires to rise quickly, leaving a gas bubble below. Cold air then rushed in, mixing with the gases and setting the 'bubble' alight. As the fires burned, more oxygen was sucked in and the process repeated itself. The inferno became larger and hotter, peaking at more than 1,000 degrees Celsius and climbing two miles into the sky.[22] The fire sucked all of the oxygen out of the cellars. Those in them gasped, put their faces to the ground, choked, and died. Then their bodies were incinerated.[23]

On the streets, howling winds were deafening, and they tore through the streets with a force that ripped tiles and doors from buildings, smashing windows, and carrying the debris through the air, crushing anyone in its path.[24] People with bloody feet stepped over rubble, bodies, and the wounded, ignoring the last as they cried, 'Take me with you, please take me with you!'[25] Mothers struggling against the wind felt their babies torn from their arms. Trees three feet thick were uprooted. Death had a random, godless quality. Some people burst into flames, while those a few feet away from them were spared.[26]

The inferno raged for five hours. At its peak, 133 miles of houses were on fire. The great city of Hamburg was dying. At 02:25, an hour after the bombing began, the senior officer of Hamburg's air defences jotted down a novel word in his logbook: *Feuersturm*.[27]

05:00: Berliner Tor

The bunker was still. The minutes ticked slowly by. The bombing had stopped, but Elfriede and Ernst-Günther had no idea of what was going on outside. The air grew worse, and people fell silent. In the early hours of the morning – Elfriede cannot remember when exactly – someone swung the bunker's steel door open, probably hoping to let in fresh air. Instead, people from outside poured in. They were refugees from the firestorm; most were burned, and some were naked. There was almost no fat left on their bodies, only burn wounds. Their tongues stuck out and hung down towards their necks. They lay where they fell and died.

Rather than fresh air, the open door brought in billows of smoke. Screams echoed through the bunker, particularly from the children. Elfriede heard confused cries for help, and yet more victims entered the bunker. Someone called out, 'Whoever can

THE DAY HAMBURG DIED

leave the bunker should do so now!' Elfriede climbed out, step-
ping over charred bodies. The view outside was extraordinary.
She thought, *Is hell like this?* The smoke burning her eyes, she
watched walls collapse, the wind and flames twist in a squall.
The inferno was unstoppable. It tore through the street and up
to the sky. Hydrants were uprooted. Burning debris was carried through the air. Elfriede recognised the old hot dog stand at
the Berliner Tor, but it, too, was picked up and swept away. All
around her, burning beams, planks, even parts of roofs, windows,
and doors were carried through the flames, dust, and ash.

Ernst-Günther and his mother emerged at approximately the
same time. 'The distant heavens,' he later remarked, 'were pitch
black, but above us it glowed red. You could hear the awful
screams of the injured. More and more came to us with burned
and torn clothes; their bodies were covered in phosphorous burns.
You could not tell whether clothes or skin were hanging from
their bodies.' Ernst-Günther recognised a neighbour who, stone-
faced, walked towards them with two suitcases – one large, one
small – in his hands. He opened them. In the bigger one was a
large object that looked like a charred tree trunk; in the other
suitcase were two smaller, but otherwise identical objects.

They were the charred remains of the neighbour's wife and
children.

Ernst-Günther and his mother sought to escape the heat in
the underground railway tunnels beneath the Berliner Tor. From
there they were taken by lorry to the Moorweide, a large park
in the middle of the city. They joined thousands of others and
waited to be transported out of Hamburg.

* * *

Elfriede and her mother pushed their way through the wind and crowds, making their way to the same subway station, where they stopped to rest. They saw screaming women lying on makeshift beds. There was one brown-shirted victim whose stomach was hugely protruded from smoke poisoning. No doctor came to him, and the efforts of others to help were fruitless. He died.

The three sat near the underground railway tracks for hours. Having no desire to climb up to the streets, they tried to find a way out by following the subway lines. They eventually made their way to the main station, the Hauptbahnhof, where they were reunited with Elfriede's father. He told them what he had seen: 'The houses in the Süderstrasse had been flattened, even the cellars were gone. There was nothing left of our house; not even one stone stood atop another. The entire street was a burning mass grave. The flames were shooting out of the cellars! The high explosives knocked the roofs off, and the incendiaries finished the job.' He closed his eyes and continued: 'On the corner of Süderstrasse and Ausschläger Weg a lorry drove into a deep bomb crater. No one survived. God, there were so many bodies. I saw people running down the street; they suddenly caught fire; they fell to the ground and died there. The air was so hot, it could suffocate you. I jumped into the cra-ter [among the bodies] and stayed there for at least an hour. [The British] dropped phosphorous, liquid phosphorous. People [cov-ered in it] jumped into the canals, but when they came up they were still burning. It was an awful fate, you can't imagine . . . so many charcoaled bodies. They were so small.'[28]

Elfriede and her mother joined thousands of other Hamburgers who fled their city. They left that night for the Lüneburger Heide (Luneburg Heath), an area of forests and villages south of the city, to which her younger sister had been evacuated. Her mother spent the next night crying for her lost belongings. And for her lost Hamburg.

The Day After

Hamburg was in ruins. For miles in every direction, all that remained of large apartment complexes were the outer walls. Approximately 35,000 people were dead.[29] Concentration camp inmates were forced to help dig out the bodies, which were thrown into mass graves at the city's Ohlsdorf Cemetery.[30]

The heat was still unrelenting, and the neighbourhood was soon full of the stench of death and the threat of disease. City officials cordoned off the area – they would eventually build a brick wall around it – until the thousands of bodies could be cleared.

In the Rathaus Karl Kaufmann – the city's Gauleiter and a committed Nazi who had urged Hitler to deport Jews east after the first bombings – had to decide what to do.[31] It was obvious that the Allies would not stop until they had obliterated Hamburg. Against orders, thousands were fleeing the city, determined not to live through (or die during) a third night of bombing.[32] Kaufmann gave the order to evacuate.[33] Over the next forty-eight hours, some 900,000 people – half of the city's 1933 population – left.[34] Hundreds of thousands climbed onto wagons, pushed carts around the hills of bodies and rubble, or boarded ships on the Elbe.

By the evening of 29 July, almost all those who could leave Hamburg had done so. The city was empty and on its knees. And once again, the bombers swept in at 01:00. Hamburg's defences had improved marginally over the raids (German defenders and searchlight operators co-operated more effectively, and ten RAF aircraft would be brought down), but radar was still hugely impaired. The RAF's targets that night were the districts of Rotherbaum, Harvestehude, Hoheluft, and Eppendorf, directly to the north of the city centre. They made up a beautiful, affluent residential neighbourhood. That night, the weather came to the neighbourhood's aid: heavy winds blew the pathfinders east, over what was left of Billbrook. As the bombers came in from the north, creepback brought bombs to the previously undamaged districts of Eilbek, Uhlenhorst, Winterhude, and Barmbek. The old centre of Barmbek was levelled, and 27,945 houses were destroyed. Fires raged, but the districts were – save for the stubborn – empty. One thousand people died.

The next two nights brought only nuisance raids, and on 3 August, Bomber Command launched the final raid of Operation GOMORRHA. A total of 749 bombers took off from southeast England. When they reached Hamburg, they couldn't see it. For the first time since the attacks began, a thick cloud had descended over Hamburg. The RAF's weather forecasters had got it wrong: not only was the weather over Hamburg not clear, it had become a thunderstorm. The pilots struggled to maintain control as their planes were knocked about the sky. Lightning flashed everywhere. The bombers jettisoned their loads where they could; the bombs fell aimlessly across Hamburg, creating local fires but causing no significant damage. The firestorm was not repeated. It was, as a local newspaper put it sixty years later, as if the heavens took pity on the razed city and said 'enough'.

Three weeks after the attack, most of the area where the firestorm had raged was still cordoned off. Rats and large cockroaches swarmed through the ruins. Somehow, Werner managed to get to the bunker at Stresowstrasse 88. He found his father's hat and his empty suitcase. He never saw his friends again.

FOUR YEARS EARLIER

THE BLITZ: BOMBING CIVILIANS AND DESTROYING HOUSES

On 1 September 1939, German planes appeared over the central Polish city of Wieluń. Their bomb bays opened.[1] The synagogue, church, hospital, and houses below exploded. Terrified residents streamed out of the city. They found little respite: Stuka dive-bombers, which would terrify civilians across Europe, strafed them. Bodies littered the roads. The operation was repeated in dozens of cities across the country.

As the bombers laid waste to Poland's cities, 1.5 million German soldiers poured across its borders from the west and north. While Germany's air force swept the few modern planes the Poles could muster from the skies, fast-moving German tanks burst through Polish positions, surrounded them, and destroyed them.[2] The Polish government desperately hoped that the British and French would honour their guarantee to intervene. On 17 September, foreign troops indeed arrived, but they were not Anglo-French: Stalin ordered his forces to attack Poland from the east. The Poles put up a resistance that can only be described as heroic and managed to inflict 45,000 casualties on the Germans, but the outcome was never in doubt. By October, it was over. The Germans, at this point 'enthusiastic advocates of unconditional surrender', had utterly crushed the Poles; more than 100,000 Polish soldiers were dead.[3]

During and after the campaign, Wehrmacht tactics showed uncompromising brutality. Over the course of a three-week campaign, German forces burned 531 towns and villages (with Warsaw and the province of Łódź suffering particularly heavy damage).[4] On 25 September, two days before the Polish surrender, the Luftwaffe launched an incendiary raid on the centre of Warsaw, dropping 632 tonnes of bombs – at that point, the largest air raid in history.[5] 'Dante's description of the Inferno,' wrote the Polish-Jewish diarist Chaim Kaplan (whom the Germans would later murder in Treblinka) 'is mild compared to the inferno raging in Warsaw.'[6] The bombing of the Polish capital was not, strictly speaking, terror bombing: it was designed to aid an advancing German army and was akin to shelling during a siege.[7] But it was a horror to those on the ground, and it left between 2,500 and 7,000 people dead.[8]

Next on the list was Rotterdam: On 13 May 1940, the Wehrmacht was outside the city. The general in command of the 9th Panzer Division warned the Dutch defenders that, unless they surrendered, their city would suffer 'complete destruction' at the hands of the Luftwaffe. The Dutch duly surrendered, and on 14 May, General Schmidt of XXXIX Corps ordered Luftwaffe units to postpone the bombing.[9] In spite of that, one hundred bombers appeared over the city. Schmidt made frantic attempts with red flares to recall the bombers, and over forty returned. The remaining bombers nonetheless destroyed, with the help of leaking oil installations, 2.8 square miles of the city and killed 850 people.[10] The German army entered Rotterdam unopposed.

By late summer 1940, it was Britain's turn. On 7 September 1940, a Londoner named Colin Perry was cycling over Chipstead Hill, Surrey. He heard the by-now-familiar drone of planes overhead and looked up to see whether they were British fighters. They were not. 'Directly above me were literally hundreds of planes, Germans! The sky was full of them. Bombers hemmed in with fighters, like bees around their queen, like destroyers around the battleship!'[11]

Over the course of the day and into the evening, German bombers hammered the London docks and the surrounding East End neighbourhoods, among the poorest in the city. As an inferno consumed the docks, the destruction spread through the Isle of Dogs, West Ham, Bermondsey, Stepney, Whitechapel, Poplar, Bow, and Shoreditch. In one Bow church, people knelt on the ground, wept, and prayed. They were spared; some four hundred others were not.

The next night, the Germans were back. More than 170 bombers hit the East End again, killing another 400. On 9 September, still more – 200 – bombers arrived by day, killing 370.

As the bombers hammered the city, those Londoners who sought public shelter first made for the capital's dirty, dank, and in many cases disease-ridden public shelters. Later, they headed to the Underground stations. The government initially did not want to open Tube stations to the public, but local opinion forced its hand: within five days, 'there was a stampede to the stations'.[12] Crowded onto station floors, escalators, and platforms, 120,000 people sought safety in London's literal underground.[13]

They were not always safe there. On the 19th, as German bombers continued to hammer the capital, bombs landed near the Tube station at Balham. The roadway caved in, the mains burst, and the water gushed into the station below. Ballast, sand, and water mixed together, and cascaded down the escalators and steps. Slime began filling the station. 'All you could hear,' remembered one air defence worker, 'was the sound of screaming and rushing water.' The next morning, sixty-four Londoners lay dead with a pile of sludge on top of them.[14]

In relation to the enormous size of London – then as now a city of eight million – the numbers in the shelters and Underground were small. Only four per cent of Londoners sought shelter in Tube stations; the majority, befitting a city of houses, opted to stay in their homes.[15]

The September attacks were the first serious daylight raids on the capital and part of the Battle of Britain, Hitler's effort to use bombing to prepare for an invasion. It has no clear starting date: air raids occurred sporadically in June and July and intensified during August. At that time, the German Luftwaffe launched a costly but effective campaign against Britain's industrial production, fighter bases, and shipping infrastructure. Although the targets were industrial, imprecise bombing – there was little in the way of aiming technology at this point in the war – meant that neighbourhoods were also hit. In July, 258 civilians were killed; in August, the figure was three times that: 1,075 people, including 136 children and 392 women.[16]

In the last weeks of August, Luftwaffe commanders deduced from intelligence reports that Fighter Command was a spent force.[17] Following a long-established plan, the German air force shifted targets as a prelude to an invasion.[18] The Luftwaffe bombed industrial, military, and transportation targets around large urban centres.[19] German bombers hit Bristol, Liverpool, and Birmingham at night. On 2 September, Göring ordered the systematic destruction of targets in London. Three days later, Hitler directed the Luftwaffe to undertake a general campaign against urban targets, including the capital, and against British morale.[20] 'The object of the attack,' writes historian Richard Overy, 'was to do serious damage to London's capacity as Britain's major port, to undermine the infrastructure necessary for the war economy as well as to intimidate the population. German bombing was intended to affect morale indirectly, rather than undermine it by deliberately indiscriminate or terror attacks.'[21]

For the next nine months, the Luftwaffe launched raids on London and other British cities. On 17 September 1940, the Germans dropped 350 tons of bombs on London, more than the total tonnage dropped on the entire country during the First World War.[22] By April 1941, they would drop three times that figure – more than a thousand tons – in a single night.[23] In November of that year, the Luftwaffe launched its most infamous raid of the war, obliterating Coventry. Five thousand people were killed. At the same time, a series of raids on industrial targets in heavily populated cities – Liverpool, Manchester, Sheffield, Portsmouth, Plymouth, Swansea, Cardiff, Glasgow, and Belfast – targeted their residential neighbourhoods. The attacks seemed wholly indiscriminate to anyone on the ground. In the capital, raids that began in the East End extended westward, hitting the Palace of Westminster, Buckingham Palace, and West London's more affluent neighbourhoods. The rich fled to the countryside, turning some of London's most fashionable streets over to the lower-middle and working classes.[24] On 10 May 1941, the worst night of German bombing, 1,436 people died, and the capital's famous landmarks were hit: Westminster Abbey, the Law Courts, the Royal Mint, and the Tower of London.[25] By the time the Blitz ended, 40,000 Britons had been killed and 750,000 made homeless. The dead ranged in age from an eleven-hour-old baby to a hundred-year-old pensioner.[26] A million and one-quarter homes had succumbed to the bombs.

The Blitz was not only a horror; given the Germans' own aims, it was counterproductive. Luftwaffe raids on aircraft targets were costly in bombers and airmen's lives – probably too costly to sustain for long – but they had the effect of wearing down British defences.[27] Night-bombing of city targets, by contrast, allowed British fighter defences to regroup.[28] British morale famously failed to buckle; rather, it hardened. Londoners, traditionally divided by class, wealth, and postal code, came together, and they became the heroes of the free world.[29] More than anything else, the bombing of London swung neutral opinion to Britain's side.[30] When Hitler drew an end to the campaign in preparation for his attack on the Soviet Union, he left a UK that was physically scarred but morally and psychologically strengthened – and determined to give it back to the Germans.

The question was how. When Britain declared war on Germany, the RAF was made up of four main commands: Bomber, Fighter, Training, and Coastal. The offensive component was Bomber Command, which in 1939 had 349 bombers organised into five groups, spread out across the East Midlands and East Anglia.[31] During the initial year of the war, the first wartime commander-in-chief, Sir Edgar Ludlow-Hewitt, pursued a cautious strategy. He was bound by the government: before the start of the war, the Cabinet had publicly endorsed the (unratified) 1923 Hague Rules of Air Warfare: subject to a reciprocity condition, the intentional bombing of civilians was illegal; only identifiable targets could be attacked from the air; and such attacks could only be undertaken if the harm to civilians was negligible.[32]

The restrictions on Bomber Command 'were consistent with the widely held view in Britain that indiscriminate bombing was the hallmark of barbarism, whereas self-restraint was a feature of being civilised'.[33] But they also reflect realism: Chamberlain had no desire to provoke retaliatory attacks on British cities, and Ludlow-Hewitt knew that if he launched an aggressive war the Germans would wipe out Britain's bomber force within weeks.[34] During the first seven months of the Bomber War – until May 1940 – Bomber Command limited itself to leaflet campaigns (dropping Allied propaganda over Germany) and largely ineffective raids on naval targets.[35]

Ludlow-Hewitt's caution was warranted, but it cost him his job: he was replaced on 4 April 1940 by his protégé, Sir Charles Portal. Portal, educated at Winchester and Christ Church, Oxford, was a child of the RAF. He joined the Royal Flying Corps (RFC) in 1915 and rose quickly to the rank of lieutenant colonel by the end of the war. He was among the first airmen to drop bombs on the Germans. When the RFC became the RAF in 1918, he stayed on, and by 1927, he was running a squadron. After a stint in Aden, where, in a harsh example of colonial power, he bombed rebellious tribesmen into submission, he became a lecturer at the Imperial Defence College.[36] Three years later, he was promoted to air vice-marshal and appointed Director of Organisation within the Air Ministry. As he took over the post, the RAF was in the midst of a belated and rushed effort to expand in the face of growing German air power. Portal was significantly involved in the development of new heavy bombers (Stirlings, Halifaxes, and Manchesters) and the building of airfields. In 1939, Portal was again promoted, joining the Air Council, which was responsible for running the RAF.[37] From there, he was appointed commander-in-chief of Bomber Command.

Shortly after Portal's appointment, the Germans launched their invasion of the Low Countries. The bombing of Rotterdam provided the RAF with the excuse for a shift in strategy; the reason was the Germans' surging invasion westwards.[38] Portal was informed that he could target rail and oil installations east of the Rhine. It did not go well. The main British bomber – the Blenheim – was a slow and fragile aeroplane that was no match for German fighters.[39] During the June and July raids, many aircraft would turn back. Those that did make it often missed the target. The bombing was, in fact, so imprecise that the Germans, seeing bombs scattered across hundreds of miles, were genuinely unsure of what the target was. The RAF suffered high casualties in the process. On 2 July, twelve aircraft took off for raids on oil targets; ten turned back, and one of the two aircraft that continued was destroyed. The story was the same throughout the rest of the month.[40]

From then, things only got worse. On 13 August, as the Battle of Britain was picking up, twelve aircraft were sent to attack a German airfield at Aalborg in northern Denmark, the site of an earlier disastrous raid.[41] Twenty miles from the target, German fighters – Messerschmitt 109s – attacked them. The fighters strafed the formation mercilessly all the way to the target. When the fighters broke away at the last minute, German flak guns opened fire. It was a massacre. All twelve aircraft were shot down, and only nine of the thirty-three aircrew who left England survived – as prisoners. One was blind in one eye, and another had a broken back. Throughout the war, Bomber Command's casualty rates would continue to be high, and the psychological effects on those who survived were often profound. On one early 1941 raid, a pilot watched the head of an observer be sheared off by a cannon shell.[42] The gunner climbed to the front of the plane and dragged the body back so that the pilot would not have to be behind a headless corpse all the way home, but it was too late; the pilot never flew again.

As British bombing produced few results, and as the German war machine went from success to success, constraints on Bomber Command started to fall away.[43] In July, pilots were given discretion in choosing any military or military-economic targets (which were themselves defined increasingly broadly). In September, the policy of bringing back unused bombs was abandoned in favour of an order to bomb anything worth bombing. As London suffered the Blitz in September and October, all constraints on bombing were lifted, and on 30 October, Bomber Command was ordered to target 'morale' through 'heavy material destruction

– 34 –

in large towns'.[44] 'The decision,' writes historian Richard Overy, 'paved the way for the escalation of the RAF campaign during 1941 and 1942 into full-scale city bombing.'[45]

On 16 December 1940, 134 bombers – Wellingtons, Whitleys, Hampdens, and Blenheims – set out for Mannheim. They bombed the centre of the city successfully and returned home. The mission killed 34 people, injured 81, and bombed out 1,266. The War Cabinet authorised the raid – a forerunner of area bombing – in retaliation for heavy German bombing of English cities, especially Coventry and Southampton.[46]

By then, Portal was no longer commander-in-chief of Bomber Command. He had been promoted to Chief of Air Staff on 4 October 1940. Sir Richard Peirse, an uncompromising advocate of precision bombing, replaced Portal as commander-in-chief. Throughout the autumn of 1940 and the spring of 1941, oil remained the first target when weather allowed, with German barges as the second (Bomber Command would destroy some 12 per cent of the German fleet).[47] The RAF made a valiant effort, but poor precision meant that the Germans hardly realised that oil was the intended target.

As the bombing war progressed without producing results, Portal began to lose faith. He was instinctively a supporter of precision bombing. In 1940, he held the view 'that bombers were best employed against coherent target systems and precise objectives'.[48] But he was nonetheless moving towards area bombing. In July, he made almost casual mention of the possibilities of attacking German morale. At that time, the aircraft industry was the first target, oil the second. The difficulty with both, Portal (then still commander-in-chief) wrote, is that the targets were 'isolated and in sparsely inhabited districts', meaning that 'the very high percentage of bombers which inevitably miss the actual target will hit nothing else important and do no damage'. Where attacks dispersed over the widest area of Germany, they would increase 'the moral effect of our operations by the alarm and disturbance created over the wider area'. Here, less than a year into the bombing war, were the seeds of area bombing.[49] Four months later, Portal – now issuing rather than receiving the directives – wrote to Peirse and instructed him to attack electricity and gas plants located in the centre of Berlin and other German towns. Bombers on these runs should carry 'high explosives, incendiary and delay-action bombs with perhaps an occasional mine'; the first sorties would 'cause fires, either on or in the vicinity of the targets so . . . they should carry a high proportion of incendiary bombs'.[50] The prime minister was moving in the same direction. 'We have seen,' he wrote with typical Churchillian prose on 2 November 1940, 'what inconvenience the attack on the British civilian population has caused us, and there is no reason why the enemy should be freed from all such embarrassments.'[51]

RAF strategy would remain focused on precision bombing of oil, aircraft, and, from the spring of 1941, U-boat targets, for the rest of the year, but the policy's days were numbered. It had not produced results: bombs continued to miss their target, and those that hit did little evident damage. A successful precision-bombing campaign required good weather, good visibility, and limited defence. These three conditions were rarely, if ever, met. David Butt, a minor official in the Statistical Department, used reconnaissance photos and Bomber Command's own reports to determine bombing accuracy. He concluded that, at best, only two out of every three of the bombers dropped their loads within a five-mile radius of their target. It was, writes Max Hastings, 'the low-water mark in the wartime fortunes of Bomber Command'.[52]

If it was impossible to bomb precisely, then there were only two choices: bombing imprecisely or not bombing at all. British forces had been driven from the Continent, and re-establishing a British military presence was out of the question.[53] The Soviets had become an ally in July 1941, but until December they would be wholly engaged in a defensive conflict. Their survival was more in doubt than that of the British. And the Americans were still not in the war. An end to bombing was unthinkable, and with precision bombing increasingly discredited all that was left was area bombing.

Still, few people at this point or any other in the war were prepared to countenance the deliberate killing of German civilians as an end in itself; it had to produce some measurable good for the war. The concept of 'morale', which would be worn down through city bombing, seemed to offer hope towards that end.

Portal, who had by late 1941 finally converted to area bombing, put the case for targeting morale to Churchill in a September 1941 memorandum.[54] 'It must be realised,' he wrote,

> that attack on morale is not a matter of pure killing, although
> the fear of death is unquestionably an important factor. It
> is rather the general dislocation of industrial and social life
> arising from damage to industrial plant, dwelling houses,
> shops, utility and transportation services, from resultant
> absenteeism and, in fact, from interference with all that goes
> to make up the general activity of a community . . .
>   [T]he morale of the country as a whole will crack
> provided a high enough proportion of town dwellers is
> affected by the general dislocation produced by bombing.

Bombing the Germans into submission required will, but above all it required money. 'The strength required to obtain decisive results against German morale,' Portal concluded, 'may be estimated at 4,000 heavy bombers and that the time taken would be about 6 months.'[55] Britain's daily availability of bombs was approximately five hundred at this point.

Churchill responded two days later with a letter that – in the light of his earlier support for Bomber Command – was surprisingly blunt and dismissive. 'It is very disputable whether bombing by itself will be a decisive factor in the present war. On the contrary, all that we have learnt since the war began shows that its effects, both physical and moral, are greatly exaggerated . . . The most we can say is that it will be a heavy and I trust seriously increasing annoyance.'[56]

Portal waited five days to reply. When he did, he gave the prime minister a short history lesson. 'Since the fall of France,' he wrote,

it has been a fundamental principle of our strategy that victory over Germany could not be hoped for until German morale and German material strength had been subjected to a bombing offensive of the greatest intensity. This principle was clearly stated [by you] more than a year ago . . . and has been reaffirmed by you on several occasions.

In their recent review of General Strategy, which you approved, the Chiefs of Staff [i.e. senior personnel from the Army, Navy, and Air Force], stated: 'It is in bombing on a scale undreamed of in the last war that we find the new weapon on which we must principally depend for the destruction of economic life and morale . . . After meeting the needs of our own security, therefore, we give the heavy bomber first priority in production, for only the heavy bomber can produce the conditions under which other offensive forces can be deployed.[57]

Portal then threw the matter back into the prime minister's lap:

I feel bound to restate these facts, because I find them hard
to reconcile with your minute of 27 September. The Chiefs
of Staff Committee have regarded the bombing offensive on
the scale on which we hope to wield it in 1943, as a weapon
calculated, if not to break Germany, at least to reduce her
strength to the level at which our Armoured forces could
hope to intervene successfully on the Continent. If this is
a gross over-estimation of the power of the bomber, and
if the most we can hope to achieve with our bomber force
is a heavy and increasing annoyance, then, as I see it, the
strategic concept to which we have been working must
dissolve, and we must find a new plan . . .
It is my firm belief that the existing plan is sound and
practical. But other plans could be drawn up. We could for
example return to the conception of defeating Germany
with the Army as the primary weapon. I must point out
with the utmost emphasis that in that event we should
require an Air Force composed quite differently from that
which we are now creating.

Portal ended his note with a *coup de grâce:* 'If, therefore, it is
your view that the strategic picture has changed since the issue
of your original directive I would urge that revised instructions
should be given to the Chiefs of Staff without a moment's delay.'

Churchill declined the offer. He was not entirely comfortable with area bombing, but he was still less comfortable with
the idea of shifting Britain's strategy from the Royal Air Force
(and the Navy) to the Army. Britain was in no position to
launch an invasion of the Continent in 1941, and even if it were,
Churchill recoiled at the prospect of a return to the Somme or

Passchendaele.[58] Britain had no option but to fight back with the RAF; the RAF could only bomb, and the experience of the last two years of the war had made it clear that the only chance for bombing was area bombing. Churchill was not convinced – nor was Portal, for that matter – that area bombing would win the war, but he hoped it would produce some kind of effect.

Churchill wrote back on 7 October and gave his qualified support to the campaign:

> Everything is being done to create the Bombing force desired on the largest possible scale, and there is no intention of changing the policy. I deprecate, however, placing unbounded confidence in this form of attack . . . It is the most potent method of impairing the enemy's morale at the present time . . . [However,] even if all the towns in Germany were rendered uninhabitable, it does not follow that the military control would be weakened or even that war industry could not be carried on. It is quite possible that Nazi war-making power in 1943 will be so widely spread throughout Europe as to be to a large extent independent of the buildings in the actual homeland. A different picture would be presented if the enemy's Air Force were so far reduced as to enable heavy accurate daylight bombing of factories to take place. This however cannot be done outside the radius of fighter protection.[59]

This prescient letter was hardly a ringing endorsement of area bombing. Indeed, it was a call for targeted attacks on the German air force, which the Americans would press so successfully from late 1943, followed by a return to precision bombing of factories. But it was enough for Portal. 'I am now completely reassured,' he wrote on 13 October, 'that you accept the primary importance of our bomber operations and of the building up of the bomber force on the largest possible scale.' With Churchill's knowledge, if not undiluted support, the RAF had moved towards a policy of destroying Germany's ability to wage war by destroying its cities. There was no better person to implement this policy than the new commander-in-chief of Bomber Command.

3

BOMBER HARRIS TAKES OVER

According to legend, in early 1942, a young police officer pulled over a Bentley speeding on a country road near Uxbridge, west of London. The driver had a stern look and piercing eyes. The officer told him, 'You're liable to kill people at that speed.' The driver looked at him coolly and responded, 'Young man, I kill thousands every night.' He was Air Chief Marshal Sir Arthur Harris, commander-in-chief of Bomber Command. The story might well be apocryphal, but like many apocryphal stories it contains an underlying truth.

Harris was born in Cheltenham on 13 April 1892, raised in India (his parents were in the Civil Service), and, with money short (one brother had gone to Sherborne, the other to Eton), was sent back to an obscure boarding school in Devon.[1] After school, he emigrated to Rhodesia, where he drifted between a series of working-class jobs before settling down to farming on the eve of the Great War (he received a settler's allotment of 2,000 acres).[2] When war broke out, Harris signed up, with a little guile and a lot of pestering, for the 1st Rhodesian Regiment.[3] He served a year in the South West Africa campaign, setting sail for London when those operations ended in July 1915.[4] When he arrived, tens of thousands of men were volunteering for all branches of the armed services. Harris was keen to be one of them, but he could not find an opening. After rejecting the Cavalry ('I had no faith in horse warfare,' he later wrote) and being rejected by Artillery, he remembered an advertisement he had seen for the Royal Flying Corps (RFC).[5] Exploiting a connection of his father's in Kitchener's office, he jumped to the front of the queue, went through two months of desultory training, and become a fully qualified RFC pilot on 29 January 1916.[6] Harris was sent to London to defend the capital against German Zeppelin raids. This experience, he wrote, 'first brought about the conception of an air force independent of the other two services, and of independent air operations'.[7] Ten months later he was sent to France. There, in the summer of 1917, he experienced combat in a manner that would define his view of war forever. As he and his colleagues in No. 45 Squadron flew above the Battle of Passchendaele, they witnessed an appalling slaughter that eventually resulted in 250,000 casualties and cost the lives of 100,000 British and imperial troops.[8] He concluded then that it was worth bearing, or inflicting, any price to avoid a repetition of that horror.[9]

He did not see the end of the battle, though, as a debilitating flu sent him home. While he was back in England, Prime Minister Lloyd George combined the Royal Flying Corps and the Royal Naval Air Service (the Navy's air force) into a single Royal Air Force. The RAF came into being on 1 April 1918, with Hugh Trenchard, a man with an almost religious faith in bombing, as its first chief of the air staff.[10]

After recovering from the flu, Harris saw out the end of the conflict on training operations in preparation for a return to France. By autumn 1918, his squadron was ready and he was given a date to fly: 11 November, the day of the Armistice.

Harris was offered a permanent commission in the RAF and was allowed to retain the rank of major. He was posted first to India, then to Iraq, where the RAF helped see off Turkish incursions and tested bombing techniques on rebellious tribesmen.[11] In his words: 'When a tribe started open revolt we gave warning to all its most important villages, by loud speaker from low-flying aircraft and by dropping messages, that air action would be taken after 48 hours. Then, if the rebellion continued, we destroyed the villages and by air patrols kept the insurgents away from their homes for as long as necessary until they decided to give up, which they invariably did.'[12] The next sentence is revealing: 'It was, of course, a far less costly method of controlling rebellion than by military action and the casualties on both sides were infinitely less than they would have been in the pitched battles of the ground.'[13]

After two and a half years in Iraq, Harris returned to England in 1924 to go through the Army Senior Officers' School and then to assume command of No. 58 Squadron. With Trenchard's support, he was sent to an Army staff college in January 1928.[14] There, he developed his ideas on bombing and became a convinced Trenchardian disciple, sharing the chief's view that future wars would be won by bombers who brought the war directly to the enemy's cities, industries, and people. Harris left the college in 1929 and was posted to Egypt, where he did a tour of duty at Headquarters RAF Middle East in Cairo.[15] While in the city, he gave a 1931 internal RAF lecture on bombing: 'What is air bombing today but a reversion to the principle employed by the first intelligent ape, who gave up man handling and fights on the ground or in the branches because he conceived the more adequate and less risky result to be obtained by pitching a coconut down upon his adversary?'[16] The 'exploitation of range', he concluded, would allow the bomber to destroy enemy headquarters and enemy nerve centres.[17] There is no record of the audience's reaction, but the script was sent back to London. It landed on the desk of an official at the Plans Branch of the Air Ministry: Charles Portal.[18]

Harris returned to England in 1932, completed a flying course, and took over command of a base and its resident squadron in West Wales in March 1933.[19] Five months later, on 11 August, he was told to report for duty at the Air Ministry. In 1937, he and two other Directors of Plans – Tom Phillips and Colonel Ronald Adam – drafted a document entitled 'Appreciation of the Situation in the Event of War against Germany in 1939'. It is often quoted for its exaggerated prediction of 150,000 casualties in the first week of a German air attack, but it got much else right: France might be unable to cope with an assault by Germany; developing Britain's industrial output and restricting that of Germany might well be decisive; and the intervention of the Soviet Union could decide the war. As Harris's biographer put it, they 'succeeded in identifying two of the most crucial factors that were to lead to the defeat of Germany, the others being the protection of the sea lanes . . . and the intervention of the USA.'[20] The report also argued, oddly in light of subsequent events, that demoralising the Germans by attacking their cities would be impractical and unrealistic. Harris stayed at the Air Ministry until 1938, briefly commanding the No. 4 Group in Yorkshire, and was then sent to the United States to purchase aeroplanes for the RAF. He claimed to enjoy his time there, but the trip did not go well: the Americans tapped Harris's conversations, and he had to suffer through an afternoon and evening with an aircraft manufacturer 'afflicted with verbal diarrhoea to an extent I have never known before or since'.[21] Harris then had a final posting abroad, to Palestine. He again helped put down rebellious tribes – for whom he seemed to have some respect (or at least he expressed no disrespect) – and worked with the civil authorities – for whom he had none. 'There are two things you can get from aiding civil power,' he later wrote, 'and two things only – brickbats and blame. If you do not mind either of these things it can be at times quite amusing, especially if you are in a position to watch the machinations and the wriggles of "the civil power" itself.'[22]

In September 1939, Harris and his wife were in Norfolk, staying with their friends Jean and Adeline Tresfon. On the night of 3 September, two days after Germany invaded Poland, the Harrises and Tresfons were sitting around the fire listening to a crackling radio. Prime Minister Neville Chamberlain, his voice full of melancholy, announced, '. . . this country is' – pause – 'at war with Germany.' It was, Harris remarked, 'uninspired and uninspiring . . . about as stirring as a school-master confirming the fact that mumps had broken out in his prep. school.'[23] The four of them sat in silence for a few minutes. Jean turned to Harris and asked, 'How long will this one be?'[24] 'Five years,' replied Harris. And he ran to the phone.

The lines were complete chaos, and Harris could not get through to the Air Ministry. He finally demanded that the operator give him 'immediate priority'.[25] The term was meaningless, but it worked.[26] He reached Portal and said he wanted a job. Portal replied with words to the effect of 'I'll see what I can do.'

Four days later, Harris's phone rang. Portal would see him in London. There, Portal told Harris that he was to take over as Air Officer Commanding (AOC) of No. 5 Group, Bomber Command at Grantham.[27] He would serve there until 1940, when Portal was promoted to commander-in-chief of Bomber Command. Portal then contacted Harris again and asked him to become Deputy Chief of Air Staff, reporting to Portal and Vice Chief of Air Staff Wilfrid Freeman.[28] Harris viewed a return to desk work with horror but felt he had little choice but to agree.

His fears were soon confirmed. The hours were appalling.[29] He arrived at the office at 08:30 every morning and rarely returned before 01:00. He often would have to work until three or four in the morning; sometimes he didn't go home at all. After three or four weeks without a break, he would be given forty-eight hours to recover. And then the whole thing would start again.

On one of those many late nights, 29 December 1940, Harris was at a desk when he heard a great roar. He left his office and climbed up to the Air Ministry's roof to see what was happening. London was ablaze.[30] The Luftwaffe had launched its massive incendiary attack on the City; St Paul's Cathedral rose from a vast lake of fire and smoke. At steady intervals, the air would fill with the roar of an arriving bomber stream, followed by a swish as incendiaries fell into the fire below.[31] Harris called Portal to view the scene. They stood in silence for a few minutes. As they were turning away, Harris quietly remarked, 'They are sowing the wind.'[32] He later claimed that it was the only time he felt vengeful.[33] There is every reason to believe him: the claim that the RAF bombing of German cities was revenge for the Blitz is one of the great myths surrounding the bombing war.

Harris's earlier work – his speech in Cairo, his 1937 paper, and his pronouncements during the war – had caught the attention of Portal, who by then had come to share Harris's faith in area bombing. Portal quietly waited for the chance to make Harris his protégé. It came on 6 December 1941. On that day, Sir Richard Peirse resigned as commander-in-chief of Bomber Command after receiving much blame for poor performance. On 10 December, Sir Archibald Sinclair, a friend of Churchill, former Liberal leader, and Secretary of State for Air, saw the opportunity to move Peirse sideways.[34] Following the Japanese attack on Pearl Harbor, Sinclair needed a new air commander-in-chief in the Far East.[35] He saw his chance and suggested to Portal that Peirse take the job.[36] Harris's experience and his contacts in the United States (he had left the desk for a tour of the US) made him a likely candidate to replace Peirse.

A likely candidate, but not a certain one. Harris's style had already made him enemies. Lord Halifax, in particular, thought he was crude, domineering, and patronising towards the Americans.[37] During Harris's study trip to the States, his habit of speaking his mind had left his hosts offended. Against this, however, Harris had an inestimable advantage: Churchill's support. Although they differed in background, learning, style, and articulacy, they shared a flair for the dramatic. Both liked to present the struggle against Germany in grand, almost mythical terms. Whether this was enough to explain Churchill's affection for Harris is not clear, but for whatever reason he remained throughout the war strangely in thrall to Harris. 'Like Beaverbrook,' observes historian Gerard J. de Groot, 'Harris had a peculiar influence over Churchill which he used to great effect. Obstacles to the expansion of the bomber campaign miraculously dissolved after his arrival. Although he never got all he asked for, his ability to influence Churchill meant that the Prime Minister essentially allowed Harris to wage a private war.'[38] That war began with a mid-December phone call from Portal to Harris, offering him the job. Harris accepted. Portal replied, 'Splendid! I'll go and tell Winston at once.'[39] Harris sailed from the United States to England and took up his new post on 22 February 1942.

A week before he did, the Air Ministry drafted a new directive, issued on 14 February. For the first three years of the war, Bomber Command had been limited, first, by the need to protect private property; then, by the need to avoid bombing east of the Rhine; and finally, by the need to target industry rather than civilians. In early 1942, *before* Harris took power, all of this changed. According to the new directive, precision bombing was to be abandoned, and from that day forward, bombing was to be 'focussed on the morale of the enemy civilian population and in particular of the industrial workers'. To stave off any ambiguity, Portal clarified the directive in a follow-up communication the next day: 'Ref the new bombing directive: I suppose it is clear that the aiming-points are to be the built up areas, not, for instance, the dockyards or aircraft factories . . . This must be made quite clear if it is not already understood.'[40] The directive specified 'Primary

Industrial Areas' – Essen, Duisburg, Düsseldorf, Cologne – and 'Alternative Industrial Targets', including Lübeck and Rostock, Bremen and Kiel, Hanover, Frankfurt, Mannheim, Stuttgart, and Schweinfurt.[41]

For Harris, the timing could not have been better. The directive gave him exactly what he wanted, and he made no bones about it. Although not one to court publicity, he agreed to be filmed for public consumption a few weeks after taking office. As the newsreel rolled, Harris barely looked at the camera, exuding an air of bored contempt. He outlined his bombing philosophy in cool, clipped tones: 'The Nazis entered this war under the rather childish delusion that they were going to bomb everybody else and nobody was going to bomb them. At Rotterdam, London, Warsaw, and a half a hundred other places they put that rather naïve theory into operation. They sowed the wind and now they are going to reap the whirlwind . . . There are a lot of people who say that bombing can never win a war. Well, my answer to that is that it has never been tried yet and we shall see. Germany, clinging more and more desperately to her widespread conquests and even seeking foolishly for more, will make a most interesting initial experiment.'[42]

He nonetheless had to move carefully. Bomber Command was a wounded animal, and the vultures – in the form of an Army and, above all, a Navy hungry for more air support – were circling above it. Even more worryingly, political support was beginning to waver. On 25 February 1942, Sir Stafford Cripps, then Lord Privy Seal, rose in the House of Commons. Cripps was a devout Christian and pacifist. A vegetarian and teetotaller, he hailed from the far left of the Labour Party. In 1936, the party had to repudiate Cripps's argument that it would not 'be a bad thing for the British working class if Germany defeated us'.[43] In 1942, Churchill brought him into the Cabinet to shut

him up. It didn't work. 'A number of honourable Members,'
Cripps began,

> have questioned whether, in the existing circumstances, the
> continued devotion of a considerable part of our efforts to
> the building-up of this bomber force is the best use that we
> can make of our resources . . . I would remind the House
> that this policy was initiated at a time when we were
> fighting alone against the combined forces of Germany and
> Italy, and it then seemed that it was the most effective way
> in which we, acting alone, could take the initiative against
> the enemy. Since that time we have had an enormous access
> of support from the Russian Armies . . . and also from the
> great potential strength of the United States of America.
> Naturally, in such circumstances, the original policy has
> come under review . . . I can ensure the House that the
> Government are fully aware of the other uses to which our
> resources could be put, and the moment they arrive at a
> decision that the circumstances warrant a change, a change
> in policy will be made.[44]

Another disastrous raid – one producing little damage but losing many planes and airmen – might have given Cripps and those
of his ilk the excuse they needed to draw down the bombing war.

Harris was determined to not let that happen. Over the next
three years, he would fight two parallel battles: a military one
with the Germans, and a rhetorical one with the opponents of
bombing. He would receive qualified help from individuals
whose commitment to bombing, albeit bombing of a very different type, made them air purists in Harris's mould: the Americans.

4

THE AMERICANS

In December 1949, Bruce Simmons, a chauffeur, travelled to a modest ranch near Sonoma, California.[1] He was checking in on his employer, a US general. When he entered the semi-darkened bedroom, he saw the general lying in bed. There was no sign of movement. Alarmed, he bent over and put his face very close to the general's, checking for any sign of life. Suddenly, the general's eyes opened and he roared, 'What the hell do you want?' Simmons bolted upright and jumped back. The general let out a loud laugh, and said, 'You thought I was gone, didn't you?'

It was Henry Harley ('Hap') Arnold, the commanding general of the US Army Air Forces. At first meeting, one might be tempted to conclude that Arnold was Harris's American alter ego. He was irascible, gruff, and at times crude. He was ruthlessly driven and had no tolerance for those with a leisurely pace. He had even less tolerance for failure and could treat his subordinates with great cruelty. In one instance, the consequences were tragic. On a Sunday in early March 1942, Arnold called a meeting to sort out a bookkeeping issue: he consistently had fewer planes than official tallies stated he should. A lower-level staff officer, Steve Ferson, 'slowly and methodically' explained to Arnold that some planes were marked 'accepted' (i.e. delivered) even though a part was missing.[2] This was done because the manufacturer needed the money to produce planes for subsequent orders. When Arnold saw that his list of acceptances differed from Ferson's, he laid in to the hapless officer. Standing across the desk from him, Arnold

thrust his head forward and screamed. As the harangue continued, Ferson's face turned crimson and his veins bulged. He began
to sweat profusely. Ferson opened his mouth, as if to defend himself, but he never uttered a word. He pitched forward and landed
face-first on the carpet in front of Arnold's desk. He was dead
from a massive heart attack.[3] Although Harris's temper was also
legendary, it never killed a man.

Henry Arnold was born on 25 June 1886, in Pennsylvania, to a
provincial doctor of German descent, an austere and puritanical
man who dominated his household and refused to let his children
speak at dinner. Against Henry's will, Dr Arnold signed him up
for the entrance exam at West Point when the doctor's preferred
choice, Henry's older brother Tom, refused to sit it. To his father's
surprise, and Henry's horror (he was no keener on a military
career than Tom was), the boy received the second-highest score
on the exam.

At West Point, Henry resumed his indolent ways. He gradu-
ated in 1907 with a mediocre class standing of 60 out of 110 and
failed to make it to the cavalry branch he had initially striven for,
instead being assigned to infantry.[4] After two unhappy years in
the Philippines and another two in the United States, he wrote
to Washington in 1911 and asked to be detailed for aeronautical
work with the Signal Corps. The War Department sent back an
official letter asking him if he would be willing to train under the
Wright brothers in Dayton, Ohio, as a pilot. When he showed the
letter to his commanding officer, the man drolly replied, 'Young
man, I know of no better way for a person to commit suicide.'[5]

After two months' instruction under the Wrights, completed
in June 1911, Arnold was a fully trained pilot.[6] He was one of
exactly two in the US Aviation Service, but soon there would be
twenty-six more. Of this early cohort, ten died in plane crashes,
twelve quit after a few months, and four died of natural causes.

Hap was one of the survivors. After a glittering year in which he achieved a number of aviation 'firsts' for high altitude, distance, and speed, a near crash on 5 November 1912, almost ended it all.[7] He swore never to get in an aeroplane again and transferred to a desk job in Washington.

In 1914, Arnold returned to Manila, where he and his new bride were forced to share headquarters with one other officer and many cockroaches. The latter were so large that Arnold's wife tried to kill them with a broom and failed.[8] Two years later, William 'Billy' Mitchell, the founding father of American air power, asked Arnold to reconsider a career in aviation. Arnold had still not set foot in an aeroplane since his near crash. He had to decide whether to try again or to bring an end to his aviation career, and to the anomaly of an air force man afraid to fly. On 18 October 1916, he flew as a passenger; a month later he soloed; and in mid-December he was in the air for more than forty minutes, flying upside down and putting the aircraft through stalls, spins, rolls, and loops.[9] 'Hap' was back.

After a frustrating attempt to build an air force during the First World War, Arnold was demoted to major and transferred to Rockwell Field in San Diego, where he served as commander. Despite the demotion and the more provincial focus of his work, Arnold was ecstatic. He was away from the desk and was commanding troops.

The transfer was more fateful than he could have recognised. Arnold had two people to help him in San Diego. The first was Carl Spaatz, who was assigned to Arnold as his executive officer. The second was Ira C. Eaker, who served as their adjutant. The three men would have a defining influence on the development of the US Air Force.

Spaatz's background was similar to Arnold's. His upbringing was rural – he was born in Boyertown, Pennsylvania, on

28 June 1891 – and his father was a member of the rural liberal professions (he owned a family newspaper). Spaatz was of German descent: his grandfather migrated to the United States from Germany and the newspaper, the *Boyertown Democrat*, was originally published in German, the language his paternal grandmother spoke until the end of her life.[10] He attended West Point and ended up with a class standing of 57 – three above Arnold. His 'conduct' ranking was much worse: 95. He excelled at wit, along with bridge, poker, and the guitar. West Point failed to instil in him a love of learning, but it did equip him with two things he would carry for the rest of his life: a love of flying and a reputation for honesty.[11]

With less fuss than Arnold, Spaatz went from West Point into the infantry, and from there he moved into his chosen branch: the Aviation Section of the Signal Corps. Spaatz could have chosen the safety of a desk, but he insisted on fighting at the front. In September 1918, he reported for flying duty with the 2nd Pursuit Group, which had entered combat five weeks earlier. On 15 September, he shot down his first German aeroplane. Eleven days later, a daring dogfight earned him the Distinguished Service Cross and made the *New York Times*. The headline read: FLYING OFFICER SHOOTS DOWN THREE PLANES – TWO GERMAN AND HIS OWN.[12] When his wife, Ruth, saw the headline, she exclaimed, 'That has to be Tooey [Spaatz's nickname]!'[13] Spaatz's determination to gun down the enemy had led him to neglect his fuel. He ran out of petrol and crashed in no man's land. Luckily, the French got to him before the Germans did.[14]

While Spaatz was flying across enemy lines, the third in the air force trio – Ira Eaker – was serving as an infantry officer at Fort Bliss, Texas. In November 1917, Eaker saw an aeroplane try without success to clear the South Franklin Mountain after take-off.[15] When the plane returned, it landed close to Eaker, who ran to help. He had never seen an aero engine before, but he climbed on and saw a loose spark plug lead.

'Maybe this is your trouble,' Eaker remarked.

'Let's find out,' the pilot replied. He showed Eaker how to turn the propeller and got back into the cockpit. The engine sprang back to life.

'You know so much about airplane motors,' the pilot said, '[that] you ought to come to the aviation section of the Signals Corps.'

'How do I do it?' Eaker asked.

The pilot was a recruiter. 'Fill out this form and send it in,' he replied, 'and you'll probably get a call to fly.'

In October 1918, after flight training in Austin and San Antonio, Eaker was transferred to Rockwell Field, where Arnold and Spaatz appointed him post adjutant.[16]

Eaker came from very little: he was born on 13 April 1896 to struggling Texan farmers.[17] While Spaatz and Arnold attended West Point, Eaker's education was at the rather undistinguished Southeastern Normal School in Durant, Oklahoma.[18] What he lacked in prestige he did not make up for in physical appearance: Arnold was towering and handsome, Eaker short and balding. Eaker nonetheless had several assets which he husbanded carefully. Whereas Arnold and Spaatz were the Army equivalent of spoiled Ivy League students yawning over their books,[19] Eaker had a deep and abiding love of learning. Through sheer determination, he became an intellectual, an accomplished writer and speaker. His soft Texan accent and gentle demeanour made him appear the gentleman, Arnold the vulgarian.

In the inter-war years, what would become the United States Air Force would develop in tandem with the careers of Arnold, Spaatz, and Eaker. All three were disciples of Billy Mitchell, the

American counterpart of Hugh Trenchard, who, like Trenchard, was a believer in city bombing. Destroying 'vital centers' (that is, cities), he claimed, was 'more humane than the present methods of blowing up people to bits by cannon projectiles or butchering them with bayonets'.[20] Mitchell had been the first American airman to arrive at the Western Front, the first to fly over enemy lines, and the first to be seduced by the promises of air power.[21] The son of a US senator, he had fought in the Spanish–American War, dressed in sporting fashion (high cavalry boots and expensive tailored suits), studied at several European universities, and spoke fluent Spanish.[22] His elegance had a rougher edge: he drank heavily, had a bitter divorce from his first wife, pushed his staff to the breaking point, and by 1925, had 'alienated practically everybody above him in the chain of command, including his commander in chief, President Calvin Coolidge'.[23]

Mitchell took inspiration from his experiences on the Western Front – the prospect of streaking forward over enemy formations in seconds while armies struggled to advance a few inches – and from the writings of Italian theorist, air commander, and fascist General Giulio Douhet.[24] In Douhet's view, the advent of air power meant that future wars would be offensive, short, violent to a superlative degree, and targeted at the enemy's homeland. Such war would be total and Cromwellian in its brutality: 'War is war . . . . Any distinction between belligerents and non-belligerents is no longer admissible today either in fact or in theory. Not in theory because when nations are at war, everyone takes a part in it: the soldier carrying his gun, the women loading shells in a factory, the farmer growing wheat, the scientist experimenting in his laboratory. Not in fact because nowadays the offensive may reach anyone; and it begins to look now as though the safest place may be the trenches.'[25] Douhet's vision was, by his own account, 'dark and bloody' and required that combatants kill before they

– 56 –

were killed: 'the picture grows darker still when one realizes that any defense against aerial attacks as it is commonly envisaged is *illusory*.'[26] The only option is to send out 'an offensive aerial force of our own which would go in search of the enemy and destroy him in his nest . . .'[27] Yet this dark vision was the foundation of the bombers' dream: only an independent, aggressive air force could secure the nation's security; it alone could win wars; and as it did the navy and army would shrink in size, resources, and importance.[28]

Whereas Douhet's project had something of genocide to it, Mitchell's was, or was meant to be, humane (though his views were never entirely consistent).[29] Air wars would be violent, but fewer people would die. Constructing an image that seduced generations of aviators, Mitchell believed that a dazzling bombardment would knock out the pillars of the enemy's war machine, destroy the people's will to fight, and lead to a quick surrender before the Army and Navy had even mobilised. The wars of the future might be nasty and brutish, but they would be – above all, in comparison with the prolonged slaughter of the First World War – short.

Still at relatively young ages, Arnold, Spaatz, and Eaker all risked their careers for Mitchell. Mitchell's penchant for publicly condemning the Army and Navy, which opposed both an independent air force and Mitchell's radical ideas for a reorganisation of all services under a new Department of Defense, came to a head on 5 September 1925. Following the crash of the USS *Shenandoah*, a Zeppelin, during a flight regarded by Mitchell as a dangerous propaganda exercise at his expense, he read a prepared statement to reporters. The crash, which left fourteen men dead, occurred on the heels of another tragedy – the crash, again with the loss of life, of Navy seaplanes off Hawaii. 'I have been asked,' Mitchell told the newsmen, 'from all parts of the country to give my opinion about the reasons for the frightful aeronautical accidents and loss of life. My opinion is as follows. These incidents are the direct result of the incompetency, criminal negligence, and almost treasonable administration of the national defense by the Navy and War Departments.'[30] Mitchell was court-martialled. Spaatz and Arnold bravely spoke in his defence, while Eaker worked quietly behind the scenes to help shape it.[31] Mitchell was convicted of insubordination and given a five-year suspension at half pay. Refusing to be silenced, he resigned on 1 February 1926 and pressed the case for air power as a civilian, but the audiences dwindled, his argument became repetitive, and his claims were increasingly delusional and paranoid.[32] He continued to spend beyond his means – a tendency not helped by the 1929 stock market crash – and he got involved in another high-profile trial, this time lobbying to impeach a Massachusetts judge who blocked the extradition of an African-American man to Virginia for a murder trial on the grounds that the trial would not be fair.[33] He remained cantankerous and contrarian, life-loving and hard-drinking until the end. On 19 February 1936, a body ravaged by alcohol, riding, and hard work gave out, and he died of heart failure.

For their part, Eaker, Spaatz, and Arnold survived the trial, although Arnold was banished to Kansas for a time. They remained loyal to their mentor and his cause but, bruised by their cross-examination, they drew at least one powerful lesson from it. 'There must be something to this public relations business,' they were reported to have said to each other. 'I guess we'd better learn it.'[34] They would.

Montgomery, Alabama, is infamous for its role in the civil rights movement, but it also played an important role in the history of American air power. In 1910, at a muddy site occupied by a few wooden hangars, the Wright brothers opened their flying school.

In 1922, the air force designated the site Maxwell Field and, in
1931, transferred its Air Corps Tactical School from Langley,
Virginia. Over the subsequent decade, some of the most famous
and infamous men in the history of American air power – Eaker,
Spaatz, LeMay, and Arnold – would pass through its doors and
they, along with less well-known permanent personnel at the
school, would develop American ideas about air power.

One of the faculty lecturers was Lieutenant Colonel Harold
L. George, a veteran bomber pilot who had served in the First
World War and was the 'anonymous warrior'[35] who provided
much of the intellectual basis for what would become America's
Second World War strategic bombing campaign. During his
three-year stint at the school (1933–6), he worked with a small
team.[36] Together, they drew on the ideas of Mitchell and Douhet,
as well as the British military theorist B. H. Liddell Hart and
the Prussian general and theorist Carl von Clausewitz,[37] and
added their own, rather American, twist. Mitchell and especially
Douhet had said little about targets (except that, in 'vital centres',
everything was a target) other than the aircraft industry and the
opaque goal of destroying 'morale'.[38] George and his colleagues
thought about nothing but targets: they wanted to identify the
critical pillars of a modern industrial economy and how bombing could knock them – and with them, the enemy's war-making
capacity – out.[39]

Doing so required money, and the Air Corps Tactical School
had little of it. They could not hire economists, and they were
forbidden to study the economies of Japan or Germany. To get
around these constraints, George and his colleagues studied the
American industrial system as a proxy (an imperfect one, as
the two economies were and are very different) for the German
one. Through this work, they developed the idea of an 'industrial web': modern economies were delicate and interconnected

machines that were entirely dependent on the same set of key supports.[40] All industries needed steel, ball-bearings, and electricity. All industries needed railroads to transport these materials and to deliver their finished products. Given these facts, what was needed, then, was not Douhet's war of extermination, but rather a precise and relentless bombing campaign against the producers of steel, ball-bearings, electricity, and similar products.[41] If bombing could destroy these 'choke points', the wartime economy would collapse and, with it, the will to fight on.

Out of these theories emerged daylight precision bombing, America's plan for bringing the war to Germany. The question was how to accomplish it, and it is here that George's ideas showed their American origins: he had an overwhelmingly optimistic faith in the ability of ingenuity and technology to overcome difficulties.

Added to these beliefs was, at least at the start, a critical view of bombing civilians, which the Americans viewed as pointless and immoral. On the former, as one general put it in 1944, 'There was a memorandum on 29 October which said that no German cities would be bombed as secondary targets unless they had military targets adjacent. We said we would never bomb a German city. We will bomb a military target within the bounds of a German city, but not a German city. That is largely because of the fact that the Eighth Air Force does not believe that the morale of Germany is vulnerable to a decisive degree . . . [Hitler] has made the morale of the German civil population highly invulnerable to either [Allied] propaganda or morale attacks.' Otherwise, there would have long been a rebellion against Hitler: 'Never before in the history of man has a nation been subjected to any pounding like the Germans have.'[42] This conclusion was based on contemporary evidence: Arnold asked a 'Committee of Historians' in 1943 for their analysis of the likelihood of a German collapse in the face of sustained bombing.[43] The nine scholars, including distinguished historians of war and revolution (Bernadotte Schmitt, Edward Mead Earle, and Louis R. Gottschalk), concluded that the Nazi control apparatus 'gives no encouragement to the supposition that any political upheaval can be anticipated in Germany in the near future . . . . It seems clear that bombing alone cannot bring about [the] defeat [of Germany] in the spring of 1944.'[44]

The Americans also, at least initially, viewed city bombing as immoral: 'The Tactical School,' Haywood S. Hansell, a member of George's team, later wrote, 'opposed the concept which was generally described as an attack on enemy morale. The idea of killing thousands of men, women, and children was basically repugnant to American mores.'[45] Like British moral commitments earlier in the war, which were equally genuine, these principles would be greatly compromised before the end of the war against Germany and abandoned altogether over Japan. But they informed early American thinking on air power. Daylight precision bombing was thus a perfect synthesis of American attributes of the time: a belief in the importance of morality in politics, optimism, and a commitment to technological pioneering.[46]

In 1933, the optimism and idealism were in place, but the technology wasn't. At least the lecturers at the Air Corps Tactical School *thought* it wasn't. In fact, in 1931, Carl L. Norden, a Dutch inventor who had emigrated to the United States in 1904, had developed an idea to help naval aircraft bomb with greater precision. Resembling an oversized camera, the bombsight allowed aircrew to input airspeed and altitude on the bombing run. The bombsight would calculate the trajectory of the bomb and the moment when it should be released. The bombsight was originally designed for purely defensive purposes, and the Navy ordered almost a hundred thousand of them to protect the US coastline. The faculty at Maxwell Field did not hear about this until the mid-1930s, but when they did, they believed it could change the course of warfare. In truth, the bombsight was far less accurate than the Americans had hoped, and was useless in cloud cover, but in the mid-1930s, it served as a shot in the arm to American air advocates.

By 1935, what would become the United States Air Force had three apostles of air power: Arnold, Spaatz, and Eaker; it had the abstract creativity and empirical research of George and his colleagues at Maxwell Field; and it had the technology it believed it needed to translate the theory of precision bombing into a reality. It lacked one thing, however: an aeroplane.

5

BUILDING THE EIGHTH

On 12 September 1938, President Roosevelt and his adviser and
New Deal architect, Harry Hopkins, were in a car in Rochester,
Minnesota, where the president's son was undergoing surgery.
According to Hopkins, the radio was on, and they were listening to Hitler's speech at a huge Nazi rally in Nuremberg. The
German dictator ranted and threatened Czechoslovakia with
invasion if it did not submit to his demands. When the speech
ended, Roosevelt, who understood German, snapped off the radio
and turned to Hopkins. He told him to look immediately for new
aircraft factory sites on the West Coast.[1] Roosevelt 'was sure
then,' Hopkins wrote, 'that we were going to get into war, and he
believed that air power would win it'.[2]

The US Congress did not agree and refused to provide the
funds. Without the money, only two thousand planes were produced in 1939. All of this changed in early 1940, however. In May,
as the Germans invaded the Low Countries, Roosevelt issued a
public call for an annual output of fifty thousand planes – some
twenty-five times the figure produced in 1939! Congress quickly
provided the money. After spending years begging for funds
to build a handful of bombers, Hap Arnold – now chief of the
Army Air Corps – found that 'in forty-five minutes I was given
$1,500,000,000 and told to get an air force'.[3]

Arnold had the money; he now needed the power. In 1940,
Roosevelt had appointed Henry L. Stimson his Secretary of War.
Stimson was a Harvard-educated lawyer, the son of a Union

soldier in the Civil War, and an upper-class New Yorker.[4] His upbringing emphasised the puritan virtues of work and abstention (although he lived very comfortably) and the not uncommon early-twentieth-century view of war as a cleansing antidote to the soft materialism produced by American affluence.[5] 'Every man,' he wrote in 1915, 'owes to his country not only to die for her if necessary, but also to spend a little of his life in learning how to die for her effectively.'[6]

One of Stimson's first acts was the appointment of a fellow New Yorker, Robert Lovett, to the new position of Assistant Secretary of War for Air. Lovett was a wealthy stockbroker, an experienced pilot (he had flown Navy combat planes in the First World War), and a student of RAF administration. He had a talent for packaging his ideas and for handling difficult people, not least of whom was Arnold. 'When I became impatient, intolerant, and would rant around, fully intending to tear the War and Navy Departments to pieces,' Arnold wrote, 'Bob Lovett would know exactly how to handle me. He would say, with a quiet smile, "Hap, you're wonderful! I wish I had your pep and vitality. Now . . . let's get down and be practical." And I would come to earth with a bang.'[7]

In 1941, Lovett produced a plan for reorganising the Air Corps and giving it more autonomy. Roosevelt accepted it. The Army Air Corps was replaced by the Army Air Forces. A new Chief of the Army Air Forces (who was also Army Deputy Chief of Staff for Air) controlled the entire organisation. With the support of General George Marshall (Chief of Staff of the United States Army, its professional head), the position went to Arnold. Marshall wrote later: 'I tried to give Arnold all the power I could. I tried to make him as nearly as I could Chief of Staff of the Air without any restraint.'[8]

The Air Staff was made up of old Maxwell Field lecturers: Kenneth Walker, Haywood Hansell, and Laurence Kuter, among others. They produced a document known as AWPD-1, named after the Air Staff's Air War Plans Division. The plan envisioned four roles for the air forces in the coming war: supporting the defensive strategy in the Pacific during the initial phases of war; waging an unlimited strategic offensive against Germany as soon as possible; preparing for an invasion of the European continent; and preparing the invasion of Japan by waging an unlimited strategic air offensive against its homeland. Although a more measured document than the one produced earlier by Britain's Directorate of Plans, it was still beholden to the bombers' dream. 'If the air offensive is successful,' AWPD-1 read, 'a land offensive may not be necessary.'[9] Working long hours, Hansell, Walker, and Kuter rehearsed the document with each other until they knew it by heart.[10] The three men then presented it to Marshall, Stimson, and Hopkins. The lecturers, as it were, flew on a wing and a prayer. At a time when the United States had thirteen B-17s, they spoke of thousands. The large figures, Hansell later said, 'scared us very badly at the time'. But the presentation went over well. It was then leaked to the *Chicago Tribune* – probably by Hansell himself – and the public reaction was strongly supportive. The leak ensured that the details of the plan were publicised *before* the draft was sent on to the Army, which would have almost certainly reworked it.

From beginning to end, Arnold's conduct of the air war was driven by two goals: the strategic and the political. The first was to do maximum damage to Germany and Japan's ability to prosecute the war. The second was to advocate for air power's role in defeating Germany as an argument in favour of service autonomy: a US air force independent of army and navy control and at least equal to the other two services in respect, prestige, and funding. The two goals naturally overlapped, but the political added a twist: 'dramatic results from strategic bombing,' writes historian Thomas R. Searle, 'became the means by which the

USAAF hoped not only to help win the war, but also to pursue its post-war goals.'[11] The Japanese, much more than the Germans, would come to understand what this meant in practice.

Having already won two wars – over money and power – Arnold now needed to win another – over strategy. His opponents were not in the US military (everyone agreed on daylight precision bombing) but across the Atlantic: the British.

In May 1940, Arnold sent Spaatz to London. Officially, he was there as an 'Assistant Military Attaché (Air) to Britain'; unofficially, he was a 'high-class spy' studying the air war and the state of Britain in it.[12] Although it was a low point in Britain's war, Spaatz formed prescient views about the limits of German air power and the ability of the British to hold out.[13] A year later, Arnold visited. By this point, America's entry into the war seemed likely. Arnold expected to meet Portal, then Chief of Air Staff and overseeing an air war that was still formally committed to precision bombing. Beyond Portal, Arnold held out hope for a meeting with Lord Beaverbrook, Churchill's Minister of Aircraft Production. To his surprise, he was treated as a minor celebrity. When he arrived for an overnight stay in neutral Portugal, three members of a UK delegation, led by Air Marshal John Slessor (Assistant Chief of Air Staff [Plans], who worked directly under Vice Chief of Air Staff Wilfrid Freeman and Portal), were waiting for him. After allowing Arnold a bath and change, they pelted him with questions: What could the Americans do about the U-boat campaign, which threatened the UK with starvation? What could they do about the B-17 (delivered by Roosevelt to England), which was useless in combat? And, above all, did he really believe that precision bombing would work?

Despite his quasi-hero's welcome, the trip nearly went badly. The British were appalled by how unprepared Arnold was. Portal was shocked to learn that he had arrived without an agenda for

his visit. Arnold, for his part, found Portal defeatist and demanding (although his words might have been coloured by resentful-
ness and defensiveness over his failed visit). They would 'talk
about squadrons whereas we would talk about groups'. Things
looked up, however, when he met Beaverbrook, who was 'the one
man in London with ideas as large as his own' – perhaps because
he, too, was a North American.[14] Beaverbrook agreed immediately to Arnold's request for two each of Spitfires, Hurricanes
(both fighters), and Wellingtons (medium bombers) for study, and
invited him to view 'everything the British had'.[15] Most reveal-
ingly, from Arnold's perspective, Beaverbrook told him that the
Germans had reduced British aircraft production by up to one-
third as a result of factory bombing.[16] Another of Beaverbrook's
comments left a lasting impression on Arnold. At a 21 April dinner, Beaverbrook asked him: 'What would you do if Churchill
were hung and the rest of us were hiding in Scotland or being run
down by the Germans? We are up against the mightiest Army
the world has ever seen.'[17] When Arnold left London, he had the
impression that the British were setting their sights far too low
and that the gloom that had overtaken the country might lose
them the war. He reserved his most scathing views for Peirse. In
contrast to the leaders of Fighter Command, who were actually
fighting, Peirse was 'pathetic'.[18]

As so often, Arnold's words said as much about him as they
did about the target of his ire. They reflected his gruff impa-
tience, his tendency to exaggerate the importance of individuals
(as opposed to equipment and weather) in ensuring a mission's
success, and his inflated sense of what the US air forces could
and would achieve, particularly early in the war. It is true that
Bomber Command's performance at this point in the war was
less than distinguished, but Peirse was hobbled by a small bombing force dissipating in strength through unavoidably imprecise

attacks on numerous targets.[19] Arnold would soon enough face similar challenges.

In August 1941, Roosevelt and Churchill met in Newfoundland. There, they outlined the principles that would guide their countries' approach to war. Neither country would seek territorial expansion. Both would foster the freedoms of all people, vanquished and victors. The United States had served notice on Hitler that his enemies had its sympathy. It had also, though this captured less attention at the time, served notice on the British Empire.

Marshall had invited Arnold to attend the conference, and while Roosevelt, Churchill, and their aides drafted the charters, Arnold met with the generals and admirals, whom he held in something close to contempt. The 'British long-range plan,' he wrote in his diary, 'is to keep giving as little as possible in remote areas where they can meet Germans on even terms, always hoping for a break – a miracle – an internal breakdown of [German] morale.'[20] They had no long-term plan that envisaged total victory or even the invasion of the Continent. Yet, they wanted four thousand heavy American bombers at a time when the United States was producing five hundred a month.[21] All of this was true enough to a point, but Arnold failed to consider, or at least mention, several factors complicating the British position: the toll the country suffered through the Blitz and two years of the war; the fact that it was the only European power standing against Hitler; and that British production was stretched whereas US production had great slack.

Arnold returned to Washington in August and spent the next four months building the US air forces and resisting British requests for more planes, which he argued were needed to defend the American homeland. Events appeared to prove him right.

The Japanese attack on Pearl Harbor destroyed 188 American aircraft and damaged another 159. The aircraft had been left in tight formations to prevent sabotage, thus forming ideal targets for the incoming attackers. Four hours after Pearl Harbor, Japanese bombers scored another trick, destroying twelve B-17s they caught refuelling in the Philippines.

With the United States now in the war, the effort to build its air forces took off. The US air forces would have four commands: Bomber and Fighter Commands, as well as Ground-Air Support Command and Air Service Command (responsible for supply and maintenance). Eighth Bomber Command was organised into combat wings, which were in turn composed of three bomb groups (made up of squadrons) that operated together on air raids. Each combat wing was part of a larger structure, first called a bombardment wing (there were two – the 1st and the 2nd in 1942) and later an air division (eventually made up of three to five combat wings).[22]

Arnold's next move was to bring onboard Ira Eaker, who had taken over fighter defences on the West Coast after Pearl Harbor. Arnold met with him in Washington on 8 January. 'You're going to England. I want you to fly over there and negotiate with the British for headquarters, airdromes, communications, all the stuff we'll need. Understudy the British and work out the plans. Then I'll get you some bombers and crews. You'll be in charge of the Eighth Air Force Bomber Command.'[23]

That night, not yet used to the new stars on his shoulders, Eaker and his wife, Ruth, accompanied Arnold to a dinner in Washington for Portal and Harris.[24] Wine flowed throughout the long meal, and over after-dinner drinks, Harris subjected Arnold to a harangue on precision bombing. The account comes from Eaker's sympathetic biographer, but the language on both sides rings true.[25]

'I bloody well don't think you can do it,' Harris began in a characteristically truculent mode. 'We tried it. We know. We've even tried it with your Fortresses.'

Arnold, now accustomed to this argument, replied, 'Sure. You tried it with one or two B-17s at a time. We don't plan to do it that way. We're going to send them out in mass formations.'

Harris was not to be moved. 'It doesn't matter a tinker's damn what you send them in,' he shot back. 'The Boche have too many fighters, too much flak, too much bloody power against that West Wall to make it worth the losses. God knows, I hope you can do it, but I don't think you can.'

Looking at Eaker, he said, 'Come join us at night. Together we'll lick them.'

Eaker, ever the gentleman, sought a compromise and in so doing produced a phrase that would become legend.

'Yes,' he said, 'we'll bomb them by day. You bomb them by night. We'll hit them right around the clock.'[26]

The famous 'bombing around the clock' strategy thus originated not in agreement but rather its opposite. Harris, and Portal, wanted the Americans to make cities their primary daytime targets, but Eaker would not be drawn in.[27] The Americans would bomb by day, the British by night. It was an agreement to disagree.[28]

On 4 February 1942, Eaker left to take up his assignment in England. He and six staff officers undertook a long trip to London. After a complicated journey, he finally arrived in the capital on 21 February, a day before Harris took over Bomber Command. After three days in London, Eaker and his staff moved on to Bomber Command headquarters near High Wycombe. Harris was there to greet him. Although he and his wife, Jill, had themselves just moved in, he insisted that Eaker stay with him until his headquarters were ready. They lived at

Springfield, an elegant, wide, eighteenth-century house. After the war, rumours circulated to the effect that the house was bombproof, but it wasn't.[29] The only bombproof part of the house is a panic room within a bathroom, with a bullet-proof window, which was not installed until the 1980s, when the RAF had the Irish rather than the Germans to fear. In fact, both the house and the town itself – a typical provincial English town filled with streets of terraced, working-class houses – were chosen for their ordinariness. German reconnaissance flights over High Wycombe would see a normal, mainly residential town. Harris did not, however, want for comfort. The house has large rooms, a dining hall, and a grand lawn. It is stately but unpretentious and housed both the Harrises and the Eakers comfortably.

The two men could not have been more different: Harris liked a drink; Eaker barely touched the stuff. Harris was hearty, gruff, and provocatively offensive; Eaker was shy and eager to please. Harris was cold and aloof with his staff; Eaker was informal and completely approachable. For all that, the two men got along during their stay, and developed a friendship that would outlast the war. Harris could have a monster of a personality, but he never let his disagreements get in the way of friendship with those whom he held in genuine affection.

After Harris's warm welcome, Eaker received a less enthusiastic one from Major General James E. Chaney (Commanding General, US Army Forces in the British Isles), who had overseen the skeleton staff the Americans had in England. Chaney and Eaker, like most airmen, had known each other for some time, but Chaney was hostile to the American plan for a separate air force under Eaker and Spaatz. He wanted Eaker and his men to join the existing London-based air staff of thirty-five officers, only four of whom were airmen.[30] Eaker outflanked him: he pointed out that he was there to understudy the

RAF and that he could not do that from London. Fortuitously, he received an invitation from Harris to share space at RAF Bomber Command. Eaker seized upon it immediately and he, his six accompanying staff members, and eventually fifteen additional officers, all moved in.

Until US air forces had their own infrastructure in the United Kingdom, Eaker had to play his hand carefully. The British were still pressuring the Americans to join in the area bombing campaign and, when expressed by Harris, that pressure was not subtle. Throughout early 1942, Harris urged Eaker to bomb cities and to kill German workers. 'It took,' he told Eaker, 'only a year or less to build a tank or a plane but it took 20 years to build skilled workmen, and skilled workmen in short supply would affect war production as much as loss of their factory.'[31] Eaker steadfastly told Harris and Portal that his orders from Arnold were to bomb by day, that American planes and crews were not trained for night bombing, and that precision daylight bombing could be made to work.[32] The disagreement did not, however, stand in the way of broader co-operation between the two air forces. Harris turned over five long-established bases in East Anglia, and the Air Ministry agreed to build another sixty. Eaker could not have been more pleased.

It was also necessary to secure permanent headquarters. General Chaney suggested tents, but Eaker was able to kill that idea. He also got his way on the location: in High Wycombe, within five miles of RAF Bomber Command. Harris and Eaker drew a five-mile radius around Bomber Command headquarters, and Eaker scouted the area.[33] The only suitable building was the Wycombe Abbey School for girls, a manor house set on a verdant campus, its walkways shaded by linden trees. After facing some resistance (girls from the colonies were in the school, and they could not return home),[34] Eaker moved in three weeks later.

Although formally part of a joint strategy, over the next three years the Americans and British would effectively fight parallel but separate air wars against Germany. While the Americans were preparing for their war, Britain's, under Arthur Harris, would begin in earnest.

6

LIGHTING GERMANY ON FIRE

The bombing force that Harris took over in 1942 was small: 407 bombers. Of these, only 136 (29 Lancasters, 62 Halifaxes, and 45 Stirlings) were heavy bombers, all of which were four-engine bombers.[1] A force of that size could be wiped out over the course of a few high-loss raids. Harris viewed the situation with his usual clarity. He sought to increase the number of bombers, to expand his crews, and to make sure that both had a better chance of surviving.

All three problems had, as Harris saw it, a single solution: successful raids that inflicted a great deal of damage on Germany at little cost to Bomber Command. A new development in navigation technology, an area in which the British were always ahead of the Americans, helped. This radio navigation system, named Gee after the first letter in *grid*, was developed in 1940–1. As two transmitter stations in England (a 'master' and a 'slave') simultaneously sent signals, a Gee apparatus in an aircraft picked up the signals and measured the difference between the times at which they were received, thus showing its distance from the two stations.[2] The navigator plotted the plane's position on one line of the chart created by the apparatus. The master and a second slave station (there were three in total) transmitted another two signals, which allowed the navigator to plot a second line on the chart. The airline was at the point where the two lines intersected.[3] For the first time in the bombing war, RAF aircrew had a precise measure of where they and their targets were. The only downside was time: the Germans would eventually figure out what the British were up to and jam it. The RAF gave it six months.

Harris made his first move, without Gee, in an unusual precision raid on the Renault works at Billancourt, west of Paris, which produced trucks for the Wehrmacht. On the night of 3 March, he sent in three waves of bombers. Tightly concentrated – 121 planes passed over the target in an hour – the first wave marked the target with flares, while the second and third blasted the target with high explosives.[4] The factories suffered severe damage; only one aircraft was lost, though the bombs killed three hundred French people.

In a subsequent series of raids on industrial targets in Duisburg, Cologne, and Essen, he instructed his crews to mark the targets with flares using Gee alone.[5]

By the end of March, the technical pillars of Harris's strategy were being put in place. Gee would guide a first wave of aeroplanes to mark the target with flares. Subsequent waves of bombers would hit the target with high explosives, blowing off roofs and transforming buildings into tinder, and incendiaries would light the target on fire. With navigation technology, markers, and concentrated bombings, Harris was ready to bring his war to Germany.

The question that remained was one of targets. At this point in the war, Harris avoided Germany's major industrial cities: Düsseldorf, Essen, Stuttgart. They were heavily defended and, in the case of Stuttgart, hard to reach. Harris instead sought a city whose destruction would be so complete that the world would take notice. 'I wanted my crews to be well "blooded", as they say in fox-hunting, to have a taste of success for a change.'[6] Such a city would have three attributes: it would be easy to find, poorly defended, and likely to burn.[7] The commercial port city of Lübeck, with its mass of densely knit, wooden houses, fitted the bill. 'It was built,' as Harris noted, 'more like a fire lighter than a human habitation.'[8]

Like other Hanseatic cities such as Hamburg and Bremen, Lübeck was built around trade. The city radiated out from its central market around which wealthy trading families had built their famous gabled houses. The city's old centre was small and compact – half a mile wide by one mile long – and bounded by canals on all sides. Its two most important public buildings were the cathedral (for which Henry the Lion, the city's founder, had laid the cornerstone in 1173) and the Church of St Mary. Both were famous for their paired steeples.[9] By 1940, the entire city core was under a preservation order, but, in 1942, it was only lightly defended by five heavy and three light flak batteries.

Lübeck, Northern Germany

In the early evening of 28 March 1942, the sun was setting. It was the night before Palm Sunday. Around 23:15, the first air-raid warning rang out.[10] No one paid any attention. Lübeckers told themselves that the city would not be bombed because Churchill's grandmother lived there.[11] She did not; it was a myth, variants of which were heard in many German cities. Pathfinders appeared above the city and marked it with their gently descending flares. At 23:29, the first wave of incendiary and 250-pound bombs hit the city, landing near the harbour in the south.[12] 'We couldn't believe it,' wrote the members of Flak Group 161 later. 'Many, probably most of us never thought the enemy would actually attack this city of ancient architectural wonders . . . but attacked it was . . .'[13] Nearly twenty minutes later – at 23:48 – a second and far more powerful wave of bombs hit the city. High explosives and incendiaries rained down on the area around the main station and the city's famous cathedral. One hit a house on the corner of Ritterstrasse and Gothlandstrasse,[14] outside the main aiming point, killing eleven members of a family who were celebrating a birthday. Only one boy and his grandmother, who were not in the house, survived. Fires started in the Grosse Burgstrasse, in the southwestern corner of the old city.[15] They quickly spread through the neighbourhood, surrounding St Jacob's Church and the adjacent school.[16] The flames continued to move, and the incendiaries started hundreds of new fires that spread westward, consuming the Königstrasse and the Breite Strasse (which ran north–south, parallel to each other) along with the Kuhberg and the Johannisstrasse (which also stood parallel). They reached the Kohlmarkt and the adjacent Church of St Mary's almost exactly in the middle of the old city. As this was happening, bombs lit fires in and around the Aegidien church, to the southwest. Surrounding the church was the Kaufmannsviertel, the merchant's district, made up of tightly knit narrow streets. The fires tore through them and began leaping over the buildings into neighbouring streets. As they did, high explosives shattered houses, providing more oxygen and new pathways to the flames.

At 01:00, a final wave of bombers hit the city. A combination of high explosives and thousands of incendiaries landed across Lübeck: in the east, south, and west. One high explosive landed in the Mühlenstrasse, in the southeast of the old city and just feet from the cathedral, and hit the city's water mains.[17] Firemen tried to put out the flames, but the pipes bringing water from the Trave Canal, in the north of the city, were broken. In the Johannisstrasse, flames shot up from the roof of the Karstadt department store and then spread, leaping out of the spires of St Mary's Church. Nearby, the Rathaus (town hall) and St Petri Church also burned, as did the Cathedral. A neighbouring museum was hit by the first wave of bombs and the fires jumped across to the great church.

Firefighters did not have the blaze under control until 10:00 the next morning. It was too late for the bells of St Mary: thirty minutes later, they fell, crashing through the great organ made by

Arp Schnitger, the famous north German organ builder.[18] Thirty minutes later, the cathedral's northern tower collapsed; at 14:00, the southern tower met the same fate.[19]

Two hundred acres of the old town had been demolished. All of the churches were shells. The Kohlmarkt was flattened. More than 320 people were dead, 130 seriously injured, and 15,000 homeless. Bombing destroyed 1,063 houses and 21 public buildings.[20] Twenty-five industrial concerns were hit, two significantly: Drägerwerk (which made breathing equipment for U-boats) lost 30 per cent of its power supply, and an armaments factory was seriously damaged.[21] The harbour suffered only light damage. Losses among the RAF were tolerable: twelve bombers did not come back.[22]

Although Lübeck's historic centre had been ravaged, the effect of the raid on industrial production was minimal. The city was operating at 80 to 90 per cent output within days.[23] The Heinkel factory, which suffered during the raid, recovered within weeks.[24] There was no evidence of the widespread panic, fear, and demoralisation promised by Portal and Harris. Instead, newspaper reports spoke of the 'heroes' that were the flak operators,[25] of 'Lübeck's heart' that was 'tougher than English bombs', and of the help that poured in from neighbouring cities and beyond. The dead were declared 'soldiers' who fell for a Germany that would never forget them. Above all, the city would recover from the 'great crime' committed against it by the 'British murderers'. 'It made us,' wrote Lübecker Günther Becker, 'harder and more resilient, and we believed even more in Germany's ultimate victory.'[26] The bravado likely reflected the fact that the bomb load and destruction, while awful for those who suffered directly, remained relatively limited. Lübeck would not be bombed again, but such sentiment elsewhere would not withstand the overwhelming force of future heavy bombing raids.

For all the official defiance, the Germans feared another

attack: not on the city, but on the harbour. A full four months after the attack, on 24 July 1942, the Staatskommissar in the mayor's office in Lübeck wrote to the local Luftwaffe command in Hamburg begging for more air protection from direct attacks on the harbour.

For the moment, this did not matter to the RAF. The photos of Lübeck's skyline, covered in billows of smoke from the city's shattered cathedral, made the destruction alone seem like a great achievement. And from a technical point of view, it was. In 1941, a raid involving a hundred bombers over the course of four hours would have been considered a great accomplishment. Now, one year later, Harris managed more than twice the number of bombers in half the time.[27]

One of those impressed by city bombing was Churchill's scientific adviser, Lord Cherwell. Cherwell was courageous, wealthy, and – when he wanted to be – disarmingly charming. He was also vain, arrogant, and unforgiving to the point of vengefulness. He was born Frederick Lindemann in Baden-Baden in 1886 (of a German father who had migrated to England in 1870), studied in Darmstadt, and took a Ph.D. from the University of Berlin. He always viewed his German birth and descent as a handicap, one which he perhaps tried to overcome by being violently anti-German.[28] 'Lord Cherwell entertained,' write historians Sir John Wheeler-Bennett and Anthony Nicholls, 'an almost pathological hatred for Nazi Germany, and an almost medieval desire for revenge was a part of his character.'[29] Throughout the war, Cherwell was the most consistent advocate, after Harris, of levelling Germany.

When war broke out in 1914, Lindemann made several unsuccessful attempts to use his scientific background to support the war effort before he was offered a position at the Royal Aircraft Factory at Farnborough.[30] From there, he was accepted into the Royal Flying Corps, where he developed a mathematical theory of aircraft spin recovery.[31] Spin occurs when one wing loses lift while the other retains it, sending the plane spiralling downwards with the pilot disorientated by the earth spinning as it rushes towards him. Spin was ill-understood at the time (the great wartime writer, Constance Babington Smith, called it 'an Act of God'), and during the First World War it plagued British pilots. By 1917, one of them, chief Farnborough test pilot Frank Goodden, had had enough. Relying only on hearsay, he took a plane up, put it into a spin, and – against all intuition and logic – pushed down on the stick. The plane entered a nosedive, but picked up crucial speed, allowing Goodden to pull out of it. Lindemann was then brought in to do the mathematics. He calculated the necessary speeds and angles and then took a plane up himself. Without a parachute and facing certain death if it went wrong, he repeated Goodden's experiment, this time memorising the vital instruments. He confirmed that the trick was to fight human inclination: rather to press the stick down, to nosedive, to accelerate, and only then to pull out of the dive. What's more, he concluded that the stresses on the plane were not, as thought, rotation but, rather, the pull-out from the dive. It was a major breakthrough, and Lindemann's method is still in use.[32]

In 1919, Lindemann took up a chair in experimental philosophy and became director of the Clarendon Laboratory. He saw Nazi Germany for what it was earlier than most people in the UK, and he urged preparation for war. In the 1930s, he was also active in helping distinguished German-Jewish scientists. In the summer of 1933, Cherwell visited Germany to interview scientists and made his recommendations to the UK Academic Assistance Council. With Cherwell's help, more than a dozen scientists found positions in Britain. They included Albert Einstein, who became a fellow at Christ Church – Portal and Lindemann's

Oxford college. In the college's senior common room, there is a photo album of present and former college fellows. In it, not far from Cherwell himself, the casual observer stumbles across the familiar uprush of white hair. In a very Oxonian way, the photograph is not marked in any particular manner, and it does not even have the great scientist's name below it.[33]

Although kind to those closest to him, Cherwell could in no way be described as sociable. In his favour, his foreign origins and the rumour that he was Jewish (-*mann* being a common name ending among German Jews) likely created a wall between him and other students (Christ Church's quaint name for fellows) at his college.[34] Cherwell was, however, rigid and unforgiving. All those who worked with him – first at Christ Church and later in government – had to be careful. Although Harris had little time for Cherwell,[35] the two men shared more than a passion for bombing: both saw little difference between constructive criticism and personal slight. Those who crossed him, whatever their motive, were never forgiven. Roy Harrod, a Christ Church economist, recalled a 1920s conversation between Lindemann and another economist, who ventured a figure on the value of British exports. Lindeman offered another.

The matter was subsequently looked up, and my colleague wrote to the Prof. to acknowledge the fact that his, the Prof.'s, *guess* had been nearer than his own. The word 'guess' was quite fatal; the Prof. never forgave him. I remember that many years later the Prof. had to consider a proposal put forward, and objected to it. 'Why did you object, Prof.?' I said. 'The proposal seems a very reasonable one.' He made some specious criticisms which struck me as quite unconvincing. Then it suddenly flashed across my mind that the proposal was associated with the name of

my unfortunate colleague, who had accused the Prof. of
'guessing' some twenty years before.[36]

At one of Cherwell's rare visits to High Table, he came across
an idea that would have an important influence on the bombing war. Cherwell had been Churchill's scientific adviser since
1940. On one evening in August 1942, a young physiologist, Solly
Zuckerman, the son of Eastern European Jewish immigrants to
South Africa and an Oxford zoologist who conducted early experiments on the effects of bombing, was sitting next to Cherwell.[37]
Zuckerman worked at the Ministry of Home Security, which was
responsible for civil defence. The two men found themselves in
agreement on Bomber Command: despite the poor results, the
case against bombing had not been proved. More importantly,
there was no other way of hitting the Germans. Zuckerman suggested to Cherwell that there might be one way of proving the
case: survey the damage done by the Germans in their raids on
English cities and generalise the results back to German ones.[38]
Cherwell immediately took to the idea. He threw his support
behind the survey and gave Zuckerman three specific questions:
How many tons of bombs would it take to break a town? And
how should the bombs be delivered – in one sharp attack or over
a number of nights? If the latter, in what ratios should the total
load be distributed and over how many nights? Zuckerman carried out the survey with the help of John Desmond Bernal, a
London University scientist. They chose Birmingham and Hull
as, respectively, typical manufacturing and port towns. Cherwell
sent requests to Zuckerman and Bernal for data and had an
almost complete tally of the bombs dropped during air raids fed
to David Butt in the Statistical Department.[39] Butt analysed the
results and then presented them to Cherwell. They, but not the
Zuckerman-Bernal report itself, formed the basis for a minute he

drafted for Churchill. It was ready on 30 March, and Cherwell
sent the following to the prime minister:

> The following seems a simple method of estimating what
> we could do by bombing Germany. Careful analysis of the
> raids on Birmingham, Hull and elsewhere have shown that,
> on average, one ton of bombs dropped on a built-up area
> demolished 20–40 dwellings and turns 100–200 people out
> of house and home.
>
> We know from our experience that we can count on
> nearly 14 operational sorties per bomber produced. The
> average lift of the bombers we are going to produce over
> the next 15 months will be above 3 tons. It follows that
> each of these bombers will in its lifetime drop about 40 tons
> of bombs. If these are dropped on built-up areas they will
> make 4,000–8,000 people homeless.
>
> In 1938 over 22 million Germans lived in 58 towns of
> over 100,000 inhabitants, which, with modern equipment,
> should be easy to find and hit. Our forecast output of heavy
> bombers (including Wellingtons) between now and the
> middle of 1943 is about 10,000. If even half the total load of
> 10,000 bombers were dropped on the built-up areas of these
> 58 German towns the great majority of their inhabitants
> (about one-third of the German population) would be
> turned out of house and home.
>
> Investigation seems to show that having one's house
> demolished is most damaging to morale. People seem to
> mind it more than having their friends or even relatives
> killed. At Hull signs of strain were evident, although only
> one-tenth of the houses were demolished. On the above
> figures we should be able to do ten times as much harm to
> each of the 58 principal German towns. There seems to be

little doubt that this would break the spirit of the people.

Our calculation assumes, of course, that we really get one-half of our bombs into the built-up areas. On the other hand, no account is taken of the large promised American production (6,000 heavy bombers in the period in question). Nor has any regard been paid to the inevitable damage to factories, communications, etc., in these towns and the damage by fire, probably accentuated by the breakdown of public services.[40]

The scale of destruction promised captured Churchill's imagination, and he passed Cherwell's minute on to Portal and Sinclair with one sentence added: 'What do you think of this?'

Portal and Sinclair wrote back effusively. Lord Cherwell's calculations were 'simple, clear, and convincing'.[41] Seeing the opportunity, they then argued that the 'necessary scale of destruction of Germany' would only be achieved if further conditions were met: more squadrons, more resources for target finding, and authority for the RAF to focus on bombing Germany alone.

Cherwell's letter seems to have swayed the prime minister, who had only months before come close to writing the campaign off. Throughout the war, Churchill's attitude to the bombers and bombing shifted in a way that frustrated the airmen then and confuses historians now. He would, as in his September 1941 note to Portal, dismiss the airmen's promises as overblown; in the next note, he would blast his airmen for failing to accelerate the campaign. One day he would appear the guardian of European culture; the next he would be prepared to flatten Hamburg or Dresden just to have something in hand at his next meeting with Stalin. Infuriated at the depths to which the Nazis would sink, he at times called for the levelling of everything that stood in Germany. At others, he would read reports of the bombing, and doubts would creep in. In the summer of 1943, after viewing film of ravaged Ruhr cities, he wept and asked Jan Smuts (prime minister of South Africa and field marshal in the British Army), 'Are we beasts? Are we taking this too far?'

Churchill's oscillations partly reflect what one observer called 'the promiscuity of his conversation': Churchill would rattle off judgements and injunctions on a vast array of topics, often contradicting his own earlier statements in the process.[42] They also reflected the fact that he was under overwhelming pressure and followed a gruelling schedule. Every day, he woke up around 08:00.[43] His staff would bring him a cooked breakfast, which he would eat in bed. His chief secretary, Kathleen Hill, followed soon afterwards with his boxes. The prime minister did not get out of bed; it became a desk, and he got straight to work. Two hours later, his valet would arrive, draw his bath, and lay out his clothes. Hill would leave with the typing.

The rest of the morning was occupied by meetings with Chiefs of Staff or the War Cabinet. Midday would be broken up by a good lunch with his wife, Clementine, and possibly a few others, followed by at least an hour's sleep and another bath. If the House was sitting, he would go there to take questions, followed by drinks in the smoking room. He would then head to Downing Street, where there were more meetings and telephone calls, often to Roosevelt. Churchill might then dictate a few more letters to Hill before going for dinner.

Dinner was usually the longest event of the day, accompanied by champagne and a quality claret or burgundy. There were about twelve people around the table, often including Portal and his wife. As was the practice at the time, the women attending would eventually retire to another room, and the servants would bring brandy and cigars. Churchill would hold forth over a wide range of conversations, falling reluctantly silent only if two or more of his guests entered a debate. Although ever tending towards monologues, he welcomed interruptions in his own conversations – provided they were short.

At 23:00, as others joined their wives and went home, Churchill would head to his office. The night secretary would come in regularly to ensure that a tumbler of whisky and soda was ready. Churchill would work, drinking regularly, until 03:30 or 04:00. He would then get up, say goodnight to the secretary as he passed through his door, and collapse into sleep for a few hours.

Added to this crushing schedule was a hatred of detail – above all, mathematical detail.[44] The complex calculations that Portal added to his September 1941 letter bored Churchill, so much so that Portal apologised in advance. Bombing, however, was all about numbers: of bombs, bombers, and bomb loads; of houses, factories, and buildings; of miles flown and acres destroyed. Churchill's time constraints and distaste for detail led him to rely on the judgement of those he trusted. He had no time for Harris's predecessor, Peirse, and only intermittently had patience for Portal. But he listened to Cherwell, right to the end of the war.[45]

And this meant, by definition, that he did not listen to others. One who was shocked by the minute and its logic was Cherwell's Oxford colleague, Sir Henry Tizard. Tizard had played a key role in the development of radar, but by the early 1940s his influence was on the wane. He had disagreed with Cherwell more than once (on 12 December 1942, he wrote that an Air Ministry memorandum assumed that night bombing was going to win the war when it would not) and experienced the wrath of the 'Prof.' for daring to do so.[46] Tizard finally decided to pack in the dark art of politics for the more genteel world of the Oxford common room. He was likely not cut out for political life anyway. In an interview with an American researcher, he suggested that American and British scientists could work in a vacuum isolated from political considerations. 'Between scientists,' he said, 'there are no barriers except language.'[47] This is probably never true, but it was certainly not true in wartime. In 1942, Tizard became president of Magdalen College, Oxford. His last act was to speak out against Cherwell's minute. On 15 April 1942, he wrote directly to Cherwell:

> I am afraid that I think that the way you put the facts as they appear to you is extremely misleading and may lead to entirely wrong decisions being reached, with a consequent disastrous effect on the war. I think, too, that you have got your facts wrong . . .
>
> I conclude therefore (a) that a policy of bombing German towns wholesale in order to destroy dwellings cannot have a decisive effect by the middle of 1943, even if all heavy bombers and the great majority of Wellingtons produced are used primarily for this purpose.
>
> (b) That such a policy can only have a decisive effect if carried out on a much bigger scale than is envisaged [in your paper].[48]

Tizard's objections were not primarily moral. As point (b) implies, he was willing to carpet-bomb the Germans. He simply doubted that it was technically possible to do so and that, even if it were, it would deliver what Cherwell promised. Bomber Command could expect at most seven thousand bombers by mid-1943, not the ten thousand Cherwell promised; bombs would hit, at most, 25 per cent of their targets; and the next generation of radar navigation and bomb aids necessary to perform better would not be available before spring of 1943 at the earliest. Above all, such a large transfer of resources might lose the war elsewhere, notably in the Battle of the Atlantic.[49] Given all of this, bombing on the scale envisaged by Cherwell 'would certainly be most damaging, but would not be decisive unless in the intervening period Germany was either defeated in the field by Russia, or at least prevented from any further advance'.[50]

Tizard was not alone in his scepticism. When Cherwell's memorandum made its way to Zuckerman, he was taken aback, as it contradicted his and Bernal's report.[51]

In neither town was there any evidence of panic resulting from a series of raids or from a single raid. The situation in Hull has been somewhat obscured, from this point of view, by the occurrence of trekking [people leaving town at night], which was made possible by the availability of road transport which was much publicised as a sign of breaking morale, but which in fact can be fairly regarded as a considered response to the situation. In both towns, actual raids were, of course, associated with a degree of alarm and anxiety which cannot in the circumstances be regarded as abnormal, and in which in no instance was sufficient to provoke mass anti-social behaviour. There was no measurable effect on the health of either town.[52]

Neither Tizard's nor Zuckerman's views mattered in the end. Only Cherwell had the ear of the prime minister. Cherwell wrote back to Tizard with a dismissive reply. 'My Dear Tizard, many thanks for your note. I would be interested to hear what you think wrong with my simple calculation, which seemed to me fairly self-evident . . . My paper was intended to show that we really can do a lot of damage by bombing built-up areas with the sort of air force which should be available.' Whatever gap there might be between the figures and the facts, bombing German cities would be 'catastrophic' for the enemy.[53] Whether from conviction, distraction, or lack of interest, Churchill accepted Cherwell's standard for judging the bombing war – acres of dense cities flattened – and Portal's call for more money.

7

KILLING THE BOCHE

In April 1942, General Marshall and Harry Hopkins arrived in London. They were there to pursue two goals. The first was to brief General Chaney on Arnold's assumption of direct command over all US air forces. What this meant, though they did not have to say it, was that Chaney was being sidelined. The second was to convince the British of the need for a 1942 invasion of the Continent. The Germans were 140 miles from Moscow, and Stalin was demanding the opening of a second front. Although a Soviet counter-offensive had repelled the Germans from the Soviet capital, the German army was far from defeated.

Marshall did not inform Eaker of these developments, but he kept in close contact with him. He praised Eaker's work, lunched with him and Harris, and brought Eaker along to dinner at Chequers, the prime minister's country house. A partnership was established at one of these dinners. It was a good night, and the company was glittering: Lend-Lease Ambassador Averell Harriman; the British First Sea Lord, Sir Dudley Pound; and Harris. The conversation, over wine and then whisky, was about bombing: when would the Americans get their bombers? Could the British borrow them? How could they best take the offensive to Germany, and then to Japan?

In the midst of these exchanges, Marshall offered his views. 'I don't believe,' he said, 'we'll ever successfully invade the Continent and expose that great armada unless we first defeat the Luftwaffe.'

Eaker looked at him and replied, 'The prime purpose of our operations over here . . . is to make the Luftwaffe come up and fight. If you will support the bomber offensive, I guarantee the Luftwaffe will not prevent the cross-channel invasion.'[1]

Harris, unsurprisingly, did not add his agreement, but he may not have even taken part in the exchange. He was in great spirits that night, extolling his city bombing programme and boasting about levelling Lübeck.[2]

And boast he could. In the wake of the Lübeck raid, everything was going Harris's way. Portal and Cherwell gave him the intellectual justification he needed, and his directive allowed him a free rein to bomb Germany. Harris was certain he could repeat his success over northern Germany. On 22 April, he wrote to Arnold brimming with confidence: 'Come on over and let's clean up! 1000 bombers per raid, instead of 2–300 as now, and we've got the Boche by the short hairs . . . Ira [Eaker] will have sent you the Lubeck and other photos by now.' He then added a few sentences that generously interpreted the truth: '[Ira] and I see eye to eye in all such matters – and indeed in all matters. He's a great man. I do not thereby infer that I am also! But I find myself in invariable agreement with him – except perhaps that I think he will find it necessary to go easy with the daylight [bombing] stuff until he has felt his way . . . . Extraordinary how many people can think of ways of employing air power except the right one! I know you have your problems too. Frightening the codfish all over wide open spaces will never win a war. Bombing Germany and Japan will win this one – or else.'[3]

Harris's next try was over the Baltic city of Rostock. Over four nights starting 23/24 April, Bomber Command attacked the old core of the densely packed city. Despite heavy defences, the raids were another destructive success: 60 per cent of the city destroyed and two hundred people killed.[4]

In the days following the Rostock raid, Harris reflected on Bomber Command's success. Under his leadership, the Command had by then destroyed 780 acres of Germany's cities, effectively squaring the UK's account with Germany. But it wasn't enough. The army and navy would be quick to point out that neither Lübeck nor Rostock was well defended, and that their destruction could not prove Bomber Command's ability to take out larger targets.[5] The press coverage was good: the *New York Times* put the Lübeck raid on the front page, but the story was brief.[6] It left Harris hungry for more. He needed something bigger, something that would make the world stand up and take notice.

This search for the dramatic led him to alight upon the '1,000' plan. The idea was to put one thousand bombers above a German city in one night and to attack it with the greatest concentration of air power in the history of the world.[7] The plan was bold — and rather mad. There was no chance that the Air Ministry would support it; as Harris was conceiving the plan, they were grumbling about the rate at which he was going through bombs. So, he went above their heads. He called Portal and put the idea to him. Portal loved it, and then called Churchill. On Sunday, 24 May, Harris visited Churchill at Chequers, and the two spoke about the broad details of the raid over whisky and soda until 03:00. The idea appealed squarely to the prime minister's flair for the dramatic. He agreed to a loss of one hundred bombers, or a 10 per cent casualty rate.[8] Harris drove the ten minutes between Chequers and Springfield, humming contentedly.[9]

With Portal and Churchill on board, Harris assigned the job of finding a thousand aircraft to his deputy, Robert Saundby, a veteran of First World War air campaigns and a like-minded supporter of area bombing. Saundby had just over 800 aeroplanes at his disposal: 485 in Bomber Command's four operation Groups (Nos. 1, 3, 4, and 5) and 330 in its two training groups (91 and 92).[10]

Coastal Command – then in the middle of the Battle of the Atlantic – first offered 250 aircraft, but then baulked at the gimmicky nature of the whole idea.[11] Saundby persuaded RAF Flying Training Command to provide another twenty-one clapped-out planes, but that still left him just under 200 short. Harris took the brave, if not foolhardy, decision to use crews who had not been fully trained, and by mid-May, Bomber Command had 1,046 aeroplanes ready. As RAF airman Jack Pragnell remarked sixty years later, 'They got everything that would move into the sky.'[12]

The next question was which city would be the target. The obvious choice, Berlin, was too far away and too heavily defended. The next most obvious choice was Hamburg, Germany's second-largest city and Europe's largest port.[13] What was more, the River Elbe served as a user-friendly map leading right into the heart of the Hanseatic city. On 27 May, the day originally chosen by Harris for the Hamburg raid, thick clouds covered England and northern Germany.[14] A raid in such conditions risked collisions over the target area and during landing.[15] Such a disaster would have been fodder for Harris's critics. He postponed the operation for twenty-four hours, but Hamburg was once again covered by clouds.[16] The operation was postponed until 29 May, and then for the same reasons until 30 May. The pressure was beginning to mount on Harris. The longer he waited, the stronger his critics would become.

On the morning of 30 May 1942, Harris walked into the operations room at Bomber Command headquarters in the village of Walters Ash, near High Wycombe. He sat at his desk and tensely waited for the meteorological reports. At 09:10, the meteorological officer gave him unexpected news: while northern Germany would be covered in cloud, there was a chance that it would break up in eastern England. Saundby added, 'The home base will, on the whole, be clear of cloud.'[17] Harris remained stone-faced.

He slowly pulled a cigarette pack from his pocket, flicked the bottom with his thumb, and retrieved a protruding Lucky Strike.[18] He set it within a cigarette holder he retrieved from his right breast pocket and placed the holder firmly between his teeth.[19] Still silent, Harris put a finger on the charts in front of him and slowly traced a path from England towards the European continent. It passed Brussels and Leuven in Belgium towards the German border. He continued to move it past Aachen and the liberal, Francophile city of Düsseldorf. Then, he stopped. He turned to his senior Air Staff officer, his face still expressionless, and said, 'The Thousand Plan. Tonight.'[20] His finger rested on Cologne.

8

COLOGNE

30 May, 20:00: North Yorkshire

Near the town of Leeming, the crew of 10 Squadron gathered for their briefing.[1] The ritual was the same throughout the war. The men would take their seats, and the briefing officer would tell them whether there was to be a raid. If no, they would slip off to the local pub for a night's entertainment. If yes, they would prepare to fly over Germany.

At 20:00 on 30 May, the chatter in the room died down as the briefing began. The briefing officer began with a formula designed to convey drama and singleness of purpose: 'Gentlemen, the target for tonight is COLOGNE. Tonight, gentlemen, though, the raid is no ordinary one. We shall be bombing with one thousand aircraft!' The men cheered. They were not itching to kill Germans but believed that so many bombers implied safety. 'We were not thinking of bringing victory any nearer,' one remarked forty years later, 'but of staying alive longer.'[2] The briefing continued: 'Cologne is a highly industrialised centre . . . [It has] light and heavy engineering . . . factories for guns, tanks, vehicles used on the Russian front. [It is also an important] railway centre. [Finally, there are] chemical factories at Ehrenfeld, Kalk, and Mulheim lying on the east of the river . . .'[3]

Some of the men wondered which of these would be the target. The engineering works? The train station? The factories across the river from the centre of Cologne? The men of 'Shiny 10', as the squadron was known, were veterans of precision bombing.

During the 'Battles of the Barges', they had attacked the ports of Lorient, Le Havre, Antwerp, Cherbourg, Boulogne, and Calais. Against a barrage of flak, they had taken out moving barges of the German invasion fleet.[4] Tonight, however, they would bomb neither ships nor factories. An intelligence officer then took the floor, raised his cue, and let it rest on a point not far from Cologne's famous cathedral. 'The central point is right here. At the Neumarkt. Look carefully. It's just this western side of the river.' It was the very centre of the city. 'The age of terror bombing,' writes Eric Taylor, 'was about to begin.'[5]

Twelve miles to the north of RAF Leeming, a similar briefing was finishing at RAF Croft. Air Vice-Marshal Roderick took the stage, pulled out a piece of paper and read a statement direct from Harris himself. 'The Force,' it began,

> of which you are about to take part tonight is at least twice
> the size and more than four times the carrying capacity
> of the largest Air Force ever before concentrated on one
> target. You have the opportunity therefore to strike a blow
> at the enemy, which will resound, not only throughout
> Germany, but throughout the whole world. In your hands
> lie the means of destroying a major part of the resources
> by which the enemy's war effort is maintained . . . . Press
> home your attack to your precise objectives with the
> utmost determination and resolution in the foreknowledge
> that, if you individually succeed, the most shattering and
> devastating blow will have been delivered against the very
> vitals of the enemy. Let him have it. Right on the chin.[6]

That night, more than nine hundred bombers reached Cologne. Wave after wave hammered the city. Forty-five minutes into the raid, one pilot, Micky Martin, could not believe his eyes as he approached the vast red glow ahead of him.[7] He flew in low – at four thousand feet. The fires seemed to lick his wings as he flew past the silhouette of the great cathedral, rising above the rubble around it. Martin crossed the city three times, wondering whether it was worth it to drop his bombs. At last, he dropped them on the city's battered railway station, close to the Cathedral itself.

As the fires raged, Cologne's fire and air defences lost control of the city. Searchlights crisscrossed the sky aimlessly, unsure of which of the hundreds of aeroplanes to trap in their glare. The flak guns began to run out of ammunition, and one by one, they fell silent, leaving Cologne almost defenceless.

Almost, but not entirely. Bomber Command lost forty air-craft on the mission. One of those was piloted by a 21-year-old Leslie Manser.[8] Manser's plane and its seven-member crew were 'coned' (trapped in searchlights) over Cologne. As Manser tried to shake off the lights, flak guns sprayed the underbelly of his plane, wounding the rear gunner. He dived from seven thousand to one thousand feet. Manser could have then ordered a bale-out, but he feared the consequences for his crew of going down over Germany. Instead, he brought the aeroplane up to two thousand feet. The port engine burst into flames. The plane was losing speed and altitude fast. Smoke began to billow into the cockpit. Manser ordered the bale-out. The plane was bucking against him, but he held the controls tightly, keeping it stable enough for a safe jump. The other six members baled out successfully. As they were slowly carried to earth by their billowing white parachutes, they watched their plane, with Manser still at the controls, explode in a ball of flames.

Down below, the citizens of Cologne had the first taste of what awaited many other German cities in the course of the war. Under the city's streets, tens of thousands of citizens cowered in cellars. In earlier raids on Cologne, the all-clear signal rang after a few minutes. That night, it didn't come. Instead, civilians heard the drone of bombers flying over their city, punctuated by the great crash of landing bombs. Gertrud Freischlader was eighteen years old at the time and worked as a bookkeeper.[9] She was with relatives that night in the Auguststrasse, in the north of the city, and they went to the cellar together. The detonations shook the house, and dust and dirt fell from the walls and ceilings. Every so often, the drone would stop and she would think, *It's finally over*. But then another wave would come in and the whole thing started again. 'It just wouldn't stop . . . when every second, every minute is an eternity, the fear, it becomes so unbearable.'[10]

Across the city, 2,500 fires – 1,700 of them classified as 'large' by the local fire brigade – were started.[11] They tore through the Hohestrasse, which had followed the course of the Roman main street, and they consumed the western gallery of St Mary's in the Capitol, an eleventh-century church.[12] Those who had taken shelter in cellars cowered in fear of the bombs. They struggled to breathe through the clouds of dust from the flying debris and the stifling heat as their city burned around them. Gertrud was among them, and they were the lucky ones. The unlucky died in their living rooms or bedrooms, or out in the street. They were buried alive by collapsing roofs, crushed by flying debris, or shredded by high explosives. In the morning, rescue workers had to collect hundreds of charred and crumpled bodies. The only consolation was that it could have been far worse. The city's water mains held under the strain of intense bombing. A call went out to Düsseldorf, Duisburg, and Bonn, and before the bombing was over, 150 fire departments had sent equipment racing for Cologne. The casualties numbered between 469 and 586, the highest figure yet but only some 30 per cent greater than in Lübeck, a smaller city attacked by many fewer planes.[13] Cologne was badly damaged, but – thanks in part to relatively modern, wider streets – not levelled.

* * *

On the evening of 30 May, as fleets of squadrons were taking off for Germany, Arnold, Eaker, Portal, Harriman, US Ambassador John Gilbert Winant, and Dwight D. Eisenhower, who had just replaced a sacked Chaney as overall commander of the US army forces in the British Isles, were dining at Chequers. Arnold had arrived in the UK a week earlier to persuade the British to allow aircraft shipments, previously promised them by the Americans, to be given to Eaker instead. The Americans at this point hoped for an early invasion of the Continent. At midnight, Churchill stood up and announced, 'Gentlemen, at exactly this moment one thousand of our bombers are attacking Cologne!' He made a less dramatic, but equally important remark to Eaker that same night: 'Perhaps your programme is too ambitious.'[14] The prime minister was serving subtle notice of his opposition to the American plan for invading France early, putting forward instead his preferred option: an invasion through North Africa.[15]

At this point in the war, as Harris was hitting Cologne, the United States had only 1,871 men in England – mostly ground staff – and not a single aeroplane.[16] The next day, Winant sent an urgent message to President Roosevelt: 'England is the place to win the war. Get planes and troops over here as soon as possible.'[17] Roosevelt would, but for the moment it was the British who brought the war to Germany.

GÖRING AND SPEER

Hermann Göring was the most colourful figure in the senior Nazi hierarchy. As a young man, he was rakishly handsome, with haunting pale eyes. Throughout the 1930s and into the war, his hunger for food, luxury, and fame had been insatiable. He became fatter and fatter. Heavy perfumes, large rings, mountains of clothes, and even lipstick were standard features of his wardrobe. Göring would never take a trip to Paris or Vienna without trolling through the shopping districts for fine clothing, art, and jewellery. This decadence horrified the sombre and snobbish soldiers and bureaucrats who met him.¹ When Göring attended the first launch of Germany's ill-fated wonder weapon, the V-2 (*Vergeltungswaffe* 2, or revenge weapon 2) rocket, the officer in charge – Generalmajor Walter Dornberger – looked at him with disgust.² 'Soft Morocco leather riding-boots of glaring red with silver spurs,' Dornberger later wrote, 'a very voluminous greatcoat of Australian opossum fur with the hide turned outwards. Platinum rings with big rubies . . .'³ In an odd sort of way, Göring's flamboyance endeared him to Hitler. The Austrian was himself always keenly aware of his status as an outsider, and he indulged Göring's vulgarity and ostentation precisely because they made him so different from the austere German bourgeois and aristocratic classes.⁴

Göring's odd personality also earned him a few sympathetic remarks from his British adversaries. The British have always been much more celebratory of eccentricities than the Germans, and the English upper class found Göring's dress and manners amusing rather than offensive. As one of his critics, Sir Eric Phipps, British ambassador to Berlin from 1933 to 1937, put it, 'Lunching with the Warden of New College [Oxford], General Göring might pass as almost civilised.'[5] Göring's oddities and his charm might encourage the view that he was less sinister than the other senior Nazi colleagues, even harmless. He was anything but. When the Reichstag fire broke out on 27 February 1933, Göring launched an indiscriminate wave of repression, instructing the Prussian police to shoot anyone who demonstrated and giving the SA (the *Sturmabteilung*, Ernst Röhm's brownshirts) a free hand to terrorise left-wing opponents.[6] The Prussian police largely ignored the order, but the SA went on a rampage.[7] A little over a year later, Göring played a decisive role in the Night of the Long Knives. On 30 June 1934, partly in response to Göring's prodding, Hitler moved against Röhm, the dictator's erstwhile friend and ally. On that infamous day, Göring presided over the liquidation of his enemies.[8] He oversaw the expropriation of Jewish property and the Aryanisation of the German economy, and he ensured that both policies were carried out ruthlessly. He was the driving force behind the decision to impose a fine of one billion marks on Germany's Jewish community following Kristallnacht.[9] After Hitler launched his war, Göring worked closely with the SS on the 'recruitment' of slave labour.[10] Even friends and colleagues were not immune; the latter he drove to intense frustration and, in two cases, to suicide.[11]

Göring was born in Bavaria on 12 January 1893 to an economically insecure family that, as historian Richard Overy puts it, 'hovered on the fringes of aristocratic and royal life in Prussia for two hundred years'.[12] Following his father (who was a soldier before entering the German diplomatic service), he opted for a military career.[13] As was the case for so many Germans of his generation, the First World War and its aftermath defined Göring. The Kaiser awarded him the prestigious *Pour le mérite* in June 1918 for his services as a fighter pilot, but Germany's defeat and the post-war economic chaos that followed it destroyed the livelihood and sense of security enjoyed by Göring's family.[14] After the war, he became an uncritical subscriber to the 'stab in the back' theory.[15] He met Hitler in 1922 and was captivated by the Austrian's ability to convert his inchoate rage and frustration into words. Göring led the SA without distinction, fled to exile following the November 1923 putsch, returned to Germany in 1927, and entered the Reichstag as a Nazi deputy in 1928.[16] By 1939, he was in charge of a rambling empire that controlled the police, the air ministry, and industrial policy across an increasingly centralised Germany. As more territories fell into German hands, Göring established an economic empire, based on pure exploitation, extending eastward. From 1937 to 1942, when Speer bested him, this bullying narcissist enjoyed an unmatched degree of autonomy over both the German *Luftwaffe* (Air Force) and the entire German economy.[17]

To add to his own glory, Göring made a point of surrounding himself with mediocrity and incompetence. His appointee in 1936 to head German aircraft production, Generaloberst Ernst Udet, allegedly told a friend, 'I don't understand anything about production. I understand even less about big aeroplanes.'[18] Udet's chief merit was that he had been part of the same squadron as Göring, and Göring instinctively trusted him.[19] The downside for Udet was that Göring held him fully responsible for any failures. After five years of ill health, bullying, and manipulation from everyone around him, and constant harangues from Göring over his failure to increase aeroplane production, Udet killed himself. Before he died, he scrawled a suicide note blaming Göring for his death. He was formally succeeded by Feldmarschall Erhard Milch, a commander in the Norwegian campaign with close contacts to the armaments industry, having been a longstanding air ministry official. Göring reluctantly brought Milch back into aircraft production in mid-1941, first as Udet's assistant and then, during the summer, as his effective replacement.[20] He feared Milch's competence and the threat to his power implied by it, but dreaded Hitler's reaction if aircraft production continued to languish.[21]

With reason. By early 1942, Göring's star was waning fast. The Blitz, which he oversaw, had failed to bring Britain to its knees, and he had rashly staked what was left of his reputation on one claim: 'If a single bomb falls on the Ruhr [valley], you can call me *Meier* [a twit].'[22] Harris hit Essen, the heart of the Ruhr, repeatedly in March and June 1942.[23] He also bombed Duisburg and Düsseldorf along with – outside the Ruhr – Bremen, Emden, Osnabrück, Hamburg, the great medieval city of Frankfurt, the small Hanseatic city of Wismar, Aachen, Stuttgart, Kiel, and Munich. The raids made Göring and his Luftwaffe look incompetent.

In birth, upbringing, and education, Albert Speer stood apart from the grasping, lower middle class men who made up the bulk of National Socialist membership and support. He was born in 1905 in the then-prosperous bourgeois town of Mainz. Speer's father, an architect by training, had grown rich through buying, redesigning, and selling property, and it was he who convinced Albert to study architecture rather than his true love, mathematics.[24]

Speer studied first in Karlsruhe and then in Munich before finally settling at the Technical University of Berlin, where he studied with Heinrich Tessenow, an apostle of simple, unadorned architecture that was the antithesis of Speer's later bombast.[25] Tessenow took a liking to the bookish outsider and offered him, to the embitterment of his classmates with better grades, a position as his assistant. In Germany, working as a professor's assistant is highly prestigious, as professors themselves enjoy much more prestige than they do in the English-speaking world. This was especially true then, and the offer was also, at the tender age of twenty-three, a serious leg up into the world of architecture. One of those embittered by Speer's good fortune was Rudolf Wolters, an intensely close friend of Speer's who would become a hardened critic after the war.[26]

On 4 December 1930, Speer travelled to Neukölln, a working-class neighbourhood in southeast Berlin, to hear a speech by Hitler. Today, Hitler looks absurd on film. The bulging eyes, wildly exaggerated gesticulations, and shouting make one wonder how anyone could have fallen for this lunatic.[27] But there is of course much hindsight and little context in such a reaction. The crescendo of Hitler's speeches followed a carefully planned, step-by-step rhetorical escalation in which he had full control throughout. Like the climax of a drunken party, it appeared vulgar, loud, and chaotic from without but smooth, embracing, and above all exciting from within. 'Hitler's political instinct,' writes historian Magnus Brechtken, 'and his extraordinary capacity to adjust his speech to different audiences is widely recognised as the key to understanding the recognition and euphoria unleashed by his interventions. Whether industrialist, artist, or – as in [Neukölln] – academics, Hitler spoke the universal language of nationalist sentiment [*Empfindungen*] and through it made himself credible and authentic.'[28]

Albert Speer, for one, was convinced. Four months later, he joined the National Socialist German Workers Party (NSDAP) and the SA, and he was given membership number 474,481.[29] Speer attributed his decision to join the party to Hitler's intoxicating rhetoric, and it may well have solidified his choice, but his interest in National Socialism predated it: in early 1930, he had joined the National Socialist Automobile Club.[30] The NSDAP was then a right-wing splinter party that few took seriously; Speer joined the association as a true believer would, eight months before its September 1930 breakthrough (in which the party secured 18.3 per cent of the vote).[31] When Hitler spoke in that Neukölln hall in late 1930 about the unification of the 'Aryan' people of central Europe in order to 'arm themselves' against the 'racially inferior' (*Untermenschtum*), he was in Speer's case already preaching to the converted.[32]

Speer spent the next eighteen months living with his parents in Heidelberg. In Speer's versions of events, a few days before the July 1932 election, he was preparing for a three-week journey to the isolated East Prussian lakes.[33] Then, a few hours before he was to leave, he got word that the organisational head of the Berlin region (*Gau*), Karl Hanke, urgently needed to speak to him. Hanke invited Speer to Berlin to renovate the Gau's new headquarters near Potsdamer Platz. Speer immediately cancelled his trip and headed to the capital. If the call had come three hours later, Speer maintained after the war, he would have been unreachable.[34]

Recent scholarship suggests this is nonsense, a story manufactured by Speer as part of his long post-war effort to construct the myth of himself as a reluctant National Socialist.[35] It was much more likely that Speer expected the position and that he formed a partnership with Hanke: Speer would work for a National Socialist victory, and Hanke would reward him with commissions.[36] The next such commission was for one of the Nazi top three: Goebbels.

The propaganda minister set Speer to work on the renovation of a palace designed by Schinkel (Berlin's most famous architect, roughly to Berlin what Haussmann is to Paris) on the Wilhelmplatz. As he was working on it, Goebbels organised the boycott of Jewish shops on 1 April 1933, an event that Speer must have experienced personally.[37] The renovation pleased Goebbels, and he – with another recommendation from Hanke – awarded Speer the job of decorating the site for a 1 May mass rally at the Tempelhof football field, later Tempelhof Airport. At the rally, Hitler stood on a wooden platform; behind him were massive red swastika flags. Bathed in light, the red glowed against the slowly darkening night sky. It was the world's first taste of the haunting Nazi aesthetic, and Speer was its author.

Speer would have us believe that he moved seamlessly from the 1 May 1933 rally to a far more glittering prize: design of the late-summer Nuremberg rally.[38] He did not. Like all National Socialist public spectacles, the rally was scrupulously planned down to the last detail, but Speer played a marginal role.[39] 'In the summer 1933,' writes Brechtken, 'Speer had little to do with Nuremberg, and less to do with Hitler.'[40] A much-drama-tised meeting with the Führer probably never happened.[41] What Speer did in fact plan with Goebbels was the Harvest Festival on the Bückeberg near Hamelin (Hameln). It was Germany's Thanksgiving, which the Nazis made into an annual propaganda exercise designed to strengthen National Socialist support among farmers.[42] This was where Speer began his experiments with light (there is some debate about whether he invented or copied them), which would become the Cathedrals of Light so closely associ-ated with the Nuremberg rallies.[43]

Speer tells us in his memoirs that 1933 was a year in which his architectural firm flourished, the commissions poured in, and he completed projects for Hitler.[44] None of this is true.[45] He had in fact one employee – Rudolf Walters – and depended for private com-missions on the connections he was diligently cultivating with the National Socialist élite.[46] He was nonetheless getting somewhere.

At the end of January, Willy Liebel, the Lord Mayor of Nuremberg, awarded Speer the contract for the 'artistic and cultural structures' for the upcoming Nazi party rally.[47] At the front stood three massive flags — swastikas at each end and the black, red, and white Reich flag in the centre. Hitler was surrounded by dozens of soldiers, and the field was packed with thousands of spectators. The effect was intoxicating, not least on Speer himself, who was both seducer and seduced.[48]

After Nuremberg, Speer secured the contract to renovate the State Secretary's flat in the Reich Chancellery; to add a garage to the Chancellery gardens; and to renovate the neighbouring Borsig Palace as the new home of the truncated, post-purge SA.[49] Speer's tireless lobbying was central to each of these contracts, and he received the most impressive one yet – the construction of the monumental Nazi party rally grounds at Nuremberg.[50] He was handsomely rewarded for his efforts: though he would claim in his post-war memoirs to have declined payment, in fact he earned more than all his employees combined.[51] The costs to the German public purse were enormous: the equivalent of 12 billion euros.[52]

After Nuremberg, Speer assisted Werner March with the design of the stadium for the 1936 Olympics, and thereafter he received another high-profile, public commission – the German pavilion for the 1937 Paris International Exhibition. When it was finished, the Nazi eagle stared from atop an otherwise plain stone building at socialist realist revolutionaries reaching upwards from the Soviet pavilion. Then – with characteristic ambition and shameless self-promotion that was repackaged after the war as reluctant but dutiful assumption of necessary tasks – Speer set his sights on a glittering prize: the transformation of the Third Reich's capital.[53] It was a typically arrogant move: at that point, the only structure he had built in Berlin was a garage.[54]

Hitler had a complex relationship with many cities, not least Vienna, and viewed Berlin with a mixture of hatred and hope.

He loathed its liberality and permissiveness; its Jewish theatres, homosexual bars, and 'Negro bands;' its left-wing politics and educated citizens. But he believed it would, following Germany's victory, be the capital of the world. He wanted to tear out its centre and transform it into an architectural wonder that would – along the garish lines of the 'bigger, taller, better' mantra that actuated so many National Socialist projects – outclass Paris, Vienna, and Rome. On 30 January 1937, Hitler named Speer General Construction Superintendent for the Redevelopment of Berlin, and Goebbels bestowed on him the thoroughly undeserved title of professor the same day.[55]

In yet another flattering and unjustified comparison, Speer saw himself as a modern Hausmann. As the latter had transformed Paris's tiny, irregular streets into grand, uniform avenues, Speer would sweep away Berlin's neighbourhoods in favour of overblown public buildings, expansive boulevards, and clean, crisp lines. Inspired by ancient Rome and contemporary Paris, Speer proposed a radical redesign of Berlin's historic core between the cathedral and Alexanderplatz; the demolition and rebuilding of portions of the Museum Island and, most ambitiously of all, a grand north–south axis with a triumphant arch at the southern end and a massive, domed People's Hall – three hundred metres tall and dwarfing all other structures in the capital – at the northern end, next to the Reichstag.[56]

For Speer to implement his plans, he needed to clear huge swathes of the German capital: he planned to demolish between 100,000 and 130,000 flats over ten years.[57] There was, however, the matter of the people already living there: they needed to be rehoused, and there was no room in the crowded capital to do so. Berlin's mayor, Julius Lippert, opposed the plan, and he threw up every bureaucratic obstacle he could think of.[58] By September 1938, Speer had to face the fact that there would be no new apartment blocks to which he could transfer those living on the land he needed for his building projects. Speer being Speer, he did not give up. Rather, he trained his sights on the apartment dwellers who could not avail themselves of judicial, bureaucratic, or political protection: Berlin's Jews.

On 14 September 1938, Speer held a meeting with representatives of the Berlin municipal government. He had a proposal for them. 'With reference to the construction of mid-sized and large flats,' the official record notes, 'Professor Speer proposed securing the needed large flats through the eviction (*zwangsweise Ausmietung*) of Jews.'[59] By robbing Berlin's Jews of 2,500 flats of four rooms or more, Speer could convert them into smaller flats of two or three rooms and rent them to those Berliners forcibly displaced by his demolitions, generating 40 million Reichmarks of revenue in the process.[60] It was dispossession on a massive scale.

As Speer was making his plan, Goebbels enacted another: he sent his SA dogs and Hitler Youth on a rampage across the country (although they often wore civilian clothing to try to demonstrate the 'spontaneous' nature of German anti-Jewish hatred). They destroyed 270 synagogues, wrecked 7,500 businesses, killed 91 Jews, and arrested over 30,000 people.[61] Hundreds more killed themselves. In Berlin, the Nazis evicted another 8,000 of the city's most vulnerable Jews: children from orphanages, the elderly from old people's homes, and patients from hospitals.[62] Across Germany, Jewish neighbourhoods were littered with smashed furniture and artwork while fires consumed Torah scrolls, prayer books, and innumerable works of philosophy, history, and poetry.[63] Kristallnacht reflected three core tenets of National Socialism: violence, eliminationist antisemitism, and philistine vulgarity.

The arrests, murders, and suicides left more apartments vacant, and Speer moved quickly to secure them. On 11 November 1938, as Berlin's synagogues still smouldered, Speer presented his plan for the Jewish evictions to the federal economics minister.[64] By the end of the month, thanks to the support of Goebbels and Göring, he had won: on 27 November, Göring issued a writ stating that Speer enjoyed the first right of purchase (*Vorkaufsrecht*), and the first right to let, all Jewish property – flats, stores, warehouses, and so forth.[65] Speer continued his efforts over the next two years. After the war began, he officially declared four '*Judenreine Gebiete*' (districts cleansed of Jews).[66] By 1941, Speer had evicted 74,000 Jews from the Berlin property market (at that point, there were 170,000 Jews left in Germany overall).[67] As Jewish emigration was dominated by the young and wealthy, those evicted would have been disproportionately elderly and poor. The evicted Jews were crowded, in cramped and appalling conditions, into other Jewish flats, creating an informal ghettoisation in Berlin.[68] Speer's evictions, concludes historian Susanne Willems, 'linked the rebuilding of the German capital – wilfully and without uttering a single antisemitic word – directly with the persecution of the Jews'.[69] They also linked it with what became the Final Solution: as was the case across Europe, the dispossession, eviction, and ghettoisation of Jews were steps along the path to their murder. From the autumn of 1941, Jews rehoused by Speer were deported to their deaths.

Speer was much more successful in dispossessing Jews and demolishing flats than he was in building anything in their stead. Speer demolished tens of thousands of flats in a housing-poor city, and he left gaping holes in Berlin's architectural landscape before a single Allied bomb fell on the city.[70] But he built very little in their place. The Reich Chancellery was the beginning and the end of his Berlin. Today, all that remains of his architectural dreams are the location of the Victory Column (moved from its earlier position in front of the Reichstag), the neo-classical pavilions serving as entrances to underpasses leading to the Column, and street lamps running along Berlin's east–west axis, the Strasse des 17. Juni.

By a quirk of fate, Speer, the man responsible for so much of Nazi Germany's military, and therefore genocidal, successes saw his future change forever in exactly the same month that Harris's and Eaker's did: February 1942. If Harris's predecessor suffered from a lack of self-assurance and a reluctance to speak truth to power, Speer's predecessor, Fritz Todt, had the opposite problem. Todt was born in 1891 to a wealthy upper-middle-class family similar to Speer's. He joined the Nazis in 1922 and remained a committed National Socialist throughout his life.[71] After the Nazi seizure of power, he was tasked with overseeing the construction of the autobahns. He then organised the building of the *Westwall* (the Siegfried Line). In 1940, Hitler appointed him Reich Minister for Armaments and Ammunition and Inspector-General for Water and Energy. His bureaucratic empire was exceeded only by that of Göring, and Todt's was far better run. Todt's power flowed partially from his competence, but above all from the admiration, bordering on reverence, with which Hitler viewed him.[72]

On 7 February, Todt flew to see Hitler in his Rastenburg headquarters. There is no record of their discussion at the meeting, but by that point Todt no longer believed Germany could win the war.[73] The Red Army had stopped the Wehrmacht at the gates of Moscow, and the Germans were at the end of their offensive strength.[74] The Soviets still controlled vast portions of the country, and they were marshalling their resources for a counterblow.[75] Hitler had declared war on the United States on 11 December 1941, meaning that an enormous industrial power's resources were now trained on Germany. There was, Todt concluded, no way that Germany could overcome the dual effect of military stagnation on the eastern front and the threat presented by the United States. It was time, while Germany held so much of Europe under occupation, to seek a negotiated settlement to the war.[76] He likely said as much to Hitler.

On the same day, Speer arrived from Dnepropetrovsk in eastern Ukraine. German troops had taken the city on 24 August. In October, Einsatzgruppe C massacred the city's Jewish population: they marched Jews of all ages and sexes out of the city, lined them up in front of graves and sprayed them with machine-gun fire. The murders were occurring while Speer was there – they continued into March – and his meetings fit squarely within this genocidal context: a German occupation based on the murder of all Jews, the expulsion and starvation of some Slavs, and the enslavement of others.[77]

Speer went in to see Hitler after Todt's meeting with the dictator. There is only Speer's record of the conversation, so we do not know what was said. Speer claims in his memoirs that he was meant to be on the plane with Todt but that, after Hitler kept him up all night, he decided to cancel his flight.[78] This is doubtful: Speer knew all too well that having Todt out of Rastenburg gave him a further opportunity to ingratiate himself with Hitler. But telling it the way he did added an air of drama and a touch of providence given what happened next: Todt's death.

The following morning, witnesses saw Todt's Heinkel HE-111 taxi onto the runway and take off. The plane began to gain altitude and then, very suddenly, it turned and headed back towards the runway. Only sixty feet from the ground, a vertical jet of flame shot out of the fuselage. The machine plummeted. With a great crash, it broke apart on landing, setting off further explosions.

The circumstances behind Todt's death were never clarified, and they fuelled much post-war speculation. Was Speer tipped off the night before, leading him to cancel his flight? Did Hitler himself order Todt's execution? Were Himmler and the SS, without

Hitler's knowledge, behind it? Todt's own actions fuelled the rumours: shortly before his death, he deposited a large sum of money in a safety deposit box and left instructions that it was to go to his secretary if anything happened to him.[79] But these conspiracy theories – like all conspiracy theories – are hard to square with the facts. Murdering his friends was not Hitler's first instinct (as it was Stalin's), and Todt posed no threat to him. Had Hitler wanted to be rid of Todt, he could have asked him to resign on health grounds, a request to which Todt, who imagined himself an obedient, apolitical technocrat, would surely have acceded.[80]

Whatever the cause of Todt's sudden death, when the news was passed on to Hitler, Speer was the obvious successor. Hitler summoned him. According to Speer, Hitler solemnly declared, 'Herr Speer, I appoint you the successor to Dr Todt in all his capacities.'[81] This is plausible. Also according to Speer, he hesitated and stammered, saying he would do his best but suggested that his work should be limited to taking over Todt's construction tasks. This is implausible: Speer's lust for power was insatiable, and he would have seized the opportunity with glee. In early November 1939, he had pushed Göring aside and taken control over air force production; in July 1941 he took more of Göring's powers over wartime production (including some naval production); and in December 1941 Hitler granted him control over 30,000 workers in the occupied portions of the Soviet Union.[82] Todt could not be pushed aside like the lazy and substance-dependent Göring, but Todt's death opened possibilities that Speer readily seized. His pursuit of total power certainly still faced competition: Göring naturally, but also Robert Ley, Head of the German Labour Front and co-creator of the highly successful 'Strength through Joy' programme; Economics Minister Walther Funk, an enthusiastic pilferer of Jewish property; and Erhard Milch, a Göring subordinate charged with aircraft production. But Speer would see them all off: he sidelined Funk; Göring's power was by early 1942 in decline; Ley was a drunken womaniser whose corruption distinguished itself in a competitive Nazi field; and Milch, though competent as these things went, was under Göring.[83]

By February 1942, then, the die was cast. Ira Eaker and, after him, Carl Spaatz had total, if not uncontested, control over the Eighth Air Force. Arthur Harris had total, if not uncontested, control over Bomber Command. And, with Göring sidelined and Todt dead, Speer had ever-expanding control over German war production.[84] For the next three years, there would be a furious struggle between the men who wanted to destroy Germany's effort to wage war and the man who, as a thoroughly committed National Socialist, did everything he could to sustain it.

CHURCHILL, ROOSEVELT, AND THE FUTURE OF BOMBING

On 13 January 1943, Ira Eaker was just settling into his new house in Kingston upon Thames and was entertaining guests. He had been commander of the US Eighth Air Force since 1 December 1942, when he replaced Spaatz, who had been transferred to North Africa. During the soup course, a message from Eisenhower arrived: 'Proceed at earliest practicable time to Casablanca for conference, reporting there to General Patton. Conference involves method of air operations from United Kingdom.'[1]

The night before, Churchill had boarded a small plane with Charles Portal. They were bound for Casablanca, where they were to meet with Roosevelt. The meeting was originally planned as a 'Big Three' conference for Roosevelt, Churchill, and Stalin, but the Soviet leader's refusal to leave Moscow turned it into an Anglo-American summit. The meeting had been called to reach agreement on Allied tactics in the run-up to D-Day.

The flight to Morocco was not an auspicious start. The aeroplane was a 'Commando', a converted bomber. It had no central heating unit, so the RAF had installed a petrol heater in the bomb alley and linked it to heating points throughout the plane. One of these was below the feet of the sleeping prime minister. At 02:00, the point had become red hot, and Churchill's burning toes woke him. He climbed down from his bunk and woke Portal. Together, they found two other equally hot points and traced them back to the bomb alley, where two men were industriously keeping the flames going. Fumes were filling the alley and drifting up towards the red-hot points. 'I decided,' Churchill wrote later, 'that it was better to freeze than to burn, and I ordered all heating to be turned off, and we went back to rest shivering in the ice-cold winter air, about eight thousand feet up . . . I am bound to say that this struck me as rather an unpleasant moment.'[2]

At Médiouna airfield, not far from Casablanca, on the morning of 13 January, security men were on the tarmac waiting for the prime minister's plane. The Commando duly appeared over the horizon and landed safely, but security was in for a surprise. The meeting was meant to be top secret, and the plan was to whisk the British prime minister discreetly to safety. Instead, Churchill emerged in a bright blue RAF uniform that would have caught the eye of anyone within sight. Matters got worse still. After he descended to the tarmac, Churchill asked about a second plane scheduled to land. When told it was the Chiefs of Staff, Churchill insisted on waiting for them. For minutes that to the security men must have seemed like hours, Churchill stood on the empty tarmac in full view, puffing on a large cigar and waiting for the next plane to land.[3]

The Allies had cleared Casablanca of German soldiers, but the city was swarming with German agents and retained the air of intrigue depicted in Michael Curtiz's film.[4] Berlin radio delighted in reporting unpublicised events in Morocco an hour after they happened. The Luftwaffe occasionally launched nuisance raids over the city.

Since nowhere in Casablanca was safe, the security agents decided that the visitors might as well be comfortable, and they commandeered the modern Anfa Hotel and a clutch of elegant private villas.[5] The latter were reserved for Churchill, Roosevelt, and French General Charles de Gaulle. President Roosevelt occupied a spacious villa known as Dar es Saada; Churchill's Villa

Mirador was about fifty yards away.[6] When Churchill arrived, it was not clear whether de Gaulle would show (he did, petulantly), as he had refused to work with fellow French General Henri Giraud, who had the Americans' backing.[7] Giraud, though thoroughly anti-German (he became a national celebrity after making a daring escape from a German POW prison), incurred de Gaulle's wrath because he offered his services to Pétain and, in all likelihood, because Churchill and Eden considered him an alternate leader of the Free French, 'a plausible Vichyite alternative to de Gaulle'.[8]

Both Churchill and Roosevelt were in good spirits, and they set the tone of the conference. De Gaulle wasn't due to arrive until 16 January, and the first two days of the summit were conducted in a relaxed atmosphere. As Churchill put it, 'I had some nice walks with Pound and the other Chiefs of Staff on the rocks and the beach. Wonderful waves rolling in, enormous clouds of foam . . .'[9] Roosevelt was, if anything, even more at ease. The president repeatedly let everyone know how delighted he was to escape Washington's unrelenting pressure-cooker politics, and his 'mood was that of a schoolboy on vacation'.[10] Roosevelt's only complaint was of 'the Winston hours' – after-dinner drinks that lasted until two in the morning.[11]

Congeniality did not imply consensus, however. The most important differences concerned invasion tactics. The British wanted to concentrate on North Africa and delay the invasion of the European continent. General Marshall viewed the invasion of the Continent as the main priority and Allied activities in the Mediterranean as a mere diversion from the real show.

There were also disagreements over bombing. Except for Harris, all participants agreed that bombing alone would not win the war. Even Portal, an advocate of area bombing, conceded that it would be necessary to 'exert maximum pressure on Germany by land operations; air bombardment alone was not sufficient.'[12] The 1942 bombings of Bremen, Emden, Duisburg, Düsseldorf, Lübeck, Osnabrück, Hamburg, Frankfurt, Rostock, and other cities had not brought Germany to its knees, and both Portal and Churchill were starting to view Harris's promises with scepticism. There was also agreement on the overwhelming necessity of beating the U-boats at sea,[13] with the predictable exception of Harris. In June 1942, he said of Coastal Command: 'it achieves nothing essential . . . it abates little . . . it aids by preventing a few shipping losses. A very few.'[14]

Eaker arrived in Casablanca on 15 January and took his rooms. He tried to reach Arnold right away, without success. Arnold wasn't able to escape meetings until that evening, when he joined Eaker and Harriman for dinner. He told Eaker that 'the President is under pressure from the Prime Minister to abandon day bombing and put all our bomber force in England into night operations along with (and preferably under the control of) the RAF.'[15]

Eaker exploded. 'General, that is absurd. It will permit the Luftwaffe to escape. The cross-Channel operation will then fail. Our planes are not equipped for night bombing; our crews are not trained for it. We'll lose more planes landing on that fog-shrouded island [that is, the UK] in darkness than we lose now over German targets . . . . If our leaders are that stupid, count me out. I don't want any part of such nonsense!'

Arnold, himself given to flying off the handle, was amused to see the usually controlled Eaker do so. He chuckled and replied, 'I know all that as well as you do . . . [in] fact, I hoped you would respond that way. The only chance we have to go get that disastrous decision reversed is to convince Churchill of its error. I have heard him speak favorably of you. I'm going to try to get an appointment for you to see him. Stand by and be ready.'[16]

Eaker returned to his villa, took a pencil, and began outlining his argument, sending his assistant (and later biographer), James Parton, off to check the occasional fact.[17] They sat at one end of a long dining table. At the other end, Robert E. Murphy of the US State Department huddled with Harold Macmillan, trying to broker a compromise between Giraud and de Gaulle. Eaker's work was interrupted frequently by visitors. At one point, General Patton, who was overseeing security, strolled in wearing his pistols. Harry Hopkins, whose recent marriage had given him a new spring in his step, also visited. Breaking only for these brief chats, Eaker wrote all afternoon and the next day. With an eye to Churchill's distaste for others' verbosity, he limited his reasons in favour of daylight bombing to seven, keeping another sixteen in his pocket as back-up.

Eaker handed the material to Parton for typing and flew to Algiers to confer with Spaatz. The two returned to Casablanca on 19 January after Arnold arranged a meeting with Churchill.

Churchill, dressed again in his blue Air Commodore's uniform (which Eaker found 'resplendent'), came down the stairs. He said to Eaker, 'I understand you are very unhappy about my suggestion to your President that your Eighth Air Force join the RAF in night bombing.' Without waiting for Eaker's reply, he continued: 'Young man, I am half American; my mother was a US citizen. The tragic losses of so many of our gallant crews tears my heart. Marshal Harris tells me that his losses average two percent while yours are at least double this and sometimes higher.'

Churchill had this backwards – American losses had been 2.54 per cent over the preceding three months; British 4.7 per cent – but Eaker resisted the temptation to correct the prime minister.[18] He presented Churchill with his short memorandum, less than a page long, making his case. 'I hope,' he said to the prime minister, 'you will read it.'

Churchill had Eaker sit on the sofa beside him. Reading half-aloud, he absorbed Eaker's arguments. Towards the end, Churchill began to speak louder, rolling the words and adding emphasis to his rounded English vowels:

Day bombing is the bold, the aggressive, the offensive thing to do. It is the method and the practice which will put the greatest pressure on Germany, work the greatest havoc to his war-time industry and the greatest reduction in his air force. The operations of the next 90 days will demonstrate in convincing manner the truth of these conclusions. We have built up slowly and painfully and learned our job in a new theater against a tough enemy. Then we were torn down and shipped away to Africa. Now we have just built back up again and are ready for the job we all cherish – daylight bombing of Germany. Be patient, give us our chance and your reward will be ample – a successful day bombing offensive to combine and conspire with the admirable night bombing of the RAF to wreck German industry, transportation and morale – soften the Hun for land invasion and the kill.[19]

The memo still in his hand, Churchill chatted with Eaker as if the two were old friends. After Eaker argued his case further, Churchill handed the memo back to him. He said, 'Young man, you have not convinced me that you are right, but you have persuaded me that you should have further opportunity to prove your contention. How fortuitous it would be if we could, as you say, bomb the devils around the clock. When I see your President at lunch today, I shall tell him that I withdraw my suggestion that US bombers join the RAF in night bombing and that I now recommend that our joint effort, day and night bombing, be continued for a time.'[20]

Arnold was delighted. 'We had won a major victory,' he later wrote, 'for we would now bomb in accordance with American principles, using the methods for which our planes were designed.'[21] The Americans were now ready to enter the bombing war on their own terms.

Churchill might have been agreeable because he had won the other two arguments: over de Gaulle's threatened boycott and, more importantly, over the date of the Continental invasion. He did so by playing good cop and bad cop. To de Gaulle, he was the bad cop: he threatened to cut off British financial aid. To the Americans, he was the good cop: anticipating Marshall's 'diversion' argument, the British prepared what they called a compromise. The Channel crossing would be delayed from 1943 to 1944, but after clearing out North Africa, an Anglo-American force would occupy Sicily in order to ensure the relatively safe passage of ships.[22] In the view of Robert D. Murphy, US chargé d'affaires to Vichy and effectively co-chair with Harold Macmillan of the conference, this 'compromise' was very much in the UK's interest: 'The Mediterranean,' he wrote, 'was an essential link in their imperial system, and they were gravely concerned about what would happen in this area after the war . . . [By contrast], [t]o nearly all American strategists, the Mediterranean was a temporary battleground and little more.'[23]

To concentrate American minds, the British brought to Casablanca a six-thousand-ton ship, the HMS *Bulolo*, which had been turned into a reference library.[24] It was crammed with all of the essential files from the War Office and had a complete staff of file clerks prepared to retrieve the correct supporting documentation.[25] Unprepared for a debate, and in the face of overwhelming evidence, the Americans – as the British had hoped – agreed.[26] Rather than a quick fight in Africa as a prelude to a Continental invasion, Eisenhower found himself consenting to a protracted campaign in the Mediterranean. His troops would be making their way to Germany, but only gradually.[27] The compromise, writes Murphy, 'had been adroitly designed to persuade the reluctant Americans to accept the strategy which kept them fighting for two more years in this traditional sphere of British influence . . . . More than a year passed before [Eisenhower] could even get back to England to prepare at last for the kind of invasion of Europe which he and other Americans had wanted in the first place . . . . For the two years we fought there, we were a reluctant tail to the British kite . . . .'[28]

Having reached agreement on who would bomb *how*, the Allies now needed to decide on *what*. In the run-up to the conference, the Americans had put a great deal of thought into how best to defeat the German menace at sea. They agreed on the need to destroy the factories producing U-boats, the Luftwaffe planes protecting them, and the raw materials that made them. Closely following this logic, they specified five essential targets: (i) submarine yards and bases; (ii) the German air force, its factories and depots; (iii) ball-bearings factories; (iv) oil installations; and (v) facilities producing synthetic rubber and tyres. Nobody mentioned a word about cities.

The conference ended on 23 January. Roosevelt was getting ready to return to the States when Churchill came to see him. 'You cannot come all this way to North Africa without seeing Marrakesh. Let us spend two days there.'[29] Glad to have another reason to delay his return to Washington, the president joined Churchill on a 150-mile drive across the desert and saw out the day with dinner and a view of the sunset.[30]

Even before Churchill and Roosevelt went off on their journey, officials at the Air Ministry began drafting a new directive (christened 'POINTBLANK') for Harris. It was ready on 21 January 1943 and came across his desk on 4 February.[31] The directive began with these words: 'Your primary object will be the progressive destruction of the German military, industrial and economic system and the undermining of the morale of the German people to the point where their capacity for armed resistance is fatally weakened.'[32] If Eaker and the Americans had their way, there would have been a full stop after the 'economic system'. They viewed the destruction of morale through bombing as a lost cause,[33] but they agreed to insert the rest of the sentence to satisfy the British. The directive continued:

Within that general concept, your primary objectives, subject to the exigencies of weather and of tactical feasibility, will for the present be in the following order:

(a) German submarine construction yards
(b) The German aircraft industry
(c) Transportation
(d) Oil plants
(e) Other targets in enemy war industry

It went on to specify other worthwhile targets: submarine operating bases on the Biscay coast, Berlin (inserted at Churchill's insistence), and northern Italy in support of amphibious operations in the Mediterranean. The directive ended by summing up the two air forces' roles:

You should take every opportunity to attack Germany by day, to destroy objectives that are unsuitable for night attack, to sustain continuous pressure on German morale, to impose heavy losses on the German day fighter force, and to contain German fighter strength away from the Russian and Mediterranean theatres of war.

– 123 –

Whenever Allied armies reenter the Continent, you will
afford all possible support in the manner most effective.

In attacking objectives in occupied territories, you will
conform to such instructions as may be issued from time
to time for political reasons by His Majesty's government
through the British Chiefs of Staff.

Harris was unimpressed. The directive, like so many others
that issued from the Air Ministry, was based on a flawed idea:
that bombing one or more precision targets would be a panacea.
Harris was convinced it wouldn't be. The whole point of bombing, for Harris, was to take out German cities and everything
within them – all German cities, not simply Berlin. The question
was how he would continue to do so while respecting the directive. As one author puts it in the doublespeak common to Harris's
apologists, 'he felt [the directive] was open to a certain amount
of interpretation'.[34] The official history put it slightly differently:
Bomber Command interpreted the directive as allowing 'general
attacks necessary to render the German industrial population
homeless, spiritless and, in so far as possible, dead'.[35] The word
morale, sprinkled uncomfortably throughout the document, certainly helped, but it could not hide the fact that the order called
for the overwhelming weight of British and American bombs to
fall on industrial targets. Harris waited several weeks to reply,
and when he did he offered a 'commentary' on the directive. It
suggested a slight rewording, stating that 'the primary objective
of Bomber Command will be the progressive destruction and dislocation of the German military, industrial and economic system
aimed at undermining the morale of the German people to the
point where their capacity for armed resistance is fatally weakened'. Read this way, it implied that the main point of bombing was the undermining of morale rather than the destruction

of industry. Harris was convinced it gave him exactly what he wanted. The Casablanca directive, he wrote after the war, 'allowed me to attack pretty well any German industrial city of 100,000 inhabitants or above'.[36]

Although the directive was meant to wind down city bombing, not to launch a new wave of it, Harris exploited the directive's ambiguity in order to continue his city-wrecking campaign. There were only two men who could stop him: Churchill and Portal. The prime minister, following a year of bombing with few results, no longer believed Bomber Command's exaggerated promises, but he could never resist the appeal of bombing Berlin. On 27 January, he sent a note to Sinclair urging him to 'keep on the big city'.[37] Portal, for his part, knew that his subordinate was not implementing the directive, but he chose to turn a blind eye.[38] Harris continued his effort to wreck Germany from end to end.

THE RUHR

The Ruhr was Germany's industrial heartland. Bordered in the west by the Rhine (around Wesel), it extends east to Hamm, and stretches from the River Ruhr in the south to the Lippe in the north. It contains a series of mid-sized cities – Bochum, Essen, Dortmund, and Duisburg – that are actually part of Germany's largest conurbation of five million people. Before Germany's late industrialisation, the area was made up of small market towns, with the exception of the old trading port of Düsseldorf. The region's industrialisation, like so much else in German history, was rapid and jarring. Property prices exploded – in Hamborn, they rose one hundredfold in twenty years as workers poured into the area,[1] creating great demand for affordable housing. With the exception of Düsseldorf, there was no middle class to pay for the elegant turn-of-the-century apartments found in Berlin, Pforzheim, or Hamburg. The result was hastily built rental apartment blocks with small, crowded courtyards. The materials were cheap, the buildings were often badly built, and little attention was given to such matters as plumbing and safe drinking water. It was not unusual for a recently built house to collapse.[2] The region's occupants were thoroughly proletarian: uncomplicated, poor people who – to the horror of the bourgeois residents of Düsseldorf – enjoyed fairs, drink, and illegal bars.[3]

The area was Germany's industrial heartland and home to some of Europe's most important producers of oil, steel, and chemicals. In the spring of 1943, the Ruhr became the focus of Harris's war. It was the right target. As historian Adam Tooze writes, 'The Ruhr was not only Europe's most important producer of coking coal and steel, it was also a crucial source of intermediate components of all kinds. Disrupting production in the Ruhr had the capacity to halt assembly lines across Germany.'⁴ In early 1943, Bomber Command was ready to hit it. 'At long last,' Harris declared, 'we are ready and equipped.'⁵

The night of 5 March 1943 was moonless, and the industrial skyscape of Essen was barely illuminated.⁶ The old city centre was a dense pocket of narrow streets with shops and houses, a few grand, turn-of-the-century hotels, and elegant churches.⁷ A dark haze of pollution hung over the otherwise clear and cloudless city. At 20:00, eight plywood aeroplanes were streaking towards Essen. They were de Havilland Mosquitoes, made almost entirely of wood and capable of speeds greater than 400 miles an hour. They made up the Pathfinder Force and were carrying Oboe equipment, a navigation system that used ground-based radio transmitters, working in concert with a transponder on the aircraft, to identify the mission's target and mark it with flares. Once over the city, they began circling and dropping the flares. Minutes later, hundreds of bombers swept in.

At 20:37, the air-raid warning rang out across the city. Eighteen-year-old Paul Werner was on the night watch at his local school, the Burggymnasium. During air raids, it was his duty as a volunteer in the local air defence to stand ready. He would cycle through the city reporting fires, damaged buildings, craters, and broken pipes. The one place he wasn't allowed to visit was an air-raid shelter.

The signal brought eleven-year-old Horst Rübenkamp to the window. He lived in the west of the city, not far from the Krupp steelworks. He had viewed all previous raids as a game, and he found the lights, flak, and occasional explosions exciting. Tonight would be different. The sound of hundreds of bombers and hundreds of flak guns was deafening. Horst ran to his mother, and they made for the house's cellar. The noise penetrated the walls. After ten minutes, everything fell silent. The next bomb was theirs. A massive explosion shook the cellar. The lights went out. Water pipes burst, and plaster came raining down. Horst's mother grabbed his hand as she tried to climb the stairs to safety; the stairs were no longer there. The explosion and ensuing fire had left only ashes where they had been. Horst's mother lifted him up, and then scrambled over the wall after him.

When they came out into the street, houses were ablaze and bombs were falling. Dodging fires and explosions, they struggled fifteen hundred feet to the nearest concrete, above-ground air-raid shelter. Horst picked up a stone and hammered on the door. A Nazi party member opened it and ushered them inside. He told them to say nothing about what was going on outside, as it might create a panic. Covered in dust from the cellar ceiling, they took their places and waited.

Not far away, Paul Werner was at the school. One high explosive had hit its steps, smashing them and leaving a crater in its wake. Next to the school, another high explosive had destroyed a house, killing seventeen people. Across from the school, the cathedral was burning. Paul climbed up to the church attic, where the fire extinguishers were kept on the assumption that the roof would burn first. He ran down to the cellar and ordered it cleared. Twenty-four children came out into the street. Paul led them through the burning streets and to the subway near the main station. His arms and hands were covered in burns.

At 04:00, the door of the shelter housing Horst and his mother was opened. 'I could not believe my eyes,' he said sixty-five years later. 'There were smoking piles of rubble everywhere. Our house was gone, and so was our neighbourhood. Eighty per cent of it had been destroyed.' When the flames subsided, between 457 and 482 people were dead, and 160 acres of Essen were destroyed.[8] Horst and Paul stayed in the city, and a week later, on 12 March, they watched the rest of it go under in a second devastating RAF raid.

Essen was the opening salvo in the Battle of the Ruhr. Over the next five months, Harris launched more than forty raids. Bomber Command poured fifty-eight thousand tons of bombs on Germany, more than the Germans dropped during the Blitz and more than Bomber Command had dropped during the whole of 1942. One by one, the cities of the Ruhr were turned into ash and rubble: Essen (5–6 March, 12–13 March, 3–4 April, 30 April–1 May, 27–8 May), Duisburg (26–7 March, 8–9 April, 26–7 April, 12–13 May), Bochum (13–14 May, 12–13 June), Düsseldorf (27–8 May, 11 June), Dortmund (4–5 May, 23–4 May), Wuppertal (29–30 May and 24–5 June), Krefeld (21–2 June), Mülheim (22–3 June), Gelsenkirchen (25 June, 9 July), and Cologne (16 June, 28 June, 3 July, 8 July).[9] From Harris's point of view, the raids were extraordinarily successful. In mid-May, Churchill was caught up in the drama again, and he wrote to Harris asking for a list of the one hundred most important towns in the German war effort. Harris gladly complied. On 15 May, his confidence reaching a new high, Harris told Portal that 'staggering destruction [has] been inflicted throughout the Ruhr to an extent that no nation can stick it for long. If we can keep this up it cannot fail to be lethal within a period of time which in my view will be surprisingly short.'

In the middle of the Ruhr campaign, before Harris could turn his attention to Hamburg, he reluctantly launched a precision bombing raid, one that – if repeated – might have altered the course of the war.

* * *

In the early hours of 17 May 1943, Speer was still working. An assistant handed him a report. The largest of the Ruhr dams, the Möhne, had been shattered. It was one of four dams supplying the Ruhr valley with water and electricity. When it collapsed, the floods covered fifty square miles. They extinguished gas furnaces, flooded coal mines, and swamped more than one hundred factories and many homes. Over 1,200 people drowned.[10]

The 'dambusters' raid, formally known as Operation CHASTISE, is the stuff of legend, the most famous of the RAF raids.[11] The idea behind them – that a bomb could bounce into its target rather than being dropped on it – was conceived by eccentric scientist and aircraft designer Barnes Wallis.

Wallis was obsessed with bombs: how big they should be and how much they could destroy. The Möhne dam was 112 feet thick at the base, 25 feet thick at the top, and 130 feet high. Wallis originally suggested that a 10,000-pound bomb would wreck it, depriving armaments producers of electricity and people of water. In 1943, however, Bomber Command had no aeroplane capable of carrying such weight. Wallis was sent back to the drawing board. He then thought about the position of the bomb rather than simply its size: a small bomb exploding right next to the dam wall at the correct depth might do more damage than a larger one going off several feet away. After countless experiments and calculations, he concluded that a 6,000-pound bomb, if placed right up against the dam wall, would destroy it. The question was how to manage the placement. Further experiments led Wallis to the now-famous bouncing bomb. A round bomb that looked like a cement roller – technically a mine – when dropped low at the right speed and height (240 miles an hour and sixty feet above water level) would skip across the water and hit the side of the dam. The spinning motion of the bomb would cause it to roll down the side of the dam, exploding underwater like a depth charge. If the bomb created a hole, even a tiny one, in the dam, the force of the water would do the rest.

When Harris first heard of the idea, his response was scathing: 'With some slight practical knowledge and many previous bitter experiences on similar lines I am prepared to bet that this is just about the maddest proposition as a weapon that we have yet come across.' The bouncing bomb was (1) a precision bombing proposal created by (2) an inventor – the two things that Harris hated most. Harris refused to meet with Wallis and was only talked into it by Air Chief Marshal Sir Ralph Cochrane (AOC 5 Bomber Group). When he was brought in to see Wallis in March, he started the conversation on a truculent note: 'My boys' lives are too precious to be wasted on your crazy notions.'[12] Despite this inauspicious beginning, chemistry formed between the two men. Wallis and Harris had more in common than either realised. As Harris's biographer put it, they both 'mistrusted politicians, disliked senior civil servants and despised obstructionists; they possessed determination and originality far beyond most of their contemporaries; and between them they had as much diplomacy as a circus prize fighter.'[13] Rather than follow his initial insult with a swift exit, Harris listened patiently to Wallis, watched the scientist's film, and admitted that he had not been aware of all of the details.[14] On 15 March, Harris told Cochrane that he should form a special squadron and suggested Guy Gibson to command it. Gibson, a dashing young man with a lovely smile, was already known as a crack pilot who had flown a hundred missions over three bombing tours – two more than was required.

Harris remained critical and hostile – in April, he wrote, 'I always thought the weapon is [barmy] . . . get some of these lunatics controlled or if possible locked up' – but the raid went ahead.[15] By May, No. 617 Squadron was ready to attack the

Ruhr dams. On the night of 16 May, nineteen aircraft – specially designed Lancasters – took off for the Ruhr. Nine were to attack the Möhne, five the Sorpe, and five stayed in reserve. En route, the Sorpe force was savaged. Guns raked one of the planes, while another grazed the water while taking evasive action; both had to return. Another two were shot down, leaving only one aircraft to attack the Sorpe dam.[16]

Gibson's Möhne force fared better, but one plane was lost on the way when flak tore a Lancaster from the sky.[17] When Gibson's plane reached the dam, there were eight planes still airborne and ready to attack. Under intense fire in the full glare of the searchlights, Gibson's aircraft swept in low across the water. He dropped his bomb and pulled up hard. The bomb skipped across the water, hit the side of the dam, and exploded underwater. A perfect hit. When Gibson looked back, however, the dam was still standing. A second plane, piloted by John ('Hoppy') Hopgood, came in next. Hopgood's plane had already been raked by ground fire on the way over, wounding his rear gunner. He was bleeding from the head, and Hopgood could have easily returned to base with honour. Instead, he chose to press on. As he came in over the water, the Germans were waiting for him. Flak strafed his aeroplane, setting his starboard wing on fire. His bomb-aimer released the bomb. It bounced over the dam and destroyed the pumping station. The burning aircraft crossed the dam. Hopgood held it steady and ordered his crew out. His bomb-aimer and rear gunner managed to get out, the latter breaking his back when he bounced off the tailplane. Hopgood stayed at the controls as the plane went down, crashing some two thousand feet from where his crew had jumped. Over the squadron radio, someone said, 'Poor old Hoppy.'[18]

As Hopgood sacrificed himself to save his crew, a third plane attacked the dam. Micky Martin, an Australian, followed the same path blazed by Gibson and Hopgood. To draw off German fire, Gibson joined him. In what must have been an awe-inspiring and fearful sight to anyone watching from the dam, Martin and Gibson came in together, all guns blazing. Martin's bomb skipped and scored another direct hit. But the dam still held. Next on the attack was Dinghy Young, a Californian in the Royal Canadian Air Force. His aeroplane came in with Gibson and Martin on each wing tip, using their guns to draw enemy fire. Once again, the dam withstood an accurate hit. Young pulled his plane up, while Gibson and Martin swung around to join David Maltby, who was making a fourth run. The three planes came in sixty feet above the water. Maltby scored a third accurate hit, and the three planes pulled up just as the bomb exploded. The planes circled the valley, preparing for a four-plane attack. Then, suddenly, the dam cracked and collapsed. 'A wall of water twenty-feet high surged over the masonry and swept off into the night.'[19] As the water rushed into the valley, Gibson led the planes that had not dropped their bombs towards the Eder Valley dam. After three runs, during one of which Henry Maudslay's plane was caught in the explosion, the second dam collapsed. Some 25,000 tonnes of masonry collapsed, two-thirds of the water escaped the reservoirs, and 1,294 people – including 493 foreign forced labourers – died.[20] The raid had cost Bomber Command fifty-six aircrew, only three of whom survived in POW camps.[21] The surviving aircraft headed home.

A hero's welcome awaited the airmen. On their arrival, they learned that the Sorpe raid had failed to breach the much stronger earthen dam, but it hardly mattered. The bouncing bomb had been a stunning success, and the two raids showed that Bomber Command was capable of precision that no one would have imagined possible a few months earlier. The casualty rate had been extremely high – some 24 per cent – but the absolute losses – eight aircraft – were no higher than that of an average raid and were arguably tolerable given the vast degree of destruction meted out against the dams. Gibson became a national hero, though he did not enjoy his status for long. He was above all a bomber and could not forgo the thrill of the air. After writing his bestselling book, *Enemy Coast Ahead*, and going on a lecture tour of the United States (paid for by the British government in the vain hope of keeping its hero on the ground), Gibson continued to badger Bomber Command for a return to operations. He volunteered for still more bombing runs, and, in 1944, his plane went down on its way to a raid over Rheydt, a suburb of Mönchengladbach. The man who had dodged dozens of Luftwaffe fighters and tons of flak had run out of luck – and fuel. His plane crashed near Steenbergen in the Netherlands.[22] He was twenty-six years old.

After Harris took over Bomber Command, the organisation went from strength to strength. In the early years of the bombing war, Bomber Command had had difficulty getting a hundred planes into the air. Once there, some of them would become hopelessly lost, failing to find Germany, much less any particular city in it. Those planes that did reach their target would circle pathetically above it, trying to identify without radar the precision target they had been assigned. They were easy prey for the Luftwaffe, and Bomber Command suffered terrible casualties. As the Butt report to Cherwell had made clear, the bombs that did fall mostly went astray. It must have seemed futile to the surviving crew members.

In contrast to those years, the first six months of 1943 must have seemed like a miracle. Over the space of four months, Harris had taken out major German cities and brought Bomber Command to industrial Germany's beating heart. And, finally, as a definitive answer to the sniping of the Butt report, the dambusters raid had hit a target with a precision measured in inches.

Harris's command energised the RAF. The Lübeck and, above all, the Cologne raids had made the world stand to attention. In the United Kingdom, the Blitz had ended two years earlier, but only the most empathetic could fail to take pleasure at the Germans finally receiving something of what they had dished out against Rotterdam, Warsaw, Coventry, and London.[23] The aircrew had gone from being the whipping boys of the war effort – chronically short of funds, demoralised, and viewed as pointless by large sections of the army, navy, and political élite – to the public and very glamorous face of the war itself. The *Times* headline of 18 May 1943, shouted their triumph.

RUHR DAMS BREACHED *** DARING LOW-LEVEL ATTACK *** WALLS BLASTED OUT BY 1,500 LB MINES *** VAST DAMAGE BY FLOODS

Peppered with exciting reports from the airmen themselves, the story told of a secret operation that was months in the planning, of a hand-picked crew, and of the bravery and thrill of the raid itself. Air Minister Sinclair was quoted, giving full credit to Harris himself: 'Our praise is due to that resourceful and determined Commander-in-Chief, Air Chief Marshal Harris, to the staffs who planned the details of the operation, and those superbly daring and skilful crews who smote the Germans so heavily last night. It is a trenchant blow for the victories of the allies.' The article ended with Harris's own words: 'Please convey to all concerned my congratulations on the brilliantly successful execution of last night's operation. To the air crews I would say that their keenness and thoroughness in training and their skill and determination in pressing home their attack will for ever be an inspiration to the Royal Air Force. In this memorable operation they have won a major victory in the Battle of the Ruhr, the effect of which will last until the Boche is swept away in the flood of final disaster.'[24] He might as well have been looking Stafford Cripps right in the eyes.

While the United Kingdom was celebrating, Albert Speer was making his way from Berlin to the Ruhr to inspect the dams. The Sorpe Valley reservoir had taken a direct hit, and the hole was just above water level. Had it been a few inches lower, the pressure of the water would have swept the dam away. With the two successful hits, he later wrote, the RAF 'with just a few bombers [nineteen] . . . came close to a success which would have been greater than anything they had achieved hitherto with a commitment of thousands of bombers.'[25] The RAF had made one mistake: the Eder Valley dam had nothing to do with the water supply to the Ruhr, and, as a result, the long-term damage to the Germans' industrial water supply was far less severe than the British had hoped.[26] Still, Speer knew that, combined with the broader attack on Ruhr industrial targets, the RAF was hitting the right targets.[27] His relief that the dams were reparable was marred by a gnawing fear: when would the British be back?

They wouldn't. Harris had no interest in hitting the dams again. Speer rallied the workers, who feverishly set about repairing the damage.[28] 'A few bombs,' Speer observed, 'would have produced cave-ins in the exposed building sites, and a few fire bombs would have set the wooden scaffolding blazing.'[29] But they never came. On 23 September 1943, the workers managed to close the breach just before rains arrived that would have flooded the valley again. 'The British air force,' Speer noted with relief, 'missed its second chance.'[30] There could well be some literary licence and hyperbole here, but both the dambusters raid and the overall Ruhr campaign certainly threw him into a panic: he had already rushed to the Ruhr following the first raids on Essen, and subsequent raids forced him to return in May, June, and July to oversee the emergency response and to energise the workers.[31]

Harris did not have the benefit of Speer's views, and Speer for his part was not thinking about the British casualty figures: the RAF lost 56 out of 113 aircrew on the dambusters raid.[32] Such losses were a major disincentive to execute further raids, but of greater importance was Harris's indifference to the dams: he thought the advantage of the dambusters raid lay in their effect on Bomber Command morale and popularity. Cities remained the key to Germany's war effort. In the months after the dambusters raid, Harris returned to them and specifically to drawing the Battle of the Ruhr to a close. On 23–4 May 1943, 826 bombers lit Dortmund on fire. Production at the Hoesch steelworks ceased, and some 600 people were killed.[33] A few days later, on 29–30 May, almost 500 bombers attacked Wuppertal. Fires tore through the city centre's narrow streets, destroying half of the city and leaving approximately thirty-four hundred people dead. The raid destroyed five out of the town's six major factories, 211 other industrial premises, and four thousand houses.[34] 'Wuppertal,' writes popular military historian Martin Middlebrook, 'was the outstanding success of the Battle of the Ruhr.'[35]

The raid was so successful partly because air defences were poor and partly because the RAF had developed a new technique. The first wave of planes dropped the high explosives that tore off the roofs of the houses and public buildings. The second wave followed with incendiaries, which set the houses' contents and interior walls on fire. Fires spread from one building to another, and the neighbourhood was soon a conflagration. With any luck, the high explosives would also break underground waterlines, making it impossible to fight the fires. The ratio varied, but

Portal viewed the ideal as one-third high explosives to two-thirds incendiaries.[36]

This technique was again employed to devastating effect on the Rhine city of Düsseldorf on 11–12 June. The high explosives–incendiaries sequence unleashed 8,000 fires, destroyed 130 acres of the city centre, and left 1,400 people dead.[37] The industrial damage was extensive: production stopped completely at 42 war-relevant factories, and another 35 suffered partial stoppages. On 21–2 June, fires ravaged Krefeld, destroying half of the city and killing one thousand people. A precision raid the same night on Friedrichshafen did greater damage to the war effort: although only 10 per cent of the bombs hit the target – the Zeppelin works – they did much damage to it and surrounding industries. The next night, 550 aircraft destroyed 64 per cent of Mülheim, with notable, if somewhat vague, effects on industry. The night after that, Bomber Command destroyed the remaining half of Wuppertal. The raid killed some 1,800 people, destroyed 171 industrial premises and damaged 53 others. By July, Bomber Command had carried out 22 major raids. The casualties among Bomber Command aircrew were high: 7,000.[38]

From Harris's point of view, the raids were an extraordinary success. On 15 May, his confidence at a new high, Harris told Portal that 'staggering destruction [has] been inflicted throughout the Ruhr to an extent that no nation can stick it for long. If we can keep this up it cannot fail to be lethal within a period of time which in my view will be surprisingly short.'[39]

He might have been right. Although a series of area raids, the Battle of the Ruhr bombings were, given the sheer density of extractive industries across the Ruhr, in effect one large precision bombing of a major industrial target. And they had an effect. Allied sources estimated that the Krupp works lost between 25 per cent and 50 per cent of planned steel output over the summer of 1943, which corresponded to around 11 per cent of total German production, above all in steel.[40] The figure is a significant one, particularly in the context of American industrial potential. The methodologies employed were, however, inconsistent and estimates necessarily only rough ones.[41] German sources, which are probably more reliable, record a decrease in steel production of 200,000 tons; a fall in the rate of increase in ammunition production from 80 per cent to 20 per cent; a serious shortage of all manner of parts, castings, and forgings; and most significantly a flat-lining of Luftwaffe fighter production.[42] 'Allied bombing,' writes historian Adam Tooze, 'had negated all plans for a further increase in production. Bomber Command had stopped Speer's miracle in its tracks.'[43]

The problem, as Tooze notes, is that Harris wasn't interested in continuing the Ruhr campaign. Even during it, he reduced the impact of the Ruhr raids by launching attacks on the distant cities of Stuttgart, Munich, and – with Churchill's support – Berlin.[44] Having ravaged the Ruhr's cities, he felt his job was done, and he wanted to move on to bombing other cities across Germany. The move followed Harris's logic: the point was to destroy as many cities as possible, not to concentrate his destructive focus on any particular industry or region.

The year 1943 was a key one in the bombing war. Bomber Command was gaining in numbers of airmen and aeroplanes, in morale, and in destructive capability. The Americans, as we shall see, began bombing in earnest. But it was something of a lost opportunity. Some of the most famous precision raids of the war – the dambusters and the Schweinfurt ball-bearings attacks (discussed below) – occurred in 1943, when Harris sent his force to destroy the Ruhr. We will never know, but it is arguable that an RAF bombing war concentrated in its majority on the Ruhr, backed by American (and a few British) precision attacks, might have had a massive impact on German industrial production and military supply lines and, therefore, its capacity to wage war. It is worth, subject to all the qualifications about his reliability, reading Speer's post-war views on the matter. Defenders of Bomber Command are fond of quoting Speer's claim that area bombing opened a 'second front' over Germany. They are less fond of quoting his conclusions about that campaign: 'I had early recognised,' Speer wrote, '[that] the war could largely have been decided in 1943 if instead of vast but pointless area bombing, the planes had concentrated on centres of armaments production.'[45]

For his part, Harris obviously recognised the importance of oil, steel, ball-bearings, chemicals, and much else to the war effort, but he thought it pointless to single out any one of these as the silver bullet. Strangely, for a man who seemed so hostile to ideas, he took a much more subtle, abstract, and almost theoretical view of the German war economy. It was a complex and integrated machine in which the component parts depended on the operation of the whole. Industries depended on people; people depended on food; food depended on factories and transportation; transportation depended on infrastructure; infrastructure depended on industry; and industry depended on resources. To target any one industry would be to overlook this interlocking structure. Attacking a factory here or there was like a pinprick: it hurt briefly but healed quickly (factories were easy to rebuild). Bombing an entire city would take out everything in it and wreck the very complex, integrated machine on which Germany's ability to wage war depended. Added to this was the particular role of workers: without them, there could be no industry. As Harris put it, replacing a building takes a few months; replacing a worker takes twenty years. He saw little distinction between attacking the soldiers who occupied the battlefield and attacking the workers who armed them.[46] If it was morally acceptable to starve the Germans in the hundreds of thousands (as the Allies did with their First World War blockade), how could it be immoral to attack them in their cities?[47]

Area bombing, Harris also argued, was a modern, almost civilised, way to fight, and one that particularly suited Britain's circumstances. Likely drawing on his own First World War experience, he wrote to Churchill in June 1942 that '[i]nvolvement in land campaigns, especially Continental campaigns, serves but to reduce us to the level of the Horde. We are not a Horde. We are a highly industrialised, under-populated, physically . . . small island. Our lead is in science, not spawn; in brains, not brawn.'[48] It was also the best way. 'Victory,' he wrote in the same letter, 'speedy and complete awaits the side which first employs air power as it should be employed . . . [City bombing will] knock Germany out of the War in a matter of months.'

Harris's theory had been tested but not proven in the Ruhr. And it was not Harris's main target anyway. The Ruhr is Germany's most populated region, but it is made up of a series of medium-sized cities. Harris was happy to see them go under, but they were hardly Germany's largest and most famous cities: Berlin, Munich, Hamburg, and Frankfurt. Up to this point in his command, Harris had been salvaging the credibility that Bomber Command had lost during the first aimless years of the bombing war. He was able to turn to his main targets once credibility had been unquestionably restored. At the top of the list was Berlin, the capital of the Reich, among the world's largest cities in 1943 and Germany's largest by far.[49] Churchill, eager to offer something to Stalin other than the opening of a second front, was urging him on.[50] For the moment, however, the German capital was too far away and too well defended for Harris to be at all confident of a successful raid. Berlin's time would come, but for the moment

Harris looked elsewhere. He alighted on a city that was second only to Berlin in its importance, that was on a readily identifiable river, and that was easy to reach from England: Hamburg.

ENGLAND, 27 JULY 1943:
'LET US OPEN THE WINDOW'

They did not look like much: small paper strips, about a foot long and an inch wide, silver on one side and black on the other. They were tied together in a tight bundle and ready to be loaded into Jack Pragnell's aeroplane, a Halifax with 102 Squadron. Jack had joined the RAF in 1940 with his twin brother, and the two had trained together in South Africa before being assigned to different Bomber Command squadrons. He had no particular hatred for the Germans. Even the loss of his brother in the fight against Germany did not change his views. On the contrary, like many members of Bomber Command, he developed respect for his counterparts in the Luftwaffe. They alone understood, in a way that no armchair critic could, what bombing meant for the bomber. 'It was only a shame,' he later remarked, 'that they weren't on our side.' Jack's motivations were simple yet powerful. There was a war that England had to win, and he had to contribute somehow. He had considered joining the Army or the Navy, but could not bear the thought of dying in the foul depths of a submarine or crawling through mud and barbed wire. The RAF, by contrast, offered glamour. 'I had always wanted to fly,' he said sixty years later.

The strips were code-named Window. They were a further advance in a radar war conducted between the British and the Germans throughout the conflict. The idea of radar itself was a fantastic notion from the pages of sci-fi writers: deadly rays could penetrate enemy aircraft and kill the pilots.[1] The man tasked with the job of transforming this idea into reality was the one-time friend of Cherwell, Henry Tizard.

Tizard's civil service work had put him back in contact with Cherwell. Although the two men's careers followed an at times eerily similar trajectory, they were very different characters. When Tizard was in Berlin, he lived in a cold rented flat and looked with envy at the warm coats of wealthy Berliners strolling down the Unter den Linden, Berlin's grandest boulevard. Cherwell, then Lindemann, lived on that very boulevard, at the city's most prestigious address, the newly opened Hotel Adlon, opposite the Brandenburg Gate.[2] Back in England, their lifestyles continued to differ. Cherwell was a gentleman and lived the life of one. He would rise late, have a leisurely morning, and send his manservant to pick up his car – a large Mercedes – around 11:00. He would be driven to the lab to put in a few hours' work before returning to his rooms at Christ Church. They were a very grand set – one room of which was occupied, as it happened, by the author some sixty years later – overlooking Christ Church meadow and the chapel.

Tizard's was an altogether different character, unpretentious and suspicious of unjustified privilege. When he learned during the war that an official car was kept continuously at his disposal, he gave it up in favour of that most proletarian means of transportation: the bus.[3] Tizard also possessed a work ethic more like that of an American entrepreneur than an English gentleman. From 1929, Tizard had been rector at Imperial College London, and he combined that position with his civil service work. He would put in a full day at Whitehall and return to Imperial as late as midnight. He would then rouse the college secretary, G. C. Lowry, and work until three or four in the morning. Then the whole thing would start again.[4] In both committee and college,

Tizard had the gift of making everyone – professors, students, bureaucrats, and office messengers – feel that their views were of enormous interest to him.

On 28 January 1935, a committee, soon called the Tizard committee, met for the first time. Harry Egerton Wimperis, a scientist who had been researching bombing since the 1930s and on whose suggestion the Tizard committee was initiated, made a startling announcement. A short time before, he had asked Robert Watson-Watt, superintendent of the Radio Division of the National Physical Laboratory (part of the Meteorological Office, which tested radio signals in the detection of thunderstorms), to look into the possibility that a projected beam of electromagnetic radiation might destroy an aircraft. The hypothesis was a version of comic book fantasy – that deadly rays shot at an aeroplane might penetrate it, killing the pilot and crew.[5] Watson-Watt dismissed the idea in a note a few days later, but he suggested another: that enough energy might be reflected from an aircraft, with radio field strengths that could be readily generated, to create an echo that could be detected by a radio receiver on the ground.[6] An excited Wimperis presented the idea to the committee, and it requested a full memorandum from Watson-Watt. It arrived on 12 February 1935, and practical tests were hastily arranged. From these tests, the committee concluded that if the time it took for a beam to return from an aeroplane was multiplied by the speed of the signal and divided by two, it was possible to find and then track the plane.[7]

Watson-Watt's early work also showed how radar might be rendered useless: if an aeroplane sent a beam bouncing back, so might other objects near the aircraft. In 1937, R. V. Jones, then working for the Air Ministry at Farnborough on air defence, suggested that wires or metallic strips dropped from the bombers might create the impression of an assault by many thousands of planes.[8] Out of this simple idea emerged Window: metallic strips, dropped in the thousands, would render German radar useless.

Watson-Watt was nonetheless hesitant: the Germans would eventually overcome counter-measures against their radar (a point on which he was correct – see below), and therefore the moment of its introduction had to be chosen very carefully.[9] Nothing was done during the first two years of war.

On his account, R. V. Jones, pressed the idea with Cherwell, and early tests were undertaken in late 1941 and early 1942.[10] Window was on course for adoption, but then Cherwell – who 'rarely found it possible to believe in an idea unless he was at least a midwife at its delivery'[11] – intervened. He pointed out the obvious: if it worked against German radar, it would also work against the British. And then he posed a question that still shook a bombing-weary country: what if the Germans launched a new and more devastating blitz against Britain?[12] The idea horrified those responsible for defending London: Fighter Command, Anti-Aircraft Command, and Minister of Home Security Herbert Morrison. Tizard threw his weight behind Bomber Command, which was firmly in favour of Window, but it was not enough. Its introduction was delayed.

Harris was disgusted, and he did not hesitate to let the Air Ministry know. Directly addressing Cherwell's 'tit-for-tat' argument, 'it is generally wise,' he wrote in late May 1942, 'when you think of a weapon first to use it. Otherwise you lose all chance of profit before the enemy, as he will think of it and get it into service. This weapon is adjudged to be of benefit to the bomber. The bomber crews have more to face than anyone else in our war. They should be given all reasonable preference. But because we are defensively minded – and that never yet won a war – everyone else always gets preference over the Bomber!'[13] He did not, however, follow his missive with his usual insistence. He let the matter rest and only raised it again when radar-directed night fighters began imposing higher losses on Bomber Command in the summer of 1943.[14] At that time, he went directly to Churchill. The issue was finally settled at a June 1943 meeting. R. V. Jones, the young Assistant Director of Intelligence [science], Watson-Watt, and the obstinate and hot-tempered commander-in-chief of Fighter Command, Sir Trafford Leigh-Mallory, were there. All sides repeated their arguments while Churchill listened.

Finally, after an hour and a half, Sir Trafford switched sides. 'I have heard both sides of the argument,' he said, 'and I still believe that launching this weapon will wreck our defences. I am, however, prepared to take the risk.'

'Very well,' Churchill said. 'Let us open the window.'

It was a wise move. The heart of the anti-Window case was that using it would remove all moral constraints. Seeing their defences overwhelmed and their cities wrecked, the Germans would retaliate. British defences would be equally overwhelmed, and London would be open to a second, much more devastating blitz. The result would be an early form of what during the Cold War was called mutual assured destruction. As it happened, the opponents had underestimated German reticence. In one of the war's ironies, British angels were prepared to go where German devils feared to tread. The Germans had known about Window since the middle of 1942 but were horrified by the possibility that the British would discover and employ the technique.[15] The Germans would eventually learn to counter Window; in some ways, they actually benefited from it. Before any of this occurred, however, a heavy price would be exacted at Hamburg.

13

TO DESTROY HAMBURG

24 July 1943, 10:00

At air bases all over eastern England, airmen were relaxing in the sunshine.[1] The most curious went to the base's station office to hear the orders rung through from High Wycombe. The rest headed to the messes, where the operation plans were pinned to a board. There were sighs across the country: the 'ops' were on, but the airmen would not learn the target until that evening's briefing.

The pace quickened across hundreds of bases. The men headed to their aeroplanes to get them 'bombed up' and to help the ground crew check that they were ready for battle. As they approached, they saw brown paper parcels, endless numbers of them, piled up on the tarmac next to each plane. Some of the men could not contain their curiosity and opened the bags to find the silvery strips of Window. 'We couldn't make head or tail of it,' an airman of 427 Squadron later said. 'One chap peed on it to see if it reacted.'[2]

Once the planes were ready, the men had to live through the dead time between bombing-up and the 17:00 briefing.[3] Shortly before that hour, they took their places in the briefing room. Someone closed the door behind them, and the officer in charge – a flight commander or the commanding officer – pulled down the flight map. On it was a red line of ribbon leading to the target. As the men strained forward to identify the city, the officer uttered the standard phrase: 'Your target for tonight, gentlemen, is . . . Hamburg.'

The briefing followed. The officer told them about the route. The weatherman explained the conditions they would face on the way to and over the target. The armament officer discussed their bomb loads, and the signalman covered radar.

The intelligence officer then took the floor. He explained that Hamburg was Germany's second-largest city, a manufacturing hub, and a centre of submarine production. Taking it out would be of great benefit to the Battle of the Atlantic. Their target, however, was anything but industrial: the aiming point was the centre of the city, almost directly above the St Nicholas Church (Hauptkirche St Nikolai).

He briefed them on Window:

It has been worked out as carefully as possible to give you maximum protection, but there are two points which I want to emphasise strongly. Firstly, the benefit of Window is a communal one: the Window which protects you is not so much that which you drop yourself as that which is already in the air dropped by an aircraft ahead. To obtain full advantage, it is therefore necessary to fly in a concentrated stream along the ordered route. [It is equally important] that the correct quantities of Window are discharged at the correct time intervals . . . . When good communication is achieved, Window can so devastate a defence system that we ourselves have withheld using it until we could effect improvements in our defences, and until we could be sure of hitting the enemy harder than he could hit us.

'The time has now come,' he concluded, 'when, by the aid of Window in conserving your unmatched strength, we shall hit him even harder.'[4]

The officer took the floor again and asked if there were any questions. There were not. He said words to the effect of, 'It is now time to synchronise your watches. Good luck.'[5] Then he turned and left the room.

The men regrouped around 19:00 in the mess, where they had the usual bacon and eggs. Everyone knew that it would be the last meal for some of them. After eating, they donned their gear and waited to be transported to the planes.

Around 21:00, they were at their planes, and half an hour later they were ready for take-off.[6] At 21:45, Sergeant P. Mosley's Stirling of 75 (New Zealand) Squadron was the first to take off. Minutes later, hundreds of aeroplanes were screaming down runways across England. Once in the air, Mosely's Stirling was overtaken by the Lancasters in the Pathfinder Force.

At around 22:00, Jack Pragnell's Halifax took off and slowly began to gain altitude. His first job was to get the heavy plane as high in the air as possible. Down below, in Wellingborough, his fiancée, Brenda, could often hear the planes and wondered which one he was in. When they approached the English coast, his squadron joined the others high above the seaside towns below. They fell into three large bomber streams approaching the coast. By 23:00, Jack's was one of 791 aeroplanes in the skies heading out over the sea. At almost exactly this moment, Freya radar beams (which showed a plane, but said nothing about altitude) sent from the Germans' Ostend radar station, some seventy-five miles away, silently made contact with the planes and instantly relayed the message. The Luftwaffe had been warned.

About eighty miles from the German coast, three bomber streams converged into one. With the pathfinders in the lead and the bombers stretching two hundred miles behind them, a vast armada of aeroplanes was droning towards Hamburg.[7]

Northern Germany

Stade is a small Hanseatic town situated between Hamburg and Bremen, ringed with half-timbered houses following the curve of the city's harbour. In 1943, its airfield housed a massive, bomb-proof bunker. Inside was a raised balcony overlooking a huge, frosted-glass screen, some fifty feet wide.[8] From the balcony, Generalleutnant Walter Schwabedissen, cigarette in hand, looked down on the screen and the fighter-control officers, who manned the radios, below. On the screen itself, projected points of light represented each plane in the air – white spots for enemy planes, green spots for German planes – with details of each plane's position and flight direction.[9] From his vantage point, Schwabedissen oversaw air defence for whole of northwestern Germany.

00:30: The German Coast

Hundreds of German fighter planes hovered, circling in tightly organised boxes, over the coast. They made up the Kammhuber Line, brainchild of General Josef Kammhuber. He was the son of a Bavarian farmer had lived through Verdun, and was among the troops retained in Germany's small post-Versailles army.[10] He was sent secretly to the Soviet Union for flight training at the end of the 1920s, and when he returned he was instrumental to Germany's efforts to set up a strategic bombing force. When the war started, he was one of three chiefs of staff in the Luftwaffe, Hans Jeschonnek and Hans-Jürgen Stumpf being the others. He clashed several times with Göring, and likely tiring of his imperious boss, requested active duty. He was sent to France but was quickly shot down and captured. After France fell, he was released and sent back to Germany to continue his service. General Hubert Weise, responsible for co-ordinating northern Germany's air defences, put Kammhuber in charge of the first dedicated night-fighter organisation (12th Air Corps) and co-ordinated it with searchlight and anti-aircraft auxiliary batteries in northern Germany and the Low Countries.[11]

The result was the Kammhuber Line, which linked the three spokes of air defence – flak, fighters, and searchlights – in a single, integrated defence system.[12] The first spoke was made up of the fighter forces, which were organised into 'boxes' (*Himmelbetten*, meaning 'canopy beds' or 'heavenly beds') stretching along the North Sea coast from Denmark to the mouth of the Scheldt.[13] Each had a radius of about twenty-two miles and was linked with radar trackers, which covered the twenty-two-mile range and could follow a bomber in every direction.[14] From the ground, vast searchlights illuminated the darkened sky. When a bomber entered a box, the night control officer would use the radio to direct the fighters to exactly the point where the bomber crossed over the searchlight.[15] From that moment, the fighter had a few minutes to identify and engage his target; the whole thing would be over in ten minutes.[16] The bomber either would be spinning towards the ground or he would have made it through the box; fighters did not give chase.

The next obstacle was a chain of searchlights further east, about eighteen miles deep, stretching from the Skagerrak Strait (between Norway and Denmark) and ending in northern France.[17] The searchlights were grouped into quadrants made up of three subgroupings of nine sixty-inch searchlights. In the centre was a main searchlight. Guided by radar (the 'Würzburg Giant'), the centre light and those around it rotated 360 degrees in concert. Behind the wall of light, the fighter squadrons (*Helle Nachtjagd*) were waiting to attack. This was a massive, unprecedented, co-ordinated death trap that only awaited the go-ahead from Schwabedissen.

00:30: RAF Bomber Stream over the North Sea

Jack Pragnell's flight engineer climbed to the back of his plane. He took out a stopwatch, which would allow him to throw down the bundles of Window exactly every sixty seconds. Around him, seven hundred other flight engineers were doing the same. They would continue to do so for the next two hours.

At half past midnight, the pathfinders had the German coast – and thus the Kammhuber Line – in their sights. They approached it, waiting for the flak and the fighters. Their breath quickened, and their hands gripped the controls more tightly. From the back, the rear gunner's eyes strained against the darkness, trying to pick up enemy fighters. The coast was closer. Three . . . two . . . one . . . and . . . nothing.

The pathfinders streaked over the Kammhuber Line unimpeded. Hundreds of bombers followed them. Whereas dozens upon dozens of Luftwaffe fighters might normally have attacked the bomber stream, only a handful – drawn by the pathfinders' first flares – were there tonight. They only managed one 'kill', an unfortunate Lancaster.

00.30: Stade

Schwabedissen and his officers, wreathed in cigarette smoke, watched their screen intensely. Scores of white dots – bombers they had known about since 23:00 – were making their way across it. Radio operators relayed the bombers' positions to Luftwaffe fighters, who had already engaged. Then, suddenly, the tail of the bomber stream began to expand while the front continued to surge forward.[18] The bombers seemed to be reproducing themselves. Reports from radar stations along the coast all said the same thing: *'Gerät durch Störung ausgefallen!'* ('Equipment

ineffective due to interference!')[19] Schwabedissen yelled, 'What
the hell is going on here?'[20] But they had no better idea than he
did. Down below, radio operators patched through calls to radar
stations throughout the northwest; they were all told the same
story: there were not hundreds of bombers but, rather, thousands
– and seemingly more by the minute. Some radar screens showed
general 'fuzz' rather than distinct blips, as if a solid wall of bombers, several miles wide, was moving across Germany.[21]

In the air, the confusion was total. German fighters followed
instructions, only to find themselves not in the middle of the
bomber stream but in an empty sky without an enemy aeroplane
in sight. Some were ordered to turn to port, then starboard, then
port again with dizzying speed. Others were sent around in endless circles. As one Luftwaffe pilot said, 'The radio reports kept
contradicting themselves. Now the enemy was over Amsterdam
and then suddenly west of Brussels, and a moment later they
were reported far out to sea . . . [In a typical exchange, a comrade
suddenly shouted] "Tommy flying at us at great speed. Distance
decreasing . . . 2,000 yards . . . 1,500 . . . 1,000 . . . 500 . . . gone."'[22]
They were fighting phantoms.

The pathfinders were leading the bombers up the Elbe river
and towards the outlines of the city. As the planes approached,
the crews grew nervous. Despite the promising words about
Window, veterans of even a few raids were all too familiar
with the violent ritual. The regular, steady drone of the engines
would be interrupted by gunfire, searchlights, and the sound of
a nearby bomber going down. Planes not hit by flak would be
'coned' and had at most a few seconds to go into a deep dive
before the flak guns took aim. The dive itself was no guarantee of
salvation. The searchlights sometimes followed the plane down.
Other times, pilots shook off the searchlights only to be trapped
in the dive. Unable to pull up, they dived into the ground. Some

crashed into other bombers, handing the Germans two kills rather than one.

Thanks to Window, that night was different. For the first time in the bombing war, bomb-aimers could do their job without mortal fear of the flak that was spraying wildly and aimlessly around them.

At exactly 00:57 – right on schedule – two Lancasters of 83 and 97 Squadrons and one Halifax of 405 Squadron opened their chutes.[23] All three planes dropped the first line of high explosives, and the Halifax marked the city with yellow target indicators, which guided other aircraft to the aiming point. The next wave of pathfinders dropped more yellow markers and white flares.[24] The yellow target indicators guided the other pathfinders into the city, and the white told them where to drop their red indicators (red took priority over yellow when the Main Force started bombing).[25] Within a few minutes, some forty red target indicators were cascading down over Hamburg, forming a rough rectangle over the city centre.[26] Minutes later, some seven hundred bombers swept in over the northwest of the city,[27] over Eimsbüttel and into the city centre, towards Altona (west of the centre) and Wandsbek (northeast of the centre).[28]

They were aiming for the middle of the city, near the Rathaus and River Alster, at a point above the St Nicholas Church, the city's tallest structure. The goal on 25 July 1943 was to drop the bombs within three square miles of the church, destroying a pear-shaped area covering 3 miles by 1.5 miles.[29] It was the centre of administrative, cultural, and residential Hamburg.

The first high explosives landed southwest of the city centre just before 13:00. They were designed, in the words of one Bomber Command veteran, to 'open up' the houses. Since November 1941 – that is, months before Harris took over Bomber Command – the British had been thinking about how to make Hamburg burn.

It was in that month that the Bombing Operations Directorate in the Air Ministry selected Hamburg from a list of potential targets.[30] Using tests of models of German roofs and drawing on the advice of German émigré architect Walter Gropius, the Air Ministry concluded that destroying Hamburg required a mix of (a) high explosives that would destroy windows, crater the streets, and disorientate firefighters, and (b) a concentrated wave of incendiary bombs (25,000 per square mile).[31] Fires would consume civilians and overwhelm fire services, while delayed-action bombs would 'render suspect for several hours the whole area of ground covered by each stick of incendiaries . . . [The fire brigade] will approach the area with the certain knowledge that they may be blown to pieces at any moment throughout the whole night [although] . . . the "All Clear" signal has been sounded.'[32] The result would be an inferno that killed as many people and destroyed as many buildings as possible.[33] This was a deliberate, meticulous plan developed in the Air Ministry and tested by Harris over Hamburg.

The plan worked. The high explosives sliced into the houses. Shingles, dust, brick, cabinets, beds, tables, children's toys, and whatever else was in the flat followed the bomb down with a deafening crash. Seconds after drawing the house into itself, the process was reversed: the bomb detonated. Within the blink of an eye, shingles became dust; wood, brick, stone, and – if the house was occupied – body parts exploded outward in vast arcs in all directions. The house then either collapsed or stood gutted. The shattered roofs, blown-out windows, and debris were manna for the incendiary bombs. Fires spread along the floors and walls, and out of the windows. Very quickly entire neighbourhoods were ablaze.

As the pathfinders were coming in over the city, Hamburg's defences sprang into action. Searchlights came on, and the great

flak guns began to fire. Hamburg had among the most extensive air-raid defences in the Reich: fifty-four heavy flak batteries, twenty-six light ones, and twenty-two searchlight batteries.[34]
But they were of no use. Window was reaching the peak of its
effectiveness. Radar controllers could provide no information
on the incoming planes; searchlight operators flashed their lights
randomly across the sky or pointed them directly upward, and
the guns sprayed barrages of flak indiscriminately, in all directions. Experienced pilots reaching the city could not believe it:
they were not caught in searchlight cones, which all but promised
death, and they suffered no targeted bursts of flak.

The bombing of Hamburg occurred in six waves. The first five
waves lasted eight minutes, during which more than a hundred
planes dropped a line of bombs on the city.[35] Each high explosive
was followed by a quick, violent flash and the delayed echo of the
explosion. The 4,000-pound bombs created a still larger, though
slower, explosion. Between these flashes were thousands of twin-
kles, as incendiary bombs set the houses, clothes, cars, and, in some
cases, people on fire. In the last wave, sixteen planes finished the
raid at 01:50. Five minutes later, a straggler, a main force Halifax
that would no doubt have been brought down had German
defences been operating, passed over the city and dropped its load.
Then, an intact bombing formation turned from the city, banked
north, and flew home. For the bombers, it was over.

For the city, it was not. Hamburg would burn for days. Fifteen
minutes after the first bombs hit, the telephone link between the
area's fire station and the central station was knocked out, and
the bulk of Hamburg's firemen responded to calls from the southeast of the city, which was suffering only relatively mild effects of
scattered bombing.[36] Calls went out to Lübeck, Kiel, and Bremen,
but their fire engines would only arrive early the next morning.[37]
Within a single hour, the RAF had dropped 2,284 tonnes of

bombs, including on average 17,000 incendiaries per square kilo-metre.[38] Before they died down, the fires created a perimeter six-teen miles in circumference, and fifty-four miles of streets in west-ern Hamburg were in flames.[39] In the city centre, the Rathaus had been hit, and St Nicholas Church was destroyed.[40] The house in which Johannes Brahms was born, in the Speckstrasse, was rub-ble. Twenty high explosives had hit the Hagenbeck Zoo, leaving more than one hundred animals dead or dying.[41] Fifteen hundred people were dead,[42] and the bombing had only begun.

The raid had been one of the easiest in the RAF's history. Of the 791 bombers that left for Hamburg, only a handful failed to return. Mechanical problems led forty-five to turn back before reaching the German coast, another two jettisoned their load just inside Germany (dropping a bomb load anywhere on German soil constituted a sortie), and five crashed. Two Halifaxes – from 51 and 158 Squadrons – strayed badly off course and were brought down by German fighters well north of Hamburg. One came down when a Stirling dived to escape a searchlight and crashed into another plane head-on. The pilot of the Stirling, Flying Officer Geoff Turner, managed to bring his plane safely back to England, despite having lost a four-foot section of the plane's starboard wing. After he touched ground in England, he had less than two months to live: Turner and his entire crew were shot down during a 23 September 1943 raid on Mannheim.[43]

The next major raid was the firestorm – and the end of Hamburg.

AFTER HAMBURG

GERMANY'S NIGHTMARE

By mid-1943, as the air war got worse and worse for Germany, Speer's career got better and better. He assumed ever larger shares of his rival's authority. In February 1942, he had also taken over all of Todt's responsibilities, in the days after the latter's death, while simultaneously seeing off attempts by Ley, Funk, and Bormann to limit that power.[1] On the 14th, Speer assembled workers from the Reich Ministry for Armament and Munitions in the courtyard of the Ministry's headquarters next to the Brandenburg Gate, and he gave a rousing speech. 'However great our grief over [Todt's] death is, that of the Führer is greater still. We all want to ease his pain through indefatigable labour. The success or failure of our work will determine Germany's victory. I have vowed to the Führer that I will dedicate my entire strength to achieving this goal, and I know that I can count on all of you. Sieg Heil! Sieg Heil! Sieg Heil!'[2] To signal his support to his new employees and to secure theirs, he integrated his 'Baustab (Construction Staff) Speer' into the Organization Todt.[3]

Speer threw himself into his new responsibilities with typical determination and typical amorality. On 19 February, he arranged the publication of a Führer order stating that anyone who knowingly published false information on resources, materials, equipment, or labour needs would be imprisoned or, in extreme cases, executed.[4] He worked closely with Himmler to implement these measures.[5] Speer extended his efforts to include the camps: he seconded two managers to concentration camps to root out corruption and inefficiencies in production.[6] Speer and Himmler were, and would remain, partners in devoting every effort – including the widespread use of forced labour inside and outside of concentration camps – to furthering Germany's war.[7]

With Ley and Funk otherwise occupied, his main rivals were Göring and Milch. Twice in February, Speer visited Göring in his lavishly and – being Göring – garishly dedicated country estate, Carinhall (named for his deceased wife).[8] The Reichsmarschall was still hoping to tame and control the young minister, but Speer – being Speer – bested him. He was conciliatory and soothing. With feigned sincerity, he assured Göring that he had no intention of reducing the latter's competencies, and offered what he hoped would seem like a major concession: he, Speer, would perform his duties 'within [Göring's] Four Year plan'.[9] This was, in fact, meaningless; Göring's role as Commissioner of the Four Year Plan was at most ceremonial, without the powers that Todt and, above all, Speer had assumed. But the promise left Göring 'deeply satisfied'.[10] By early March, the two men agreed on a title: Speer would be the 'General Authority (*Generalbevollmächtigten*) for Production within the Four Year Plan'.[11] Göring thus signed himself out of industrial and armaments policy and tied his star to an air war that was already going badly.

That was spring 1942. In summer 1943, Speer was in front of the Central Planning Committee (*die Zentrale Planung*), an overarching body presided over by Speer and Milch that co-ordinated supplies of raw material across the German economy.[12] From Speer's February 1942 power grab, he and Milch (responsible for armaments production for the Luftwaffe until 1944) had been equal partners in the German war effort.[13]

After the RAF attacks, Speer had been briefed on what happened in Hamburg: smashed water pipes, hurricane winds, cyclone-like firestorms, blazing asphalt, and incinerated civilians.

As he reported to the committee, the words he spoke seemed to be a vindication of Harris and his whole bombing strategy. 'If the air raids,' intoned Speer, 'continue at the present scale, within three months we shall be relieved of a number of questions we are at present discussing. We shall simply be coasting downhill, smoothly and relatively swiftly . . . We might just as well hold the final meeting of [the] Central Planning [Committee] in that case.'[14]

Over the next few days, apocalyptic reports continued to come in. According to his own account, Speer was devastated by the attack and went to visit Hitler personally. 'I told him,' Speer wrote after the war, 'that armaments production was collapsing and threw in the further warning that a series of attacks of this sort, extended to six more cities, would bring Germany's production to a total halt.'[15] It is possible that he said this to the Führer, but it is equally possible that this is a narrative technique typical of Speer and his indulgent biographer, Joachim Fest: present an insoluble problem, land Speer on the scene, and achieve a miraculous solution.[16]

Speer, in any case, had little to do with Hamburg's recovery; it was instead Hamburgers themselves who turned the situation around. Hamburg's workers turned up for their shifts in the days and weeks after the bombings, and they worked with enthusiasm and determination.[17] Within three days, the Tiefstack power station was up and running, another followed after twenty days, and even the completely destroyed Barmbek station was back in service by the end of October.[18] Telephones were working by the end of August; gas supplies, all but knocked out, were restored to the vast majority of the city by the end of November; and 97 per cent of the city had running water by the following spring. Industrial production staged an equally impressive recovery: by the end of 1943, aircraft production was at 91 per cent of pre-raid levels; the badly hit chemical industry was at 71 per cent; and the manufacture of electrical goods, optics, and precision tools had exceeded its late July levels. The British raids had hardly touched the shipbuilding firm Blohm and Voss (the British weren't trying to destroy it, and the Americans missed), and U-boats were entering the water again by the end of September.

Against this backdrop, Hamburgers' morale improved sharply. Indeed, within a few weeks, a pervasive sense of total apocalypse had been replaced by a sense of triumph, of pride in survival. Rather than destroying morale, Hamburgers had a new sense of community; they had pulled together in the face of an unimaginable catastrophe.[19] This is perhaps less surprising than it seems. Like James Joyce's snow, Harris's bombs rained down on both the living and the dead, the innocent and the guilty, the collaborator and the resister. When one survivor took a hand reaching out from the rubble of a bombed house, he did not ask if it belonged to a Nazi. Even those with the most reason to hate the Germans were not immune: in some cases, hidden Jews went through the streets helping bomb victims.[20] The bombing made Hamburgers, always a proud people, love their wounded city more than ever.

Speer nonetheless had every reason to worry. Since becoming armaments minister in 1942, he placed the German economy in the full service of the Wehrmacht and made strenuous efforts to increase war-related industrial production.[21] He created the Central Planning Committee to oversee German industrial production, rationalised steel and coal production, and linked the production of arms with the production of their component parts.[22] It gave him and Milch authority over 90 per cent of armaments production, with Speer in the superior position not because of his formal responsibilities or competence but because of his connection to Hitler, who transmitted his priorities through Speer down the chain of command.[23] Speer, as ever, greatly over-claimed credit: many of the rationalisation efforts had begun long before he became armaments minister,[24] and he passed off as his own several key innovations conceived of and implemented by others.[25] The increase in production, embedded in a concerted Goebbels–Speer propaganda effort designed to rally the home front in favour of war, was nonetheless real enough: the rate of armaments production continued to rise until the summer of 1944.[26]

The sudden surge in productive effort resulted in bottlenecks. The growth increase was reaching natural limits, and it was particularly vulnerable to disruption.[27] At exactly this moment, from the summer of 1943, the Americans began their bombing campaign in earnest.

On the evening of 16 August 1943, the men of the US 351st Bomb Group were having beers at the RAF base at Polebrook, in Northamptonshire.[28] They had only two each, since they might need clear heads in a few hours' time. They were in bed by ten o'clock.

A few hours later, they were awoken. Orderlies shouted at them, and the drowsy men got out of bed and made their way to the mess, where they met good and bad news. The good news was that they were being served fresh rather than powdered eggs, and an unusually large number of cooks were there to prepare them to the men's liking. The bad news was that this could only mean one thing: they were being sent out over Germany.

At 02:00 in bomb groups across England, the men went to their briefings. It followed the same ritual everywhere and used the British format. Each briefing took place in a classroom-like venue, with a large, covered map of Europe at the front. Once the men had taken their seats, the briefing officer removed the cover. Some men groaned and put their heads in their hands;

others cursed, and a few even stood up and shouted abuse. The marker showed a route from England deep into Germany. One formation was to execute a precision raid over aircraft factories at Regensburg; another was to bomb Schweinfurt. And they were to have no fighter cover. The bombings were undertaken following a 3 June 1943 joint directive, which updated POINTBLANK: in the light of the threat posed by the Luftwaffe to plans for invading the Continent, UK Bomber Command and the US Eighth Air Force were to concentrate on targets associated with the aircraft and ball-bearing industries.[29] The briefing ended, the crews hurried to their planes, and they and ground support began loading the bombs. By 05:00, the force was ready to take off.

The order to take off was to be given by Eighth Bomber Command headquarters, fifty miles from the nearest bomber base.[30] There, its head, Fred Anderson, was studying the weather reports. Born in Kingston, New York, Anderson had attended flying school at Kelly Field in Texas in the late 1920s. He was widely known as a fiercely aggressive commander who looked with an admiring eye to Harris's area bombing campaign. Commenting on the Eighth's engagement with the Luftwaffe, he once said that 'if it comes up here where we get one of those damn cities that we can see and have our force on . . . there won't be a damn house left.'[31]

Frustrated with the slow pace of the US bombing war,[32] the ever-impatient Arnold had forced Eaker to take on Anderson as the new commander of the Eighth's Bomber Force in Europe. He had arrived in July, and Schweinfurt was his first test. Anderson was in phone contact with the two commanders in charge of the missions: Brigadier General Williams, of the 1st Bombardment Wing responsible for Schweinfurt, and Colonel Curtis LeMay, of the 4th Bombardment Wing responsible for Regensburg. Of the two men, LeMay would become by far the most infamous, viewed with reason as a ruthless airman who rained fire down on Japan.

But, like Harris, he was more complicated than the caricature. In the spring of 1938, he had heard about a military plane that crashed into a crowd at a Colombian air show, killing sixty people and mutilating many others. That night, he dreamed of the time his brother had fallen from a barn roof onto a pile of broken bottles. A few days later, LeMay, on the start of a South American tour, attended the funeral of the Colombian victims. Viewing the weeping relatives, he remembered airmen who had died in training missions. LeMay thought 'how very much alike we are after all'.[33] Similarly, speaking after the war of Germany, he said that '[y]ou drop a load of bombs, and, if you're cursed with any imagination at all, you have at least one quick horrid glimpse of a child lying in bed with a whole ton of masonry tumbling down on top of him; or a three-year-old girl wailing for *Mutter . . . Mutter . . .* because she has been burned. Then you have to turn away from the picture if you intend to retain your sanity.'[34]

On 17 August 1943, as LeMay awaited the order, the skies above Anderson at headquarters were clear, but clouds covered all of the bomber bases. Almost four hundred planes were to take off in rapid succession, and doing so through clouds would inevitably lead to collisions. Anderson told LeMay and Williams to wait an hour. He did, but another hour later things hardly looked better. Anderson rang LeMay and Williams and asked them if he could wait yet another hour. LeMay told him that he could not: the Regensburg force had to fly on from Germany to North Africa and needed to land there by daylight. The most he could offer, LeMay told Anderson, was thirty minutes.

At 06:40, the weather had cleared somewhat, but not much. Anderson had to decide whether to call off the whole thing, send up LeMay's force alone, or take the risk and send up both forces together.[35] None of the options was appealing. Sending them together would lead to crashes. Delaying the mission might be career suicide, as Arnold was demanding results. And sending only one of the forces would mean that the Regensburg mission's chief advantage – as a diversionary raid to draw off Luftwaffe fighters, thereby allowing the other planes to bomb Schweinfurt more effectively – would be lost. Under enormous pressure, Anderson made his call: he ordered LeMay to prepare for immediate take-off, and had Williams delay. LeMay put down the phone and ran to the car standing outside his headquarters. The car sped along the fourteen miles between LeMay's headquarters and Snetterton Heath, the base of the 96th Bomb Group. When he arrived, LeMay got out of the car in his flying clothes and his driver carried his parachute and kit to the plane. Archie Old, who had hoped the delay meant he could fly the lead aircraft, asked LeMay, 'What in the hell are you doing here?' LeMay was there to lead the mission.[36]

The B-17s flew with fighter escort until Antwerp, where dwindling fuel supplies forced the fighters to pull off. The Germans were waiting, and they attacked the Americans with force. LeMay pushed on. Emergency hatches, exit doors, prematurely opened parachutes, aeroplane parts, and bodies shot past them in the slipstream.[37] The Americans soldiered on. The target was hit successfully and the city of Regensburg itself was untouched. LeMay's force suffered high losses – twenty-four aircraft, or 16 per cent of the planes that went out.[38]

A full four hours after LeMay's bombers took off for Regensburg, some two thousand men of the 1st Bombardment Wing were still grounded. They had been awake for eleven hours and waiting in or around their planes for five. A mission had never before been delayed so long. 'Perhaps the thing that still remains most vivid of the memory of that long and arduous day,' one veteran later wrote, 'was the awful wait as take-off was postponed again and again. If there be a limit to human endurance of that sort of thing, we must have approached it that day.'[39]

Two hours later, Williams's bombers were crossing the English coast and flying over the North Sea. At 12:30, German radar picked them up. At the Dutch coast, they were met by eight squadrons of Spitfires that would accompany them to Antwerp, fifteen minutes away.[40] The Americans loved the Spitfires. They were often flown by Poles, who – motivated by an intense hatred for the Germans – were particularly aggressive. Regulations at the time told the Americans to treat only planes that turned towards their formation as an enemy.[41] But if the Poles saw a Luftwaffe fighter in or on the other side of an American formation, they would come straight at it.[42] Wiggling their wings, they would blast right through the formation to hunt the Germans down.[43]

At Antwerp, American P-47s met them and flew with them until Eupen, in eastern Belgium, which the head of the bomber force passed at 14:10. One bomber had already been shot down, and several more had to turn back. But the bulk of the force was on its way to Schweinfurt, fifty minutes away. They had, however, reached the limits of their escort range, and from Eupen they had to continue alone.

Wilbur Klint of the 303rd Bomb Group was the co-pilot in one of the B-17s. He had flown his first mission the day before, as part of an American raid on Le Bourget airport at Paris. As the bombing formation came towards the target, a small number of fighters turned on them. As they opened machine-gun fire, the wings lit up, and looked like long neon tubes. The formation blasted past the fighters with no difficulty. 'We were young and confident,' Wilbur observed six decades later, 'and I thought, this is a piece of cake.'

Schweinfurt would be anything but. At Eupen, Wilbur watched the P-47 escort fighters turn away. They were on their own. Almost immediately, pilots in the leading aircraft made out black dots coming towards them, seemingly straight on. They were German Luftwaffe fighters, dozens of them, bearing down on the B-17s. Within seconds, the Germans were all over them. They flew straight at the Americans, all guns blazing. Out for blood, the fighters attacked mercilessly. They fired upside down. They fired as they did mid-air rolls, bearing down on the B-17s. American pilots saw dozens of aircraft sailing right at them and then, at the last second, diving and shooting past. 'I witnessed,' a waist gunner in the 384th Bomb Group later reported, 'something that mankind will never see again . . . a parachute invasion of Germany. There were planes in flat spins, planes in wide spins. Planes were going down so often that it became useless to report them.'[44] The attacks would come in waves, every ten minutes or so. A group of fighters would finish their attack, land to refuel, and come back up again. 'They kept coming and coming and coming and coming,' reported one navigator, 'and we still had miles to go before the target.'[45]

The bombers pressed on. Ineffectively trying to dodge the incoming fighters, they absorbed round after round of bullets from the front and flak from below. Flaming bombers fell away on all sides. By the time they reached the city's three ball-bearing factories – which produced 70 per cent of Germany's ball-bearings – thirty-two bombers had been lost. The remaining 298 began bombing at 16:00 local time, unloading 265 tons of high explosives and 115 tons of incendiaries on the factories and, in some cases, the surrounding neighbourhoods.[46]

It was a beautiful, clear day when Wilbur's B-17 reached Schweinfurt. Still under fighter attack, the crew approached the target area. As they turned at the initial point where all of the bombers began their bomb runs, the flak guns opened. Shells began exploding all around and shrapnel began ripping holes in the fuselage. As it did, the bomb bays opened. The lead bomber dropped his bombs, and the B-17s behind him followed.

The moment the group was out of flak range, the German fighters were back. Under heavy Luftwaffe attack, the Americans flew north out of Schweinfurt, banked west, and continued on to Eupen and the waiting Spitfires. By the time they reached England, they had lost thirty-six heavy bombers, a staggering casualty rate of 20 per cent. Each one of them represented 22,500 hours of labour.[47] The Schweinfurt raid shook American confidence.

They paid a high price, but they exacted a heavy toll. The Americans were only able to drop thousand-pound bombs (the British had 4,000-pound bombs by this point), and one-third missed their targets and landed on houses. Nonetheless, they meted out significant damage, causing a 34 per cent loss of ball-bearing production.[48] The following day, Hans Jeschonnek, the Luftwaffe's Chief of Staff, shot himself.[49]

The day after the raid, on 18 August, Schweinfurt was at its most vulnerable. The Luftwaffe had lost forty-seven fighters in the previous battle and would be less able to defend the city. The American bombing had blown off factory roofs, collapsed the upper floors, and punched great gaping holes. The ball-bearings machines on the ground floor were exposed.[50] The Germans waited for the follow-up raid. It never came. Given their losses, the Americans were in no position to launch one. That left it to the RAF.

The British Air Staff had been pressuring Harris to bomb Schweinfurt throughout late 1943.[51] 'It is essential,' Norman Bottomley, Deputy Chief of Air Staff, wrote to Harris on 23 December 1943, 'that the attempt to achieve within the time available the maximum destruction of the major built-up areas in Germany should not be allowed to prejudice the implementation of the Joint Anglo-American policy of employing the night bomber force whenever possible for the destruction of vital centres associated with . . . vital industries, e.g. ball-bearing and fighter assembly plants; these industries have been accorded the highest priority in the combined bomber offensive plan . . . Your night bomber forces would make the greatest contribution by completely destroying those vital centres which can be reached by day only at a heavy cost; examples are Schweinfurt, Leipzig and centres of twin-engined fighter industry.' Drawing on an intelligence report, Bottomley continued: 'Whereas the German people feared the night attacks, Hitler and the German High Command feared the daylight precision attacks on individual factories. Hitler openly boasted that he could, by means of his party organisations, control the morale of the population for some considerable time . . . . The Air Staff must take a somewhat less confident view than [you do] of the possibility of causing the enemy to capitulate by reason of area attacks alone . . . .'[52] Bottomley was third in the chain of command after Portal, and the man from whom, in Harris's words, 'on policy and strategy I take my instructions.'[53] You would not have known it. In his reply, Harris wrote: 'Hitler's record as a prophet is not such as to inspire confidence . . . . It is surely impossible to believe that an increase by more than one half of existing devastation [through city bombing] within four months could be sustained by Germany without total collapse.'[54]

In the days after the American raid, Harris responded with delaying tactics, finding one excuse after another not to bomb Schweinfurt.[55] On 18 August 1943, when Schweinfurt was at peak vulnerability, Harris sent his bombers to destroy the V-2 factories at Peenemünde instead. In a tightly executed attack, three waves of bombers hit the plants. Sixty-one planes from 6 Group (formed from Royal Canadian Air Force crews in January) made up one-half of the third wave, and the lion's share of the losses. A full 20 per cent of the crews dispatched would not return – a figure four times the maximum acceptable loss rate.[56] Trassenheide, the concentration and labour camp next to the facility, was also hit by stray bombs, killing – according to German figures – some five hundred forced labourers.[57]

The Germans responded to the raid by redoubling production through slave labour. At the end of August, forced labourers from Russia, Poland, and France were transported from Buchenwald to the newly founded Dora concentration camp.[58] In October, the SS created the Mittelbau concentration camp, which included Dora and other subcamps, some forty in total.[59] The forced labourers were working for Mittelwerk GmbH, founded in September by Karl Hettlage, a close associate of Albert Speer.[60] It was one of many examples of close co-operation between Speer and the SS. Surrounded by dirt and vermin, thousands of slave labourers worked in appalling and dangerous conditions, losing their lives through exhaustion, injury, and untreated illness.[61] To compel those alive to continue working, Hettlage made an example of those killed and strung their corpses from the rafters.[62] Between September and March alone, 5,000 of the 17,000 people delivered to Mittelbau-Dora died.[63] When Speer visited the site on 10 December (a viewing he denied at Nuremberg), there were thousands of corpses lying on the ground.[64]

Eisenhower suggested after the war that the raid knocked V-2 production back six months; more conservative – and realistic – estimates place the delay, caused by the bombing itself but also by frantic efforts to relocate production, at six to eight weeks.[65] In either case, the famous raid mattered relatively little for the course of the war. Peenemünde was an important hit, but the V-1s and V-2s were – and always would be – less central to the German war effort than oil, transportation links, or ball-bearings. Harris was right in saying that some precision targets were panaceas (but, naturally, wrong to suggest that they all were). V-1s and V-2s would prove ineffective terror weapons when they were finally produced and, more importantly, without ball-bearings, there would have been no 'wonder weapons' because there would have been no production. The main benefit for the Allies was that the Germans wasted so many men and resources on such a gimmicky project; the August bombing raid served that end.

Schweinfurt mattered for the war effort much more than Peenemünde, and here luck was on the Germans' side. LeMay's Regensburg raid, a tactically more successful attack with a lower casualty rate, had diverted aeroplanes that might have added to the destruction at Schweinfurt. And the RAF did not follow up, not on 18 or 19 August or on any other night in 1943. The Air Ministry had urged Harris to attack Schweinfurt as the weakest link in the German war production chain, and it did so again in December, ordering him to bomb Schweinfurt at night.[66] Harris refused on the grounds that he could not hit a small city with certainty, and that bombing Schweinfurt would be a waste of time when there were bigger cities to destroy and 'only four months left [to do it]!'[67]

If we are to believe Speer, Harris did the Germans a great favour. According to his account, Speer waited each day for the bombers and worried about Berlin-Erkner, Cannstatt, and Steyr. 'In those days we anxiously asked ourselves how soon the enemy would realise that he could paralyse the production of thousands of armaments plants merely by destroying five or six relatively small targets.'[68] Instead, the British 'continued [their] indiscriminate attacks upon [German] cities'.[69] Harris gave the Germans the breathing space they needed: without a further attack, and drawing on large reserve stocks, they were able to cushion the American blow.[70]

No good deed goes unpunished. In the United States, Arnold's whole precision bombing project was coming under renewed attack. On 14 August, he was at the QUADRANT conference, a meeting in Quebec of Roosevelt, Churchill, and William Lyon Mackenzie King along with the Combined Chiefs of Staff, the supreme Anglo-American military authority from 1942. The main argument was over when the British would commit themselves to invading the Continent. Arnold had written in a memorandum of record back in May that 'it is becoming more and more apparent that the British have no intention of invading France or Continental Europe.'[71] Arnold had the impression that Churchill was using an attack on precision bombing to divert attention from the subject of a Continental invasion. This might have been paranoia; some of his evidence came from a conversation between Marshall and Simmons that was overheard by his chauffeur.[72] Arnold was in any case determined to put up a staunch defence of American daylight bombing. He found an unexpected backer in Charles Portal.

On the opening day of the conference, 14 August, Field Marshal Sir Alan Brooke, Chief of the Imperial General Staff, summarised the 'present situation in the European theatre', and gave the floor to Portal.[73] Exaggerating somewhat, Portal opened with the claim that 'the German Air Force was now completely on the defensive . . . [while] the United Nations Air Forces . . . were everywhere on the strategic offensive.' Less than a year after pleading with Eaker to join the night offensive, Portal gave the RAF campaign short shrift. 'The night offensive,' he continued, 'is steadily increasing. Radio aids to navigation have proven immensely effective. Certain steps are now being taken to baffle the defences which have resulted in a decrease in casualties from five-to-six percent to only three percent.'[74] This out of the way, Portal turned to the Americans: 'The daylight bombing – the most important phase of all – is being extraordinarily effective. The first object of POINTBLANK was to knock out the fighter factories and to destroy fighter planes in the air to achieve complete mastery in the air over Germany. The forces available to the Eighth Air Force had done remarkable work but the programme is behind schedule for reasons, however, which are quite understandable. The targets are being hit, the enemy aircraft are being shot down and a high percentage of the aircraft are returning safely, but it is a great battle which hangs in the balance.'

Arnold saw his opening and jumped in. 'It is difficult,' he added, 'to confine a discussion on the air war to Europe since available resources must be spread between all theatres. Early estimates, based on British experience, of the replacements of men and machines have proved too low in the case of the operations of the Eighth Air Force . . . There is [also] the problem of war-weary crews. General Eaker has at present some 800 aircraft, but only 400 crews.'

Whatever the differences between Arnold and Portal, they were less important than emphasising the importance of air power in the face of army, navy or political opposition. Those differences, in any event, were decreasing by the summer of 1943 as Portal began to lose faith in Harris's area bombing, for precisely the same reason he had earlier lost faith in precision bombing – its failure to deliver results. Picking up from Arnold's points, Portal continued: 'The battle against the German fighter forces is a vital battle . . . . If the German strength is not checked in the next three months, the battle might be lost . . . . It is impossible,' Portal concluded, 'to judge the strength which the German fighter forces might obtain by next spring if our attack is not pressed home.'

Again and again, Portal came back to the decisive importance of the American daylight campaign. 'On the one hand, German fighter strength is stretched almost to breaking point, and in spite of their precarious situation on the Russian and Mediterranean fronts, they have found it necessary to reinforce their fighter forces on the Western Front from these sources. On the other hand, the expansion of German fighter strength is continuing and has increased 13 percent this year. It had been hoped that this expansion would by now have been stopped. The Eighth Air Force, who were achieving a great task with their existing resources, believe they can achieve even greater successes if their strength is increased.' It was imperative, Portal argued, to ensure a victory in the battle for air supremacy by autumn 1943. Without it, the Germans, 'by conservation of their strength and by the development of new methods of defence, might be in an unassailable position by the spring.' The key to winning this battle was to put an end to the constant drain on the Eighth's forces: 'To achieve our object diversions from the Eighth Air Force should be stopped, loans of aircraft from the Eighth Air Force to other theaters must be returned and the bomber command of the Eighth Air Force must be built up and reinforced to the maximum possible.'

Drawing heavily on a British intelligence report, Portal stated that:

Germany is now faced with imminent disaster if only the presence of POINTBLANK can be maintained and increased *before* the increase in the GAF [German Air Force] Fighter Force has gone too far . . . . The daylight 'Battle of Germany' is evidently regarded by the Germans as of critical importance and we have already made them throw into it most, if not all, of their available reserves.[75] If we do not now strain every nerve to bring enough force to bear to win this battle during the next two or three months but are content to see the Eighth Bomber Command hampered by a lack of reinforcements just as success is within its grasp, we may well miss the opportunity to win a decisive victory against the German Air Force which will have incalculable effects on all future operations and the length of the war. And the opportunity, once lost, may not recur.

Quoting directly from the report, Portal ended with a ringing endorsement of the American strategy: 'The doubling of the German S.E. [single engine] fighter force on the Western front and the allocation of this increase to Belgium, Holland and Northwest Germany are attributable solely to the development of Allied day bombing of Germany. The defence of Germany against these attacks has in fact become the prime concern of the GAF . . . . There can be no doubt that Germany regards the defence of the Reich against daylight air attack as of such supreme importance that adequate support for military operations in Russia and the Mediterranean has been rendered impossible.'

If Arnold arrived at the meeting feeling beleaguered, he left victorious.[76] Portal's views were accepted without substantial debate. Eisenhower returned the Eighth's three Bomb Groups of B-24s. Arnold himself set about increasing the number of service personnel in the Allied Air Forces. By December, forty-five thousand enlisted men and officers would arrive in the United Kingdom.

After the conference, Arnold travelled to England. He arrived in good spirits, and took the losses at Schweinfurt in his stride. Employing a calculation that might have served Bomber Command well, he pointed out that a 15 per cent loss in one raid was no worse than 5 per cent over three.[77] Arnold gathered two impressions while he was in England.[78] The first was that his B-17s were taking a beating; in addition to the losses, those that returned had been ravaged by bullets and flak. The second was that the losses were worth it. He pored over British and American aerial photographs showing extensive damage to German industry. He was particularly impressed with the Schweinfurt photos.

Although the raid was costly, it had inflicted a great deal of damage on German industry.

A great deal, but not enough. The Germans' frantic efforts to secure alternate supplies had not gone unnoticed. By the end of August, Swedish and Swiss sources were sending reports to England. Photo reconnaissance revealed frenetic repairs at Schweinfurt. And ULTRA (intelligence secured using Enigma to decrypt German codes) revealed how worried the Germans were about a follow-up attack and how urgently they were building up their forces.[79] Arnold told Eaker, 'I know you'll get to it as soon as the weather permits.'[80] Curtis LeMay, for one, was ready to go.

US forces were, however, not. Mindful of their losses, they paused to regroup. The losses they sustained on the first Schweinfurt raid ruled out a quick follow-up. Instead, the Americans looked to easier targets, and to easier bombing in the run-up to the second Schweinfurt raid. The targets were limited to cities in the western reaches of Germany: Emden (2 October), Bremen (8 October), and Münster (10 October). In the first two raids, the Americans experimented with a new radar technique, H_2X. Through a signal under the aeroplane, H_2X produced a rough outline of the earth's surface, distinguishing water, forests, and cities. It allowed the Eighth to bomb through the dense cloud covering Germany in winter. The problem was that the radar could not make out factories. The Americans continued to aim at precision targets, but they were effectively bombing blind. It would look and feel like area bombing to anyone on the ground.

Then, on the morning of Sunday, 10 October, members of the 95th Bomb Group were told that 'unlike all previous military and industrial targets attacked to date by the 8ᵗʰ Air Force, . . . today you will hit the centre of [Münster], the homes of the working population of those marshalling yards. You will disrupt their lives so completely that their morale will be seriously affected and their will to work and to fight will be substantially reduced.'[81] A young Group Navigator, Captain Ellis Scripture, was 'shocked to learn that we were to bomb civilians as our primary target for the first time in the war'.[82] The son of devout Protestant parents, he was particularly appalled by the fact that the aiming point was to be the steps of the Cathedral just as Mass would be ending. Scripture approached the Group commander, Colonel John Gerhart, and said he couldn't fly the mission. Gerhart replied: 'Look, Captain, this is war . . . spelled W-A-R. We're in an all-out fight. The Germans have been killing innocent people all over Europe for years. We're here to beat the hell out of them . . . and we're going to do it . . . You have no option! If you don't fly, I'll have to court-martial you . . . . Any questions?' There weren't any. The bombers hit the centre of Münster, leaving seven hundred people dead. Like the British before them, the Americans were being pushed towards indiscriminate bombing by the logistical and climatic challenges of daylight precision bombing, by the death toll it imposed on their forces, and by the Germans' dogged determination to keep fighting.

It took time to recover from the August losses, but in October, the Americans were back. On the 14th, Wilbur Klint of the 303rd Bomb Group was once again over Schweinfurt, part of the second American raid on ball-bearing production. His group took off from Molesworth, joined the bombing formation, and flew on to Germany.[83] Just beyond the border, the escort fighters reached the end of their range and pulled off. Then, as Eaker put it, 'the Hun sprang his trap'.[84] Immediately, a row of single-engine fighters flew at the bombers, firing 20mm cannons and machine-guns just before they dived. Then, large formations of twin-engine fighters attacked in waves, firing rockets from underneath their wings. In the meantime, the single-engine fighters had reformed, and they attacked, this time from all sides. No sooner were they done than the twin-engine fighters reformed, launching rockets from the front and the back and blasting a single formation until their rockets were expended. 'I had no idea the Germans had so many airplanes and so many different types,' Klint later said.

American bombers were falling out of the sky left, right, and centre. Once a B-17 got into trouble, the pilot – if he had any control at all – would pull off from the formation to avoid a mid-air crash. The bomber was then finished. The fighters would sweep in for the kill. From his cockpit, Klint saw two B-17s hit by rocket fire; they disintegrated. In front and below him was a sea of parachutes. The German attacks, Eaker wrote, 'were perfectly timed and coordinated and skilfully executed . . . . One of our combat wings was practically wiped out.'[85]

The surviving bombers pressed on. As Klint approached the target, the fighters were replaced by a barrage of flak. After hearing 'Bombs away!' he flew on, into the waiting fighters, which continued their attack all the way to the border.

According to Speer, he got word of another attack on Schweinfurt during a conference with Hitler.[86] Speer asked for a recess and left the room to telephone Schweinfurt. He couldn't get through. Communications with all factories were down. Finally, by going through the police, he managed to get on the line one factory foreman, who sketched a picture for Speer: a direct hit had shattered machinery, lit the oil baths, and sent fires racing through the buildings. His factory was hardly unique. Armaments production again went down substantially.[87]

The dramatic tension and personal heroism have all the hallmarks of Speer's self-flattering story-telling filtered through Joachim Fest's journalist skills, but the point is clear enough: the raid was immensely costly to the Americans, but it imposed heavy losses on the Germans. British sources confirm Speer's story.[88]

In the darkest hours after the raid, as the Americans were reeling from the loss of sixty bombers, Eaker had bravely told Arnold that 'we are convinced that when the totals are struck yesterday's losses will be far outweighed by the value of the enemy materiel destroyed.'[89] He was right.

In response to the crisis, Speer appointed one of his closest associates, Philipp Kessler (a general manager from industry), as special commissioner for ball-bearing production. They managed to import small quantities of ball-bearings from Sweden and Switzerland. Factories were ordered to use substitutes. The Germans were able to keep production going, though at a sharply reduced level, until the Schweinfurt factories were repaired. According to Speer, 'what really saved us was the fact that from this time on the enemy to our astonishment once again ceased his attacks on the ball-bearing industry.'[90]

The Germans' efforts had in fact been picked up by Air Staff in the UK, who once again urged Harris to attack Schweinfurt.[91] Harris of course had no intention of hitting Schweinfurt, and no raid followed. Instead, he turned his attention to a much larger target: Berlin.

15

THE BATTLE OF BERLIN

On 19 August 1943, Churchill wrote a letter to the Air Ministry. He stated his satisfaction with the Regensburg and Hamburg raids (curiously, as the purpose of the two raids was very different) and urged attacks on Berlin. It was one of several such requests made in 1942 and 1943 by Churchill, who believed that such raids would help – and impress – the Soviets. Portal passed the prime minister's letter to Vice Chief of Air Staff Sir Douglas Evill, who conveyed the news to Harris.[1]

Churchill was pushing at an open door. Harris had long viewed Berlin as important, if not key, to the air war against Germany. He had specifically declined follow-up raids on Schweinfurt so that he could preserve his forces for the German capital. He wrote back to Churchill immediately. He wanted to attack Berlin 'as soon as the moon wanes'.[2] The battle, however, would have to be 'prolonged' and would require '40,000 tons of bombs'. The load was five times that dropped on Hamburg.

The only problem was that Berlin was not covered by the joint Allied directives, which ordered attacks on aircraft and ball-bearing production. These aims had just been reaffirmed at the QUADRANT conference. Portal wanted to see Harris implement the directive, but he was reluctant to interfere with Harris's role in interpreting it as he saw fit. And, in any case, Churchill – whom Harris continued to visit regularly at Chequers – could override any directive.[3]

The Air Ministry was frustrated, above all by Harris but also by what they saw as Portal's indulgence of him. As Sidney Bufton, Deputy Director of Bombing Operations at the Air Ministry, told Martin Middlebrook after the war,

Portal showed extraordinary patience, hoping that Harris would conform. There was much correspondence over a long period. Harris replied with his tactical reasons why he would not conform with the directives, and all the time was doing his own thing. We suspected that we were being put off but we had nothing cast-iron and, as a background, Harris had this access to Chequers where he went at least once a week. In a way, it was subversive, going behind Portal's back, and in my opinion he was thoroughly disloyal to Portal in pursuing his own idea of how to win the war.[4]

Yet, the Air Ministry was also seduced by the image of German cities consumed by flames. As Bufton admitted, 'Hamburg had come like a bolt from the blue. We didn't mind if Harris was able to mount a successful repetition on any industrial area, Berlin or anywhere else, as long as he intended to start towards the specific targets eventually.'[5] Even among his critics, Harris had won himself some freedom.

On the evening of 23 August, Harris launched the opening raid in the Battle of Berlin. By 20:00, more than six hundred bombers were streaking towards Berlin, their bays packed with the bundles of Window that had proved to be their salvation over Hamburg. When they reached the Kammhuber Line, it seemed to work again. The bomber stream sailed past the boxes and lost only two aircraft, at least one of which fell from the sky because of mechanical problems.

Around 00:35, a 7 Squadron Lancaster, piloted by Charles Lofthouse, was over Berlin. He was one of the pathfinders, whose job it was to mark the city. Then, very suddenly, the dark plane turned bright white. It had been coned. Lofthouse tried to escape it, but failed. He fired off the colours of the day (identifying himself to other RAF aircraft) and tried to shake off the searchlight. Again, no luck. Then a 'great bright "whoosh" of tracer' streamed past the cockpit. He was under fire: 'I don't suppose anyone saw the attacking plane; the gunners must have been blinded by the searchlights. This coloured tracer just raced by us and the damage was on the port side. The wings and engines were badly hit.'

While the engineer frantically tried to put out the engine fire, the navigator, Denis Cayford, bravely asked if he could try crawling out onto the wing to put out the fire there. As this would have meant certain death, Lofthouse said no. Lofthouse ordered his crew to drop the bomb load and shouted, 'Abandon!' He later recalled:

> The flames were very fierce by now, stretching back from each engine, and there was a large hole in the wing between the two nacelles, with flames coming out of it, being beaten back by the airflow. The crew started [baling out]. The flight engineer put my parachute ready beside me. The wireless op came forward and gave me a thumbs-up to indicate that the boys at the back had gone. Cayford came back at that stage, went back to his 'office' [the navigator's bay], and then went forward and out. He told me later that he had come back for a gold signet ring from his girlfriend, which he always took off when flying because it got so cold. That horrified me because I was fighting the controls hard by then, but I managed to get out.[6]

Lofthouse broke his arm as he jumped, and his parachute came down in a tree. He was hanging outside the window of a wooden barrack building, easily visible to anyone inside. The building was used by concentration camp labourers sent to work in the fields and was watched over by camp guards. Lofthouse was a POW within seconds. But he was alive, as were – he would learn later – the rest of his crew.[7]

Many others were not so lucky. Flight Lieutenant Kevin Hornibrook's plane, a 158 Squadron Halifax, was coned as it flew towards the aiming point.[8] The bomb aimer, Pilot Officer Alan Bryett, recalled that they '. . . hadn't gone more than a minute or two, still coned, when the rear gunner shouted, "Fighter approaching!" . . . Almost at the same moment, there was a burst of machine-gun fire which we heard striking in the mid-upper area and then we started to burn there.'[9]

As Kevin took evasive action, Bryett went to the mid-upper section of the plane to see if he could put out the fire. As he arrived, he saw the gunner getting out of his turret. He had been shot in the face. Unable to see, covered in blood and bone fragments, he staggered around the back of the plane. The other gunner had also been shot and wasn't moving. Then,

> We were attacked again. I went back to [Kevin]. We had our intercom and he shouted 'Don't bale out.' But the intercom was very bad and crackly and I think that some of them only caught the last two words. The wireless operator, the navigator and the flight engineer all went out . . . One gunner was probably dead, the other probably dying and three men had baled out, leaving just Kevin and myself.

Kevin struggled with the controls, but the fire had burned through the control cables. The plane went into a sudden dive, 'with a terrible screaming sound'. The G-force threw Kevin and Alan back against the seats. Alan later said, 'We were going to go down in this bloody plane.'

As the plane dived towards the ground at incredible speed, Kevin, struggling against the G-force, grabbed the latch of the escape hatch (just forward of the pilot's seat) and wrenched it open. Still hanging on, he reached back and got hold of Alan. He pulled him towards the hatch, and pushed him out with his feet. As he did, he said, 'I'll follow you.'

Alan came out of the plane and almost immediately crashed into a dense forest; Kevin never got out. Alan saw the flames burst upward as the plane exploded three or four hundred yards away.

Kevin was a 21-year-old Australian with a brother, Keith, a year younger than him, also in Bomber Command. They were the only sons of a Brisbane couple. A year after Kevin died, Keith's plane went missing in operations.

One and a Half Hours Earlier

There were only a few Luftwaffe fighters placed across the Kammhuber Line as the RAF bombing stream approached. They knew, as did Schwabedissen, that Window made their radar useless, so they simply waited. A few pilots tried to attack the bombing stream without radar, hoping to identify the bombers visually. One may have managed to take down a Halifax. The others simply waited as the bomber stream flew past. Following their order, they hung back and made no effort to pursue. They knew that something was waiting for the bombers in Berlin.

Over Berlin, hundreds of fighters, including all of the crack crews that had previously been assigned to boxes along the Kammhuber Line, were circling. They had no radar and no contact with ground control. Their only help from below was an agreement from the local flak command to restrict the range of the flak to about twelve thousand feet, so the fighters could circle safely above it, and the support of two hundred search-lights lighting up the Berlin sky.

The searchlights were operated by anti-aircraft auxiliaries (*Luftwaffenhelfer*). The young boys, usually around fifteen and rarely older than seventeen, were drafted and lived in barracks together. There they waited for the alarms that called them to the flak guns or searchlights. Werner Schenk, who was an anti-aircraft auxiliary from January 1944 to February 1945, recalled the cadets' typically cheeky Berlin humour. '*Heil Hitler* (Hail Hitler!)' one boy would say; '*Heil du ihn doch!*' another would reply ('You heal him!' – playing on the double meaning of *heil*).[10] During one raid on Berlin, anti-aircraft fire brought down an Allied bomber. The auxiliaries saw a para-chute coming down and made for it en masse. The airman, who had no doubt heard the stories of airmen being lynched by the SS or furious citizens, must have feared for his life. The fear would have been more than justified: German police or soldiers would generally save Allied airmen from civilian wrath, but Nazi functionaries and the Gestapo gladly left them to the fate and/or sealed it.[11] Over the course of the war, at least 350 Allied airmen were murdered by the Germans.[12] But this time the RAF airman was descended upon by a horde of grinning boys who could not contain their joy at having arrested an enemy combatant. They were finally real soldiers.[13]

At 00:40, as planes came in over Berlin, Hans-Werner Mihan was manning a machine-gun, but the height of the planes meant that he was a spectator rather than a participant in the battle.[14] He watched the searchlights twist in every direction, trying to cone one of the incoming bombers. Wave after wave of them crossed the city. All around him was the sound of blazing flak guns. The ground shook under the weight of the bombs. Fires and exploding aeroplanes lit up the sky. Deadly flak splinters hit the ground around him; he was more afraid of them than of the bombs. 'It was,' he wrote after the war, 'a symphony of hell.'

Above Berlin, German fighters swept in on the bombers. They were above, below, and around the British. One was Peter Spoden, flying a Messerschmitt 110:[15]

> I had never seen so many aircraft at one time before. There must have been thirty or forty of them. Some were night fighters, but the majority were four-engined bombers. Most of the planes seemed to be flying from south to north, but the tracer was going in every direction. There were searchlights – hundreds of them – and they caused me to lose my orientation. I saw one Lancaster in a steep dive, trying to get out of the searchlights, and another which dived steeply and then reared up and actually looped right over – I swear it. [The battle] was terrible for a kid like me, and I think it must have been just as bad for the British boys. It was the most intensive night battle of the war I ever saw, a terrible inferno, still following me in nightmares in the next decade.

Peter felt paralysed. His heart was pounding. Then a bomber came directly into view in front of him, caught in the searchlights. From about two hundred yards away, Peter opened fire, aiming at the fuel tanks between the two engines. He scored a direct hit. For a few minutes, nothing seemed to happen; then the plane went down. Peter didn't see any parachutes.

His next sighting was a Stirling. Peter fired, but the pilot corkscrewed abruptly and unpredictably, which saved his life. The plane disappeared into the darkness. Peter flew on, and then spotted another Stirling well ahead of him. As he flew towards it, something unexpected happened. The Stirling turned and flew back towards him. Peter fired right into it, scoring a hit. Then the Stirling dived underneath him. As it did, the tail gunner sprayed bullets into the underside of Peter's Messerschmitt.

I heard the hit in my fuselage and a small fire started behind me. I checked with the crew but received no answer; the intercom was not working. When the heat of the fire became unbearable, I shouted, 'GET OUT!' four or five times as loud as I could. Then I jettisoned the cockpit canopy and went out myself. It was not easy; I found out later that my left thigh had been hit by a bullet and the bone was broken.

As Peter flew through the air, the crashing machine's tail plane caught him. His stomach was flat against it, his head over its top, and his feet underneath, pinned by the force of the air. For a few minutes, he was trapped there, hurtling towards the ground. He thought he was finished. His plane was coned, and he braced himself for friendly fire. In fact, the searchlight commander below had recognised Peter's plane as a Messerschmitt and hoped the searchlight would help him. Somehow, Peter managed to free himself from the tail plane, pulled his chute, and passed out.

He landed unconscious in a private garden.[16] As he woke up, he felt dull pain all over his body. He looked up to see a crowd of civilians and an SS man. They had mistaken him for an RAF airman and were beating him. He shouted at them in German and they stopped.

The defence technique employed by Peter and the other fighters was called '*Wilde Sau*' (Wild Boar), and it was the brainchild of Hajo Herrmann.[17] Incredibly, Herrmann had never been in a fighter plane; he was a bomber pilot who had flown a long string of operations over the United Kingdom.[18] By early 1943, he had a staff appointment with the Luftwaffe, working on strategies to counter the mounting effectiveness of Harris's bombing campaign. Even before Hamburg, it was clear that the Kammhuber Line was not working; fighters would pick off a few bombers as the bombing stream flew past, but the majority of planes always made it. When Herrmann surveyed German defence capabilities, two features stood out.[19] The first was that, with the Blitz over, the Luftwaffe had a surplus of trained bombers who were skilled at flying blind. The second was that single-engine day fighters could be produced more quickly and in larger numbers than twin-engine night fighters. From this, Herrmann developed the idea that single-engine fighters should be placed above German cities. Rather than having one shot at the British bombers crossing the Kammhuber Line, they would have many. Over a German city, the fires, searchlights, and flares illuminated the incoming bombers, making them easier targets for multiple attacks by the German fighters. His unit was named Jagdgeschwader (fighter wing) Herrmann, but later renamed Jagdgeschwader 300 (JG 300). Herrmann probably did not like the omen: most Luftwaffe units had been named after dead heroes.[20] The Luftwaffe allowed Herrmann to try out Wild Boar over Cologne. The results were inconclusive, but he was allowed to create a group of thirty fighters and try again.[21]

Three weeks later, after the catastrophe of Hamburg, Herrmann's quirky idea – until then indulged like a German equivalent of Wallis's bouncing bomb – was thrust front and centre stage in Luftwaffe strategy. A few days after the firestorm, a conference of twin-engine commanders was held in Holland. Herrmann presented his idea. Whatever doubts they might have had, the commanders had little choice. Until a new technique was found for responding to Window, both single- and twin-engine fighters would be used in Wild Boar tactics. The Luftwaffe gave the fighters one full Wild Boar practice run, during the 17 August 1943 Peenemünde raid. Despite a clever RAF diversion force of a few Mosquitos that held most of the fighters back, the run was a success for the Luftwaffe and a slaughter for the bombers: forty were shot down that night.[22] The fighters did not save Peenemünde, however. The RAF's costly but successful precision raid destroyed the factory trying to produce Hitler's 'wonder weapons', delaying production by six to eight weeks.[23] Nonetheless, within a month of Hamburg, the Germans had rendered Window ineffective. The Wild Boar fighters were sent to Berlin. On the first night of the raid, 23 August, they killed 298 RAF aircrew, including Kevin Hornibrook.

The next two nights of the Battle of Berlin would go equally badly for Bomber Command. On 31 August and 1 September, it lost 333 men – 225 died and another 108 were taken prisoner. By contrast, eighty-seven Berliners lost their lives. Only ten out of almost four hundred aircraft managed to bomb Berlin that night; the rest dropped their load on the Brandenburg countryside.

On the night of 3–4 September, 130 aircrew died and ten were taken prisoner. After two more costly raids – on Mannheim, over which Bomber Command lost thirty-four bombers, and on Munich, where it lost sixteen – the weather over Berlin worsened. Bomber Command had lost one-third of its four-engine strength and one-quarter of its aircrew in nineteen days. It could not continue; Harris decided to delay the Battle of Berlin until Bomber Command could respond to Wild Boar.

That took almost six weeks. With more heavy bombers, the Lancasters, better radar, and better weather, Harris was again ready to attack the German capital. On 3 November 1943, Harris wrote a letter to the prime minister in which he took stock of the bombing war.[24] Bombing had 'virtually destroyed' nineteen cities, including Cologne, Hamburg, Hanover, the Ruhr cities of Düsseldorf, Remscheid, Bochum, Krefeld, and Mülheim. The Hanseatic city of Rostock, Charlemagne's Aachen, and the medieval city of Kassel had also gone under. The Kassel raid of 22–3 October created a second firestorm, destroyed 59 per cent of the city, and killed 5,600 to 9,600 people.[25] The city was obliterated, but – as in Hamburg – armaments production was back up to 90 per cent of pre-raid levels within three months.[26]

Along with Berlin, Harris believed that there were some sixty cities (including Leipzig, Dresden, Erfurt, Weimar, Frankfurt, and Munich) left to destroy. When that was done, Bomber Command would only have to 'mop up the few small coal and steel towns' in the Saar and 'when the occasion serves . . . tidy up all around' by taking out Solingen, Witten, and Leverkusen. But it would not come to that. Harris concluded: 'I feel certain that Germany must collapse before this programme, which is more than half completed already, has proceeded much further.' The key was getting the Americans to join in, as Harris argued to Churchill:

> We have not got far to go. But we must get the U.S.A.A.F. [US Army Air Forces] to wade in in greater force. If they will only get going according to plan and avoid such disastrous diversions as Ploesti [Germany's main oil supplier, in Romania] . . . we can get through it very quickly. We can wreck Berlin from end to end if the U.S.A.A.F. will come in on it. It will cost us 400–500 aircraft.
>
> It will cost Germany the war.[27]

Over seven months, from August 1943 to March 1944, Bomber Command attacked the capital nineteen times; 10,813 bombers dropped 17,000 tons of high explosives and 16,000 tons of incendiaries, killing 9,390 civilians.[28] Two thousand, seven hundred aircrew died. As always, the bombs did much damage: the opera house in Charlottenburg, much of Potsdamer Platz, many museums, all were destroyed. But Berlin was not 'wrecked'. It continued to function as an administrative and commercial capital and the seat of some important industries, notably AEG and Siemens. Although a few of the latter were 'caught' by bombing, most bombs hit targets of no importance to the war effort; in some cases, bombing may have even aided that effort: when retail shops, hotels, and other businesses unrelated to the military were destroyed, their workers were immediately transferred to more productive tasks.[29] Berlin's solid, modern architecture, wide streets and open spaces (thousands of bombs landed pointlessly in the Tiergarten), and sheer size (nineteen times larger than Paris) meant that it could withstand bombing far more readily than Germany's older, more compact cities. Harris promised that an average monthly bomb tonnage of 13,500 would lead to the Reich's collapse. Throughout the Battle of Berlin, however, he dropped a monthly average of 14,915 tons on German cities without bringing the country remotely close to collapse.[30] As Alec Coryton, Assistant Chief of Air Staff [Operations] (and former AOC of 5 Group), noted in November, even if Berlin had been destroyed, it is doubtful that it would have meant the end of the war.[31] The city simply never enjoyed the same singularly important industrial, financial, cultural, and governmental role played by the British capital. The elusive search for a levelled Berlin was motivated by symbolism rather than sound strategy.

The first of April 1944 came and went without the promised German capitulation. The failure of the Berlin campaign did not discourage Harris. Rather, he looked to a whole new set of cities. While the Berlin campaign was still under way, 596 aircraft destroyed the ancient city of Augsburg on 25–6 February under the fire of only token flak defence.[32] On 1–2 March, Stuttgart was hit, destroying the Neues Schloss and killing 125 people.[33] On 18–19 March and again on 22–3 March, Frankfurt was hit, flattening the old centre and ending 'the existence of the Frankfurt which had been built up since the Middle Ages'.[34]

Throughout this period, the British death toll climbed: in January 1944, Harris lost 6.1 per cent of aircraft sent to Berlin, and 7.2 per cent of those which went to Stettin; in a February raid on Leipzig and a March raid on Berlin, the casualty rate was greater than 9 per cent.[35] Six days after the end of the Berlin campaign, on 30–1 March, Harris dispatched 795 aircraft for an attack on Nuremberg. Although the city – like all German cities – had some industries, none of these, with the exception of a small aircraft repair plant on the outskirts, was specified under the Casablanca and POINTBLANK directives.[36] Like Berlin, Nuremberg was appealing more for its symbolism than its industrial importance: Harris wanted to flatten the city of the Nazi party rally. The raid was a disaster: 95 planes, or 11.9 per cent of those that took off, did not return.[37] The casualty rate was a staggering 20.6 per cent. Nuremberg itself got off relatively easily: 265 buildings of little or no industrial importance were destroyed, 75 people (including 15 foreign workers) were killed, and 11,000 were made homeless. Ironically, many pilots mistook Schweinfurt for Nuremberg and successfully dropped ten blockbusters (4,000-pound bombs with light casings), three hundred other explosives, and thousands of incendiaries on a city that Harris claimed they could not attack.[38]

After two years, the failure of the bomber dream and its costs were obvious to everyone but Harris himself.[39] For the moment, however, he had to deal with what he called a 'diversion':[40] Operation OVERLORD – the invasion of the European continent.

SPINNING THE BOMBING WAR

The Times was the most venerable institution on Fleet Street. Founded in 1788, it was Britain's newspaper of record for almost two centuries. Throughout the war, it recorded Bomber Command's successes but almost never its failures. From the beginning, but particularly as Harris ramped up the bombing war, it was the most important voice of Bomber Command.

And it was generally loud and proud. Following a 9 March 1942 raid on Essen, the paper reported:

> During the heavy air attack on Essen and objectives elsewhere in the Ruhr on the night of March 9, a small number of aircraft bombed the August Thyssen Steelworks, which lie between the town of Hamborn and the Rhine. Photographs taken during the bombing fully confirm the pilots' reports that there were large fires in the area of the works, and that high-explosive bombs were accurately aimed at the fires. There can be little doubt that substantial damage was done.[1]

The reports rarely described the destruction of cities or the killing of civilians. Only two reports, over the last three years of the war, could be construed as anything close to an accurate picture of area bombing. In August 1942, Sinclair, the British Secretary of State for War, gave a speech at Swansea, the Welsh port city that had suffered so much during the Blitz. In a speech rallying the beleaguered citizens, he informed them that:

> We intended to press home our attacks on Germany
> ruthlessly . . . . The destruction which Bomber Command
> has wrought in Germany and in German-occupied territory
> in recent months has been terrible . . . . Bomber Command
> has destroyed between a quarter and a third of the whole
> of Cologne . . . . The effect of Bomber Command's mighty
> raids are well exemplified in this extract from the diary of
> a German soldier killed far from home on one of Hitler's
> many battle-fronts. 'The last mail made an overwhelming
> impression. On everybody's lips are the words "Cologne
> and Essen". Relatives wrote terrible things. Max was
> informed that "life had come off the rails and people simply
> could not recover after this dreadful disaster".'[2]

In a similar vein, *The Times*'s aeronautical correspondent provided a report on the extent of bomb damage in Germany on the
first day of 1943. He had been briefed or given information by
Harris or someone close to Harris, as he measured bomb damage with a technique favoured by the commander-in-chief: acres
destroyed. 'The damage caused by the *Luftwaffe* in Britain during
1940 and 1941,' the correspondent wrote,

> and that caused by the R.A.F. in Germany during 1942
> made an interesting comparison. The City of London
> contained less than 120 acres of devastation. In Bomber
> Command's big raid on Cologne more than 600 acres
> were devastated. In Lübeck more than 40 per cent of the
> property, totalling over 200 acres, had been destroyed
> or damaged beyond repair. The damage in Rostock was
> greater, in proportion to the total area, than in any other

city, being about 70 per cent. No city in the world had a
greater acreage of damage than Cologne. Other damage
caused by the R.A.F. included: Duesseldorf, more than 380
acres; Mainz, 130 acres; Karlsruhe, 360 acres; Emden, 60
per cent destroyed; Bremen, nearly 20 per cent; Aachen, 30
per cent (nearly 160 acres); Muenster, 260 acres devastated;
and Nuremberg, 106 acres.[3]

The only discussion of people as distinct from buildings came
on 21 June 1943. Most likely relying on Swedish reports on
German morale, *The Times*'s diplomatic correspondent wrote,

The signs are that German propaganda is now going to play
up the R.A.F. attacks as vigorously as it had hitherto played
them down. Goebbels's speech at Wuppertal on Friday,
in which he described the sufferings of the victims of
bombing, is now said to have 'broken the spell' – meaning,
presumably, that facts which have been suppressed are to
be disclosed in the future.

Hans Fritzsche [sic], the wireless commentator [NB: who
worked for Goebbels and controlled the German press],
said on Saturday of Goebbels's speech – 'The spell was
broken that had thus far lain over the sufferings of that
part of our people which is exposed to these terror attacks.'
. . . Now all Germany was to be told of the sufferings
and sacrifices of the bombed districts . . . . Large-scale
evacuation from the Ruhr is taking place, and the housing
of the refugees in what are regarded as safe areas is not
proving easy. Some of the bombed-out people have not been
sympathetically received, and in the German Press there
have been complaints of this lack of considerateness.[4]

Such relatively honest reports were not the only ones consuming column inches. Equally typical was a *Daily Sketch* report on the bombing of Lübeck: 'Lübeck, important German U-boat building yard on the Baltic and thirty-five miles north-east of Hamburg, was still on fire late yesterday. RAF long-distance bombers pounded this vital port on Saturday night . . . . Surface vessels, as well as submarines are built in the Lübeck yards. The port is also used for sending military supplies to Norway, Finland and the Northern Russian front . . . . [Twenty minutes] after the start of the attack at about 10:30pm . . . the fires had spread right across the port.'[5] But the port hadn't been the centre of the bombing at all; the old city was.

In a similar vein, a *Times* report on Hamburg in the summer of 1943 stated:

Air bombing reached a new intensity on Tuesday night,
when the R.A.F. made their fourth successive night attack
on Hamburg, which experienced its sixth raid in 72 hours.
In 45 minutes – five minutes shorter than on Saturday in
the first of the present series of raids – a total exceeding the
previous record weight of 2,300 tons of bombs was rained
on the still blazing docks and industrial quarter, causing
damage which it is expected will far exceed that caused in
any previous attack.[6]

Tuesday was 27 July 1943, the target area was residential working-class Hamburg, and the 28 July firestorm left over 35,000 people dead.

A few weeks before Hamburg, the Archbishop of Canterbury wrote to Sinclair for clarification. 'I am bombarded,' he wrote, 'by statements that we have evidently changed our policy in bombing and are now deliberately destroying cities irrespective of military objectives. I have continued to say that I see no evidence of this . . . but I should be grateful if you could let me have a line to assure me that this is correct.'⁷ Sinclair was glad to: 'It is no part of our policy wantonly to destroy cities – regardless of military objectives – as the German Air Force attempted to do . . . [though] we cannot attack factories without damaging the surrounding buildings.'⁸

The equivocation was deliberate; the British government feared a public reaction against the area bombing campaign. As Air Marshal Sir Richard Peck put it in June 1944, '[it] has always been my endeavour to avoid reference to acres of devastation and emasculation of cities in statements of Bomber Command's work, because I have always foreseen that this would be bound to lead in the long term to reactions against bombing.'⁹ Another Air Ministry official claimed a month earlier – and against all evidence – '[o]ur attacks are neither indiscriminate [author's note: basically true] nor deliberately aimed at civilian objectives but are expressly directed to the one aim – German war industry and transport [author's note: completely untrue].'¹⁰

Despite the dissimulation, the story was getting out. With some imagination, Sinclair's vengeful rhetoric and Fritzsche's stories of evacuations could have conveyed the idea that not all Germans could be successfully evacuated from their cities. With a little more imagination, the rather dry figures on acres destroyed might have provided the reader with a view of what German cities were starting to look like in early 1943. Likewise, some reflection might have led a reader to conclude that, if large numbers of civilians were being driven out of their homes, some of them, perhaps many of them, must be dying in the process. And in some cases pictures conveyed the proverbial thousand words: the Air Ministry regularly published photographs showing whole blocks of residential streets turned to rubble, and in at least one case organised an exhibition in which official comments recorded with pride the destruction of the centres of Lübeck, Rostock, Mainz, and Cologne.[11]

Others spoke in more direct terms about the bombing. Throughout the war, Vera Brittain, a pacifist and activist, published pamphlets denouncing RAF bombing as murder. In a March 1944 issue of *Fellowship*, an American religious publication, one of her ritual attacks on Allied bombing was accompanied by the signatures of twenty-eight noted clergymen and anti-war activists.[12] 'Christian people,' the text read, 'should be moved to examine themselves concerning this participation in this carnival of death.' The result was a flurry of controversy in the American media.[13]

Brittain's views were certainly unrepresentative of wider currents of opinion, but the British were never uniformly or consistently vengeful in their attitudes towards Germany. Throughout the war, the government was sensitive to public opinion on bombing, and watched it closely. The results were inconclusive. According to polls conducted by Mass Observation, during the worst of the Blitz, the public was evenly divided over revenge attacks – 45 per cent in favour, 45 per cent against.[14] In answer to the more specific question, posed by the British Institute of Public Opinion, of whether the German civilian population should be a target for attacks, the answers varied for reasons that are not entirely clear. In 1940, support for such attacks stood at 45 per cent; in 1941, it rose to 55 per cent; in 1943, it peaked at 83 per cent.[15] In 1944 and 1945, it fell off again.[16] Even these figures need to be treated with caution: answers to public opinion questions depend greatly on when and how they are asked. It is one thing for people to say they support attacks on the 'civilian population'; it is another to say so after seeing the pictures of burned and maimed children. Someone who called for revenge attacks after seeing their hometown bombed might (or might not) have changed his or her views with the passage of time.

In the end, the contemporary conversation about bombing Germany in wartime Britain was ambiguous and contested, not least because the government wanted it to be. Enough information – including pictures and occasional apocalyptic imagery conjured up by politicians ('a crescendo of destruction') – leaked out during the war to give the curious a clear picture of what was going on.[17] Still, the press reports were vague enough, and the claims of industrial targets and precision capabilities sincere enough, to allow everyone to believe what they wanted to. For those who wanted to smash the Huns where they lived and breathed, they had more than enough evidence to suggest that the RAF was doing exactly that. For those who wanted to believe that Britain was mainly bombing industries, there was no end of official statements to confirm it.

There was also a third possibility, a fairly banal one: supporting the bombing of Germany instinctively without thinking much about what it meant in practice. No country had ever been bombed on the scale that Germany was being bombed, and it would have been difficult to imagine exactly what it was like for civilians on the ground. After the war, aircrew reported that, in the air and under a barrage of flak, they thought little about the civilians in the cities as they bombed them. If the tens of thousands of feet between aircrew and civilians created moral distance, how could the six hundred miles between London and Berlin not?

The Air Ministry sat in a large, sandstone corner building on Whitehall. It is a slightly bombastic, largely inter-war structure. The Air Ministry issued bombing directives, was responsible for RAF publicity, issued press releases, and provided instructions on what could and could not be said to the press. On 21 October 1943, Air Commodore Howard Williams had been authorised by the Ministry to write a story for the *Daily Telegraph* on the bombing campaigns from the previous July. 'Bomber Command's nightly average on Germany,' Williams wrote, 'was equal to the Luftwaffe's effort for the whole 100 days on Britain [during the Blitz] . . . the total load on 35 of our larger-scale raids was 50 tons more than the Luftwaffe's greatest effort against Britain' – 450 tons on Coventry in 1940. 'The campaign,' he continued, was providing 'direct help to Russia':

When Gen. Smuts stated this week that some 2,000,000 people were engaged in Germany in meeting our air offensive in some form or other, he more than confirmed Sir Archibald Sinclair's estimate that some 750,000 were employed in active defences and another 750,000 on the passive side. In addition hundreds of thousands of workers are in the repair and ancillary industries. Many of these would otherwise be fighting the Russians.

The article also added that 'the effect of the night and day bomb offensive on events on the Russian front is known to be very appreciable.'

Williams went on to explain the difference between area bombing and precision bombing. 'Comparing our "area bombing" by night [with precision bombing by day],' he wrote, 'an RAF commentator pointed out that the enemy's cities were now great labour camps, employed almost solely on the war effort.'

The purpose of the night attack, he added, was to destroy Germany's capacity to wage war by 'striking out of her hands the weapons she seeks to use against us'.

While it is not practicable at night to bomb precise targets, as by day, a very high measure of precision occurs over the target area. The effect is to smash not only arms factories and their satellites, but [also] the virtual barracks of those who work in them, driving sometimes literally millions to their shelters below ground.

It has to be remembered that every man who works in these industrial 'divisions' is only doing so because he is of more use to the enemy's war capacity than he would be as a soldier.

At this point in the war, Williams concluded, Germany's aircraft factories were one of its 'high spots', central to the war in general and the 'Russian campaign' in particular: 'We have long known that the German fighter force has been steadily increasing since last January. It is now disclosed that there are about a third more fighters now operating against Air Chief Marshal Sir Arthur Harris by night and Gen. [Ira] Eaker by day.'

The result was that massive numbers of fighters had been drawn off the eastern front. Of the 2,750 fighters available to Germany, the RAF estimated that 1,900 were on the western front, 300 on the Mediterranean front, and 550 on the eastern front. The consequences for Germany were disastrous:

When it is realised that some 550 fighters, of which probably only 60 per cent are serviceable, have to cover the entire Russian battle front of 600 miles, the extent of the enemy's shortage can be gauged . . . .

The one thing on which the Germans are relying to stave off defeat is their fighter force, which, by night and day, is being whittled down by every conceivable means in our power.[18]

Harris was not briefed on the letter; he read it in the *Telegraph*. It made him furious. The article suggested that the targets of Britain's bombing campaign were industrial, that the most important of these targets was fighter production, and that the point in drawing off and destroying fighters was to help the Soviets. He sat down and penned a response to the Air Ministry. In a 25 October letter, Harris exhorted the Ministry to modify urgently its policy on press releases. He wrote that the Ministry had failed to convey the fact that 'the position of Germany as a result of 8 months' intensive bombing and the advance of the Russian armies across the Dnieper is such that the possibility of her collapse at a very early date must be seriously envisaged.'

If Germany collapsed, the Air Ministry would have wholly failed to make clear Bomber Command's decisive role in it:

The manner in which the aim and achievement of the combined U.S.–British Bomber Offensive have been presented both in the Press and public pronouncements by authoritative speakers in both Britain and the United States has encouraged the view that it is in the nature of an experiment or a side-show which is important but is not the major part of the United Nations' war effort in the European Theatre . . . . No one could possibly gather from casual reading of the British Press that the enemy openly admits the results of our bombing to be his most serious problem, ie, of greater importance than the advance of the Red Army.

This 'writing down' of Bomber Command was, Harris concluded, the outcome of deliberate policy. So also, it must be assumed, is the fact that the quite considerable space which is nevertheless devoted to the part of Combined Bomber Offensive entrusted to Bomber Command misrepresents both the aim and achievement of that part. This misrepresentation consists in the continued suggestion that Bomber Command is concerned, not with the obliteration of German cities and their inhabitants as such, but with the bombing of specific factory premises. What all official talks and handouts emphasise is not that Cassel [sic] contained over 200,000 Germans, many of whom are now dead and most of the remainder homeless and destitute, but that the Henschel Locomotive works and various other important factory premises were in or near the city.

The problem with this presentation was that it gave the impression that the Americans and the British were trying to do the same thing, but that the Americans were simply better at it. This, Harris continued, made Bomber Command's exploits seem 'dull and unconvincing' compared to those of the Soviets, the Allied armies in Italy, or the US Eighth Air Force. The truth was exactly the opposite:

The aim of our Bomber Force which went to Cassel [sic] on October 22/23 was to wreck the city . . . . In the course of the proceedings, the Henschel Works and a number of other factories probably got damaged, and this makes the loss to the enemy all the greater. But the fundamental purpose was to knock another great German city out of the war and add it to the growing list of those which are now liabilities and not assets to the enemy from the point of view of morale and production. By obscuring this purpose, we simply rob the whole operation of its point.[19]

Even worse, it gave the crews the impression that 'the authorities are ashamed of area bombing'. This could not stand. Men could not to go on 'risking their lives to effect a purpose which their own Government appears to consider at least as too disreputable to be mentioned in public'.

Unless the British people were told the truth of the bombing campaign, they would never understand its importance in bringing about Germany's defeat:

> The fact that bombing has won the war and forced the
> German armies to give in to the Russians will never be
> accepted in quarters where it is important that it should.
> Nobody will believe ex post facto that for 8 months Bomber
> Command was winning resounding and indeed decisive
> victories and that they were nevertheless deliberately
> represented as of less importance than very minor
> encounters with the enemy at sea and on land.

To avoid such a 'deplorable result', the Air Ministry needed a new publicity strategy. Above all, the aim of the US and, especially, the UK claims should be 'unambiguously stated':

> That aim is the destruction of German cities; the killing
> of German workers; and the disruption of civilised life
> throughout Germany. It should be emphasised that the
> destruction of houses, public utilities, transport, and lives;
> the creation of a refugee problem on an unprecedented
> scale; and the breakdown of morale both at home and at the
> battle fronts by fear of extended and intensified bombing,

are accepted and intended aims of our bombing policy.
They are not by-products of attempts to hit factories.

The success or failure of Bomber Command, Harris concluded, should be 'publicly assessed in terms of the extent to which they realise this policy'.[20]

Alarm bells began ringing in the Air Ministry, and officials penned frantic minutes to each other rejecting Harris's claims. On 28 October, Sir Arthur Street, Under Secretary of State in the Air Ministry, wrote to Portal about the matter. 'In my public statements,' Street stated, 'I always emphasise that our objectives are the centres of war power and that the damage to built-up areas, though inevitable and huge, is incidental. If we were to abandon this line and to adopt as the principal measure of our success the number of men, women and children killed and the number of houses burnt out rather than the numbers of factories destroyed, we should provoke the leaders of religious and humanitarian opinion to protest.'[21] 'There must,' he concluded, 'be no departure from our present line without consultation with me.' Air Marshal Sir Richard Peck, Assistant Chief of Air Staff, was given the job of drafting a response to Harris. Before he did so, he wrote to Bottomley and asked him directly about the Allies' policy on bombing civilians. In his reply, Bottomley stated that 'there is no indication [in the directive] of any deliberate attack upon the civilian population as such. It would be quite wrong to say that destruction of civilian lives is an accepted and intended aim of our bombing policy; nor is the aim the destruction of German cities as such unless those cities have an important part in the military, industrial or economic system of the enemy.'[22]

Over the next three weeks, the Air Ministry produced multiple drafts of a response to Harris. On 15 December, it went out with Street's signature. The letter made several attempts to minimise the differences between the Ministry and Harris. On the question of the armies', navies', and Soviets' contributions, the minister argued that it was

> obliged to exercise great discretion in drawing comparisons between the importance of land and air operations. Whatever high hopes [the Council] may entertain for the results of the combined bomber offensive, the fact is that the British and United States Governments have made plans for major land operations on the Continent at a comparatively early date. In framing their publicity policy, the Council cannot ignore this basic concept of Allied strategy. Nor can they ignore the vast significance of the Russian land offensive which jointly with the bomber offensive is placing Germany under a strain that may at any time prove fatal. Subject only to these considerations, the Council will continue to stress in their publicity the critical importance of the bomber offensive and the outstanding achievement of air power in creating the conditions of victory.

But, in the end, the response had to address directly Harris's claim that the bomber offensive was aimed at 'the destruction of German cities, the killing of German workers . . .' 'The Council,' Sweet wrote,

> recognise, of course, that night attacks directed against the German war economy involve the virtual destruction of those German cities which are essential to the enemy's war effort and that such destruction entails heavy casualties to the civil population and disruption of the organised life of the community . . . but your directive neither requires nor enjoins direct attack on German civilians as such.

Sweet denied that the Ministry was concealing 'from the public the immense devastation that is being wrought to German industrial cities . . . . Every one knows that, in attacking the sources of Germany's war potential, Bomber Command is bound to destroy large areas of German cities.' This 'widespread devastation,' was, however, 'not an end in itself but the inevitable accompaniment of an all-out attack on the enemy's capacity to wage war.' To say any more than this, Sweet concluded, would be politically unwise. 'It is,' he wrote,

> desirable to present the bomber offensive in such a light as
> to provoke the minimum of public controversy and so far as
> possible to avoid conflict with religious and humanitarian
> opinion. Any public protest, whether reasonable or
> unreasonable, against the bomber offensive could not but
> hamper the Government in the execution of their policy and
> might affect the morale of the aircrews themselves.
>
> The Council are therefore unwilling to change the
> emphasis of their publicity. They do not, however, wish
> to imply that the objects of your Command should be
> represented as confined to the bombing of specific factory
> premises.[23]

A devious character would have interpreted this wink-and-nod as an open invitation to carry on, which it probably was. But Harris was not devious. As he wrote a week later, the ministry's answers to his questions were, 'in spite of [my] most careful examination . . . ambiguous'. With regard to the Soviets and the Western ground forces, Harris did not want to imply that their successes or their significance should be ignored. Rather, he explained:

[I] asked simply that adequate emphasis as distinct from
occasional and casual references should be made to the fact
that these successes have been made possible largely by the
Bomber Offensive, and also to the truth, of which the enemy
is well aware, that the reduction to ruins of Berlin, Hamburg,
Cologne and many other cities is of incomparably greater
significance to the German people than the recovery by the
Soviets of the ruins of Kharkov, Kiev and Gomel.

The point of these bombings, Harris continued, was not to kill
the old, invalid, and very young. Indeed, doing so would be irra-
tional. Children, the handicapped, and the aged consume more
than they produce and are thus a drain on the German war effort.
The logical corollary of this, however, was that it was rational to
kill civilians who were productive. The Ministry was therefore
wrong in implying

that *no* German citizens are proper objects for bombing.
The German economic system, which I am instructed by
my directive to destroy, *includes* workers, houses and public
utilities, and it is therefore meaningless to claim that the
wiping out of German cities is 'not an end in itself but the
inevitable accompaniment of an all out attack on the enemy's
means and capacity to wage war'. I repeat that the cities of
Germany including their working population, houses and
public utilities are literally the heart of Germany's 'war
potential'. That is why they are being deliberately attacked.[24]

Harris blasted the Ministry for the contradictions in its letter. The
Ministry had in the same two pages claimed that cities were legitimate targets ('the objects of Bomber Command are not confined
to . . . specific factory premises'); that they were not legitimate

targets ('widespread devastation is not an end in itself'); and that the real objective could not be specified for fear of alienating 'religious and humanitarian opinion'. As a result, Harris was 'completely unable to discover from the Air Ministry letter whether or not [he was] in agreement with the views of the Air Council'.[25]

Not without reason. The Air Ministry and the government shied away from a full statement of what Bomber Command was up to. When Labour MP Richard Rapier Stokes asked the government whether 'on any occasion instructions have been given to British airmen to engage in area bombing rather than limit their attention to purely military targets', the reply was: 'The targets of the Bomber Command are always military, but night bombing of military objectives necessarily involves bombing of the area in which they are situated.'

As Harris well knew, this was false, or at least highly misleading. He was by nature an honest man, and he was confident in his policy and that the British people would support it. He also suspected that, if he allowed the Air Ministry to continue its dissimulation, it and the UK government would be allowed to escape responsibility for a policy that, Harris believed, they had supported from the beginning. 'I submit,' he wrote, 'that this is far too serious a matter to be left in this position of obscurity. If the authorities are in doubt that cities, including everything and everybody in them which is a help to the German war effort, are the objectives which Bomber Command in accordance with its directive is aiming to destroy, they should at once be disabused of this illusion, which is not merely unfair to our crews now but will inevitably lead to deplorable controversies when the facts are fully and generally known.' It was a prescient statement.

For Harris, the question was more than one of publicity. It went to the very cause for which thousands of young men were dying:

It concerns the whole aim and scope of the activities of
Bomber Command, since, unless my interpretation of the
situation . . . is accepted without ambiguity or evasion of
the issue, it is clear that our crews are being sacrificed in a
deliberate attempt to do something which the Air Council
do not regard as necessary or even legitimate, *namely
eliminate entire German cities* . . . . It is not enough to
admit that devastation is caused by our attacks, or to
suggest that it is an incidental and rather regrettable
concomitant of night bombing. It is in fact produced
deliberately and our whole [Pathfinder Force] and
navigational technique is primarily designed to promote
it. This is the truth which cannot be denied without
implying that Bomber Command is attempting to do the
same thing as the Americans do occasionally and doing
it comparatively ineffectively. Failure to assert it openly
will, as I stated in my previous letter, inevitably affect
adversely the morale of our crews and I would urge that
this rather than the appeasement of the sentimental and
humanitarian scruples of a negligible minority should be
our primary consideration.[26]

Harris's letter, as ever a model of clear thought and frankness,
left the Ministry with little choice. It could no longer pretend
that there was no difference of principle between it and Harris.
Instead, it had to tell Harris directly whether his own view of
the bombing war accorded with official policy as dictated by the
POINTBLANK directive and interpreted by the Ministry. In its
reply, the Ministry noted that there could be no question that the
'indirect and inevitable consequences' of attacks on 'factories,
industrial premises, public utilities and means of communication' would be 'heavy casualties to the population of the city and

destruction of buildings and monuments which are not them-selves universally recognised as legitimate objects of attack'. But this, the Ministry argued, was as far as it went:

> What is in dispute is whether, in order to maintain the morale of Bomber Command air crews and avoid unfair comparison with the methods adopted by the U.S.A.A.F. in their daylight attacks, it is necessary to include in the definition of avowed targets for direct attack civilian workers and the whole of a city including dwelling places and cultural and religious monuments.
>
> The Council cannot agree that it is.

The argument was effectively that made by the Americans: the effect might be the same, but the motivation is different, and that matters.

> War itself is regrettable. So too are almost all the consequences of war and the conscience of all humanitarian people, and not merely of a negligible minority, would be shocked if such a misdescription were applied to the objects of our attacks as to lend colour to the German description of them as 'terror' raids.

Throughout this debate, Harris certainly had a point. That he was deliberately bombing the centres of cities was hardly a secret, nor was the obvious fact that many Germans lived in the centre of those cities. A November 1943 joint report by the Ministry of Economic Warfare and Air Intelligence cited damage to housing as one of the great accomplishments of the bombing offensive; argued that the bombing of Hamburg in the summer had had great negative effects on morale; and concluded that 'the increasing death toll [due to bombing] is the important factor and coupled with military failures the general attitude is approaching one of "peace at any price" and the avoidance of the whole-sale destruction of further cities in Germany.'[27] How Bomber Command was to destroy housing and cities without intention-ally killing German civilians, Harris might reasonably have sug-gested, was the authors' secret. Moreover, Hamburg was hardly an exemplar of precision bombing. The Air Ministry also had detailed reconnaissance photos showing shells of residential hous-ing in the centres of Cologne (1,785 acres devastated), Dortmund (460 acres), Düsseldorf (1,275 acres), Hannover (560 acres), Kassel (300 acres), Wuppertal (240 acres).[28] For Sweet to claim that the levelling of one German city centre after another amounted to incidental damage was disingenuous.

The matter cannot, however, rest there. The Council had no moral objections to area bombing as such: '[We] have no com-punction whatever in publicly justifying the adoption of area bombing as a stern necessity of war involving though it must as an indirect but inevitable consequence heavy casualties to the civil population whoever they may be.' The point of area bombing, however, had to be to destroy industry, not to kill civilians: '[We] are unable to agree that it is necessary to this justification to imply that a deliberate attempt is made to take the lives of German civilian workers.'[29] The distinction might seem like hair splitting, but it was not. Under the Ministry's understanding, area bombing was justified so long as it was the only or the best way to destroy industry, as well as much else. The above-mentioned Economic Warfare/Air Intelligence report also cited damage to the fighter production, synthetic oil plants, ball-bearing factories at Schweinfurt, and steel produc-tion, and the reconnaissance photos also included damage to the docks in Hamburg, to Frankfurt and Dortmund's inland ports, to Berlin factories, diesel engine production in Cologne, and to the Krupp works in Essen. Harris, by contrast, viewed all these targets as pointless: it was more effective to destroy cities and the people in them, regardless of any concomitant damage to industry. This fundamental difference of interpretation would grow more important as the war continued, and as the case for area bombing grew weaker, it set the stage for a final battle between Harris and his direct superior, Charles Portal.

TAKING OUT THE LUFTWAFFE

In early 1944, Hap Arnold sent a memo to Carl Spaatz. It instructed him to 'seek out and destroy the German Air Force in the air and on the ground without delay. The defensive concept of our fighter command and air defense units must be changed to the offensive.'[1] Arnold was preaching to the converted. 'Destruction of the Luftwaffe,' Anderson noted after the war, 'was priority number one. [The entire] war was hinged – even strategically – to a successful defeat of the German Air Force, the German fighter forces.'[2] It was the clearest lesson of the second Schweinfurt raid. On the morning of 15 October, as sixty American B-17s lay on German soil, Eaker penned a passionate letter to Arnold:

> This does not represent disaster; it does not indicate that
> the air battle has reached its climax. Our answer to this
> challenge [will be]:
>   1. More fighter cover at longer range;
>   2. Multiple attacks by 7 or 8 combat wings of 54
>   bombers;
>   3. Greater emphasis on counter Air Force operations,
>   striking all fields with mediums and pressing
>   destruction of aircraft factories and repair
>   establishments with heavies;
>   4. Bomb through clouds when his fighters will often be
>   fogbound.[3]

Urging Arnold to rush replacement aircraft, crews, and fighters, and to supply droppable tanks for fighters (allowing greater range), Eaker ended his letter on a defiant note: 'We must show the enemy we can replace our losses; he knows he cannot replace his. We must continue the battle with unrelenting fury. This we shall do.'

Spaatz had arrived back in the UK in December 1943. He had commanded the United States Eighth Air Force, but he took over the Americans' North African campaign in November 1942, before they began bombing Germany. He returned to England to assume full command over US Air Forces in Europe and to prepare for the invasion of the Continent. Spaatz worked with Sir Arthur Tedder, General Eisenhower's chief deputy at Supreme Headquarters Allied Expeditionary Force (SHAEF). Spaatz was given overall command of a new organisation, the United States Strategic and Tactical Air Forces in Europe (USSTAF), which co-ordinated both the Eighth Air Force and the Fifteenth Air Force (US heavy bombers based in Italy). The USSTAF was effectively the Eighth in new clothes, and Eighth Air Force Bomber Command was officially disbanded. Eaker, very much against his will, was pushed out and 'promoted' to command Allied air operations in the Mediterranean. Major General James ('Jimmy') Doolittle (a hard rock miner, amateur boxer, daredevil stuntman, MIT Ph.D. in aeronautics, and hero of the April 1942 bombing raids on Tokyo) was brought in to replace him, and Major General Frederick Anderson became Doolittle's chief of operations. In a final move, Major General Nathan F. Twining was transferred from the South Pacific to assume command of the Thirteenth Air Force.

For Doolittle and Spaatz, there was no question that defeating the Luftwaffe was USSTAF's overriding goal. When Doolittle entered the office of General William Kepner, the Eighth's fighter

chief, he saw a sign that read: THE FIRST DUTY OF THE EIGHTH
AIR FORCE FIGHTERS IS TO BRING THE BOMBERS BACK ALIVE.[4]
'Take that damn thing down,' Doolittle ordered, 'and put up
another one saying "The First duty of the Eighth Air Force is to
destroy German Fighters."'

'You mean,' Kepner replied, 'you're authorising me to take
the offence?'

Doolittle replied, 'I'm directing you to.'

Of all the causes of American air force losses – bad weather,
faulty equipment, flak and fighter defences – the Luftwaffe was
the most important. The German air force was a vicious foe. Escort
fighters were able to offer a great deal of protection to American
bombers, but the Luftwaffe quickly developed a technique for
dealing with them. When incoming US bombers were picked up
on radar, the German fighters would go up but hover just beyond
the limits of the escort fighters' range. Once the escorts turned
back and the bombers continued on alone, the Luftwaffe swept in
for the kill. It was often, and by no means only over Schweinfurt,
a massacre. Ridding the skies of the Luftwaffe had to be done, for
the US Air Forces and for POINTBLANK. Only if the Luftwaffe
was knocked out could Allied bombers attack submarine, tank,
and oil targets. Recognising this, the Eighth Air Force and Air
Ministry drew up plans in early 1943 for altering POINTBLANK
priorities: destroying the German fighter force, previously priority two, became priority number one.[5] Eaker and Portal agreed,
and they presented it to the Combined Chiefs of Staff at the May
1943 Trident conference.[6] These discussions became the basis of
the 1 June 1943 directive. The force they set out to destroy was
an ever-growing one: German fighter production had increased
throughout the summer and into the autumn of 1943.[7]

The outlines of the plan for destroying the Luftwaffe had been
sketched out by Eaker at least since the April 1942 dinner at

Chequers. The idea was to deliver a massive blow against the German aircraft industry. Eaker formalised the plan of attack in Operation ARGUMENT (the 'Big Week'), which envisaged continuous, co-ordinated strikes by the Eighth Air Force, the Fifteenth Air Force, and Harris's Bomber Command.

Spaatz's idea for destroying the Luftwaffe was contained in the words 'seek out and destroy'; he may have in fact suggested them to Arnold. Until 1944, the fighters played an important but essentially defensive role. They would accompany the bombers on their flight to Germany and defend them against any Luftwaffe fighters they met. Otherwise, the striking force – a very large one by early 1944 – would be on the ground or in training flights, waiting for the next precision bombing run. Spaatz transformed this defensive role into an offensive one. On bombing missions, the fighters would not simply accompany the bombers into Germany. Instead, they would surge ahead and seek out Luftwaffe fighters, attacking them and knocking enough of them out of the air to allow the bombers to get through. Spaatz decided that, whenever he could, he would send out his dogs. The goal was 'nothing less than the annihilation of the Luftwaffe. The strategy [was] to bait them and kill them. Send in the bombers – the bait – to destroy the aircraft factories and then massacre the planes and pilots that came up to defend them.'[8]

The idea was a bold one, but it faced a powerful opponent: time. Spaatz knew that his forces, both bombers and fighters, would be called away to support Operation OVERLORD, the invasion of the Continent. He had until 1 April – only ninety days – to ruin a large, powerful, and modern air force.[9]

The first forty-five days were lost to poor weather and to arguments within the Allied Air Forces about the proper command structure. For an all-out war on the Luftwaffe, Spaatz needed the involvement of not only the Eighth Air Force, but also British Bomber Command and the Ninth Air Force, the latter of which was built to support the Allied invasion of the Continent. In this, he ran up against Sir Trafford Leigh-Mallory, head of Fighter Command and, from August 1943, the Allied Expeditionary Air Force (a complex and rambling organisation that was part of SHAEF and was to co-ordinate Allied Air Forces in the run-up to D-Day). Spaatz viewed Leigh-Mallory, not without some justification, as pompous, haughty, and naïve. Leigh-Mallory could be highly inarticulate, which made his pomposity even more annoying, and his inability to be shaken from an idea once he adopted it as his own made Arthur Harris look like a model of flexibility. His view of a fighter's role was thoroughly defensive: his four years of experience defending the United Kingdom had convinced him that there was no point in trying to get the Luftwaffe to fight if it did not want to.[10] Finally, the head of the Ninth Air Force, General Lewis Brereton, wanted to keep it independent of both Spaatz *and* Leigh-Mallory. As Brereton saw it, the Ninth would spend the time in the months leading up to D-Day on training exercises, with a few raids being launched on V-1 production sites. Added to all of this was general uncertainty about how the Allied command structure would operate once Eisenhower assumed control of the integrated British–American forces.

The whole matter came to a head in mid-February. Spaatz undercut Leigh-Mallory, who played his last hand by writing directly to Portal, who acted as the agent for the Combined Chiefs of Staff in matters relating to the air war. Portal, increasingly on side with the Americans, threw his weight behind Spaatz. 'I have had the various directives looked up,' Portal wrote to Spaatz on 15 February, 'and it seems quite clear that A.C.M. Leigh-Mallory is bound . . . [to] lend maximum support to the strategic air offensive,' and to do so on both cloudy and clear days.[11]

Having sidelined Leigh-Mallory, Spaatz then took care of Brereton. At a 19 February meeting, Brereton, facing a united front of Doolittle, Spaatz, and Anderson, agreed that the Eighth would issue primary orders to the Ninth, either through Brereton or directly.[12] Spaatz then put the matter in writing after the meeting. Brereton received an official letter: 'The Commanding General, USSTAF, will exercise control of all administrative and training matters pertaining to the Ninth Air Force and will assume direct responsibility to higher headquarters for the proper performance of those functions.'[13] If Brereton thought of objecting, he didn't for long; Spaatz's administrative control of the Eighth and Ninth gave him power over promotion.

Spaatz was gaining full control of American Air Forces, but not of the capricious northern European weather. To help him understand it, Anderson enlisted the help of yet another eccentric professor, Irving P. Kirk of Caltech. Kirk researched fifty years of European weather patterns, leading right up to February 1944, and theorised that weather patterns repeated themselves.[14] On 18 February, he rang Anderson with his findings: on 20 February, a high-pressure system would settle over central and southern Germany and it would last for several days. Spaatz leaped on the news and gave Anderson permission to schedule a maximum strike on the morning of 20 February.[15] He still faced opposition outside the air forces – Churchill refused to transmit a cable to Eaker requesting help from the Fifteenth and doubts were raised about the P-38s – but Spaatz, with Anderson urging him on, refused to be knocked off course.[16]

Spaatz and Anderson were staking the entire American armed forces on the musings of a probably nutty professor.[17] The price of this folly seemed to become clear on the evening of 19 February. Heavy clouds hung over England and reconnaissance flights to Germany could find no break in them. The next morning promised icing conditions. Doolittle recommended postponing, and William Kepner, the leader of Eighth Fighter Command, agreed. Anderson, ever the risk-taker, argued the opposite, urging Spaatz on and assuring him that the operation was worth two hundred bombers. Spaatz stayed up all night listening to the conflicting advice. As dawn broke, he'd had no sleep. But he'd made up his mind. He put a three-word message through to his base commanders: 'Let 'em go.'[18]

On 20 February, more than one thousand bombers and nine hundred fighters took off for Germany.[19] Six combat wings flew unescorted to targets near Posen and Turow. The other ten and the entire fighter force headed off to the massive assembly and component plants in the Brunswick/Leipzig area. When the ten combat wings entered German airspace, the professor was proved right: the sky cleared quickly and completely. Incredibly for February, there was snow in Los Angeles and bright sun in Leipzig.[20] The leading bombers were accompanied by nine hundred fighters (P-47s, P-38s, and P-51s). They had new 150-gallon tanks that allowed them to fly all the way to Hanover, some 400 miles from their base. Just as they were ready to break off their escort on the left side of the bombing formation, they saw a stream of Messerschmitt fighters. The Germans were planning – following a tried and tested technique – to attack the fighters from below, blasting them as they remained glued to the bombers. This time, however, it was different: the Americans attacked them. The Thunderbolts swooped down onto the Luftwaffe fighters, chewing into them. Only one Messerschmitt escaped undamaged.[21] The Americans did not lose a single plane.

While the Thunderbolts were engaging the Luftwaffe, the six other combat wings flew to northern Germany and the Ninth Air Force sent 135 medium bombers to attack airfields in western Germany. The largest force ever dispatched by the Eighth Air Force was hitting the Luftwaffe left, right, and centre.

That night, some twelve hours after his men left, Spaatz was waiting nervously for news. He was determined to see POINTBLANK through to completion, and he was willing to lose hundreds of bombers to do it. Anderson, who was even more gung-ho than Spaatz, was prepared to see seven thousand American pilots and aircrew die – two-thirds of his entire crews and one-third of the number of Marines that would die taking the Pacific – to see the Luftwaffe destroyed.[22] But a large number of losses at this early point in Spaatz's war on the Luftwaffe, even if (as at Schweinfurt) they inflicted heavy losses on the Germans, would have been severely damaging. It would have given fodder to Churchill and other opponents of precision bombing and strengthened the hand of those, such as Brereton, who opposed the concentration of power and authority in Spaatz's hands. As the evening wore on, group after group reported, and the story was always the same: they had losses of only one or two, often none at all.[23]

The attacks had damaged four plants producing Luftwaffe night fighters/bombers (Ju 88s), and two others producing day fighter aircraft (Bf 109s). More importantly, only twenty-one American heavy bombers and four fighters had been lost, half the figure lost on a raid on the same targets on 11 January and one-third of the losses of Schweinfurt/Regensburg. Of the men who went out, all but 214 came back. On the other side, the Germans had lost 150 fighters. Spaatz was ecstatic, 'on the crest of the highest wave he had ever ridden'.[24] He had every reason to be: the raids were the beginning of the end for the Luftwaffe. In February, the Germans lost one-third of their fighters and one-fifth of their crews; in March, they lost half their fighter aircraft; and by May, the loss rate of a typical mission hovered around 50 per cent.[25]

In the five days after the launch of 'Big Week', until the weather turned, the Eighth and Fifteenth Air Forces fought their way to and from targets deep inside Germany. The Americans attacked shipyards in Rostock, railway and power stations in Berlin, aircraft-production facilities in Brunswick, Daimler-Benz in Stuttgart, Messerschmitt factories in Regensburg and Augsburg, and more.[26] The Luftwaffe fought back viciously, but the American fighters responded with aggressive attacks. Big Week cost the Americans 266 bombers, 2,600 aircrew (killed or captured), and 28 fighters. Half of these losses occurred on the last two days of the battle, when the Germans exploited mistakes that left bombers unescorted or without sufficient escorts.[27]

Harris joined in on Big Week, but he did so on his own terms. On 19 January, Bottomley had forwarded a Chiefs of Staff memorandum affirming, under Casablanca, German fighter aircraft industry as the primary bombing target and requested Harris's views.[28] Harris ignored the reference to aircraft industry and forwarded to Bottomley a January 1943 report outlining twenty-two German towns attacked and the effect such attacks would have on aircraft production.[29] He then ordered more city attacks. From 20 to 25 February, the RAF bombed the centres and/or residential sections of Leipzig, Berlin, Aachen, Stuttgart, Munich, Kiel, Augsburg, Düsseldorf, Duisburg, and Schweinfurt.[30]

Alexander Witzigmann was a seventeen-year-old anti-aircraft auxiliary who manned one of Germany's great flak guns. He was one of 750 such operators defending the heavily protected capital. Across the city, there were hundreds of searchlights, heavy gun batteries, flak towers, and rocket launchers (single guns). Operating together, they were meant to create a ceiling of death over Berlin.

On 6 March, which came to be called Bloody Monday, Alexander watched a fifteen-mile-long parade of American bombers thunder across the capital.[31] 'I was so frightened,' he said, 'by the display of strength by the enemy [that] I began to shake.'[32] Their targets were the ball-bearing plant at Erkner, the Bosch electrical equipment factory at Kleinmachnow, and the Daimler-Benz aircraft engine plant at Genshagen, all on the outskirts of the city; if these were covered by cloud, the long-suffering Friedrichstrasse railway station, right in the heart of Berlin, would become the target.[33]

The Luftwaffe was ready for them. Determined to defend the capital, fighters lined up fifty abreast and flew head-on into the bombers. Searchlights coned the incoming aircraft, and flak blasted them. When they were within five hundred yards of the Americans, German fighters fired a single half-second burst before pulling up violently. These daredevil, almost proto-kamikaze techniques cost the Americans dearly: seventy-five bombers.[34] But it also cost the Germans: escort fighters shot down forty-three German fighters (at the cost of eleven escorts).[35] And although the ball-bearings factory in Erkner was hardly touched – many of the bombs hit the town, killing and maiming seven hundred people – the raid succeeded in its overarching mission of damaging the Luftwaffe. In New York, reporter James B. Reston wrote, 'The time of what was once called air-raids has passed. The Allied Army of the air has started a campaign of attrition against the Luftwaffe which must be recognised as one of the decisive military campaigns of the war . . . . From now on the Allied leaders of this campaign will send their aerial artillery anywhere in Germany where the German fighters are made and to any point where German fighters will give battle.'[36]

Harris had always counselled against hitting the same targets successively, as it gave the Germans a clear warning of what to expect. But, two nights later, on 8 March, the 100th Bomb Group was back, blazing exactly the same trail across Germany's skies. At Dümmer Lake, in northern Germany and the scene of the majority of the 100th's losses, the first wave of escort fighters, Thunderbolts, turned away. They should have been replaced immediately by Mustangs, but they weren't: the second wave of escorts was late. The Luftwaffe saw their chance and attacked: German fighters flew en masse into the 45th combat bombardment wing, flying just ahead of the 100th. The leader of the shot-up 45th was lost and confused, and he missed the turn to Berlin. Major John M. Bennett, head of the battle-scarred 100th, moved his wing to the front and led the Eighth Air Force into the German capital.

Where Adolf Galland, Inspector of Fighters (essentially the head of the German fighter force) was waiting for them. He had deliberately saved up the bulk of his fighter forces for the Eighth's bombing run.[37] As Bennett's and the other bombers came over Berlin, they responded to Galland's tactics by bearing straight ahead, and the B-17s blasted through the fighters. As the bullets pelted them from the front, flak hit them from below. The aeroplanes and men shook. Hot shrapnel blasted through the bottoms of the planes, killing some men and castrating others. By the time it returned to England, the Eighth Air Force had lost thirty-seven bombers and eighteen fighters. But they had again exacted so heavy a toll on the Germans that, three nights later, the Luftwaffe stayed on the ground during a precision raid on Berlin. Only six American bombers and a single fighter were lost.

Over the course of the March 1944 raids, the Americans suffered terrible losses – 153 bombers in just three raids – but they imposed equally terrible losses: forty to fifty German fighters per raid. By the time the Americans paused, they had destroyed 6,259 German aircraft. The Germans had lost another 3,608 to accidents as well as 2,262 pilots.[38] Fighter production peaked later in the year, but it could not keep up with the rapid destruction; the Luftwaffe was being drained of all fighting strength.[39]

18

GERMANY'S ACHILLES HEEL

Oil had been on target lists from the earliest days of the war, but
the major refineries were out of the range of early RAF bomb
runs, and the few raids on closer targets produced few results.
In February 1944, Spaatz became a convinced advocate of new
attacks on oil facilities. As air attacks on the Luftwaffe produced
early results, Spaatz ordered the formation of a USSTAF planning committee to consider future targets. With Spaatz urging them on, the committee produced a report on 5 March. It
called for combined RAF–USSTAF attacks on oil targets across
Germany and into central Europe. If fourteen synthetic oil plants
(which extracted oil from coal) and thirteen refineries could be
destroyed, 80 per cent of German production and 60 per cent of
readily usable refining capacity would also be destroyed.

Spaatz's urgency was driven by the British as much as the
Germans. Solly Zuckerman, who had fully supported Spaatz's
attacks on the Luftwaffe, had been studying attacks on communications (that is, transportation) infrastructure in the
Mediterranean theatre. He became convinced that the best way
to weaken Germany in the run-up to D-Day was by destroying
the country's transportation system, and above all its large railway centres and rolling stock.[1] Sounding rather like Harris on
cities, Zuckerman argued that a country's railways were its nervous system: if you damaged one part of it, you could cripple the
whole.[2] Specifically, destroying these transportation nodes would
paralyse the Germans as they tried to get men and materiel to

Normandy. Zuckerman calculated that about 40 per cent of all Allied bombs – 45,000 tons out of a total pre-invasion programme of 108,000 – should hit transportation targets. The work would be roughly divided between the RAF and the Eighth and Ninth Air Forces. Zuckerman presented his conclusions in early 1944, which were not radically different from those of a 1943 report by the Ministry of War Transport.[3]

The plan, proposing attacks on rail targets, went before a newly formed Allied Air Forces Bombing Committee on 10 January, passed through several other committees, and finally reached Eisenhower and Tedder on 1 February. The plan proposed attacks on rail targets, and they liked it. The report convinced Tedder of the merits of attacking transportation. Eisenhower was similarly won over, but one of the plan's merits had nothing to do with bombing at all: the integration of all available air forces complemented Eisenhower's assumption of overall command. As the plan circulated, the battle lines quickly became clear. Eisenhower, Tedder, Leigh-Mallory, and Zuckerman supported the plan; the prime minister, the bulk of the War Cabinet, the War Office, the Air Ministry, Bomber Command, and Spaatz opposed it.[4]

Added to this mix was an institutional debate. Tedder was given the job of reconciling differences between Eisenhower, who wanted total control, and Portal, who wanted autonomy for RAF Coastal, Fighter, and Bomber Command. Tedder – who saw air power as complementary to the Army and Navy – was able by April to get all parties to agree to a compromise.[5] Eisenhower would have overall direction of the strategic air forces for a limited period, only until September 1944.

Throughout February and March, the debate raged over transportation versus oil as the priority bombing targets. Tedder's support for transportation was matched by his suspicion of oil, as he had been 'led up the garden path before'.[6] He doubted that refineries could be knocked out and believed that any damage that was inflicted would be counteracted by aggressive German conservation. Spaatz responded that attacks on northern France would not bring the Luftwaffe up into the air and that the inevitable civilian casualties would destroy French goodwill towards the Americans and British.

As the argument rolled on, Eisenhower grew increasingly irritated. In late March, he threatened resignation: 'I am going to take drastic action and inform the Combined Chiefs of Staff that unless the matter is settled at once I will request relief from this command.'[7] Spaatz, Tedder, Eisenhower, Harris, and Leigh-Mallory, along with representatives from the War Office, Air Ministry, and Joint Intelligence Committee, met on 25 March to have it out. Spaatz and Eaker had already spent the morning lobbying Eisenhower, but the general would not show his hand.[8]

When the meeting started, Tedder was in the chair – a crucial advantage. He secured general agreement that the Luftwaffe, including ball-bearing production, remained the highest priority and that the air forces would only target oil or communications (again, transportation) *after* they targeted the German Air Force. Tedder then put the case for the transportation plan, and Eisenhower got immediately behind it. 'Everything I have read,' Eisenhower said, 'convinces me that, apart from the attack on the [German Air Force], the Transportation Plan was the only one which offered a reasonable chance of the air forces making a real contribution to the land battle during the first vital weeks of OVERLORD.'[9] He continued: '[In fact, there is no] real alternative.'

The argument was not going Spaatz's way, and he did himself no favours. When he presented the oil plan, he highlighted the transportation plan's problems *without* emphasising strongly enough how the oil plan would aid OVERLORD. His wooden, unpersuasive manner of speaking also did not help his case.[10]

After Spaatz's speech, Anderson came in with the unhelpfully honest admission that the oil plan would not guarantee decisive influence during the initial stages of OVERLORD. What it would do, however, was have a devastating effect on the enemy within six months. The transportation plan, by contrast, might not significantly benefit OVERLORD or the Allies' war effort overall. At this point, a British oil expert from the Ministry of Economic Warfare offered his 'help': attacks on oil would drive down German supplies by 25 per cent in three months, and would significantly affect German production (they would 'feel the pinch') within four to five months.

Portal leaped on this. The official's comments 'showed conclusively that the oil plan would not help OVERLORD in the first few critical weeks'.[11] Eisenhower agreed, and that settled it. Transportation, not oil, would be the primary target in the run-up to the invasion of the Continent.

Arthur Harris had been unusually quiet during the discussion. He naturally detested the transportation plan, as it was precision bombing *par excellence*. With his characteristic gruff wit, he wrote to US Assistant Secretary of War for Air Robert Lovett that 'our worst headache has been a panacea plan devised by a civilian professor whose peacetime forte is the study of the sexual aberrations of the higher apes. Starting from this sound military basis he devised a scheme to employ almost the entire British and US bomber forces for three months or more in the destruction of targets mainly in France and Belgium.'[12] Bombing transportation, Harris told Spaatz, would 'never work'.[13]

A few weeks before the 25 March meeting, Harris had pleaded with Portal to go in for an all-out area bombing of Germany. 'Any serious reduction of our rate at striking at German production,' he wrote, 'will inevitably make possible industrial recovery which would, within quite a short period, nullify the results achieved by tremendous efforts during the past 12 months.'[14]

Portal decided to call his bluff. On 4 March, he ordered Harris to undertake precision raids on marshalling yards in France. The results were impressive. On 6–7 March, Bomber Command blasted railway tracks, rolling stock, and railway installations, doing 'enormous damage'. The next night, the RAF dropped 300 bombs on railway yards at Le Mans; they destroyed 250 wagons, hit six locomotives, sliced through many railway lines, and burned out a store of railway sleepers.[15] Only thirty bombs fell outside the target, killing thirty-one French people. Not a single aircraft was lost on either raid, and it was crystal clear that Bomber Command was capable of a high degree of precision. Less obviously, the raids also showed that the cantankerous commander-in-chief would, when push came to shove, obey a direct and unequivocal order. When the 25 March meeting took place, Harris's success left him unable to make a tactical case against transportation targets. His views on all 'panaceas' were well known, and restating them would have gained him nothing. Instead, he reserved his invective for Leigh-Mallory, who let it be known that he was reluctant to go down to posterity as the man who killed thousands of Frenchmen. Harris shot back: 'What makes you think you're going to go down to posterity at all?'[16]

Spaatz left the 25 March meeting disappointed, but not dejected. Although transportation won out over oil, he was still left with much that he liked. For his part, Harris had been assigned twenty-six rail targets in France, so he could not go on bombing cities while Spaatz was diverted from his own preferred targets. More importantly, the overall agreement on the importance of destroying the Luftwaffe gave Spaatz a wedge into oil attacks. If bombing oil targets brought a fierce Luftwaffe response, then oil targets would fall squarely within his primary order to destroy the Luftwaffe.[17] At the same time, poor weather limited the number of direct raids on transportation, freeing up surplus bombers for oil.[18] After a long fight over transportation and oil, it was proving possible to hit both.

Within a week of his 25 March defeat, Spaatz regrouped and made his case to Portal and Eisenhower. In a 31 March memo, he defended his oil plan with a clarity that had escaped him six days earlier. 'The effect from the Oil attack,' he wrote,

> while offering a less definite input in time, is certain to be more far-reaching. It will lead directly to sure disaster for Germany. The Rail attack can lead to harassment only. In weighing these two, it appears that too great a price may be paid merely for a certainty of very little.[19]

As oil depended, like everything else, on transporting it first, the two targets might be viewed as complementary. Knocking out both oil production and the trains that brought the men and equipment to repair the damage would be disastrous for Germany's war effort.

Spaatz sketched out the target priorities for the two air forces. The Eighth would attack:

- The Luftwaffe and ball-bearing production.
- The nineteen rail targets in occupied countries, already selected through the Transportation Plan.
- The thirteen major synthetic plants.

At the same time, the Fifteenth Air Force would target:

- The Luftwaffe and ball-bearing production.
- Rail transport in Romania and selected targets in southern France.
- Synthetic oil targets in southern Germany.[20]

Spaatz envisioned a two-part attack: first, a concentrated raid on Germany's main supply of crude and refined petroleum (in Romania), which would cut production and force the Germans to rely even further on synthetic oil; and, second, concentrated air attacks on synthetic oil production (in Germany) that would, over several months, cripple German industrial production.[21] By March 1944, Germany's main source of crude and refined petroleum was to be found in Romania, at the sprawling refineries of Ploesti. In 1943, they had supplied two million tons of oil.[22]

Changing the mind of either Eisenhower or Portal was not easy. The Supreme Commander remained convinced that the transportation plan would provide the greatest support for the invasion. Portal maintained that oil fell outside POINTBLANK, and in late March he sent out an official minute ruling out Ploesti as a target.[23]

Spaatz went ahead anyway. On 5 April, the Fifteenth Air Force launched a raid on Ploesti. As required by the transportation plan, the target was the town's marshalling yards.[24] The bombers, however, 'missed' the yards and hit the adjacent refineries. A few days later, they 'missed' again, and scored another direct hit on Ploesti. Spaatz was convinced that the raids had been successful, but he could not launch a full-blown oil campaign without Eisenhower's support.

He also faced British opposition. On 10 April, the British War Cabinet and British Chiefs of Staff invoked an escape clause in the air agreement, declaring V-1 flying bombs, then under production, a threat to the security of the British Isles. Tedder phoned Fred Anderson to give him a new bombing directive: Operation CROSSBOW, the destruction of German long-range missiles and missile sites, had priority over POINTBLANK.

Both the British government and UK Chiefs of Staff had for months considered taking out the launching sites. On 18 January, the prime minister asked for a report on gassing them.[25] Portal had to point out that the Vice-Chiefs of Staff had already considered such a proposal in late 1943, along with the related idea of gassing German civilians.[26] The Vice-Chiefs had rejected the latter because it would cost Britain the moral high ground and invite retaliation, and they concluded – not surprisingly – that gas attacks on projector sites did less damage than high explosives.[27]

Spaatz was livid about CROSSBOW, and on the night of 19 April he went to inform Eisenhower. The timing turned out to be bad: minutes before Spaatz arrived, Eisenhower had learned that the commanding general of the Ninth's Air Force Service Command, Major General Henry J. F. Miller, had got obnoxiously drunk in a London hotel and proceeded loudly to take bets that the invasion would come before 15 June.[28] It was not an auspicious start, but Spaatz made good by having Miller arrested and confined to his quarters. Spaatz then vented his anger over Tedder's decision to grant V-1 sites priority. If they worried the British so much, the RAF should be sent to destroy them. The case was clear and Eisenhower agreed.

Spaatz then used the chance to reopen the oil debate. He argued that two recent raids on transportation targets at Berlin and Kassel together had cost the USSTAF only fifteen bombers. Although a great relief, it meant that the transportation attacks were not luring out the Luftwaffe. Oil attacks, Spaatz argued, would. Eisenhower would not be swayed. He repeated his arguments against moving from transportation to oil. But then he relented. No one knows exactly what Spaatz said to change Eisenhower's mind – the two men made a point of leaving no official record – but he probably threatened resignation. Spaatz was permitted any two days before the invasion to hit oil. Then it was back to transportation.

* * *

Spaatz was ready to go, but the weather was not. It was not until 12 May that the skies were clear enough, and then only over England and Germany (Ploesti remained covered in clouds). Synthetic oil plants in eastern Germany would have to be the target. That day, 15 combat wings – 886 bombers and 735 escort fighters – took off from English bases and streaked across Germany.[29] Their targets were synthetic oil plants at Zwickau, Merseburg-Leuna, Brüx (the city of Most in today's Czech Republic), Lützkendorf, Böhlen, and Zeitz. They flew across the English Channel towards Frankfurt, where the bulk of the force banked northeast towards Zwickau.

German radar picked up the bombing formation as it approached the Dutch coast. Galland, who had deliberately preserved his fighters as the Germans tried frantically to recover from previous precision attacks, guessed where the bombers were headed. He sent up four hundred fighters to attack.[30] At Frankfurt, a mass of German fighters attacked the leading division, which was low on escorts because one of its fighting groups had mistakenly rendezvoused with a trailing division.[31] The remaining escort fighters were overwhelmed. Within forty minutes, the Germans downed thirty-two bombers – some two-thirds of the total forty-six bombers lost on the mission.[32] Two others were lost to fighters, twelve to flak.

After these early kills, however, the Luftwaffe ran out of luck. Subsequent bombers were better protected, and the fighters engaged the Germans in ferocious dogfights, bringing down sixty-five aircraft for the loss of only seven fighters.[33] They protected the majority of the bombers and enabled them to fly on to oil targets. They blasted synthetic oil plants with 1,718 tonnes of bombs.

The effect was decisive. 'On that day,' Speer wrote after the war, 'the technological war was decided.' 'Until then,' he continued, 'we had managed to produce approximately as many weapons as the armed forces needed, in spite of their considerable losses. But with the attack of [the American daylight bombers] upon several fuel plants in central and eastern Germany, a new era in the air war began. It meant the end of German war production.'[34] As ever with Speer, we cannot know if he really believed that at the time. The raid certainly did nothing to dent his enthusiasm for prosecuting the war. On 12 May, he described the task of rebuilding and striking back at the Allies as 'the greatest contest in the history of the world'.[35] But there is one thing we do know: the raids destroyed in one day 90 per cent of Germany's fuel production.[36]

On 13 May, the day after Spaatz's oil raid, ULTRA intercepts produced an order from Luftwaffe Operations Staff in Berlin. It called for the stripping of heavy and light anti-aircraft guns from the eastern front and from plants manufacturing fighters in Oschersleben, Leipzig-Erla, and Wiener Neustadt.[37] They were to be sent to Zeitz, south of Leipzig, and Pölitz (Police in today's Poland, near Szczecin) to protect hydrogenation plants. Spaatz was ecstatic: the Germans obviously dreaded attacks on oil, even more so than on fighter production, and they were gathering their air forces around oil targets. He had successfully predicted both. A week later, another ULTRA intercept produced a second order, this time to convert an even higher percentage of motor transport to power supplied by inefficient wood fuel generators.[38] Oil attacks were working. Even Tedder came around: 'I guess we'll have to give the customer what he wants.'[39]

On 28 May 1944, Spaatz sent out more than four hundred bombers to attack synthetic oil plants at Ruhland, Magdeburg, Merseburg-Leuna, Lützendorf, and Pölitz. The results were devastating. At Merseburg-Leuna, Italian forced labourers added to the chaos by pouring fuel on the flames.[40]

The results of the 28 May raid were more devastating than that of 12 May. The two blows wrecked German oil production, which fell from 180,000 tons in March to 54,000 in June.[41] Looking back at the campaign after the war, Galland noted that 'it is difficult to understand why the Allies started this undertaking so late, after they had suffered such heavy losses in other operations. Right from the start, fuel had been the most awkward bottleneck for [Germany's] conduct of the war.' The oil campaign was 'the most successful operation of the entire Allied strategical air warfare' and the 'fatal blow for the Luftwaffe'.[42]

A further Ploesti raid occurred almost exactly a week before a vast armada of troops landed at Normandy. As they did, more than six thousand planes – from Bomber, Fighter, and Coastal Command, the Second (tactical) Air Force of the RAF, and the Eighth and Ninth American Air Forces – were flying overhead. They were prepared for bitter resistance from the Luftwaffe, but none came. Only 320 aircraft – making odds of 1 to 20 – were there to meet them.[43]

The air forces' support for ground troops was impressive, but their greatest contribution to Normandy occurred well before 6 June 1944. Over five months, they destroyed the factories producing fighters, used decoys and attacks to draw out the German fighters, and shot them out of the sky by the hundreds. The transportation plan, despite Spaatz's scepticism, had also produced results. Bombing had almost entirely dismembered the rail network of northern Belgium and France, choking off the supply channels feeding the German army.[44] As the German army was dependent to the end on rail lines for strategic movements, their destruction was particularly crippling.[45] But the transportation plan had other effects. Trucks that tried to move towards the front found themselves blocked by blown-out bridges. German fighters that had hoped to land at little- or never-used bases in northern France found them ravaged by bombs. Any lorries or trains that managed to find a route to the front were blasted by

Allied fighters. 'The Allies have,' the commander of the 2nd Panzer Division reported, 'total air supremacy. They bomb and shoot at anything which moves, even single vehicles and persons . . . . The feeling of being powerless against the enemy's aircraft . . . has a paralysing effect.'[46] The morale that mattered in a totalitarian state – the morale of its military and political leaders, rather than its citizens – was being undermined.[47] And it was being undermined by precision bombing.

OIL AND BABY KILLING

On 7 June 1944, Portal was sent a message originating from Luftwaffe Operations Staff that Enigma cipher machines, located at Bletchley Park, had intercepted. It read:

As a result of renewed encroachment into the production of a/c [aircraft] fuel by enemy action, the most essential requirements for training and carrying out production plans can scarcely be covered with the quantities of a/c fuel available. In order to ensure the defence of the Reich and to prevent the readiness for defence of the GAF [German Air Force] from gradually collapsing, it has been necessary to break into the strategical reserve.[1]

Portal was a pragmatist. He had once believed that area bombing would win the war. When the evidence suggested otherwise, he changed his views. In early 1944, he was very sceptical about the effectiveness of oil targets; when the evidence showed how effective those targets were, he changed his mind again.[2]

Portal sent a copy of the decryption to the prime minister and added a note: 'I regard this as one of the most important pieces of information we have yet received.' He recommended to Churchill an all-out attack on synthetic oil plants by all Allied strategic bombers as soon as they were free. Piecemeal and sporadic attacks by small forces would only give the Germans time to increase flak and smoke defences. Churchill replied with one word: 'Agreed.'[3]

On 3 June, Bottomley asked Harris for his views on bombing oil targets as soon as OVERLORD allowed him to.[4] Harris waited ten days to reply and then stated that the targets could be destroyed with thirty-two thousand tons of bombs, perhaps less, but that it would be a waste of bombs to do so. Harris also reminded Bottomley that any plans would have to go through the deputy supreme commander, Tedder. Tedder had already signed on. Thus, through an informal arrangement between Eisenhower and Spaatz and between Tedder and, reluctantly, Harris, oil became an unofficial RAF target.[5]

Later in the month, Eisenhower made public the formerly clandestine oil plan, and the attacks continued. Throughout the month, the Eighth Air Force launched three all-out raids. On 18 and 20 June, the Eighth attacked oil facilities near Munich, losing fifty bombers. Nine days later, the Fifteenth Air Force once again hammered Ploesti.

German oil production was plummeting. In May, Germany had 715,000 tons of petroleum at its disposal; by June, it had 472,000 tons. In April, the Luftwaffe had 180,000 tons of aviation spirit; by June, only 10,000.[6] On 9 July, Enigma picked up another intercept, this time from Göring. It read: 'The deep inroads made into the supply of aircraft fuel demand the most stringent reduction in flying. Drastic economy is absolutely essential.' Three weeks later, the Americans launched a raid on Germany's single-largest synthetic oil plant, at Merseburg. The intercept read: 'Heaviest attacks so far; heavy damage – works provisionally 100 percent out of action.'[7] The impact of oil attacks was decisive and unquestionable. Up to this point, during the whole of 1944, Bomber Command had not launched a single attack on oil targets.[8]

* * *

On 7 July, both the Eighth and the Fifteenth Air Forces launched oil raids on Germany. The Eighth hit targets in central Germany; the Fifteenth bombed synthetic oil plants at Blechhammer, in Upper Silesia (today, Blachownia Śląska), sixty miles from Auschwitz.

The Allies knew about Auschwitz since April 1944.[9] On 4 April, an American reconnaissance plane had flown towards the IG Farben synthetic oil and rubber plant at Monowitz. Four miles before reaching the plant, he turned on his camera. The film rolled as he passed over the plant, and then for another four miles. On his return, he had twenty-three exposures, including three of Auschwitz.[10]

Three months earlier, on 7 April, Rudolf Vrba and Alfred Wetzler, both Slovak Jews, escaped the camp and hid themselves in a woodpile just outside it. For three days, the SS and their dogs searched the camp and its surroundings. Then, after standard procedure dictated that the search be called off, Vrba and Wetzler escaped.

Two weeks later, they arrived in Slovakia. On 25 April, the Vrba-Wetzler Report (also known as the Auschwitz Protocols) told the world of the camp and its locations, of crowded trains arriving at precise times, of the separation of prisoners, and of the ovens:[11]

At present there are four crematoria in operation at Birkenau, two large ones, I and II, and two smaller ones, III and IV. Those of type I and II consist of 3 parts, i.e.: (A) the furnace room; (B) the large halls; and (C) the gas chamber. A huge chimney rises from the furnace room around which are grouped nine furnaces, each having four openings. Each opening can take three normal corpses at once and after an hour and a half the bodies are completely burned. This corresponds to a daily capacity of about 2,000 bodies . . . . The gassing takes place as follows: the victims are brought into hall (B), where they are told to undress. To complete the fiction that they are going to bathe, each person receives a towel and a small piece of soap issued by two men in white coats. They are then crowded into the gas chamber (C) in such numbers that there is, of course, only standing room. To compress this crowd into the narrow space, shots are often fired to induce those already at the far end to huddle still closer together. Then, there is a short pause, presumably to allow the room temperature to rise to a certain level, after which the SS men with gas masks climb on the roof, open the traps, and shake down a preparation in powder form out of tin cans labelled 'CYKLON. For use against vermin.' . . . [T]he total capacity of the four cremating and gassing plants at Birkenau amounts to 6,000 daily.

The report was sent to Rezso Kasztner (also known as Rudolf Kastner) of the Jewish Agency Rescue Committee in Budapest.[12] Rather than disseminating the information to that country's Jews, Kastner showed the report to Adolf Eichmann, head of the Jewish section of the SS. Eichmann feigned an interest in negotiating to keep the report secret.

Kastner, however, didn't have the only copy. Another copy, together with an additional eyewitness report on deportations from Hungary (the 'Mordowicz-Rosin' report), was forwarded by Slovak Jewish leaders to Dr Jaromir Kopecky, the Geneva representative of the Czechoslovakian government-in-exile.[13] Kopecky sent both reports to Gerhart Riegner of the World Jewish Congress in Switzerland. Riegner had a summary of the report forwarded to Elizabeth Wiskemann, an expert on Czechoslovakia at the

British legation in the Swiss capital, Bern, urging that the BBC broadcast the details.[14] Wiskemann then sent the summary immediately to Allen Dulles, head of US Intelligence in Switzerland. On 16 June, Dulles forwarded it to Roswell McClelland, the War Refugee Board's representative in Switzerland. The Board had been established by Roosevelt in January to 'rescue the victims of enemy oppression'. Dulles attached a note: 'Seems more in your line.'[15] McClelland cabled John Pehle, the head of the Board, in Washington: 'There is little doubt that many of these Hungarian Jews are being sent to the extermination camps of Auschwitz and Birkenau in western Upper Silesia where, according to recent reports, since early summer 1942, at least 1,500,000 Jews have been killed . . . . It is urged by all sources of this information in Slovakia and Hungary that vital sections of these [railway] lines and especially bridges . . . be bombed as the only possible means of slowing down or stopping future deportations.'[16] Two days later, another cable arrived, this time from the Orthodox community in Bratislava, urging the bombing of railways and of towns that served as major railway junctions.[17] On 24 June, Pehle went to see John McCloy, Assistant Secretary of War and another Stimson protégé. Emphasising that he 'had several doubts about the matter', Pehle made clear to McCloy that he was not requesting that the War Department take 'any action' beyond 'appropriately explor[ing] it.'[18]

The report was definitive proof of Auschwitz (the concentration camp) and Birkenau (or Auschwitz II, the gas chambers and crematorium), and what was happening there. Much information on the Nazi murder of Jews had leaked out and been reported, and by 1942 the Allies knew the name and location of four of the death camps: Chelmno, Treblinka, Sobibor, and Belzec.[19] Auschwitz-Birkenau, the principal site of mass murder, nonetheless remained shrouded in secrecy. Specific information about the camp – through ULTRA intercepts, for instance – had come to the Allies some time before, and by mid-1943 a number of officials had enough details to determine the site and purpose of the installation.[20] It is, however, a matter of debate whether they had analysed the disparate pieces of information in a systematic enough way to know with certainty at that point. By June 1944, they had. By the time the Allies had the knowledge, they also had the capability: bombing Birkenau required in practice heavy bombing missions from northern Italy. By April 1944 at the latest, the Fifteenth Air Force was capable of destroying Auschwitz in four precision raids, spread over several weeks and involving some seventy-five bombers each.[21] Doing so would have diverted 7 per cent of the Fifteenth's bombers from the oil offensive. Only a raid on the camp itself would have worked: bombed rail lines were easily repaired, and the more ambitious project of taking out the rail nexus leading to Auschwitz-Birkenau would have required a massive diversion of air power.[22]

In June, the Eighth Air Force began flying missions in support of the Soviet summer offensive from bases near Kiev ('Operation FRANTIC'). An attack on Auschwitz from Soviet bases would have required Stalin's approval, however, and he viewed any such attack as a diversion from aiding the Soviet summer offensive.[23] It is possible that low-level raids by RAF Mosquitoes, flying from bases near the Adriatic Sea, might also have destroyed Birkenau in June 1944, but it is doubtful that they could have covered the distance undetected, or had enough impact to destroy Birkenau if they did.[24] The Fifteenth, by contrast, could have done the job. By this point, 250,000 Jews had already been deported from Hungary to Auschwitz.

On 2 July, a few days after the report reached McCloy, Spaatz launched a series of heavy raids on military targets around Budapest. They had nothing to do with the deportations or with diplomatic efforts to stop the deportations by Sweden, Roosevelt (who appealed to the Hungarian people to help Jews to escape and to 'record the evidence'), and the Vatican.[25] The puppet government in Budapest interpreted the bombing as reprisals, panicked, and halted deportations on 6 July.[26] Approximately 300,000 Jewish lives were temporarily saved.

The day before, Chaim Weizmann and Moshe Shertok, two of the most senior representatives of the Jewish Agency for Palestine in London, went to see UK Foreign Secretary Anthony Eden.[27] Much of their conversation concerned the tragically hopeless proposals by Joel Brand of the Zionist Rescue Committee to negotiate with the Gestapo over trading Allied goods for Hungarian Jews. But they also raised the issue of bombing. The same day, Eden sent an account to Churchill. He reported Weizmann's appeal that 'we should do something to mitigate the appalling slaughter of Jews in Hungary', and suggested himself bombing the railway lines and the camps, 'so as to destroy the plant used for gassing and cremation'.

Churchill replied on 7 July, the following day. Negotiation was a non-starter: 'On no account have the slightest negotiations, direct or indirect, with the Huns.' Bombing, however, had the prime minister's support: 'Get anything out of the Air Force you can, and invoke me if necessary.'[28] The same day, Eden wrote to Sinclair: '[b]oth the Prime Minister and I are in agreement with [Weizmann's] suggestion* that something might be done to stop the operation of the death camps by (i) bombing the railway lines leading to Birkenau (and to any other similar camps . . .); and (2) bombing the camps themselves . . . . Could you let me know,' Eden continued, 'how the Air Ministry view the feasibility of these proposals? I very much hope that it will be possible to do something. I have the authority of the Prime Minister to say that he agrees.'[29]

On 11 July, the Jewish Agency intervened again, sending a note to Roosevelt urging the bombing of Auschwitz itself. Doing so

would 'give the lie to the oft-repeated assertions of Nazi spokes-
men that the Allies are not really so displeased [with] ridding
Europe of Jews' and would 'convince the German circles still
hopeful of Allied mercy of the genuineness of Allied condemnation of the murder of the Jews.'[30]

Eight days later, Sinclair replied with a cursory report stating
that 'bombing the plant is out of the bounds of possibility for
Bomber Command, because the distance [from the UK to Upper
Silesia] is too great for the attack to be carried out at night.' The
Americans might launch an attack by day, but, Sinclair argued,
there wasn't much point: 'even if the plant was destroyed, I am
not clear that it would really help the victims.' (Eden scribbled
next to this: 'He wasn't asked his opinion of this; he was asked to
act.') 'Nevertheless,' Sinclair concluded, 'I am proposing to have
the proposition put to the Americans, with all the facts, to see if
they are prepared to try it.'[31]

They weren't. McCloy had already blocked the proposal on 4
July. 'The War Department,' he wrote to Pehle, 'is of the opinion that the suggested air operation is impracticable. It could
be executed only by the diversion of considerable air support
essential to the success of our forces now engaged in decisive
operations and would in any case be of such very doubtful effi-
cacy that it would not amount to a practical project.'[32] McCloy,
who blamed the proposal on a 'bunch of fanatic Jews', maintained for decades that the decision was his own, but in 1986 he
attributed it to Roosevelt. 'I remember talking one time with [the
president] about it and he was irate: "Why the idea! They'll say
we bombed these people, and they'll only move it down the road
a little way . . . We'll be accused of participating in this horrible
business."'[33] There is no written record of the conversation.[34]

On 1 August 1944, eight weeks after D-Day, the Poles launched
the Warsaw uprising in the futile hope of liberating themselves

from the Germans before the Soviets reached the city. Two full RAF squadrons, relying on volunteers, flew missions supplying the Poles for six consecutive days. Flying from Italy, they passed over Auschwitz on their way to the Polish capital.

During this period, the debate over bombing Auschwitz continued. On 26 July, unaware of the Americans' rejection of the idea, the Air Ministry planned to raise the issue with Spaatz. A week later, Bottomley reported that he had been 'most sympathetic' but wanted more information about the 'precise location, extent and nature of the camps and installations at Birkenau'. The Ministry passed a request for photographic intelligence to the Foreign Ministry, but never got a reply.[35] Meanwhile, Allied bombers continued to fly over Auschwitz and reconnaissance flights seeking evidence of bomb damage to industry brought back photographs of the camps. One of these photos, near the end of the month, showed Jews walking from a train towards a gas chamber.[36] On 7 August, American bombers hit oil refineries at Trzebinia, thirteen miles from Auschwitz.[37] One week later, another appeal, from the World Jewish Congress, to bomb the gas chambers and crematorium at Auschwitz was again rejected by John McCloy as a costly diversion unlikely to succeed.[38] On 27 August, 350 US bombers again hit Blechhammer, and two days later they bombed Trzebinia again.[39]

Three months after McCloy's 4 July cable, Pehle forwarded another recommendation that Auschwitz be bombed, this time from the Polish government-in-exile. It was sent along to Spaatz on 3 October. It was the first and last time that the War Department sent a proposal for bombing Auschwitz to an air force official in the European theatre.[40] General Frederick Anderson urged him 'to give no encouragement to the project . . . . There is the possibility of some of the bombs landing on the prisoners . . . . In that event the Germans would be provided with a fine alibi for any wholesale massacre that they might perpetuate.'[41] The matter went no further.

Months before Anderson's dismissive communication to Spaatz, Shalom Lindenbaum arrived at Auschwitz with his father in a sealed goods wagon. A week later, he and other Jews who had arrived with them were summoned for a roll call near the camp gate. They were:

> afraid that it was our turn, because normally before dusk
> there were no transports to other camps. On the nearby
> road, which led to the sauna (bath house) and gas chambers
> a new transport, which had arrived from ghetto Lodz, as
> we later learned, passed by. There was no doubt where
> they were taken . . . . I ran ahead to my father in order to be
> together in what seemed to be our last hour.
>
> [Then,] Allied bombers appeared in the sky. It will be
> difficult to describe our joy. We prayed and hoped to be
> bombed by them, and so to escape the helpless death in the
> gas chambers. To be bombed meant a chance that also the
> Germans will be killed . . . . We were deeply disappointed
> and sad when they passed over, not bombing.
>
> Fortunately we were taken back to the barracks,
> after a search of our bodies. But we didn't speak about
> our unexpected return, survival, only about the Allies'
> reluctance to bomb the gas chambers.[42]

The chance flyover of Allied bombers may have saved Shalom's life. As the Allies never tried, we will never know how many others might have been saved by bombing. In the end, the Germans deported 509,000 Jews from Hungary; they sent 120,000 to work as forced labourers; they murdered the other 389,000.[43]

* * *

While the final chapter in the Jewish – and European – tragedy was coming to a close, Spaatz's overwhelming concern was oil. While he was bombing oil targets, the seductive if elusive target of morale was brought back onto the agenda. On 21 June, Harris – having forgotten his June 1942 prediction that 'once we get a footing on the continent our last bomb will have been dropped on Germany'[44] – asked Portal to schedule a joint US–Bomber Command daylight raid on residential Berlin.

The backdrop to the meeting was continued German assaults on London. In January, in response to its inability to protect Berlin from the air assault, the Luftwaffe had launched Operation STEINBOCK, a second night-time strategic bombing offensive against London and mostly coastal targets. The raids, some thirty over four months, had little effect, but they caused concern in the Air Ministry at the time, particularly as pathfinding techniques and bombing accuracy appeared to improve in February. Then, from June 1944, unmanned aircraft (the V-1) launched from the Continent sailed over London, then stopped and crashed down on the city. The military effect was negligible, but it was pure terror bombing, and thousands of Londoners were dying.[45] Pressure for retaliation was growing; Churchill wanted something done.

Under Harris's plan, two thousand bombers – double the number of the famous thousand-bomber raid two years earlier – would drop sixty-five hundred tonnes of bombs on Berlin. Portal supported the idea, as did Eisenhower. In a note to Churchill, Portal argued that, at the least, such a raid would 'be a pretty good answer to the results achieved in the last few days by the "flying bomb"'.[46] Harris – with an eye to poor weather and Doolittle's reluctance to share his fighter escorts – cancelled the mission. Instead, the Eighth Air Force sent one thousand bombers over Berlin. One-third of them bombed industrial targets in the outskirts; the others bombed the city centre. The Americans were further relaxing their moral constraints.

On Saturday, 1 July Churchill was in a meeting with the Chiefs of Staff. Out of the blue, he came up with a new idea for seeing off the V-1s: Britain should 'announce [its] intention of flattening out in turn the lesser German cities if the "CROSSBOW" attack is continued.'[47] Such cities would be 'small towns of 20,000 inhabitants or fewer, well known for historical or other associations, and not particularly connected to the war effort.'[48] The idea was not entirely new – Anthony Eden, the foreign secretary, had suggested it back in 1943 – but Churchill's intervention revived it.[49]

There were suddenly two plans on the table: one for flattening Berlin, the other for ignoring Berlin and flattening dozens of provincial cities. Churchill's chief of staff, General Hastings Ismay, threw his enthusiastic support behind the second idea. Sir Douglas Evill (who succeeded Freeman as Vice-Chief of Air Staff) countered that the policy would be immensely costly: the obliteration of a single city would require up to seven hundred sorties, whereas Churchill and Ismay's plan assumed that only one hundred or so would be required. Seeing that Churchill was committed to the idea, he appealed for time: the Chiefs of Staff should be given the chance to think it over. Churchill agreed.

The next day, Evill worked to kill the idea. He spoke with Tedder, who rejected the attacks as 'wickedly uneconomical'.[50] He also had Alec Coryton from Operations Planning prepare a short report on the proposal.[51] The report included a list of fourteen towns that could be destroyed by joint US–British bombing:[52] Wiesbaden, Mainz, Solingen, Saarbrücken, Bielefeld, Freiburg, Bonn, Osnabrück, Koblenz, Kaiserslautern, Oldenburg, Worms, Pirmasens, and Speyer.

The report concluded that attacking the towns would 'have little effect upon the German war effort, is unlikely to impinge upon the confidence of the German High Command, and would impinge upon the morale of only some 1.9 per cent of the population of Germany'.[53] It might actually have given the Germans the idea that the V-1 attacks were working (if not, why retaliate?). Most importantly, it would distract from the oil campaign: '[t]he opportunities available for the prosecution of our strategic attacks against enemy oil production, which Intelligence suggests may well have a decisive influence upon Germany's military capabilities, are few . . . . If the proposed policy of retaliatory attacks is adopted in full it will mean the abandonment of many, if not all those opportunities over the next one or two months.'[54]

Evill added pencil edits to the list – Mainz had already been destroyed, and Osnabrück and Saarbrücken had been 'well-hit' – and attached it to his note. He concluded by saying, 'I expect that you will wish to take steps to scotch this idea in the C.O.S. [Chiefs of Staff] on Monday.'[55]

On 3 July, Portal arrived at the meeting prepared. He argued that Churchill's threat would be the equivalent of an invitation to negotiate; that the Germans would not alter their behaviour to save militarily irrelevant towns; and that bombing them would divert Allied air forces from attacks on oil, communications, and the battle in France.[56] The committee agreed to 'further careful consideration and discussion at a future date' – an old bureaucratic trick for shelving an issue.

Churchill, however, was in a vengeful mood and was not prepared to let the matter rest.[57] At a War Cabinet meeting that evening, he ordered his Chiefs to take up the issue the next day.[58] On the 4th and again on the 5th, Portal argued still more forcefully against the proposal: 'No threat is likely to deter Hitler in his present fix. Indeed, it may well encourage him to order more F.B.s [flying bombs] and make still further efforts to increase the scale of attack.'[59] The only effect would be to distract bombers from military targets, including V-1 launch sites. The Chiefs of Staff agreed to a report on all aspects of retaliatory bombing, including poisonous gas. The report was turned around within hours. With significant input from Portal, it repeated the Chief of Air Staff's arguments about costs, diversions, negotiating, and retaliation.[60] It also argued that such wanton destruction was inconsistent with liberal democracy and Britain's moral stance. The Germans did not face the constraint of 'moral scruples or public opinion' and would win in a tit-for-tat game of destruction. Britain would surrender the moral high ground by adopting a policy of reprisals:

> We have hitherto always maintained consistently in all public statements regarding our bombing policy that it is directed against military objectives and that any damage to civilians is incidental to our attack on the German war machine. This is a moral and legal point of great importance, both now and in the maintenance of our position after the war, and it would be greatly weakened should we now for the first time declare that we intended deliberate attacks on the civilian population as such.[61]

On 5 July, the Chiefs of Staff approved the report, but – perhaps unable to shake off the lingering belief that still more bombing might bring results, or as a sop to Churchill – left the door open for future destruction of small cities. 'The time might well come,' the Chiefs agreed, 'when an all-out attack by every means at our disposal on German civilian morale might be decisive.'[62] In the end, the Chiefs recommended to the prime minister that the methods of such an attack should be examined and all possible preparations made. Despite Portal's objections, the train had left the station.

In the United States, a similar argument was being played out. In June 1944, an intelligence officer in Washington, Colonel Lowell P. Weicker, drew up several plans for destroying German morale by blasting small German towns. Throughout June and July, an official under General Charles P. Cabell, the USSTAF Director of Plans, worked to scuttle the idea. The official's name was Colonel Richard D. Hughes. Hughes had worked in the Air War Plans Division and came to London to serve on the Enemy Objectives Unit, which selected the target systems most vital to the Nazi war effort.[63] He was no sentimentalist; Hughes believed the Germans should suffer for what they had done. It was just that there were plenty of ways to make them suffer without killing them, and killing them would do nothing to serve Allied interests during the war or after it. Hughes attacked Weicker's plans as yet another stab at the 'will of the wisp of "morale"'.[64] Nazi repression made German resistance impossible, so terror bombing would only serve as confirmation of German propaganda. It would lead to a reaction among the American people against 'indiscriminate area bombing', and would – not least – violate the principles to which the country had committed itself. Although the United States may have at times been hypocritical on moral issues, the country nonetheless 'represented in world thought an urge towards decency and better treatment of man by man'.[65] The Japanese might shoot American POWs, but the Americans would never do the same to the Japanese. 'Hot blood is one thing,' Hughes added. 'Reason and the long view is another.' Cabell, who was a principled opponent of indiscriminate area bombing, agreed, and he asked that Spaatz reject the plan. Eisenhower, however, had the last word, and though he did not order the bombing of small towns, he told Spaatz to be ready to bomb the centre of Berlin at a moment's notice.[66] But notice was not given, at least not in 1944.

While all of this was going on, the case for attacking oil was growing. On 9 July, the day of the ULTRA intercept confirming how deeply affected German oil supplies had been, the British Air Ministry announced the formation of a joint Anglo-American oil targets committee, which was to keep the Axis oil position under review, to assess the damage inflicted, and to determine the priority of further attacks.[67]

A week later, Harris, asked by Churchill to intervene in the debate, resuscitated his 1943 proposal for a British–American area bombing offensive that 'could eradicate any German town except Berlin in one combined (though not necessarily simultaneous) attack' and be repeated 'on every occasion when the weather permitted'.[68] Destroying the German night and day fighter forces would be a side benefit, and then the armies would enjoy a 'walkover'. Harris did note Bomber Command's excellent results in taking out flying bomb supply sites and supply dumps, but these results did not affect his views on the feasibility and purpose of precision bombing.[69]

During the month of July, then, two different committees were established: a joint Anglo-American committee to look at oil, and a working committee (made up of Air Staff, Foreign Office, Ministry of Economic Warfare [MEW], and USSTAF representatives) to look at morale. At the end of the month, they both reported. The joint committee concluded that 'Germany will be unable to continue the struggle beyond December given intensive fighting on three fronts and the continued success of Allied air attacks.' Thanks to bombing, the report noted, Germany was consuming 300,000 more tons of oil each month than it produced. This was fact. At the same time, the working committee offered its recommendations. On 22 July, the committee argued that the point of a morale attack was 'to influence the minds of the German authorities in such a way that they prefer organised surrender to continued resistance'. The target for a morale-

busting campaign would be Berlin. A few months after Harris's
five-month-long effort to 'wreck the city from end to end', the
committee promised that twenty thousand bombs, delivered in
a four-day and three-night round-the-clock bombing raid, would
disrupt government services, destroy communications, and lead
to an overall breakdown of morale. This was fiction.

Three nights later, Harris launched just such a campaign on
a different city. Over four nights – from 25 to 29 July – Stuttgart
was flattened. Dating from the thirteenth century, the city had
grown up in a series of narrow valleys. Its old city core centred
around the castle, the town hall, and the market square. Elegant,
densely packed commercial buildings, set alongside houses with
sloping roofs, radiated out from the core. At 01:38 on 26 July,
474 bombers razed the city.[70] The first wave of high explosives
destroyed the town hall and knocked out the water mains under
the market square. The houses burned and collapsed, bury-
ing the remaining water hoses. By morning, the palace was an
empty shell. Over the course of the raids, 1,171 people died, and
most of the city centre was obliterated.[71] Stuttgart joined an
ever-growing list of dead cities.

The following week, on 3 August, the working committee presented its final draft to the British Chiefs of Staff. By then, Portal
had successfully deflected the conversation away from destroying German towns.[72] That left Berlin: Harris's plan for bombing
the city's residential neighbourhoods was still on the table, and
the Chiefs of Staff had left open the possibility of a massive area
raid in their 1 August memorandum. The Directorate of Bombing
Operations did some calculations on the bombing needed for a
raid – code-named 'THUNDERCLAP'[73] – that would devastate
Berlin. It suggested that two thousand Eighth Air Force bombers
drop five thousand tons of bombs on two and a half square miles
of central Berlin. The attack would take place during daytime,

when the area had a population of 375,000 people.[74] If the Eighth achieved a bomb density of two thousand tons per square mile, they would kill 110,000 and maim or otherwise seriously injure another 110,000.[75] In order to bomb 'for purely moral effect', wrote the Director of Bombing Operations, Bufton, on 1 August, 'that attack must be delivered in such density that it imposes as nearly as possible a 100 per cent risk of death to the individual in the area to which it is applied.'[76] What's more, 'the target chosen should be one possessing the maximum traditional and personal associations for the German people as a whole. The administrative and governmental centre of Berlin best fulfils these conditions.'[77] If the Eighth didn't do the job on the first day, the Fifteenth could pelt the area with incendiaries on the next. Such death and destruction, the Air Staff subsequently argued, would be a 'spectacular and final object lesson to the German people on the consequences of universal aggression'.[78]

Despite the failure of area bombing to deliver results, and the clear evidence that precision bombing of oil was working, few people in the British military command were willing to give up entirely on the idea of area bombing. Tedder showed great interest in the idea of attacking morale, and even Portal seemed for a while to favour it.[79] In the end, the plan foundered – at least temporarily – on the rocks of American opposition. General Robert McClure, director of SHAEF's Psychological War Division, suggested that, given the destruction Germany had suffered, only an even larger raid – one that the Division must have known would be impossible – would have any success.[80] McClure then attempted to take the terror out of terror bombing by recommending a series of warnings and the establishment of safe areas for civilians.[81] Cabell was far more direct: he dismissed THUNDERCLAP as another 'baby killing scheme'.[82] As Major General Laurence Kuter, by then Spaatz's Assistant Chief of Staff for Plans and Combat Operations, argued, 'It is contrary to our national ideals to wage war against civilians.'[83] The policy was not only morally untenable; it would not work. Drawing the obvious conclusion from the previous two and a half years of the RAF's bombing campaign, Kuter noted that the 'area bombing of Cologne, Berlin and [other] cities has apparently not created large scale absenteeism in industry. Apathy and discouragement mark the German population; these are doubtful qualities from which . . . to generate revolt.' Kuter also raised questions about British motives: 'Since any such attack will feature U.S.A.A.F. units in the limelight, we should consider whether the recent buzz bomb attacks have not instilled in the British Government a desire for retaliation in which American air units will be called upon to share with the R.A.F. Bomber Command the onus for the more critical features of area bombing.'[84] He was not alone in this view. Speaking before the debate over THUNDERCLAP, Cabell observed that 'the British were building up this terrific resentment on the part of [bombed] peoples, whereas we were being looked at as being a little "pure" in our motives . . . I feel that the British are now anxious to have some of that odium shared by other nationals – in other words, by the United States.'[85] On the Air Ministry proposal itself, Cabell was even more to the point. 'I have just read the great opus: "Operation THUNDERCLAP",' he wrote to Hughes. 'To my mind . . . this would be a blot on the history of the Air Forces and of the US. We should strongly resist being sucked into any such venture. It gives full rein to the baser elements of our people.' The cause of civilisation and world peace, he concluded, would not be advanced an iota 'by killing more women and children'.[86] On 27 August, Spaatz wrote to Arnold: 'I have been subject to some pressure on the part of the Air Ministry to join hands with them in morale bombing. I . . . have maintained a firm position that our bombing will continue to be precision bombing against military objective[s]. So far my stand has been supported by Eisenhower.'[87] Although pressure in favour of bombing Berlin seemed to be emerging from the 'highest levels' (most likely a reference to Churchill), 'I personally believe that any deviation from our present policy, even for an exceptional case, will be unfortunate.' Picking up Kuter's point, he ended with a prescient remark: 'There is no doubt in my mind that the RAF very much want to have the U.S. Air Forces targeted with the morale bombing aftermath, which we feel will be terrific.'

Arnold was not willing to let the proposal die, for he was always more aggressive and bloodthirsty than his generals (when German booby traps were found in Italy, he wasted weeks trying to convince US government officials to make booby-trapped pens, pocket watches, and wallets for the US air forces to drop on German soil).[88] On 8 September, he called for a joint British–American plan for 'an all-out, widespread attack, of perhaps six or seven days duration, against Germany'.[89] By then, however, the vision had subtly changed. Rather than flattening Germany's small cities, the goal would be to get enough planes above them and do just enough damage to impress on the Germans how pointless continued struggle was – 'a stinging rather than numbing blow' as Cabell, who still opposed the idea, put it.[90] Both bombs and leaflets would be dropped. When the plan demanded by Arnold was duly produced ten days later, it suggested the targets should be military rather than industrial and should allow for the easy rebuilding of the towns after the war.[91] It failed to conclude whether hitting Germany's small towns would work (though it noted that, if it did not work, the war would 'be drawn out over a long period that would be highly costly for the Allies'). The proposal was shelved.

By this point, Churchill had moved on to the idea of conciliating rather than killing German civilians. On 23 August, he suggested that the Allies publish a list of fifty to one hundred German war criminals 'who will be executed if they fall into the hands of the Allies'.[92] 'At the present moment,' he continued, 'none of the German leaders has any interest but fighting to the last man, hoping he will be that last man. It is very important to show the German people that they are not on the same footing as Hitler, Göring, Himmler and other monsters who will infallibly be destroyed.'[93] Nothing came of the idea.

As the 'baby-killing' plan was grinding to a halt, the oil plan was gaining traction. On 18 August, an intercepted telegram from the Japanese ambassador in Berlin quoted Speer saying in confidence that 'the attack on oil installations was the problem to which they attached the greatest importance at the moment . . . . The only sound method of combating [such] air attacks . . . was to regain air superiority.'[94] Three days later, Bufton and Air Vice-Marshal Douglas Colyer wrote that 'serious consideration should be given to according overriding priority to the attack of oil targets by the Allied Strategical Bomber Forces.'[95] This was English mandarin speak for 'bomb oil immediately!' Doing so would cripple German production and, because planes need fuel to fly, the Luftwaffe.

The Americans were doing just that. During July, Spaatz took every opportunity to bomb oil targets. The cost over twelve raids was 247 bombers – 212 lost and another 35 written off – or 70 per cent of the Eighth's total losses for the month. The Fifteenth Air Force launched thirteen missions (out of a total of fifteen) against oil, at the cost of 196 bombers. In July alone, the Fifteenth hit Ploesti five times.

Oil was not the Eighth's only target. Spaatz also launched a series of city raids. Munich was bombed on 11, 12, 13, and 16 July; what was left of Stuttgart was hit on 16 July. The Munich raids targeted BMW and were meant to be precision raids, but weather and H2X radar's imprecision (identifying the town, but not the precise target) meant that the city was also hit. Indeed, the four Munich raids, launched through clouds with a high percentage of incendiaries, resulted in a July 1944 wartime record of Eighth Air Force bombs dropped on 'towns and cities': 9,866 tons.[96] As Anderson said on 21 July, 'We will conduct bombing attacks through the overcast where it is impossible to get precision targets. Such attacks will include German marshalling yards whether or not they are located in German cities.'[97] The intention remained the same, however: they hit industry when they could. On 19 July, clear weather had allowed a successful Eighth–Fifteenth precision raid on BMW.

When precision bombing became blind bombing, the Americans asked – as they had asked since 1943 – that history judge them on their intentions rather than on their results.[98] As Anderson said in the document cited in the last paragraph, 'We have in the past, and will continue to do so in the future, directed our efforts towards precision targets . . . . We will not, at any time, direct our efforts towards area bombing.'[99] But good intentions cannot hide the fact that, excluding attacks on transportation targets, the USAAF launched over the course of the war at least sixty-nine substantial raids (meaning more than 100 bombers each), dropping almost sixty thousand tonnes of bombs on the centres of twenty-five German cities.[100] Fully three-quarters of the American effort against German targets between 1943 and 1945 involved 'blind bombing' with H2X radar.[101]

On 7 August, the British Joint Intelligence Committee reported that the Germans had launched a vast programme for repairing oil plants. Spaatz responded by redoubling his efforts. From late August to early September, Spaatz launched ten more attacks, seven of which were directed at oil. The Fifteenth flew thirteen missions against Balkan and German oil targets.

One of the Fifteenth's missions was conducted on 10 August

1944. Walter Gilbert, a bombardier in the 450th Bombardment Group, was just above the target.[102] Flak sliced into engines one and two, sheared off half of the rudder, damaged the nose and bomb bay, and mangled the left wing. It ripped through the floor, grazing the crew and injuring the co-pilot badly. To protect the other planes, the B-17 left the formation. As the fighters swept in for the kill, First Lieutenant Vernon E. Mikkelson ordered his crew to bale out. Gilbert was immediately captured by Romanian and German troops and taken to a military outpost where he rejoined the co-pilot and nose gunner. All were well treated, according to Gilbert. For the remainder of the month, Gilbert and the rest of the crew witnessed the American bombings from captivity.

Two weeks later, in one particularly spectacular raid, the Eighth and the Fifteenth joined forces on 24 August for combined raids on synthetic oil plants. All oil production ceased, and the plant was occupied by the Soviets a few days later.[103]

20

HARRIS'S AND SPAATZ'S ORDERS

Overall command of the strategic bombing war had been returned from Eisenhower to Spaatz and Harris on 14 September 1944. On that day, Portal and Arnold issued a new directive, which Bottomley passed on to the commander-in-chief on 25 September. Compared with past directives, it was a model of clarity. It instructed the Allied Air Forces to make attacks on oil their first priority, with transportation targets and tank and motor production as the second priority. After that, it listed German Luftwaffe targets and support of the Allies' land and naval operations. Like all directives, it left open room for area attacks when these targets could not be hit: 'the bombing of important industrial areas when weather made other targets impractical'. Who judged the weather and a raid's practicality? Harris and Spaatz.

The directive effectively told the Americans to do what they had been doing, with the added benefit of satisfying Spaatz's long-held wish to prioritise oil over transportation – although Spaatz had by this point come to view the two as complementary. Both oil and transportation were precision targets, both required successive bombing raids to be decisively destroyed, and the destruction of both materially affected Germany's capacity to wage war. But there was a basic difference between the two. Oil refineries and synthetic oil plants were located outside the cities, in the countryside of central and Eastern Europe. They were usually ideal precision targets; bombing either destroyed them or it destroyed very little (a few stray bombs did land on Budapest

– 263 –

during the summer 1944 raids). The situation for marshalling yards and railway stations was entirely different. Big rail yards were located in central urban districts, next to workers' housing. The train stations, or at least the main ones, were right in the centre of the cities. Destroying these targets inevitably meant destroying houses and killing workers, and doing so intentionally. USAAF commanders acknowledged as much when they used a large percentage of incendiary bombs – the area bomber's weapon of choice – on these raids despite the fact that they did little damage to rail yards.[1]

These risks to civilians were compounded by strategy and that great wild card, worsening weather. The Eighth Air Force had adopted Curtis LeMay's policy of 'bombing on the leader'.[2] In order to concentrate responsibility for targeting (the same principle applied in the use of pathfinders), only lead aircraft were given Norden bombsights, and the others were instructed to drop their bombs as soon as they saw bombs fall from the first plane. The technique increased accuracy when the bombers arrived in a tight formation and the lead bomber hit the target, but it also ensured that when things went wrong, they went horribly wrong. If the lead pilot bombed the wrong target, they all did. And if the bombing formation stretched back too far in poor weather, the bombers behind the leader blasted whatever was just before the target. Sometimes, in the case of marshalling yards and train stations in small cities, the whole town was destroyed. 'My squadron was on the tail end of a bombing strike against a railroad yard in a small industrial town,' Eighth Air Force pilot Craig Harris recalled after the war. 'There were about four hundred bombers in front of us as we approached the target. Our shadow, if we had one, would have covered almost the entire town. The clouds were so thick that we couldn't see a thing on the ground. The lead plane carried the radar equipment. When it passed over the target it dropped its bombs, along with a smoke marker, the signal for the rest of the formation to drop. The planes at the head of the formation wasted the marshalling yard, but the rest of us wasted the town.'[3] Marshalling yards felt the weight of American bombs more than any other target in Europe: at least 25 per cent of the Eighth's tonnage fell on marshalling yards – somewhere between 175,000 and 200,000 tons (with targets also in France in the run-up to D-Day).[4]

Radar was of little help when conditions were not right. When a target was cloud-covered, H2X could identify the city but not the targets. In these situations – such as at Kassel (2 October 1944), Nuremberg (3 October), and Mannheim (19 October) – the Eighth threw its bombs at the city. They wanted to avoid hitting towns if they could, but they would hit towns if they could do nothing else. It was precision bombing in theory and area bombing in practice. Even on clear days entire towns would go down. 'We bombed the marshalling yards of Mayen,' wrote John J. Briol of the 457th Bomb Group. 'The railroads went right through the center of the town . . . . This was a little city of about 2,000 people. We blasted the yards all right and the entire city with it. I saw the whole city disappearing and I suddenly realised again what a rotten business this was.'[5] As historian Richard Overy concludes, 'The distinction for most, though not all, American raiding from British area bombing was intention.'[6]

Wasting towns – deliberately, not incidentally – was of course exactly what Harris wanted to do. On 6 September, a week before the September directive, Harris sent his bombers to attack Emden. The daylight raid, free from the recovering Luftwaffe, destroyed the city at the cost of only one Lancaster. Four days later, Bomber Command 'tore out the heart' of Mönchengladbach without losing a single plane.[7] After that, it was Darmstadt's turn: in the early morning of 12 September, a city loved by English tourists for its richly detailed residential architecture, was set alight. At five minutes before midnight, 221 Lancasters and 14 Mosquitoes dropped one thousand tons of bombs on Darmstadt.[8] A Hamburg-esque firestorm tore through the city, levelling the area imme-diately south and east of the centre and killing approximately twelve thousand people, including two hundred Italian internees buried alive.[9] Temperatures reached 1,000 degrees Celsius, and the flames could be seen 180 miles away. For the RAF, it was, as one captain reported, 'A quiet trip all around.'[10] All of the city's industry was located in the suburbs, and the incidental damage it suffered was repaired within a month.[11]

On 12 September, the RAF attacked oil refineries at Dortmund, Scholven/Buer, and Wanne-Eickel. The Dortmund refinery was badly damaged, but smoke pots and flak protected the other two.[12] Seven aircraft were lost. Also on the 12th, the RAF area raids smashed what was left of Münster (killing 144 people). The next night, Bomber Command raided Frankfurt (killing 469), and Stuttgart (killing 1,171, the city's highest death toll of the war). The RAF also hit the Nordstern oil plant at Gelsenkirchen on the 13th with 140 aircraft. Three nights later, Bomber Command devastated the centre of Kiel.[13] Overall, Harris launched fourteen area raids in September, dropping fifteen thousand tons of bombs and, thanks to the American war on the Luftwaffe, suffering a lower casualty rate of 1.8 per cent.[14]

In late September, Churchill invited Harris to Chequers to dine and discuss an ULTRA report confirming that Germany faced a crippling oil shortage. Intelligence gathered through Enigma had made this clear more than two months earlier – on 9 July – and Harris had been specifically ordered to hit oil by the 14 September directive. Either Churchill sensed that Harris was not doing his job and used ULTRA to raise the matter, or he wanted to be reassured that the city bombing campaign still had worth. In either case, Harris, citing a cold, declined the invitation and instead set out his views on paper.[15] Before altering bombing strategy, he argued, 'we should, I feel, take a more sober view of what has so far occurred on the western front. The German Army ... collapsed in the face of attack by superior and better equipped forces. But it collapsed mainly because it was beleaguered by air power.' This happy result was achieved despite giving Germany 'considerable breathers' through 'necessary and avoidable diversions' during the previous six months. Now that they were out of the way, 'we should now get on and finally knock Germany flat'.

Churchill responded right away: 'I agree with your very good letter,' he wrote, 'except that I do not think you did it all or can do it all. I recognise however that this is a becoming view for you to take. I am all for cracking everything in now on to Germany that can be spared from the battlefields.' It was exactly what Harris wanted to hear.

If September was a bad month for German cities, October was worse still. Harris launched his heaviest attack ever. In October, 80 per cent of RAF bombs fell on cities. Harris launched twenty raids, nine of them by daylight. Two of these attacks – on Kleve and Emmerich on 5 and 7 October – were requested by the Allied ground forces in order to aid advancing troops, but they were pushing on an open door. On 14/15 October, Duisburg was smashed twice in 24 hours: 5,029 tons hit the centre by day, 5,093 by night. 'The record,' writes historian Richard G. Davis, 'of more than 10,100 tons of conventional explosives dropped on a single target in a day probably still stands.'[16] On the same night, the RAF destroyed – on its fourth try – Brunswick. Fire engulfed the old city centre, and only the firefighters' determination kept the death toll to a relatively low 561. Over more than four hours, they fought their way through a ring of fire until they managed to reach eight public shelters housing 23,000 people.[17] They got all but 200 out. Without their efforts, Brunswick might have been another Hamburg. Three nights later, in Bonn, the university, many cultural and public buildings, and large residential areas were smashed. The firefighters managed to save Beethoven's house; they weren't able to do the same for 313 people.[18] The Ruhr cities of Essen, Dortmund, and Duisburg were also bombed, as were previously untouched residential parts of Cologne. Throughout September and October, the RAF's loss rate was a low 1.8 per cent.

In September, US air forces continued their assault on the Luftwaffe, dropping 5,000 tons of bombs on aircraft targets.[19] They dropped an equal amount on tanks, and somewhat more – 5,600 tons – on oil. Another 12,000 fell on marshalling yards, which had positive knock-on effects for the oil offensive: they destroyed rail lines, trains, and trucks and interfered with the Germans' race to repair the damage to oil infrastructure.

The cumulative effects of the oil and transportation campaigns were spectacular. The production of aviation fuel temporarily halted. German oil production diminished by half over the summer, and the campaign had important secondary effects. The loss of Leuna and Ludwigshafen resulted in a loss to the Germans of 64 per cent of synthetic nitrogen (used for explosives); 40 per cent of synthetic methanol (used for more advanced explosives); and 65 per cent of synthetic rubber.[20]

Harris, too, hit oil targets. In September, fourteen RAF raids were city raids, but eight targeted oil. When he did hit oil – for instance, at Dortmund on 12 September or Kaiserslautern on 27–8 September – the results were impressive. The larger size of British bombs meant that a single British raid was more devastating than an American raid. There is no question that Bomber Command played a role in the oil campaign; it simply could have done more, perhaps much more. During October, only one-twelfth of RAF bombs hit oil targets, and there was only one significant transportation raid – on 5 October, on marshalling yards at Saarbrücken. None of this is remarkable: Harris made no secret of his contempt for oil and his support for bombing cities.

And this left Portal in a dilemma. Harris was immensely popular with the British public, and the Air Ministry had spent the last two years making 'Bomber Harris' the public face of the RAF. But his obsession with bombing cities was standing in the way of the thorough execution of his orders. Not one for confrontation, Portal began by trying to reason with Harris. On 28 October, Portal and Spaatz agreed to Strategic Directive No. 2, which placed transportation again at the top, followed by oil, making those the only two target systems (except when specific requests were made by the other forces). The directive left the 'important industrial areas' exception, but Bottomley modified the language to emphasise that these areas must be clearly linked with oil and transportation. Portal then wrote a gentle letter to Harris, encouraging him to implement the oil directive. He enclosed a document called 'Notes on Air Policy to be adopted with a view to rapid defeat of Germany', which presented the American case in favour of the precision bombing of oil targets.

The letter and notes hit Harris at a particularly bad moment. On Bottomley's note, he scribbled the words 'Here we go around the Mulberry bush.'[21] These notes would have angered him at the best of times, but on Tuesday, 31 October, another Air Ministry official had questioned his judgement. 'Why,' he asked Harris, 'did you bomb Cologne last night?' The implication was clear: why did you *not* bomb oil plants? The combination of the two sets of criticism infuriated Harris, and he wrote back immediately. He began with an unapologetic defence of the area bombing campaign:

The war has already been vastly shortened by concentrating the bomber effort in the past three years

against war potential industrial targets inside Germany
. . . . A major reason for the success of the Russian
offensives has been the destruction of the German
war potential, and the chaos and confusion created in
Germany by the heavy bombing campaign . . . . There
is also no doubt that the walk-over which the armies
experienced in the invasion of France, while mainly due
to the destruction of communications in France, was also
largely due to the general shortage of equipment and man
power in the German forces, to which the general chaos
in Germany, the past strategical bombing of Germany
very heavily contributed.[22]

Whether he recognised it or not, Harris's argument had
shifted importantly over the last two years. He had once
claimed that bombing cities would avoid the need for the invasion. Now that it had occurred, he claimed to be responsible for
its success.

Harris then went on to argue that he was implementing the
14 September directive:

In his paragraph 9, the Deputy Supreme Commander
makes certain recommendations as to the best targets to
be attacked. Apart from diversions forced upon us for
tactical bombing, bombing coast guns, invested ports,
the Tirpitz, submarine bases etc. the recommendations
in that paragraph are precisely what we have been
doing and are doing . . . . The main concentration [of our
bombing] has been against the Ruhr whenever conditions
made this economical. The targets selected have been
oil targets, rail centres, canal systems and the major
centres of population . . . . Area bombing must enter into

any scheme, because in bad weather we have to use sky
markers, we must have a large target within Oboe or
G.H. range and we necessarily in those conditions paint
with a large brush.

When he was not implementing the directive, or appeared not
to be, it was a matter of the weather.

Harris was not one to let a charge go unchallenged, and he
used the letter to respond to the question about Cologne, although
Portal had not asked it. 'Cologne,' he argued

(a) was the best point at which the weather front gave
reasonable possibility of our low ceiling bombers getting
sufficiently above the . . . high cloud ceiling.

(b) It was the nearest we could get to the Ruhr.

(c) It was the furthest I proposed to send the force in . . . full
moonlight.

(d) As a most important communication centre and
industrial area it was of direct value to the Army and
generally in line with the Directive.

(e) It was big enough to be dealt with using sky mark
technique [i.e., dropping flares to mark the target]. Sky
marking requires a big, compact, and preferably isolated
target.

(f) It was already burning from previous attacks and two
important satellite areas remained to be burned. There is
something in continuity of attack, within limits, from the
morale point of view.

(g) It was as far as we could go and get back before the
bases gave trouble.

(h) Anything worth while further south would have been
outside Oboe range and would have meant flying low

inside American [range] and would [have] resulted in [the Americans] shooting at lethal height.

In the letter's last passages, Harris moved from the specific – Cologne – to the general – the nature of his bombing crusade itself. 'In the past 18 months, Bomber Command has virtually destroyed 45 of the leading 60 German cities. In spite of invasion diversions [i.e. the invasion of Normandy], we have so far managed to keep up and exceed our average of 2.5 cities devastated a month. In addition others have been "started on" to the extent where they are already damaged beyond anything experienced in this country. There are not many industrial centres of population left intact.'

Harris ended the letter with a call for a total bombing war. 'Are we,' he wrote, 'now to abandon this vast task, which the Germans themselves have long admitted to be their worst headache, just as it nears completion? [The destruction of] Magdeburg, Halle, Leipzig, Dresden, Chemnitz, Breslau, Nuremberg, Munich, Coblenz, Karlsruhe, and the completion of Berlin and Hanover are required to finish this plan . . . . Its completion will do more towards accelerating the defeat of Germany than the armies have yet done – or will do.'

In fairness to Harris, he was not in an easy position. He genuinely did not believe that bombing oil would work. It had not worked in 1940–1, and in the ensuing years, the Ministry of Economic Warfare (MEW) had come up with many 'panaceas'. The clamour continued into late 1944. As he wrote in the same 1 November letter, 'during the last few weeks every panacea monger and "me too" expert to many of whom we had already (we hoped) given the quietus in the past, has raised his head again. The Tirpitz has gone within range and the Admiralty has resuscitated a U-boat threat. The ball-bearing experts have again become vocal . . . .' Everything being said about oil had been said before, in 1940–1.

And where had that led? To high British casualties, plummeting aircrew morale, and no obvious effect on Germany.

The weather also did present a serious problem; any bombing, but above all precision bombing, required co-operative weather conditions. If the target was obscured by clouds, or if there was a storm over it, bombing was difficult, dangerous, or both. Harris was certainly right that in heavy clouds precision bombing in intention was area bombing in fact. Most importantly, Harris continued to believe in area bombing. His entire mission since 1942, if not earlier, was founded on this policy; he had publicly and repeatedly staked his reputation on it; and he had sent tens of thousands of young men to their death in executing it. It was hardly surprising that he was unwilling, just as Germany finally seemed to be collapsing, to give up on it.

The difficulty for Portal was that, while he recognised all of this, Harris was playing a double game. He was arguing at once that (a) he was bombing oil targets when he could, (b) he mostly couldn't bomb oil targets, and (c) it wasn't worth bombing oil targets. If (a) and (b) were true, there was no need to add (c).[23] There was also something patronising in Harris's letter. It was as if he were writing to someone who knew nothing about bombing, rather than to his superior and a man who had worked his way through the RAF hierarchy, much as Harris had, from its earliest days.

Harris's last paragraph, on abandoning his task, was equally ambiguous. He was shifting from a purely instrumental argument – that bombing Germany would end the war – to an absolutist one: that destroying all of German cities was an end in itself. It was an aim to which Harris would cling, with increasing tenacity, until the end of the war.

* * *

On 2 November, the day after Harris wrote about his 'vast task' of destroying Germany's remaining cities, the Eighth Air Force launched a routine raid on Germany. The Luftwaffe again surprised the Americans: a supposedly beaten force managed to get five hundred fighters in the air. The escorts were there to protect the bombers – they shot down 102 German fighters – but the show of force took Spaatz aback. Combined with the broader Allied setbacks, it showed that the Germans were not yet finished. 'It has been increasingly evident,' Spaatz wrote to Arnold, 'that the GAF was being processed to become a major threat to our deep penetrations, in daylight, into Germany.' The American victory over the Luftwaffe was 'decisive', but only because of 'almost perfect fighter cover' and 'a fortunate chain of circumstances'.[24] Arnold agreed: the USSTAF had to get the German fighters off the Continent, once and for all.

Spaatz's fears were confirmed on two further US raids – on 21 and 26 November, against Bremen – when the Luftwaffe responded again with some five hundred fighters. The Germans were clearly recouping after their devastating spring and summer losses.[25]

As Spaatz saw it, he had two options for responding to the Luftwaffe's seemingly renewed strength: *reducing* the number of bombers – to the point where adequate fighter cover could be provided – or *increasing* the number of bombers – sending out the maximum number of bombers on each mission.[26] A larger mission might ensure that, even if large numbers of bombers were lost, enough would get past the German fighters to do substantial damage. Increasing the number of bombers was the riskier of the two strategies: if a bombing formation did not have sufficient escort fighters or if substantial parts of the formation blew off course, the Luftwaffe could chew even a large force to pieces. Reducing the number of bombers was the safer option, but it came at a price: the lousy autumn weather reduced the number of raids to a handful, and a small bomber stream would result in limited damage. Spaatz decided to risk it all. On 27 November, he picked a fight with the Luftwaffe. One thousand American bombers left England in two groups. The first was made up of 515 heavy bombers, escorted by 241 fighters. It raided marshalling yards in southern Germany. The second, composed of 460 planes, headed for oil centres in northern and central Germany. The idea was to trick the Germans into thinking that the fighter force was in fact a fleet of bombers.

It worked. The Luftwaffe attacked the fighter formation, leaving the bombers relatively unimpeded. The American fighters countered viciously. They shot down ninety-eight German fighters – double the average of the spring raids – at the cost of twelve of their own. As the reports of the November operation reached Spaatz, he wrote to Lovett with confidence. 'In spite of the buildup of strength, the [Germans'] overall effectiveness has not increased . . . . [Recently], we have destroyed as much as 25 per cent of [their] forces.'[27] All that was needed was a break in the weather, and the USSTAF could finally destroy the German fighter force.

Three weeks before Spaatz rolled the dice, Portal was mulling over a reply to Harris. As he did so, the commander-in-chief bombed Homberg (twice), Oberhausen, and Düsseldorf. The Düsseldorf raid finished the northern half of the city, destroying five thousand houses and killing some seven hundred people.[28]

On 4 November, Portal wrote to Harris. He began with an apology.

Referring to my enquiry of 1st November about the bombing of Cologne in preference to oil or the Ruhr . . . I do hope that you will not resent my asking for such information as I consider it necessary to enable me to explain, and if necessary

defend, your decisions; and that you will not think that when
I do so I am ipso facto exhibiting a lack of confidence in your
direction of Bomber Command's operations. My own belief
is that true mutual confidence can only exist on a basis of
thorough mutual understanding and that the question of
amour propre or 'face' should be completely excluded.

If you concede this, I would go on to say, at the risk
of your dubbing me 'another panacea merchant', that
I believe the air offensive against oil gives us by far the
best hope of victory in the next few months. It will be
a terrific battle between destruction and repair and we
cannot afford to give a single point away over and above
the many that we shall be compelled to give away in
direct support of the land offensive and in deference to
the Admiralty's uneasiness about the coming U-Boat
offensive . . . .

[In this vein] I was very much worried about the German
recovery in oil production in October.

Portal then went on to reject each of the arguments offered by
Harris to justify his decision to bomb Cologne rather than oil.
On bad weather: there was no difference between Cologne and
the Ruhr. On cloud cover: this was true, but there were oil targets near Cologne that were ignored in favour of the city itself.
On Cologne as a rail centre: true, but oil was more important
than transport (here Portal was himself going against Strategic
Directive No. 2, which placed transportation first and oil second).
On sky-marking: it had been successfully done in the Ruhr. On
repeatedly bombing the same targets, or continuity: true, but it
was more important to bomb oil targets continually. On distance:
the Ruhr is no further from England than Cologne. Finally, on
the difficulty of reaching the south of Germany: the Ruhr is not

in southern Germany. In short, all eight reasons offered by Harris failed to stand up to scrutiny.

Portal knew his commander-in-chief well; there was little point in directly provoking him. Instead, he offered Harris an out in the form of another reason to favour area bombing over precision bombing. Perhaps, he said, the commander-in-chief had been thinking of the greater publicity benefits that came from destroyed cities. Despite this, he continued, the issues at stake were too important. 'In view of the vital importance of getting the German war finished as soon as possible and of the disastrous delay that would result from any substantial recovery of the German oil position, I make no apology for inflicting this letter upon you, and I trust that you will accept it as a sincere attempt to discharge a not altogether pleasant duty.'

Portal paused. He could not have enjoyed writing the letter, and likely looked with still less enthusiasm on the prospect of sending it on to Harris. He decided to leave it for a day.

That night, the skies were clear over central Germany, over the damaged but functioning factories in the Ruhr valley and over the benzol plants at Gelsenkirchen. As ever, the air-raid sirens went off, and the flak guns began shooting. Gelsenkirchen was not, however, the target. Seven hundred and fifty RAF aircraft flew just south of it and bombed the centre of Bochum. More than four thousand buildings were destroyed or seriously damaged; 980 Germans and 14 foreigners were also killed.[29] The same night, Harris sent 176 aircraft to the Dortmund–Ems Canal. The banks of the canal were breached, barges were stopped, and smelting coke en route to steelworks at Brunswick and Osnabrück was stranded.

Reading the reports on Bochum, Portal could not believe it. There could not have been a better opportunity to hit Germany's oil supply. He returned to his desk and continued his letter to

Harris. In the face of another affront, he raised his tone slightly. But only slightly:

> This morning I see you made an attack in clear weather which I imagine is the weather you expected since you also attacked the Dortmund-Ems canal. The destruction of Bochum as part of the Ruhr is of course very desirable and thoroughly covered by your directive but unfortunately so far as I know it contained no oil targets. To the outsider who knows the vital importance of oil it would have seemed more valuable if you could have attacked, say, Gelsenkirchen, which has two high priority oil targets and a largish, relatively undamaged built-up area into the bargain. Having risked your wrath already and in pursuance of my strong desire that we should understand each other may I ask you to let me know if you think I am wrong on this particular point . . . . My excuse for all of this is that in the light of all available intelligence I feel that the whole war situation is poised on 'oil' as on a knife edge, and that by a real concentration of effort at this time we might push it over on the right side. On the other hand if we give away anything in this battle the Germans may get into quite a strong position in the air and hold it long enough to prolong the war by several months at least. Feeling like this I am bound to put you to a certain amount of trouble but I assure that I am perfectly ready to be convinced by reasonable arguments.[30]

After ending the letter in the same apologetic style in which it began, Portal signed it and passed it on for delivery to Harris.

That night, the RAF bombed Solingen. Almost exactly a year earlier, Harris had promised to destroy Solingen in order to 'tidy up all around'. Over two nights – on 4 and 5 November – Harris shredded the old city, leaving seventeen hundred people dead.[31]

By the time Harris read the letter, his anger over the 'why did you bomb Cologne?' question seemed to have passed. He had seen nothing that would change his views on oil, and his natural stubbornness inclined him, when pushed, to push back. As Portal had all but begged him to explain Bochum away, however, Harris saw no need to be truculent. He decided to draft what was for him an unusually soothing letter. 'I agree,' he began, 'with what you say about the urgency and effectiveness of the oil plan. But in any case as the running of the Bomber offensive is now out of my hands, it is not for me to argue over the main Directive.'

The second sentence was a bit rich in the light of his 1 November diatribe against the panacea mongers, but at least Harris did not use this letter to take another swipe at them. Instead, he dealt with Gelsenkirchen:

> You ask why I did not attack Gelsenkirchen instead of
> Bochum. Gelsenkirchen is notorious from the point of
> view of the difficulty of finding and hitting the place, even
> in the best weather. It has been attacked times without
> number, and hardly a vestige of damage has ever been
> done to it. So much is this so that it has become a jest in
> Bomber Command that either there is no such place as
> Gelsenkirchen, or that it is marked wrong on the map . . . .
> I keep the most up to date photographs available of all
> the oil plants, and those taken on the 28th October of
> both the oil plants near Gelsenkirchen seemed to show no
> manufacturing activity.

Having stood his ground, Harris reverted to his emollient tone. 'I am sorry,' he wrote, '[that] you seem to think that I do not understand the importance of the oil war, because that is entirely wrong . . . . [B]efore I had received your letter, I had already impressed upon my Staff the necessity for getting on with the oil as hard as we could whenever opportunity really served. I had in fact hauled them over the coals for not putting a specific part of the force that attacked Gelsenkirchen on the oil plants. Unfortunately that attack was laid on when I was taking a day off, otherwise it would have been done.'[32]

Harris might have left it at that, but he couldn't resist a parting shot at the Air Ministry and, above all, the Ministry of Economic Warfare:

It would be of interest to know how we arrive at so exact figures of German oil production. The form in which the information reaches me savours sometimes of the type of Admiralty paper which starts with a series of assumptions and works them in three places of decimals!

Harris's claims about Gelsenkirchen were disingenuous. He had in fact launched a successful raid on the Nordstern oil plant there on 13 September, using only 102 aircraft.[33] It is also hard to credit the claim that his staff ignored his orders (a brave staff member that would be). Nonetheless, the letter seemed to keep Portal happy and Harris was able to get back to work. Over the next few days, he bombed Gelsenkirchen, Koblenz, Homberg, Harburg, and Dortmund. He was clearly feeling Portal's pressure, as three of these raids – Homburg, Dortmund, and Gelsenkirchen – were oil raids. Despite Harris's predictions to the contrary, both the Dortmund and the Gelsenkirchen raids were a success: a synthetic oil plant at Dortmund was severely damaged, and 514 aircraft bombed another plant at Gelsenkirchen before smoke obscured the target.[34] The 6 November raid on Koblenz destroyed 60 per cent of the town's historic centre, killed 104 people, and left 20,000 homeless. The city had been founded as a fortification in the year 1000 and grew up over the centuries as the seat of local monarchs and bishops. Its architecture was a mix of grand palaces and narrow, old-European streets.

As one city after another fell, Portal once again decided to respond. He could see, for only a fool could not, that Harris was making only a reluctant effort to bomb oil targets. But he felt limited by his own sense of decorum – it was not Portal's way to order his men around – and by the formal authority enjoyed by Harris. What was he to do? Portal had known Harris for more than twenty-five years and he understood better than anybody that challenging him head-on would only bring out the commander-in-chief's stubbornness. All he could do was cajole.

Portal began by casting himself as Harris's patron in a world of hostile foes, one who needed to be properly armed if he was going to repel their assaults. 'There is, of course[,] no question,' Portal wrote, 'but that the decision [about what to bomb] must lie with you alone. My concern, and my duty, however, is to satisfy myself and outsiders who may enquire, that your Command loses no opportunity of attacking the priority targets that are laid down in the directive. It is for this reason that I have felt bound to burden you with these enquiries.' Thus covering his flank, Portal then adopted a tone that was more direct and (mildly) more damning than the one found in earlier missives. Probably recognising the intrinsically subjective nature of the evidence, he stopped debating the merits of particular raids and raised the broader issue: if Harris was so committed to the oil offensive, why were so many bombs continuing to fall on cities and so few on oil? What, moreover, explained the commander-in-chief's obsession with destroying German cities?

You have been good enough to state in full the factors
which influenced you to go to Cologne rather than to the
Ruhr, and to Bochum, rather than Gelsenkirchen. I must
of course accept your decisions in these cases (but, may
I say, with the hope that the daylight attack has laid the
Gelsenkirchen bogey for ever). The issue [however] is a
more fundamental one than whether or not you could
have made a better choice in these two individual cases.
In the closing paragraphs of your letter of 1st November
you refer to a plan for the destruction of the 60 leading
German cities, and to your effort to keep up with, and
even to exceed, your average of 2½ such cities devastated
each month. I know that you have long felt such a plan to
be the most effective way of bringing about the collapse
of Germany. Knowing this, I have, I must confess, at
times wondered whether the magnetism of the remaining
German cities has not in the past tended as much to
deflect our bombers from their primary objectives as the
tactical and weather difficulties which you described so
fully in your letter of 1st November. I would like you
to reassure me that this is not so. If I knew you to be so
wholeheartedly in the attack on oil as in the past you have
been in the matter of attacking cities, I would have little to
worry about.[35]

The letter also directly addressed two claims made by Harris
against bombing oil: that an operation had to go after the easiest
target and that going after difficult oil targets would send Bomber
Command casualties through the roof. In his 6 November 1944
letter, Harris had followed his sentence on agreeing with the
'urgency and effectiveness of the oil plan' with these words:

It is my concern and constant anxiety to try to get the best overall effect out of the available sorties in the prevailing weather, and in that regard I cannot and should not . . . [miss] any opportunity of doing something valuable with some better degree of certainty by trying to do something else which in the conditions prevailing at a particular moment I regard as being too chancy.[36]

This claim, wrote Portal, made oil bombing almost a logical impossibility: 'You state that it is your constant anxiety to try and get the best *overall* effect from the effort available. Surely that would represent a falling away from the sharply defined policy of attacking oil.' Harris defined 'overall effect' as a function of the ease of the attack and its likelihood of success, and success was defined as the extent of destruction. Cities would almost always be easier to bomb than specific targets, so this calculus would almost always lead to the bombing of cities rather than oil. Given what the Allies knew by late 1944, Portal argued, 'in my view our aims now should be to go for maximum effect on *oil* whenever a reasonable chance presents itself, even though this may be at the expense of an attack with greater certainty upon a lower priority target.'[37]

In other words, since bombing oil produced more results than bombing cities, oil targets should be bombed even if it were more difficult. It was better to lose more bombers to a useful oil raid than few to a pointless city raid. Portal might have added that when Harris had in the past believed a target was worthy, he was willing to assume greater risks to take it out: Cologne in the thousand-bomber raid, Berlin throughout 1943 and 1944, and, once he had signed on, the Sorpe, Eder, and Möhne dams.

Portal also directly addressed Harris's point about repeated attacks, allowing German defences to concentrate, and the ensuing casualties among British bombers. 'I must,' he wrote, make reference to the problem of concentrating on the Ruhr. From the statistics I have available, there is little evidence so far of our concentration in this area 'putting the casualty rate up enormously'. Since 1st September, our losses in the Ruhr area have averaged only 1.3 per cent and these have been spread fairly evenly throughout the period. This rate is well below your average against some 42 of the major cities which has been 3.8 per cent since January, 1942. There would seem no reason as yet for [deviating] in our attacks on the Ruhr.[38] On the contrary, it would surely be better to concentrate against the Ruhr oil and the Ruhr now, before the enemy can solve his early warning difficulties. It will be time enough to change when heavy casualties do in fact materialize. We should if we can secure maximum effect on the Ruhr itself, and the quickest direct and indirect effect upon the Ruhr oil. Incidentally, I was delighted to see that you managed to attack the plant at DORTMUND last night without loss.

As Portal was no doubt thinking, Harris had frequently 'tested' the casualty rate if he felt a campaign important. For instance, during the early Battle of Berlin, in August 1943, Harris launched three raids with high losses before delaying the campaign.

We cannot know what was going through Harris's mind as he read Portal's latest letter, but he likely recognised that he was running out of arguments. He decided instead to play for time. He did not bother to pen a reply for almost two weeks. Gladly responding to an American request for air support for the Army, Harris sent 500 planes to destroy the medieval city of Düren. The bombing killed 3,100 people, obliterated the city centre, and left only 130 out of 6,000 houses standing. The smaller towns of Heinsberg and Jülich were also destroyed that night.

Harris finally replied on 24 November. It was one of many points during this months-long exchange at which he might have simply conceded that Portal was right and carried on regardless. But that was not Harris's style. He had plenty of guile but a visceral distaste for mendacity. He believed either that Portal was wrong on the casualty rate, or that his own argument depended on Portal being wrong. Either way, he was not going to let Portal's arguments stand unquestioned.

Rather ironically, given his low regard for experts, he challenged Portal by summarising four points from an Air Scientific Intelligence Report entitled 'The Present Eclipse of the German Night Fighters'. From it, Harris concluded that (i) Germany put an immense effort into the expansion and equipment of its night air defences; (ii) British losses were kept in bearable limits only by attending to tactics such as 'spoof' and diversions; and (iii) the retirement of the enemy to his own frontiers deprived him of much of his early warning system, making deception easier. The report, Harris continued,

stresses the fact that our low losses up to the present are due not to our ability to fight and defeat the German defences, but to our success in evading them. [The report] points out that a quite small technical advance made by the Germans might, temporarily at least, reduce our powers of invasion. This would mean an immediate and large increase in our rate of loss, as our gunners, provided as they are with a poor view and deficient fire-power, cannot hope to deal effectively with the powerfully armed and heavily armoured German night fighters.[39]

It was probably a good thing that the letter wasn't shown to the Americans. It was a patronising dismissal of the efforts made by the USSTAF to destroy the Luftwaffe. Their effort, Harris implied, had been pointless, and only his skill at moving RAF bombers around Germany had saved them. Harris added one more argument against oil targets – bombing the same target is boring for crews – and sent the letter to Portal.

Portal took more than a week to respond. During that time, the bombing went on relentlessly. On 27 November, the southern German city of Freiburg, which until then had remained untouched, was set alight. Fires tore through the narrow streets of the 875-year-old city. Within two hours, the heat and flames made it impossible for fire crews to reach the citizens or to rescue those still in cellars.[40] When it was over, only a hollow shell of the old city remained, and over two thousand people were dead.[41]

Over the course of November, Harris had dropped 60 per cent of his bombs on cities, 24 per cent on oil, and 9 per cent on transportation. American raids at the same time made clear that there was nothing inevitable in this. The figures for the Eighth Air Force were 41 per cent on oil, 33 per cent on marshalling yards, and the rest mostly on ground support. For the Fifteenth Air Force, they were: 35 per cent on oil and 51 per cent on transportation.[42] Cities were not being destroyed because 'weather made other targets impractical', but because Harris was disobeying orders.

December also opened with a city raid. On 4 December, Harris sent 244 planes to Heilbronn, a 600-year-old city of 77,500 people and no industry. In just over 20 minutes, the RAF dropped 1,249 tons of bombs on the city (40 per cent incendiaries) and 170 tons of high explosives on the rail yard.[43] The city was decimated – every building in the old town was destroyed – and seven thousand people were killed.[44] The same night, Harris also bombed Karlsruhe, killing 375 people.[45] An attack on 26–7 September

1944 had already carpet-bombed the city centre, leaving fifty dead.[46] The two raids left only burned-out façades standing in the centre, but some nearby houses and public buildings were intact. Harris would try one more time to flatten the city – on 2 February 1945 – before leaving it alone.

From late November to mid-December, Harris also bombed Münster, Cologne, Neuss, Essen, Dortmund (twice), Bottrop, Osterfeld, Duisburg, Oberhausen, Karlsruhe, Hallendorf, Hamm, and Hagen. A handful of these raids – on the Kalk Nord railway yards in (obliterated) Cologne, on a tar and benzol plant in Dortmund, on a coking plant at Bottrop, and on steelworks in Hallendorf – were precision attacks. But more than two thousand tons of bombs were dropped on Hagen, Karlsruhe, Essen, and Duisburg.

Two days after Heilbronn, Portal's letter arrived. Portal rejected outright Harris's argument about German air defences and tolerable casualty rates. 'While losses might go up on a particular raid, where German flak defences secured unexpected successes, the overall casualty rate was less than 1 per cent.' While this could, of course, change, 'there is some force in the argument that we should exploit [Germany's] present confusion by making a maximum effort while it lasts.'[47] He also rejected the argument, made in Harris's last letter, that a higher casualty rate was tolerable in 1943 but not in 1944. How, Portal asked, could Bomber Command give up the opportunity to press home a winning strategy? 'In this, the culminating phase of the war we would not be justified in pulling our punches.' The letter also reminded Harris – again – that oil and transportation were the *first* priorities.

Portal dismissed Harris's 'boredom' argument. Morale could only benefit from bombing over a strategically important target under relatively safe conditions. Bombing a city was not like visiting one; from the air, one did not look radically different from the next. The excitement of the raid flowed from its danger, the flash of lights, fires, the sound of flak. Most crews would happily do with less excitement in the form of incoming German fighters.

Portal might have left it at that. Instead – for reasons that are not at all clear – he handed Harris another lifeline: he urged Harris to see the degrees of freedom the directives allowed him.

When conditions are unlikely to be suitable for [visual] attacks on the specific targets, such as oil plants or railway centres, which is often the case in the winter, your directive makes provision for the attack of some twenty-four industrial centres throughout Germany, including Breslau, Dresden, Chemnitz and Munich. Such occasions might perhaps be exploited with the object of further increasing the enemy's uncertainty.

For the present, therefore, I feel that neither the restrictions implicit in the directives, nor their effect in terms of increased losses are as serious as your letter suggests. Whether or not the enemy can overcome his present difficulties and inflict increasing losses upon us, only time can show; in such an event, you would have unlimited tactical licence under your directive to deal with the situation. For example, should it be *essential* for tactical reasons, in order to bomb Leuna, to send out considerable forces to attack one or two other targets not specifically mentioned in the directive, that would be acceptable. It would of course be better if you could achieve your diversionary effect by attacking targets mentioned in the directive, but this may not always be possible. There has never been any question of limiting your tactical freedom.

After fairly clearly demolishing the arguments Harris had presented against oil bombing, Portal baulked. He invited Harris to reopen the debate about what was essential. He reminded Harris that there were plenty of cities that he could decimate as part of the Allied directive, and that in effect the Air Ministry would turn a blind eye when destroying a city not on the lists somehow served the directive. It was an open invitation. Harris would take it.

PORTAL PLEADS

In October 1944, Hitler's gloom about the course of the war – he had ordered a scorched earth policy for Germany in September – lifted.[1] He had a plan: the German army would launch a vast counter-offensive on the western front in the Ardennes. After a devastating blow had been dealt to the Western Allies, he would then be able to transfer divisions to the eastern front and push the Soviets back.

The idea was to assemble twenty-five divisions of Wehrmacht soldiers over a seventy-mile stretch of the front in the heavily wooded Ardennes.[2] In a surprise attack, two armies – the Fifth and Sixth Panzer Armies – would break across the Maas river around Liége and Dinant, push towards Brussels, split Allied forces in two, and eliminate the supply port at Antwerp.[3] The Fifteenth Army, meanwhile, would launch an attack towards Aachen, pinning Lieutenant General Courtney Hodges's First US Army there. Two factors evidently underpinned Hitler's thinking.[4] First, the element of surprise, which had served him so well in 1940 and 1941, would again work its wonders. Second, the need to co-ordinate a response between Churchill and Roosevelt, whom he evidently saw as strategic heads of armies in the Hitlerian mould, would delay an Allied response until it was too late.

Generaloberst Alfred Jodl presented Hitler's general plan to senior western commanders on 3 November. They thought it hopeless.[5] The army had too few tanks, too little fuel, and too few men to manage it. They could forget about taking Antwerp. At best, German divisions might reoccupy Aachen and use it as a base for a subsequent westward push.[6] More important, it would be suicide to decrease troop concentrations on the eastern front, where the Russians were likely preparing their own offensive. Jodl rejected the generals' more modest strategic objectives out of hand. The result had to be so stunning that it would 'make the western powers ready to negotiate'.[7]

Despite their objections, the generals quickly fell in line and soon touted, and in some cases perhaps shared, Hitler's delusions.[8] The problem of Allied air superiority would be solved by putting five thousand German planes in the air (the Germans struggled to secure five hundred at this point), and the armies would reach Antwerp within four days.[9] By 16 December, Feldmarschall Gerd von Rundstedt was calling for a holy war against the Anglo-Americans.[10]

On 16 December 1944, mist hung over the Allied front along the Ardennes, running along the German border from Luxembourg in the south, through Belgium, and into the Netherlands. Snow covered the ground. It was almost entirely silent. On the German side of the front, thirty divisions, six hundred tanks, and two hundred thousand German troops were amassed. Most of the soldiers were boys – around fifteen or sixteen years old. Others were old men. They were waiting for the order to attack.

At 05:30, it came. At the northern end of the front, Josef 'Sepp' Dietrich's Sixth SS Panzer Army launched a massive artillery barrage against American troops. By 08:00, all divisions had attacked. They hugely outnumbered the Americans, who had eighty thousand soldiers and four hundred tanks. The Germans also had the element of surprise. When the first sounds of gun and cannon fire were heard, the Americans dismissed it as friendly fire. It was only when they saw German soldiers moving through the forest that they realised they were under attack.

The Germans concentrated their attack on three positions: the north, centre, and south of the front. In the north, the Sixth SS Panzer Army pushed the Americans into Belgium, but they soon recovered and the Germans became bogged down in heavy resistance. In the south, Erich Brandenberger's Seventh Army broke through American lines and pushed towards Luxembourg. After they had advanced for four miles, however, divisions of the US VIII Corps blocked them, and held the new front.

In the centre, the Americans were overrun. General Hasso von Manteuffel's Fifth Panzer Army broke through. His tanks pressed forward in a deep cut of some sixty-five miles, making it within a few miles of the River Meuse.[11] Manteuffel surrounded two regiments of the 106th Infantry Division. Almost eight thousand men surrendered to the Germans, the greatest American setback of the war in Europe. Manteuffel pushed on to encircle the entire 101st Airborne Division and ordered its general, Anthony McAuliffe, to surrender. Defiant, McAuliffe gave a one-word reply: 'Nuts.' He scribbled the word on a paper, which was delivered to the Germans. They didn't know what it meant.

Spaatz was in Paris at the USSTAF's new headquarters when he got word of the German counter-offensive, later known as the Battle of the Bulge. Wild rumours circulated about Germans in Allied uniforms infiltrating the city. Spaatz's deputy, Major General Hugh Knerr, recommended that the headquarters be locked down, streets around it blocked off, and sentry boxes set up. Spaatz didn't take this suggestion, but the German counter-attack – as he later said – had 'caught us off balance'.[12]

He quickly recovered, however. Spaatz directed two of the Eighth Air Force's fighter groups to find proper continental airfields on which to base themselves.[13] He put them under the direct command of Major General Hoyt S. Vandenberg, the young and handsome Maxwell Field graduate who had become commanding general of the Ninth Air Force in August. The rest of the US bombing force – two-thirds of it – stayed west of the Rhine and awaited Spaatz's orders. On 18 and 19 December, the Eighth braved atrocious weather in England to send out missions over the Ardennes, but equally foul weather shielded German troops from most of the bombing. On 19 December, Harris – at Eisenhower's request – sent Lancasters out in foul weather to bomb rail targets at Trier. The bombers destroyed the targets, though stray bombs killed sixty Germans, including thirty nurses who died when a bomb penetrated their cellar.[14] Bomber Command's success was the exception, however, and for three days the Germans enjoyed the advantage.

It did not last. On 23 December, a new ally – an area of high air pressure from Russia – came to the Americans' rescue. The thick clouds that had provided the Germans with essential cover cleared, leaving the troops exposed. Spaatz ordered an attack. On Christmas Eve, a vast armada of American bombers flew over the German troops and hammered them. The German formations were smashed; bridges, rail lines, and airfields were destroyed; and troops were limited to night-time movement.[15] Panzer grenadier units could not reach the front, supplies and reserves could not be sent in by train, and even soldiers on bicycles found it impossible to get through wrecked railway towns. On that day, the Eighth Air Force dropped more tonnage than it had on any other day during the war.[16]

On the ground, the steady drone of incoming bombers made the Germans' already miserable task impossible. Manteuffel's advance was handicapped by a key shortage: oil. The Germans were only able to secure enough oil to supply each tank for two to three days. After that, they simply stalled. The plan had assumed that a rapid advance would allow the German army to overrun American fuel depots. It did not. In a sharp tactical move, Eisenhower, acting on intelligence reports, moved the depots well behind his lines.[17] The result was that Manteuffel's advance began to thin as it moved forward. In the north, the Sixth SS Panzer Army's Joachim Peiper and his *Kampfgruppe* (a sort of ad hoc battalion with about eight hundred men) got as far as La Gleize in Belgium.[18] As they advanced, Peiper's men murdered more than one hundred American POWs and approximately eighty civilians. Once in La Gleize, the fuel ran out. Harassed by American bombers, they abandoned more than a hundred vehicles, including six tanks, in the town and made their way back to German lines on foot. At precisely this moment, Eisenhower was moving a quarter of a million men right into the thick of the fight.[19]

As the Americans launched their bombing raids, Hitler raged in front of his generals: 'I have never in my life come to know the term capitulation.' Germany would emerge victorious, he declared, or it would be 'annihilated'. The war would decide 'the existence of the substance of our German people . . . . Elimination destroys such a race under certain circumstances forever.'[20] He was not, he continued, contemplating for one second the loss of the war: it was essential to return to the offensive.[21]

On 26 December, Patton broke through German lines. In one of the most thrilling rescue efforts of the war,[22] he had his Third Army race towards Bastogne where, encircled by the Germans, McAuliffe refused to surrender. The day after Christmas, Patton's troops entered the town.

On 1 January 1945, airmen on German squadron bases were celebrating the New Year. 'We danced, laughed, and drank,' recalled

Leutnant Gunther Bloemetz, 'until quite suddenly – on a gesture from the Kommandeur – the orchestra stopped playing.'

'*Meine Herren,*' the Kommandeur shouted, 'we will check our watches. Take-off in fifty minutes.'[23]

Every available German aircraft – some nine hundred, including both daytime fighters and night-time bombers – launched a daring surprise raid on Allied airfields in Belgium, Holland, and northern France; the goal was to destroy the Allied Air Forces on the ground 'in one stroke'.[24] The Luftwaffe caught the Allies off guard and destroyed 450 planes, including 146 from Bomber Command.[25] But the Germans lost much more: 400 aeroplanes, 237 pilots, 59 leaders, and the ability to fight on.

'The Luftwaffe received its death blow,' wrote fighter chief Adolf Galland after the war, 'at the Ardennes offensive. In the unfamiliar conditions and with insufficient training and combat experience, our numerical strength had no effect. It was decimated while in transfer, on the ground, in large air battles . . . and was finally destroyed. In this forced action [the 1 January 1945 raids] we sacrificed our last substance.'[26] The Americans' long war against the Luftwaffe – which, like the villain in a bad horror movie, kept rising from the dead – had been definitively won. The German Air Force was finished, and with it went any hope of protecting German cities.

Hitler would make one last try – Operation NORTHWIND, designed to break through US lines in France, near Alsace – but it came to nothing. German troops advanced some twelve miles, then stopped. The Ardennes offensive was lost. As Speer told Allied interrogators after the war, because of transportation raids, 'the preparations for the Ardennes offensive were brought to a standstill . . . the attack was ordered to begin although the units had only one or two fuel supply units; the entire supplies of bridge-building equipment still lay in the rear areas, whilst the rest of the supply organisation for the units was insufficient for the distant goal in view . . . . *Transport difficulties were decisive in causing the swift breakdown of the Ardennes offensive.*[27]

Over the course of the battle, German troops killed nineteen thousand American soldiers – by far the highest death toll for any Second World War battle. Another twenty-three thousand were captured and forty thousand wounded. The blow led the Allies to overestimate greatly Germany's remaining strength and shook Eisenhower's nerve; it took a full seven weeks for the Americans to recover their balance.[28] The Germans were able to launch their counter-attack, and to inflict such material and, above all, psychological damage so late in the war, because they could draw on their dwindling, but remaining, oil supplies.

Four days before the German counter-offensive on 16 December, Harris wrote again to Portal, with yet another combination of his 'I can't do it – it's not worth doing' arguments. Based on his staff's calculations, Harris concluded that knocking Germany's synthetic oil and benzol plants out of action, and keeping them there, would require thirteen daytime raids of 200 aircraft and eighteen night raids of 350 aircraft over nine months, totalling 56,500 sorties and 226,000 tons of bombs. Assuming the weather was clear on only three or four nights per month, Harris continued, it would be impossible to launch these eighteen night raids. Harris then switched arguments:

You will recall that in the past M.E.W. experts have never failed to overstate their case on 'panaceas' e.g. ballbearings, molybdenum, locomotives etc . . . . [A]fter the battle has been joined and [these] targets attacked, more sources of supply or other factors unpredicted by M.E.W. have become revealed. The oil plan has already displayed similar symptoms. The benzol plants were an afterthought. I am quite certain

that there are dozens more benzol plants of which we are
unaware and when and if we knock them all out I am
equally certain we shall eventually be told by M.E.W that
German [industry] is continuing to run sufficiently for their
purpose on producer gas, steam, industrial alcohol etc., etc.[29]

Five days after writing the letter, and one day after the Germans
opened the Ardennes offensive, the RAF obliterated Ulm, leaving
the old city shattered and 707 people dead.[30]

On 22 December, as the German offensive was thinning and
slowing due to lack of fuel, Portal replied.

The essence of the immediate task before the Allied
strategic bombers is to put out and keep out of action the
11 synthetic [oil] plants in Central Germany. These are
producing 70 per cent of the enemy's current supplies of
aviation and motor spirit. There is no doubt in my mind
that their immobilisation and the continued immobilisation
of the remaining major producers would represent by far
the greatest and most certain contribution that our strategic
bombers could make to the achievement of an early
decision in the German war. It is not expected by anyone
that your Command can do this job by itself; neither can
the US Eighth Air Force by itself. Over the winter months
it is essential, however, that no single opportunity is lost,
whether by day or by night.

Portal urged Harris to view the bombing campaign in the overall context of the war, and to be sensitive to history's judgement.
Were the Americans and the British to join in a co-ordinated
campaign against oil, using every available opportunity to attack
Germany's refineries,

strategic bombing will go down to history as a decisive
factor in winning this war. On the other hand, if by any
weakening of determination or any reluctance to implement
the policy which we have laid down our grip on the oil
position is relaxed, the vast effort we have expended against
oil will have been largely fruitless.

He then called Harris on the tension in his 'I can't do it – it's
not worth doing' arguments:

I am profoundly disappointed that you still appear to feel
that the oil plan is just another 'panacea'. Naturally while
you hold this view you will be unable to put your heart into
the attack of oil. Your letter gave me the impression that
while you have somewhat reluctantly agreed to attack Politz
and Leuna [locations of large producers of synthetic fuel at
hydrogenation plants] when occasion offers, you feel that this
is all you should be asked to contribute towards the attack
of the all-important Central German plants. I must say I
should have hoped that you would on the contrary be seeking
opportunities to attack all or any of them whenever there is
a chance of doing so, in order that the R.A.F. might play as
large a part as possible in what is by far the most immediately
profitable policy we have undertaken in this war.

The particular concern, even obsession, with cities and the
related dismissal of all precision targets became a self-fulfilling
policy. Harris did not believe in precision targets, attacked them
half-heartedly, and then took the mixed results flowing from his
less-than-total effort as evidence of the target's tactical irrelevance. 'In your last paragraph,' Portal wrote,

you again cast doubt on past estimates by the Ministry of Economic Warfare and by implication the whole principle of attacking a particular target system. You throw doubt also upon the soundness of our oil policy. If the attack of a particular target system is to be successful, it must be carried out as rapidly as possible and with the object of immobilising as many plants as possible in the system at the same time. Clearly we cannot expect to get very far if only half the plants are out of action at any one time. If we had tried harder in our attack on ball-bearings I have little doubt that full effects forecast by M.E.W. would have been achieved. I am glad to say that we have shown much more determination in the attack of oil, but if you allow your obvious doubts in this direction to influence your conduct of operations I very much fear that the prize may yet slip through our fingers. Moreover, it is difficult for me to feel that your staff can be devoting its maximum thoughts and energies to the accomplishment of your first priority task if you yourself are not wholehearted in support of it.[31]

With each exchange, Harris felt less and less inclined to soften his blows. He was offended by the suggestion that he did not follow orders and, above all, by the idea that his staff responded to his views rather than his instructions. He penned a long letter to Portal – almost twice as long as the one sent to him. The letter he drafted reflected his anger with the experts who knew nothing about bombing; with the Americans who had so long stood in the way of his campaign; with the Army and Navy for their many diversions; and with Portal, the erstwhile backer of city bombing. Harris dismissed out of hand the suggestion that his men might

be affected by his views on strategic bombing or by his contempt
for the Ministry of Economic Warfare. Reacting to Portal's argument that only a small number of plants – fewer than twenty –
were hit, Harris replied:

> I have certainly not overlooked the fact that the majority
> of output comes from the limited number of major plants.
> The point I tried to make clear was that I do not believe the
> M.E.W. know anything at all about the number of Benzol
> plants, or even oil plants for that matter . . . . I am certain
> that no feasible scale of destruction of oil plants and Benzol
> plants will vitally affect the carriage of essential supplies
> forward to their armies.[32]

As he crafted his reply, Harris reflected on the follies that had so
often been held up as the final key to victory. Remember fighter jets?

> The attacks against the German fighter forces and industry
> last year are outstanding examples of the futility of panacea
> seeking. . . . Nobody could say that every possible effort was
> not made, and brilliantly executed, in the best of conditions,
> to knock the German fighter forces on the ground and in
> their factories. But the enemy by concentrating his efforts
> and his great industrial abilities in countering the effects
> of these attacks rendered them virtually nugatory. All
> we have to show for it . . . is that we failed to achieve the
> aim. A failure both expensive and complete. If, over that
> long period of attacks on the German fighter industry, [the
> Americans] had instead joined with us in our area bombing,
> what vastly greater effects would not have been achieved
> on the enemy's war machine and will to war as a whole?
> Remember ball-bearings?

> You conclude saying that 5 per cent or even 10 per cent losses
> in successful attacks will be well worth while. Although that
> statement is by no means the equivalent, it reminds me much
> of a statement I once received from the Air Ministry that it
> was worth the virtual destruction of my force over a period
> of months, if we could knock out Schweinfurt. Where should
> we be now if I had agreed to that?

And now he was expected to believe that oil was the magic bullet. He wouldn't: 'I am afraid that nothing will disillusion me of the view that the oil plan is, for reason[s] I have given above, and on many occasions elsewhere, another panacea.' He would continue to attack oil – 'It has always been my custom . . . to leave no stone unturned to get my views across, but, when the decision is made I carry it out to the utmost and to the best of my ability' – but doing so was pointless. 'The basis,' Harris wrote, 'of the plan is wrong . . . and its pursuance is, and will prove to be, chimerical.'

Harris used the letter to address Portal's argument that history would soon judge him. He turned it on its head. 'The history of bombing,' he wrote,

> throughout this war will, when it is all summed up, show
> our repeated lapses from that essential principle of war,
> the maintenance of an objective. Three years of bitter
> struggle have gone into our area blitzing. All Germany
> openly bemoans it as their worst trial. We know that on
> more than one occasion they have nearly collapsed under
> it. As the programme nears completion we chuck it all up
> – for a panacea.

The pursuit of these panaceas, Harris believed, had already cost the Allies dearly. Just before D-Day, Harris had warned the Army that if Bomber Command were to lay off bombing Germany for five months, the country would recover all that was necessary for war production. 'The aggregate of our diversions, on the railway plan, on helping the armies and now on oil, very far exceeds the five months' estimate.' Referring to Ardennes, Harris added, 'We need look no further for the cause of what happened in this last fortnight.'

THE GERMANS DESPAIR, HARRIS THREATENS, PORTAL BLINKS

On 6 January, Harris sent his bombers to destroy the centre of Hanau. Munich's turn came the following night. More than six hundred Lancasters and a few Mosquitoes area bombed the centre.[1] Incendiaries ravaged the two cities, and Bomber Command suffered a remarkably low 2 per cent casualty rate.

The day after the Munich raid, Portal wrote to Harris. His patience had worn thin, and he decided to speak truth to truculence. 'In spite of your assertions to the contrary,' Portal noted, 'I believe your attacks on oil would be pressed home harder and more certainly if they were backed not solely by your sense of loyalty but by your enthusiasm as well.'[2] He began by pointing out that Harris's raid on the oil plant at Pölitz involved only one-third of the total possible bombing force, and therefore he, Portal, was 'not convinced by your argument that the prospect of damaging Pölitz would not have been increased had you despatched two or three times the force you did. The target is a large one . . .' He then went on to describe Harris's antipathy towards the Ministry of Economic Warfare as 'misplaced' and inimical to the war effort. The MEW did not choose the ball-bearing and oil targets alone; economists' recommendations, agents' reports, and intelligence committees in both the United States and the United Kingdom all informed the decision.

The adoption of these two policies was therefore backed
by investigations which, as far as was humanly possible,
covered all the ground and brought in all interests which
were able to help. They were clearly not merely 'panaceas
enthusiastically put forward by the amateurish, ignorant,
irresponsible and mendacious M.E.W.' and it is an
unworthy and inexcusable travesty of our conduct of the
war to suggest that our policy is determined on that kind
of basis.

His pen gaining flourish, Portal repeated and confronted the
other claims made in Harris's letter. That he had done everything
he could to destroy Germany's ball-bearing factories:

You state that you are satisfied you achieved a 'whole
series of brilliantly executed attacks of an effectiveness that
nobody would even have thought possible at the time when
the ball-bearing plan was initiated.' The facts scarcely seem
to me to support your appreciation of your achievements.

That the American attacks on the German fighter force were
futile:

Had the American forces joined with Bomber Command in
bombing cities instead of fighter production, there is every
possibility that the whole combined bomber offensive might
have been brought to a standstill. It was only by a narrow
margin that they gained the ascendency which virtually
cleared the skies for 'OVERLORD', the prerequisite
condition for its launching, and obtained freedom to
proceed to the attack of oil.

That area bombing would have proved decisive if the Americans had joined the campaign:

> [The enemy's] counter measures would have prevented
> us from maintaining such a policy to the decisive
> point. We would have been forced to precision attack
> to maintain the air situation needed to continue the
> offensive at all. The Americans did this for themselves
> in 1943/1944 with a little help from Bomber Command.
> Under cover of the favourable air situation which was
> created 'OVERLORD' was launched successfully, and
> the advance to the German frontier gave night bombing a
> new lease on life. But for this it is possible that the night
> blitzing of German cities would by now have been too
> costly to sustain upon a heavy scale. These factors must
> not be overlooked when considering the past and future
> results of area attacks.

Portal, the erstwhile backer of area bombing, ended the letter with a full – even passionate, if such a word can be used of such a gentlemanly character – embrace of precision attacks on oil:

> We have determined to exploit our period of tactical
> freedom over Germany by the attack of the vital
> element in her war economy – oil. We have reduced their
> production to 30 per cent of the pre-attack figure and her
> reserves are now virtually exhausted . . . . The completion
> of the oil plan lies so well within our capabilities that
> it can be pressured to a point at which the operational
> effectiveness of the German armies and air forces on all
> fronts will be decisively restricted; but to do this it is
> essential to hold firmly to this aim.

The energy, resource and determination displayed by the enemy in his efforts to maintain his oil production must be more than matched by our own determination to destroy it.

On 16 January 1945, Harris sent his bombers to attack Magdeburg. The historic core, with its churches, narrow streets, and elegant Rathaus, along with the *fin-de-siècle* northern suburbs, were flattened, and four thousand people were killed.[3] The bodies of thousands of women, children, and old men were piled up in the gutters. The same day, Portal and Spaatz issued Strategic Directive No. 3, making oil again the first priority, followed by transportation. The category of 'important industrial areas' to be attacked when weather demanded it was a distant third.

Having obliterated another ancient German city, Harris answered Portal.[4] The jig was up. Portal would not accept his assurances that he was doing everything he could to implement the oil directive. Although January was the peak of his contribution to the oil campaign, only 30 per cent of his bombs hit oil targets, while 40 per cent fell on cities. Harris had little to gain in restraining his views. He let Portal know what he thought of precision targets:

All strategic targets of the panacea type are dependent on the assumption that the enemy has been fool enough to allow vital bottle-necks to persist even at this stage of the war. They are also dependent on the assumption that over a definite period of time, and quite a short time, those vital targets can all, or the major part of them, be destroyed before the enemy has time to disperse them, *and thereafter be kept destroyed.*[5]

Such a bombing effort would require most of the bombers and 'all' of the good weather'. Even then the Germans would simply disperse their industries. 'Small oil plants,' Harris argued, 'especially those suited for M.T. [motor transport] and jet fuels, can be erected inside ordinary farm, village, town and city housing' with ease. Finding them, much less hitting them, would be impossible.

But above all, Harris concluded, destroying oil targets would not do any good anyway:

> On top of all this the final factor is that Germany wants so very little in the way of fuel *for the essentials with which to continue the fight defensively*. It is those last essentials which I know will be so extremely difficult to find, to deprive her of, and to keep her deprived of. It is no good knocking out 75 per cent of something if 25 per cent suffices for essentials.[6]

And doing so would further distract Bomber Command from the single most important aim of the bombing war:

> The main factor which I fear is the abandonment of priority for area attack[s] with all the vast harm they have done to the enemy war machine, in favour of a type of attack which *if it fails to achieve its objectives achieves nothing*. Nothing whatever. Worse than nothing. Because it largely relieves the enemy of his worst problem – industrial area bombing. This we throw aside just as we near our long striven for goal of destroying the 50 leading industrial cities.

The oil plan, like all precision plans before it, 'is another attempt to seek a quick, clever, easy and cheap way out. It will prove to be none of these things. If only because the enemy is neither a fool nor an incompetent. We will not deprive him of his last essentials in fuel. What we will succeed in doing will be largely

to relieve Germany of her 'worst headache' – the crescendo of
industrial civil and morale destruction which is near intolerable
to her war potential now and must soon, even in Gestapo-ridden
Germany, react to her final undoing on every front, including the
home front. And that despite the fact . . . that the U.S. bombers
have taken no serious part in area attacks.'

Given this, Harris was not prepared to follow his orders. 'I
will not willingly again lay myself open to the charge that the
lack of success of a policy, which I have declared at the outset
. . . not to contain the seeds of success, is after the event, due to
my personal failure in not having really tried. That situation
is simply one of heads I lose tails you win, and it is simply an
intolerable situation.'

If Harris were to remain in his position, he would do so to finish the job:

> The next three months will be our last opportunity to knock
> out the central and eastern industrial areas of Germany, viz.
> Magdeburg, Leipzig, Chemnitz, Dresden, Breslau, Posen,
> Halle, Erfurt, Gotha, Weimar, Eisenach and the rest of
> Berlin . . . . These places are now the mainspring of German
> war production *and the culmination and consummation of
> three years' work depends upon achieving their destruction.*
> It is our last chance, and it would have more effect on the
> war than anything else . . . . But for all the diversions,
> necessary or otherwise, these places would nearly all be
> burnt out or blazing by now. That would have been the
> consummation of our three years' effort, and it would have
> been absolutely fatal for Germany.

If Portal was not prepared to accept this, then he had, Harris
said in the letter's last lines, only one option: 'I . . . ask you to

consider whether it is best for the prosecution of the war and the success of our arms, which alone matter, that I should remain in this situation.'

It was a defining moment in the bombing war. It was not the first time that Harris had threatened resignation. If Portal had called Harris's bluff, city bombing might have ended or at least been sharply reduced, and the bombers could have been redirected towards key oil and transportation targets. Tens of thousands of civilians would not have lost their lives, more than a dozen cities would have been spared, Germany might have capitulated earlier, and thousands of Allied lives might have been saved. Given Harris's record of disobeying orders and his insolence, there was every case for sacking him. Instead, Portal backed down. He wrote to Harris: 'I willingly accept your assurance that you will continue to do your utmost to ensure the successful implementation of the policy laid down. I am very sorry that you do not believe in it, but it is no use my craving for what is evidently unattainable. We must wait until after the end of the war before we can know for certain who was right and until then I sincerely hope that you will continue in command of the [air] force.'[7] It is hard to imagine a feebler letter from a superior to a subordinate officer.[8]

Portal and Harris did not know everything that the Germans were thinking – although ULTRA intercepts meant that they knew a fair amount – but we do now. Shortly after this argument drew to its tepid close, Speer drafted a report outlining the situation facing German production in January 1945. All manner of German production – infantry rifles, flak guns, motor vehicles, tanks, fighters and other Luftwaffe aircraft, and ammunition – saw a sharp increase in production from 1942 to 1943.[9] The only notable industry displaying relatively poor increases was submarine production.[10]

From the last quarter of 1944, following the transportation plan, the oil plan, and the Western Allied advances in German territory west of the Rhine, production began to fall sharply. In his report, Speer attributed the fall to three causes: the loss of portions of the country west of the Rhine; air attacks on the Rhine-Westphalia area, which wrecked energy supplies and transportation (demonstrating again the Ruhr attacks were the most effective Bomber Command attacks); and precision attacks on other raw material production.[11] Coal production in the last quarter of 1944 was 16 per cent lower than the average for the whole year.[12] Allied attacks in the Ruhr had brought German crude steel production 'to a standstill'. Attacks on German oil production reduced synthetic oil production to one-third of its pre-attack levels; without the raids on oil and even with the loss of Romania, Germany would have had more than enough fuel to supply both the Wehrmacht and civilian sectors. Finally, precision attacks on other chemical industries – nitrogen, including methanol, carbide, and sulphuric acid – led to a severe shortage of all these products. The only targeted industry that managed to keep production at relatively high levels was ball-bearings, production of which was 83 per cent of the 1943 level by the end of 1944.

There can be little doubt who was right and who was wrong in the debate between Portal and Harris. Harris's stubbornness meant that still more German cities would be pointlessly obliterated (including, but certainly not only, Dresden); that Bomber Command's contribution to victory would fall short of its potential; and that post-war controversy over the morality of area bombing, inevitable since Hamburg, would be particularly intense.

AMERICAN AREA BOMBING

On 3 February 1945, Lieutenant John Welch, a co-pilot with the 457th Bombardment Group, was over Berlin. His plane was one of a thousand bombers flying across the capital. His aiming point was Friedrichstrasse station, close to Berlin's famous boulevard, the Unter den Linden, and to the Brandenburg Gate and the Reichstag. When Welch's plane reached the target, his bombardier released his load of 500-pound bombs on the station. 'God help them,' he whispered as the bombs hurtled towards their target.[1]

The station was crowded full of refugees fleeing the Soviet advance. As the bombs rained down, people scurried into the tunnels. One was Herie Granberg, a Swedish newspaper correspondent. 'The ground heaved,' he wrote in a report smuggled out after the raid, the 'lights flickered. It seemed the concrete walls bulged. People scrambled about like frightened animals.'[2] Clouds of dust filled the tunnels.

Outside, it was worse. Those who did not make it into the station in time were slaughtered. Bombs exploded on or around them. Flying glass and metal fragments sliced through them. When the bombing stopped, Granberg climbed out of the tunnel to find dozens of people dead and dying in the square in front of the station.

The raid also ravaged other areas of the stricken city. Large parts of Mitte (the centre), Kreuzberg (an industrial, densely populated area just south of the centre and later the heart of West Berlin's counterculture scene), and Friedrichshain (working-class east Berlin) were reduced to rubble.[3] A vast column of smoke covered the centre of the city. All utilities were knocked out. For days, delayed-action time bombs exploded, shaking the ground.[4] The attack, wrote one Foreign Office official, 'directed against the centre of the city, the government district, and the railway stations, was the ultimate apocalypse, as far as Berlin is concerned. . . . Never has the city looked so devastated as it does these days, when rain and water from the melting snow bespatter its ruins with muck, and streams of filthy water flow through the streets.'[5]

The raid was city and civilian bombing, pure and simple. 'We were told today,' a member of Welch's crew wrote in his diary, 'that if we had any scruples about bombing civilians, it was hard luck for us because from now on we'll be bombing and strafing women, children, everybody.'[6] More than a hundred thousand people were made homeless, and at least three thousand civilians were killed. Two weeks after the raid, on 17 February, German radio announced that the Wehrmacht was awarding the Order of the White Feather to Spaatz for 'exceptional cowardice' in laying a 'carpet of bombs' across a city 'crowded with hundreds of thousands of refugees, principally women and children'.[7] The Nazis' only award to those women and children was more suffering: 'The homeless masses,' Goebbels declared, 'must share whatever new disaster may befall [the capital].'[8]

Such sympathy as the Germans received came from the aircrew. 'Shacked [military slang for bombed] women and children,' wrote one bomb releaser on his aeroplane immediately after the raid. Another, a radio operator named James Henrietta, said much later, Berlin 'bothered me for a long time. In fact, it still does . . . . I'm thinking we're bombing out a lot of people who maybe were helpless victims.'[9]

The February raid on Berlin emerged from a complex set of first British, then American proposals set out over the early months of 1945. Both forces dusted off the THUNDERCLAP proposal of the previous summer. On 12 January, the Soviets launched their winter offensive. On 25 January, the British Joint Intelligence Committee issued two reports on how best to assist them. The first report argued that attacks on five targets would help the Soviet offensive.[10] The most important of them was oil. After oil, the committee recommended attacks on tank factories, on Berlin (to disrupt troop flows), and on German reinforcements moving from Italy or Hungary. It also recommended attacking sea mining operations in the Baltic. The second report – following the THUNDERCLAP proposals from the previous summer – looked exclusively at Berlin. It argued that attacks on Berlin should in no way interfere with oil or tank targets, and that destroying Berlin would neither break Germany's will to resist nor lead to the downfall of the regime. Still, the massive bombing of the capital, as eastern Germany's main transportation hub and the home of millions of refugees, 'would be bound to create great confusion, interfere with the orderly movement of troops to the front, and hamper the German military and administrative machine.'[11]

Anyone who has worked in a large, complex organisation will have noticed a curious tendency on the part of its officials to reinvent the wheel: ideas that were tried and failed in the past often return. When they do, younger people who did not hear the original arguments or view the consequences of the decisions, or older people who did but forgot them, seize on these ideas and put them into practice. The 'morale' argument was – by 1945 – tried, tested, and found to be thoroughly wanting. Yet, here it was again, repackaged only slightly as 'confusion'.

As often occurs in area bombing debates, other justifications were added. Large German troop formations were passing through Berlin. Destroying the city would also demonstrate to the Soviets an American and British desire to help them, thus improving the Western Allies' hand at the upcoming Yalta conference.[12] Finally, although no one said it, bombing Berlin seemed – as it had almost from the start of the war – the right thing to do.

The next day, the Air Staff presented their views.[13] Oil targets should absolutely remain the first priority. Tank production could be attacked only if attacks on transportation could be reduced. Mine laying would definitely produce dividends, but bombing German troop movements likely would not. As for Berlin, the Chiefs of Staff were doubtful that bombing would produce much in the way of results.

While these discussions were going on, Bottomley called Harris to hear his views. The commander-in-chief naturally loved the idea of bombing Berlin; such an attack was, he said, already 'on my plate'.[14] He recommended additional strikes on Chemnitz, Leipzig, and Dresden, as these cities were housing large numbers of refugees, which would add to the post-bombing chaos and confusion, and as they were focal points in German communications behind the eastern front.[15] Harris was ready to blast Berlin 'as soon as the moon has waned'.

Churchill then entered the argument, with a predictably decisive effect. On the evening of 25 January, he was preparing to have a drink with Harry Hopkins, President Roosevelt's envoy. Before he did, he called Sinclair. The prime minister had read the Joint Intelligence Committee's reports and spoke with the Secretary of State. Sinclair concluded from the conversation that he had been asked about the RAF's plans for 'basting the Germans in their retreat from Breslau'.[16]

Sinclair took Churchill's views to Portal the next day. Portal replied that oil targets should remain the first priority but that attacks in support of the Soviet advance could be the second. In some cases, though he did not explain which, city attacks might come first. That day, Sinclair passed this on to Churchill. 'I feel strongly,' Sinclair wrote on 26 January, 'that the best use of our heavy bombers at the present time lies in maintaining the attack upon German oil plants, whenever weather permits. The benefits of these attacks are felt equally by the Russians and ourselves and nothing should be allowed to interfere with them. There may, however, be occasions when the weather is unsuitable for attacks on the comparatively small targets presented by these oil plants but yet would permit area attacks on Eastern Germany. These opportunities might be used to exploit the present situation by the bombing of Berlin and other large cities in Eastern Germany such as Leipzig, Dresden and Chemnitz . . . . To achieve results of real value, a series of attacks would probably be required, and weather conditions at this time of year would certainly prevent these being delivered in quick succession. The possibility of these attacks being delivered on the scale necessary to have a critical effect on the situation in East Germany is now under examination.'[17]

For Churchill, the response was too equivocal. He wanted it bombed immediately. 'I did not ask you last night,' he shot back on the same day, 'about plans for harrying the German retreat from Breslau. On the contrary, I asked whether Berlin, and no doubt other large cities in East Germany, should not now be considered especially attractive targets. I am glad that is "under examination". Pray report to me tomorrow what is to be done.'

Sinclair passed the prime minister's minute on to Bottomley, who issued orders to Harris. Bottomley criticised the Joint Intelligence Committee report and told Harris,

[In] the opinion of the Chief of Air Staff . . . it would not be right to attempt attacks on Berlin on the 'THUNDERCLAP' scale in the near future. He considers it very doubtful that an attack even if done on the heaviest scale with consequent heavy losses would be decisive. He agrees, however, that subject to the overriding claims of oil and the other approved target systems within the current directive, we should use every available effort in one big attack on Berlin and related attacks on Dresden, Leipzig, Chemnitz or any other cities where a severe blitz will not only cause confusion in the evacuation from the East but will also hamper the movement of troops from the West.

'I am therefore,' Bottomley concluded, 'to request that subject to the qualifications stated above, and as soon as the moon and weather conditions allow, you will undertake such attacks with the particular object of exploiting the confused conditions which are likely to exist in the above mentioned cities during the successful Russian advance.'[18]

A similar argument was developing on the other side of the Atlantic. Arnold, always impatient for results, was increasingly strident in his demand for action. He had just suffered his fourth heart attack and was driven by the realisation that the war might finish him before he finished Germany. 'With [our] tremendous striking power,' he wrote to Spaatz, 'it would seem to me that we should get much better and much more decisive results than we are getting now. I am not criticising, because frankly I don't know the answer and what I am now doing is letting my thoughts run wild with the hope that out of this you get a glimmer, a light, a new thought, or something that will help us bring this war to a close sooner.'[19] It was an open appeal for something dramatic. And brutal.

General Marshall was impatient as well. He wanted troops out of Europe and into the Pacific, and he was prepared to try anything to get them there. Since the Germans had shown unexpected resistance, they had to be met with unexpected force. Just before Yalta, he met with Frederick Anderson and told him that he wanted Munich bombed (it would not be, at least not like Berlin), along with the cities in the Berlin-Leipzig-Dresden corridor. Eisenhower and Bradley signed on. There was no need to ask Roosevelt, as the president had for years called for hell's fury to be unleashed against Germany.[20] On 31 January, Bottomley radioed a message to Portal: oil would be the first priority, followed by Berlin, Leipzig, and Dresden.[21] With V-2 rockets raining down on London, few people disagreed with Roosevelt's sentiment.

Few, but not no one. When Spaatz presented the plan to Doolittle on 30 January, Doolittle viewed it as what it was: terror bombing. He wrote back to Spaatz, urging him to reconsider.[22] Doolittle pointed out that there 'are basically no important, strictly military, targets in the area indicated'. He dismissed the idea that Berliners could be terrorised into surrender. 'The reactions of the people of Berlin who have been bombed consistently will be very different from the people of London who have not experienced a heavy raid in years . . . . Terror is induced by the unknown. The chances of terrorising into submission, merely by an increased concentration of bombing, a people who have been subjected to intense bombing for four years is extremely remote.' Doolittle was doing nothing more than repeating the argument that Spaatz had himself made against THUNDERCLAP.[23] If Harris's obliteration campaign against Berlin hadn't worked in 1944, why would it work in 1945? But that was not all. There were other issues at stake, namely the Eighth Air Force's reputation and historical legacy.[24] 'We will,' Doolittle continued, 'in what may be one of our last and best remembered operations regardless of its effectiveness, violate the basic American principle of precision bombing of targets of strictly military significance for which our tactics were designed and our crews trained and indoctrinated.' Leave area bombing to those who believe in it: the British. If the Americans had to take part in THUNDERCLAP, Doolittle concluded, let them be assigned 'precision targets of military significance'. This appeal to conscience almost certainly had some impact, as Spaatz refused to even address it. 'Hit Berlin,' he wrote back, 'whenever [weather] conditions do not indicate the possibility of visual bombing of oil targets but do permit operations to Berlin.'

Doolittle, under a direct order, prepared every available bomber for a 2 February raid on Berlin. Heavy clouds over the capital led him to cancel it, but that night, the weather began to clear up. Doolittle knew what he had to do, but he tried once again to get Spaatz to change his mind. 'Do you want,' he cabled Spaatz, 'priority oil targets hit in preference to Berlin if they definitely become visual? Do you want center of city in Berlin hit or definitely military targets, such as Spandau, on the Western outskirts?'[25] Spaatz called him within the hour and made it clear. He told Doolittle to bomb oil 'if visual assured'; otherwise he had to bomb 'Berlin – center of [the] city.'[26]

When Doolittle's bombers were finished with Berlin, one of the dead was Roland Freisler, fanatical communist turned fanatical Nazi, representative at the Wannsee conference on the final solution, and president of the People's Court. He had sentenced Hans Scholl, Sophie Scholl, and Christopher Probst (all of Munich's White Rose anti-Hitler resistance movement) to death by guillotine. He had done the same to dozens implicated in the 20 July 1944 plot against Hitler. During the bombing, a collapsing beam crushed him. At the time of his death, Freisler was clutching the file of 20 July resister Fabian von Schlabrendorff. His death, a Foreign Office official noted in his diary, 'aroused considerable excitement in Berlin and is regarded as an act of just retribution for the revolting manner in which he conducted the case against the July 20 accused.'[27]

The February 1945 raid on central Berlin was a turning point in the bombing war. It was the moment, as historian Donald L.

Miller observes, that the Americans definitively crossed the moral threshold between the incidental and the intentional killing of civilians.[28] But it remains all but unknown outside a small circle of military history aficionados because it was displaced in collective memory by a larger and more devastating raid that month, one in which the Americans also took part: Dresden.

On 13 February 1945, at 19:57, a single wooden aeroplane, a Mosquito, took off from a barren airbase in Lincolnshire, in the north of England.[29] It joined 244 heavy, bomb-laden Lancasters in a formation on its way to Saxony.

At 22:06, radios crackled across the baroque city of Dresden. The bombers were there.

At 22:13, the first Lancasters were over the target area, which took in the entire old city, having its northern border just over the Elbe in the Neustadt and its southern border before the main station. The main station itself was outside the bombing area.

The bomb bays were opened. Thousands of high explosives hit the city centre at once. Roofs were blown off; windows shattered. The interiors of churches, museums, palaces, and apartment blocks were exposed.

A few seconds later, tens of thousands of four-pound incendiary bombs were dropped, landing in exposed corridors, concert halls, and living rooms. Beds, chairs, and paintings began to burn. The fires crossed the floors and climbed the walls. They exited through the windows.

After fifteen minutes, the first wave of bombers left the city.

By 23:00, the firefighters were losing control of Dresden. The entire old city was in flames. In the cellars and air-raid shelters below, tens of thousands of civilians, including many refugees, cowered.

At 01:20, a second wave of bombers arrived. They were meant to target the old city, but since it already was a raging inferno, they dropped their bombs instead on the southern edges of the inner city, hitting the city's Great Garden where Dresdeners were seeking refuge.

After the second bombing, the city was doomed. The fires leaped out of windows and open roofs. In the narrow streets of the city centre, fires from buildings on either side, searching for oxygen, merged in the centre, creating a ceiling of flames. It then began to move towards the ground. The fires from the fourth, third, second, and ground floors joined in the centre of the street. Still craving oxygen, the flames moved through the streets at breath-taking speed.

As in Hamburg one and a half years earlier, hundreds of these fires converged in the centre of the old city. They had nowhere to go but up. A great column of flames shot into the sky, setting off a process that created another firestorm. Dresden was dying. On the street, winds reached ninety-five miles an hour. People struggled against them, went mad, and were sucked into the flames.

By 01:40, anyone left in the cellars was dead or close to death.

But it was not over. On 14 February, the Eighth Air Force hit the city. Its aiming point – insofar as a visual raid was possible – was the centre of the city.[30] Dresden was to be another Berlin. What they in fact bombed was the Friedrichstadt station and marshalling yards in the suburbs, to which inner-city residents had fled the night before. 'It was,' historian Frederick Taylor writes, 'as if the enemy had anticipated the Dresdeners' every move, and then killed them like cattle cunningly driven into holding pens.'[31] Or at least twenty-five thousand of them.

The raid on Dresden was quickly followed by attacks on other cities. On the night of 14 February, Bomber Command attacked the centre of nearby Chemnitz, with little success.[32] The railway remained unscathed. In two days, Bomber Command had flown 1,522 sorties and dropped 5,256 bombs on the centres of German cities.[33] On 15 February, the Americans – diverted by bad weather from oil attacks on Leipzig – made a second, unsuccessful, raid on Dresden's marshalling yards. Just over a week later, Harris sent his bombers to Pforzheim. The attacks of 24–5 February destroyed 83 per cent of the city's built-up area and killed 17,600 people – 20 per cent of the city's population. '. . . That whole place,' Harris bragged at the next air commanders' conference, 'has been burned out. This attack has been what was popularly known as a deliberate terror attack.' Bomber Command, he continued has 'now destroyed 63 German towns in this fashion'.[34] A week later, on 1 March, Harris sent 478 bombers to obliterate what was left of Mannheim.[35] The next day, 858 aircraft hit Cologne. A 'carpet of bombs' spread right across the city. 'It was the end of Cologne.'[36] When the American ground troops took the city four days later, they cleared more than four hundred bodies from the streets.[37]

After Berlin, just as the precision-bombing campaign that the Americans had doggedly supported for years approached the threshold of success, they succumbed to the self-fulfilling logic of terror bombing: if destruction fails to deliver victory, as it had in Berlin, its failure was answered with more destruction. Arnold wrote again to Spaatz and urged him to organise 'widespread simultaneous attacks' by massive numbers of bombers. Operation CLARION called for a 'coordinated attack' against transportation targets by 'all available American Air Forces'.[38] Their aiming point would not be Germany's rail nexuses or even large railway stations in major cities. Rather, it would be untouched transportation infrastructure in 'undefended or lightly defended targets': small towns and villages. Waves of bombers and fighters would, taking advantage of Allied air superiority, fly in low and cover the train stations – and much around them – with bombs and bullets. 'The destruction of facilities with all means available, using bombs and machine guns and NAPALM where warranted.' The absence of significant flak or fighter defence and low-altitude attacks would allow heavy and light-medium bombers to open up 'tremendous machine gun power . . . for strafing'. The aim of all of this? Morale, this time of railway workers: 'As a result of continued pressure against transportation objectives, morale of railway employees is known to be infirm at best and it may well be that repeated attacks using all forces available will result in mass desertion from work.'[39] The raid would 'bring home the effects of the war upon German industry and people as no other method could do', pushing them perhaps 'over the brink'.[40]

When Spaatz passed the order on to Doolittle and Eaker, both objected. Oil targets should be bombed, not railway workers. If executed, Eaker wrote Arnold in an emotional letter, the plan would 'absolutely convince the Germans that we are the barbarians they say we are, for it would be perfectly obvious to them that this is primarily a large scale attack on civilians . . . . Of all the people killed in this attack over 95 percent of them can be expected to be civilians.'[41] As Spaatz had done over THUNDERCLAP, Eaker appealed to the Eighth's historical legacy: 'We should never allow the history of this war to convict us of throwing the strategic bomber at the man in the street.' Brigadier General Charles Cabell was blunter: 'This is the same old baby killing plan of the get-rich-quick psychological boys, dressed up in a new Kimono. It is a poor psychological plan and a worse rail plan.'[42]

It went ahead anyway. On 22 and 23 February, thirty-five hundred bombers and a thousand fighters prowled the territory of the Reich, bombing and strafing railyards, train stations, bridges, grade crossings, motor vehicles, and canal barges.[43] American losses were light, totalling no more than a few bombers.[44] Anything that moved was a target.

When the reports came in, the results were, or should have been, predictable: morale was not affected, transportation not significantly disrupted, and repair crews not overwhelmed. Many towns were hit heavily, including – to the Eighth's embarrassment – Stein am Rhein in Switzerland, killing sixteen people.[45] The raids did destroy much rolling stock and permanently lowered throughput capacity at several mail rail lines, but, as a US air forces study concluded, the attacks were spread out too thinly over too great an area to have any decisive effect on German troop or goods movements.[46] It is not clear what the Americans were thinking when they launched Operation CLARION, or what they expected it would achieve. A concentrated raid or a series of raids would have had a greater impact – and killed fewer people. At a press conference, air force officials put the best face they could on it by stating that they could not destroy the morale of the Germans because it had already been destroyed.[47]

On the day before Operation CLARION was launched, Brigadier General George McDonald wrote an extraordinary letter to Anderson. McDonald was the USSTAF's intelligence director, with his fingertips on the latest information concerning German oil, fighter, and broader industrial production. 'This [30 January] directive puts,' he wrote, 'the American Army Air Forces unequivocally into the business of area bombardment of congested civilian populations . . . . no intelligence available to this Directorate indicates that destruction of these three cities will decisively [a]ffect the enemy's capacity for armed resistance . . . . Nor can the elusive, if not illusionary target of morale justify the importance accorded these cities. The desideratum of morale attack is revolt. All authorities are agreed that the German people are powerless if not actually disinclined to revolt against the present controls.'[48] Referring obliquely to Arnold's (and to a lesser degree Spaatz's) frustrations with German resilience,

McDonald added that, if the Eighth's previous bombing theory and practice had been proved ineffective, 'we should face the issue squarely . . . abandon all other target priorities . . . and settle wholeheartedly to the extermination of populations and the razing of cities.' McDonald followed the directive's claims to their logical conclusion: 'If such a practice is sincerely considered the shortest way to victory, it follows as a corollary that our ground forces, similarly, should be directed to kill all civilians and demolish all buildings in the Reich, instead of restricting their energies to the armed enemy.'

In one line, McDonald cut to the heart of the contradiction of area bombing. Opposition within his own air forces, and Swiss outrage over the bombing of its territory, led Spaatz to pull back.[49] On 1 March, he cancelled the repeat of Operation CLARION, planned for 3 March, and directed his troops to bomb oil targets and Germany's rail system, and to provide support to advancing Allied troops. A new directive stated that only military targets were to be bombed.[50] As ever in the case of American bombing, intention fell well short of execution. In late February and early March, the Eighth bombed with radar guidance the 'communication centres' of (that is, train stations and rolling stock in) Munich, Leipzig, Halle, and Chemnitz. As the stations are in the centre of the cities, civilian casualties were inevitable.[51] Over March and into April, the Americans continued bombing oil targets, jet aircraft production, and jet airfields – classical precision targets where reasonable precision was possible – but also marshalling yards and rail stations, mostly using H_2X – where it was not.[52] The March 1945 campaign against German military bases included barracks, and they involved the area-bombing mix of 60 per cent incendiaries and 40 per cent high explosives.[53] And, as ever, long-suffering Berlin was shown no mercy: on 26 February, the Eighth bombed the Schlesischer Bahnhof (today, the Ostbahnhof), Berlin North station (the Nordbahnhof), and Alexanderplatz – the first two were set among dense residential neighbourhoods, and the last is the historic core of Berlin.[54]

The area bombing techniques tested over Berlin and multiple small towns in Germany would be perfected over Japan. After years of preaching, and at least trying to practise, the merits of precision bombing, the Americans launched their own carpet-bombing campaign, with murderous effect.

24

TO BOMB JAPAN

American military planners developed concrete plans for bombing Japan rather late in the day. The idea that bombs could be thrown at Japanese cities was not itself new. Following Japan's devastating 1923 earthquake, during which fires killed some 140,000 people, informed Americans knew of Japan's vulnerability to flames.[1] But the proponents of bombing Japan were generally civilians. Billy Mitchell was one of the few military exceptions: he visited the country in 1910, while stationed in the Philippines, and in 1924 the army dispatched him to the Pacific, where he produced a report over three hundred pages long.[2] It predicted in broad outlines a Japanese air attack on US forces staged in Hawaii and highlighted the possibility of lighting Japan's wood-and-paper cities on fire. Being Billy Mitchell, he was not shy about making his conclusions public. Japan's cities, he commented publicly, erected of 'paper and wood and other inflammable structures', amounted to 'the greatest aerial targets the world has ever seen . . . . Incendiary projectiles would burn the cities to the ground in short order.'[3]

As tensions with Japan rose, both members of the public and the *bien pensant* looked to air raids as a weapon against a potential enemy. In 1935, the *New York Times* – quoting a Soviet general – claimed that three tons of bombs could destroy Tokyo.[4] After Pearl Harbor, the occasional call became a chorus as American journalists screamed for the vengeance bombing of Japanese cities.

US planners took little notice, and the few military voices in favour of firebombing Japan were still exceptions. Bonner Fellers, a student attending the army's Command and General Staff School, wrote a paper praising the 'tremendous striking power of an air force directed at the paper cities of congested Japan'.[5] Fellers was not, however, in what was then the US Army Air Corps, and the only early airman of note who supported area bombing was General Claire Lee Chennault. Chennault was a romantic figure, a lover of impractical proposals, and an erstwhile supporter of precision bombing. From the later 1930s, he became – with a convert's usual zeal – an advocate of firebombing Japanese cities.[6] Armed with visions of 'burn[ing] out the industrial heart of the Empire with fire-bomb attacks on the teaming bamboo ant heaps of Honshu and Kyushu', he urged Arnold, Roosevelt, and anyone else who would listen to set Japanese cities on fire.[7] Roosevelt, quickly forgetting his 1939 appeal to spare civilians, loved the idea. Stimson hated it, but in any event it got nowhere, as Arnold and the airmen were then committed to precision bombing.

The question for the US air forces, as it had been over Europe, was how to precision bomb. Its tacticians did not start thinking seriously about bombing Japan until 1943, and when they did, they turned to the toolkit they had built up in Germany. In March 1943, Arnold ordered the Committee of Operations Analysts (COA, which itself had been created the preceding year) to specify targets in Japan. Clearly echoing earlier British plans, the COA's November report specified precision targets but opened the door a crack to area ones. The former would be shipping, aircraft, and steel; the latter would be urban areas.[8] A few months before the COA report, the Combined Chiefs of Staff outlined the broader tactical framework: the latter report, entitled 'Air Plan for the Defeat of Japan', was based on the neutralisation of Japan's air force, the destruction of its aircraft industry, and the reduction of Japanese naval and shipping resources to the point at which US forces could invade and occupy the country.[9] The proposal for area bombing Japan continued to circulate – using the COA work as a basis, Arnold prepared for the First Quebec Conference (QUADRANT) a proposal (also called 'Air Plan for the Defeat of Japan'), which included the tortured phrase 'the dislocation of labor by casualty', but at this point in the war American moral objections to bombing civilians still applied.[10] The COA reaffirmed this position as late as August 1944, when it concluded, based on German evidence, that the 'economic consequences [of area raids on Japanese cities] are not likely to be large', and that the air forces should replicate their successful European campaign against precision industrial targets in Tokyo, Kobe-Osaka, and Nagasaki.[11]

In the pre-1945 air war over Japan, the same ideas – developed at the Air Corps Tactical School by its own graduates, and through the Air War Plans Division (AWPD) 1 and 2 reports – were applied by the same men.[12] Chief among these was Haywood S. Hansell. Hansell was an old Maxwell Field lecturer, one of the authors of AWPD-1, and a firm advocate of precision bombing. Arnold established XXI Bomber Command – which would bring the air war to Japan – on 1 March 1944 and placed Hansell in charge. Following the well-established playbook, XXI Bomber Command would precision bomb by day.

Bombers require runways, so the first job of the US Air Forces was to acquire airfields within range of the Japanese homeland. Unlike Europe, in which Great Britain quickly became an American aircraft carrier within easy reach of Germany, potential bases in the Pacific presented logistical nightmares. They (a) had to be carved of the wilderness, (b) were very far from Japan, (c) lay behind menacingly tall mountain ranges, or (d) were all of the above. One air force proposal was for a ring of airfields extending north and south of Changsha, China, whereas General Joseph Stilwell (in charge of US army operations in Burma, India, and China) proposed a combination of permanent bases near Calcutta, India, and advance bases along the Changsha–Kweilin (now Guilin, 500 kilometres to the south) railroad in China.[13] As an indication of the polycentric nature of planning in the US, General Kenneth Wolfe, project director for the development of the B-29, came up with a further option: shifting the advanced bases to Chengtu (now Chengdu).[14]

Wolfe's recommendation was an odd one, as Chengtu is some thousand kilometres west of Changsha. The Joint Plans War Committee pointed out that few of the planned targets could be reached from China, and a rare moment of agreement had both the army and navy opposing the plan.[15] The US Joint Chiefs of Staff, under pressure from Roosevelt, nonetheless approved it, and the air force prepared to launch its first bombing raids from Chinese bases on 1 May 1944.[16] Finally, the Combined Chiefs of Staff approved the basing of B-29s in the Marianas, which the Americans expected to capture in October. Later, further plans for bombing from the Philippines and from the Aleutians were also drawn up.

Much of this planning was pointless, as geography made bombing from China nightmarishly difficult. All necessary supplies – fuel, bombs, bullets, and parts – had to be flown two thousand kilometres from northern India across a supply line that included the Himalayan mountains, the highest in the world.[17] The Americans had little choice but to fly over the 'Hump' to supply the Chinese army, but it made much more sense – as the chief of the navy, Admiral Ernest King, argued – to organise the bombings from the Marianas. The pressure in favour of China was political: Roosevelt was determined to demonstrate his commitment to China, and he hoped the sight of bombers flying overhead would reassure Chiang Kai-shek.[18]

Under constant pressure from Arnold, the first B-29s were produced in June 1944. They were the largest bombers ever built. The three most noteworthy technological advances were pressurised cabins (so airmen did not suffer intolerable cold as they did over Germany), speed (up to 357 miles per hour), and range (up to 3,800 miles). General Wolfe wanted to begin with night-time raids, but Arnold, consistent with longstanding American policy, overruled him. 'The limited number of operations,' Arnold wrote, 'which can be conducted from your forward bases because of logistic difficulties make it mandatory that maximum results be achieved from each operation. This requires destruction of primary targets by daylight precision bombing .... [T]he entire bomber program is predicated upon B-29's deployment primarily as a visual precision weapon.'[19]

By the summer of 1944, Hansell was ready to bring the bombing war to Japan, and he did so from China. On 15 June, as Saipan fell, his forces launched the first bombing raid: a classic US precision attack on a steel mill on Kyushu, the most southerly of Japan's main islands. Following the logistical nightmare of flying fuel and bombs over the Hump (one sortie to Japan required approximately fifteen supply trips over the Himalayas), five dozen B-29s took off from China.[20] The raid was a disaster. Following a long and tortuous fuelling routine, only forty-seven bombers managed to drop their bombs, and most missed.[21] Seven bombers crashed, six of them because of weather rather than Japanese fighters.[22] The results were poor and the casualties high.

Arnold, never a patient man, was particularly disinclined to tolerate either. He had suffered three heart attacks. Allied armies were on French soil, heralding both an eventual end of the European war and the immediate end to the bomber dream: a defeat of an enemy through air power alone. The only guarantee of an independent post-war air force was through a decisive role in the defeat of Japan. To achieve this aim, Arnold dispatched Curtis LeMay to Japan, gave him Wolfe's job, and brought Wolfe back to the United States.[23]

LeMay was something of a kindred spirit with Arthur Harris. Like his British counterpart, LeMay was gruff, rude, and appeared to make scowling an art (in fact, Bell's palsy had left the corners of his mouth paralysed). Like Harris, his determination, focus, and capacity for hard work appeared to know no limits. And, again like Harris, seeming indifference to human casualties – in the Second World War and subsequent ones – suggested an immensely callous man.[24]

No two men are identical, and there certainly were contrasts between them. Even if we dismiss his comments in his memoirs on the gruelling human cost of war as one for the history books (an eye to which Harris, perhaps to his credit, certainly never had), LeMay did not support, as Harris certainly did, area bombing from the start. Until late 1944 / early 1945, LeMay was a strong supporter of precision bombing.[25] He had tolerated high US casualty rates in order to precision bomb at Schweinfurt and Regensburg by day (with real effect in the former), and his replacement of Hansell did not signal an immediate switch to carpet bombing. For all that, two facts made Harris and LeMay more alike than they were different. First, by 1945, both men were strong supporters of area bombing (the reasons for the shift in LeMay's attitude are discussed below). Neither Harris nor LeMay was the author of hugely controversial area bombing policies, but those policies would forever be associated with their names. Second, once they had been officially adopted, each pursued his version of area bombing with murderous zeal.

In June 1945, carpet bombing was still LeMay's future. At the outset of his command, he was as determined as Hansell to make precision bombing work, but he thought attempting to do so from China was absurd. The country was chosen for all the wrong reasons – because 'our entire Nation howled like a pack of wolves for an attack on the Japanese homeland' – and bombing from it faced insurmountable obstacles. 'It did not work. No one could make it work. [The whole proposal] was founded on an utterly absurd logistical basis,' LeMay later wrote.[26] He was right.

Fortunately for the American air war, the capture of Saipan made China-based bombing operations redundant. Hansell phased them out.[27] When he arrived on Saipan, US bombing infrastructure consisted of forty hardstands (where planes rested), a bomb dump (storage), and a small vehicle park.[28] The Americans would not be ready to launch raids from the Marianas until November, and when they were, they followed the European playbook. Led by pathfinders (one of LeMay's contributions, borrowed from Harris), the bombers would destroy Japanese aircraft production. As in Germany, wrecking Japanese aircraft production would eliminate Japanese air defences, which would in turn allow the Americans to destroy Japanese industry and, therefore, Japan's ability to wage war.

It did not turn out that way. After more delays due to bad weather and much fretting (none of it quiet) from Arnold, 111 B-29s, led by Emmett ('Rosy') O'Donnell took off from Saipan on 24 November 1944. Their targets were four aircraft engine plants and five aircraft assembly plants around Tokyo.[29] First on the list was the Nakajima plant at Musashino, in northwest Tokyo, responsible, along with another nearby plant, for between 30 per cent and 40 per cent of all Japanese combat-aircraft engines.[30]

The raid did not go well. Possibly with memories of dogfights with the Luftwaffe, the Americans had vastly overestimated the numbers of, and threat posed by, Japanese fighters. But they faced another enemy: the wind. As bombers – particularly those at the highest altitudes of 33,000 feet – turned over Mount Fuji, they were hit by a powerful drift in the direction of their turn.[31] It was a jet stream originating in northern Siberia and shooting over Japan at altitudes of thirty to forty thousand feet. A Japanese meteorologist had actually discovered the jet stream in the early 1920s, but neither the Japanese nor the American forces had paid any attention to it.

The airmen certainly did. As they turned back towards their target, the jet stream added 140 miles per hour to their speed, causing them to streak past their targets at 445 miles per hour.[32] Such a tempo rendered their Norden bombsights useless, and only 24 aircraft ultimately bombed within the vicinity of the air-craft factory – to no meaningful effect.[33] The airmen returned to a certain degree of glory – they had bombed Tokyo – and Arnold was pleased with the mission.[34] But they had encountered a new and unexpected challenge.

It was a challenge the American planners would never over-come, and it made high-altitude bombing impossible. 'Over Japan, at 30,000 feet,' recalled pilot John Jennings, 'the winds were from 150 to 200 miles per hour.[35] So if you were coming into the wind, you were probably going thirty, forty, fifty miles an hour over the target. You were over the target so long they could shoot the heck out of you. All right, so we could turn around and come in downwind. That was the answer. No: now you're going over 300 miles per hour (sometimes up to 500 miles per hour) and the Norden bombsight couldn't figure out when to drop those things. So . . . we were getting nowhere.'

Nor would they get anywhere. A 27 November follow-up attack on the Musashino plant was foiled by clouds, and mul-tiple bombing efforts in December had little effect.[36] The only exception was a 13 December raid on a Mitsubishi factory, during which 16 per cent of the bombs landed on target.[37]

It wasn't enough for Arnold, and he relieved Hansell of his command on 6 January. It came as a total shock.[38] Arnold replaced him with LeMay, who would define the last and most brutal phase of the American bombing war of Japan.[39]

Hansell was widely respected among both airmen and the higher echelons of the armed forces, but the airmen quickly came to view LeMay as the toughest commander under whom they had ever served.[40] He did not yell – indeed he spoke so softly that one had to move close to understand – but he drove everyone who worked under him.[41] LeMay ordered intensive training for all bomber crews; expanded his staff as more bombers came on-line; and redoubled the precision-bombing campaign.[42] The results were not obviously an improvement on Hansell's, and the cost was at times greater. In a milder Japanese repeat of the Schweinfurt and Regensburg raids, a 27 January raid on the Nakajima plant at Musashino met heavy Japanese resistance. As the pilots of the B-29s caught sight of the Japanese coast south of Hamamatsu, the Japanese air forces sent 350 fighters at them. Using aggressive methods – notably attacking from the front to avoid the rear gunners and shooting out of the cockpit – the Japanese brought down nine bombers.[43] Not a single bomb fell on the primary target, and only a few scattered bombs hit the secondary target.[44]

Following the raid, LeMay changed tactics. Decisively. He switched from high-altitude to low-altitude bombing: rather than opening their bomb hatches at between 27,000 and 33,000 feet, the airmen would do so at between 5,000 and 7,000 feet. Flak was much more accurate at that level, and the airmen put up predictable resistance. LeMay ignored it and indeed created a further risk for the B-29s: to make them lighter and faster, he removed the guns, ammunition, and gunners from them.[45] Finally, and most dramatically, he switched from precision to area bombing. The goal would be to burn out the core of Japanese cities and, in the process, to destroy Japan's capacity to wage war. LeMay had become Harris. If all went well, the Americans would inflict massive damage on Japanese cities, which would vindicate the US Army Air Forces as an entity, inflict irreparable damage on the Japanese economy, and force Japan to surrender without the need for what was believed to be a brutal and costly – above all in lives – invasion. LeMay would test these techniques and theories over the Japanese capital.

A CRESCENDO OF DESTRUCTION

In the first two weeks of March 1945, Harris launched a series of raids under the transportation plan, but he employed his old methods: destroy the city and with it, ideally, the railway station.[1] At the end of 1943, he had argued that 'the destruction of villages or even of small towns would contribute nothing to . . . destroying the whole organised system on which the German air effort depends.'[2] That was now forgotten. On 5 March, 683 aircraft dropped almost two thousand tons on the centre of Chemnitz, devastating the old town and surrounding neighbourhoods. The fires, which raged for hours, engulfed the railway station, but the Americans had already destroyed it two days earlier. On 7–8 March, Dessau was ravaged by bombs, with the centre, as usual, the target.[3] Three days later, Harris returned to the Ruhr. On 11 March, more than one thousand aircraft bombed the centre of Essen, causing great damage to the marshalling yards and the Krupp works, and killing some nine hundred people.[4] The next afternoon, a slightly larger force wrecked Dortmund. Five days later, it was Würzburg's turn.

On 16 March 1945, Herbert Oechsner had snuck back to his home in the city after having been evacuated weeks earlier. He lived in Grombühl, a drab working-class neighbourhood. His mother had many admirers, gave birth to two illegitimate children including himself, and was rarely at home. His grandmother raised him and his one-year-old brother, Peter.

A mile to the south, in a far more affluent part of town, Heinrich Giesecke was in his parents' apartment near the city's famous cathedral.[5] Heinrich's father had done well under National Socialism and could afford a large apartment on a desirable central street. In 1938, he had stood at the flat's front windows and watched Nazi thugs throw Jews and their belongings from the house across the street. It was Kristallnacht. On the night of Würzburg's destruction, he had just finished repairing the flat's windows, which had been blown out during an earlier raid.

A mile further southeast, Hans Heer, the fifteen-year-old son of a basket maker, was lying on his bed in this parents' third-floor flat. Over his father's objections, Hans worked at a nearby airfield, where he met members of the passive resistance. His other friends, living in a school next to his house, were an equally unusual group of people in Nazi Germany: the blind. One of the partially sighted residents from the school for the blind next door had brought some wine back from a nearby vineyard, and Hans had drunk too much. The room was spinning.

Several blocks away, an eleven-year-old boy, Heinrich Weppert, was playing with toys given to him by his landlord. Heinrich's life had improved under the Nazis. When Jews in a larger apartment in Heinrich's apartment block disappeared, Heinrich's family was able to move into it. The toys had likely been left by one of the deported Jewish children.

17:00: England

Air marshals announced the targets: Nuremberg and Würzburg. No. 5 Group had a distinguished history in the bombing war: the dambusters mission, attacks on Heilbronn, Darmstadt, Brunswick, Munich, and Kassel, and the lead formation in the 13 February 1945 raid on Dresden.[6] Around 17:00, 501 Lancasters and 227 Mosquitoes prepared for take-off.

The bombers did not take the most direct route. When they reached continental Europe, they followed a south-easterly course north of Reims towards the Vosges Mountains. From there, they went northeast, crossing the Rhine, which by then formed the western front. At Crailsheim, a smaller formation of 223 bombers – 212 Lancasters and 11 Mosquitoes – broke off from the main bombing stream and flew on to Würzburg; the rest headed towards what was left of Nuremberg. They bombed southern Nuremberg, including the neighbourhoods of Steinbühl, Lichtenhof, Galgenhof, St Leonhard, and the gasworks; 529 people were killed.[7]

At 21:20, the pathfinders flew over the red, peaked roofs of Würzburg. They dropped eighteen flares, which would guide the bombers over the town. These were quickly followed by the green and red markers, the 'Christmas trees', whose slow descent lit up the Würzburg night.

A few minutes later, hundreds of bombers passed over the compact town, and the bombs began to fall. In three waves, the RAF hammered Würzburg. The first wave dropped 300,000 four-pound incendiaries. They lit the place on fire.

The high explosives followed immediately. They landed in the area bounded by Neubaustrasse, Hofstrasse, Theaterstrasse, and Bahnhofstrasse. They crashed through the roof of the Rathaus, the houses in the Domstrasse (hitting but not collapsing the roof of the cathedral), and the rococo, stuccoed Falkenhaus on the Marktplatz. Würzburg exploded.

By 21:20, ten minutes into the raid, every single street in the city was in flames. The houses in the Spiegelstrasse, a few blocks north of the river, collapsed entirely; anyone who had not left the cellars died. At Würzburg's jewel, the Residence, the roof with its magnificent fresco over the grand staircase survived the bombardment, just as its architect, Neumann, had predicted in the 1740s (he had offered to fire a battery of cannons at the Residence to prove that the ceiling would hold), but the incendiary bombs set the building alight. The fires tore through the south-wing apartments and the regal rooms. They climbed the walls and covered the ceilings, destroying everything. Much of the drapery and furniture had been moved after an earlier bombing, but the ornately decorated mirrors in the Mirror Room remained. They shattered and fell. In the Green Room, the fires charred the walls, turning the green paint black. The rococo ceiling of the White Room burned, and the roof collapsed.

In the Domstrasse, right in the centre of the town, all of the houses were on fire. The flames from the two sides of the street met in the centre and created a fire tunnel between the cathedral and the Old Main Bridge. By morning, all of the buildings would be empty shells. Only the tall, thin Rathaus (built on the base of a fourteenth-century house), its medieval tower, and the adjacent buildings would eventually be restored. The cathedral itself survived the bombing (the roof would collapse a year later), but a high explosive crashed through the southeastern side. The fires consumed the gilded altar and Riemenschneider's Madonna.

The bombers had crossed the city in seventeen minutes. The raid was over. They had not lost a single aeroplane.

20:00: On the Ground

Radio stations across the city were interrupted. A voice announced, 'A large formation is heading towards our city. Seek shelter immediately!'[8] An entire city stood up. People grabbed their children, relatives, and suitcases, and they made for the cellars.

Herbert was in his apartment when he heard the alarm. He ran up the hill to a neighbour's allotment plot. He arrived at an old shed housing a table and several chairs. He was the first to arrive and claimed a chair. A few minutes later, the rest of his family, the plot's owner, and a sixth person, a woman from Herbert's neighbourhood, arrived. They sat and waited. A few minutes later, he looked out a window facing north and saw the Christmas trees cascading down over the city. Then the bombing began. Herbert heard a man shout, '*Würzburg brennt!*'(Würzburg is burning!) He heard the whistle of a high explosive and then, nothing.

A bomb landed not far from the shed, blowing a crater into the ground. The air pressure flattened all of the garden houses, killing most of the people inside them instantly. When the hospital attendants arrived, they saw a field littered with bodies, and they began the gruesome task of piling them up for transport. Then, one of the orderlies noticed something: a small body moving among the corpses. It was Herbert. They left to find a stretcher, or its equivalent. By the time they returned, he had vanished.

Half-conscious, he had started climbing up the hill, only coming to once he was well away from the bomb site. He continued to move away from the heat, following the taut wires (used for growing the grape vines) up the hill. Some three hundred feet away, there was a sports field used as an assembly point. As he approached it, he was spotted by two people at the northern gate. Herbert collapsed, and he was taken to a small dressing room. He asked after his family, but no one knew of them or their fate. He dropped in and out of consciousness – he did not know for how long – and was taken to the university psychiatric clinic on the Füchsleinstrasse which was used as an SS hospital. He spent a week in a dark cellar without medical attention. Kindly slave labourers gave him bread and moistened sugar. Several days later, an ambulance drove him to a mental hospital at Lohr am Main. American fighters were rumoured to spray the roads with machine-gun fire by day, so the driver took safer back roads.

Herbert's grandmother and brother had burned to death; she had pulled the child into her, and the two melted together. She was so badly burned that she could only be recognised by the pattern of her knitted vest, burned into her skin. His mother suffered severe burns on the lower half of her body and was evacuated. No one ever heard from her again.[9]

20:00: Central Würzburg

Heinrich Giesecke had spent the day with his great-aunt, helping to make her apartment habitable after the windows and doors had been blown out by a previous raid. He returned home and began working on the windows in his parents flat, which had also been blown out by earlier raids. When the pre-alarm rang out, he, his brother, and his mother left their flat. They had no confidence that their own cellar would survive the bombing, so they made for a public air-raid shelter in the Mainviertel, just below the Marienberg fortress, on the other side of the River Main, overlooking the city. As they were crossing the Old Main Bridge, the full alarm rang out; they heard the planes overhead and saw the pathfinders' markers. It was time to run. When they reached the air-raid shelter, there was only standing room.[10]

In the cellar, Heinrich heard a whistle, quickly followed by the great crack of an exploding bomb. And again, and again. Within a few seconds of the first bombs, one landed near the cellar's exit. The lights went out, although the emergency light held. People in the cellar huddled closer together and covered their ears. Dust and plaster covered them as the structure shook. Heinrich noticed that something was burning. The air temperature rose as fires licked the building, and then water began coming into the cellar. One of the city's main pipes had burst; they had to leave.

Soldiers in the shelter, without whom panic would surely have broken out, let people out in turns, opening the door and rushing small groups out as flames shot in. Heinrich protected his mother, his brother, and himself by soaking a blanket they had brought with them. They came out of the emergency exit and jumped through the flames. They slipped past two houses being consumed by the fires, and dashed past burning balconies and rubble towards the steps of the Tellsteige, a stone staircase leading up to the old fortress overlooking the city. The steps were burning and impassable. From there, Heinrich tried to catch his breath and looked back at Würzburg. It was an inferno: the roofs were on fire, and the smoke and flames covered the buildings right to the Main River. The fires sucked in oxygen, and Heinrich and his family had to fight the wind to avoid being pushed back towards the fires they had just escaped.

To avoid the burning fortress, they followed the city wall to the Neutor, a seventeenth-century gateway. Soldiers at the gate urged them through, warning of a nearby munitions dump threatened by the flames. They passed through the gate and on to Zellerau, an intact portion of the city on the other side of the fortress. At around 02:00, they reached a friend of their mothers; they were safe.

20:00: Southeast Würzburg

When the first alarm went off, Hans Heer was lying in bed, still ill from over-indulging in wine. He told his father to leave him in the apartment until the air-raid sirens stopped. He then heard an official warning: 'A large formation is heading towards our city. Seek shelter immediately!' His father frantically rang the doorbell; Hans needed no encouragement. He hit the floor running and hurried with his father into the air-raid shelter. He thought, *Jetzt ist Würzburg dran* ('Now it's Würzburg's turn'). The director of the school for the blind, two nuns, and all of the school's residents were in the cellar under his father's workshop, rather than in the cellar of the four-storey house. Hans's father thought it much better. If the building took a direct hit, they would die instantly. If a high explosive landed near the building and flattened it, there would be less rubble out of which to climb. In the latter case, the relatively small size of the structure meant they would not be deeply buried, so the cellar would be less likely to become their coffin. In the 30-square-yard room, they sat and waited for the bombs to fall.

When one of the first high explosives landed, the air pressure bent the cellar's large steel door. The sounds of exploding bombs and shattering buildings became louder. Everyone in the cellar began to pray, reciting a slight variation on a devotion to the Virgin Mary: '*Maria breit den Mantel aus, mach Schirm und Schild für uns daraus, lass uns darunter sicher stehen, bis alle Feinde vorüber gehen* [Mary, make your coat a shield, and let us seek shelter under it, until all enemies have passed over us]'. In the original, it is 'storms' rather than 'enemies'.

When the bombing seemed to be subsiding, Hans's father stepped out of the shelter. Everywhere there was fire, and the workshop itself was consumed by flames. He ordered everyone out. Rubble was strewn in front of the shelter's exit, and Hans, his father, and the school director had to help the blind over it. One by one, they came out into the yard, with fires all around them. After the last person was out, the workshop collapsed. They were in the garden behind the school; it was large and surrounded by an eight-foot wall. It sheltered them from the winds that, driven by the fire, raged through the dying city. There were two reservoirs in the garden, and nuns went back and forth dousing the school residents and everyone else with water. At 23:00, they heard an explosion:

Hans's house collapsed. They had to get out of the city. They followed Hans's father, a beneficent Pied Piper, single file, each holding another's hand, out of the burning town. They crossed a railway embankment nearby, walked along Fichtestrasse and Kantstrasse, which lead south out of the city, finally finding a vineyard shed. They stayed there until the morning.

20:00: *The Wepperts' Apartment*

When the first alarm went off, Heinrich Weppert, his parents, and his great-aunt rushed to the cellar; their confidence in Würzburg's immortality had been destroyed by earlier raids. Heinrich's cousin was with them. She was from Nuremberg, and she mocked them for running to the cellar; compared to the bombing in Nuremberg, she said, the raids on Würzburg were nothing. She stayed upstairs, but changed her mind before the first bombs fell.

In a scene that was repeated across the city, the first bombs knocked the cellar lights out. There were twenty people cowering in the cellar, and they pulled blankets over their heads to shield themselves from falling dust. Heinrich climbed into his mother's arms and stayed there during the first wave of bombing. As it seemed to let up, his father left the cellar to see what had happened. When he returned, he was ashen. The entire city, he said, was on fire, and there was no point in even trying to extinguish the flames. After hastily retrieving a few items from their apartment, he ordered the family to get out. Even his normally disagreeable cousin did not resist, and their neighbour followed them out. They arrived in the street relatively early, before the fires had reached their peak, and they ran down it, past the Gieseckes' house and towards the Rathaus. They turned to the river, but the narrow passage leading to the Old Main Bridge was by then blocked by flames. His father took them back towards the centre, but they were blocked by a great rush of people fleeing the city. They turned into the Augustinerstrasse, which led out of the city. Heinrich's father knew the cellars were linked through a series of passages that would be safer than the street. He was right: a short while later, the fires reached deadly temperatures, and the houses collapsed. His father led them into the first house's cellar, followed by his mother, his aunt, Heinrich himself, his cousin, and the neighbour. As they left the first house for the second, the cellar roof collapsed, killing the neighbour instantly.

They made it out of the houses in the Augustinerstrasse, through an archway and directly to the Main. His father led them down to the riverbank and followed the water. Houses collapsed around them, spraying debris onto the bank and into the river. When they reached the Löwenbrücke (Lion Bridge), they climbed the small steps onto the bridge. There was a great crowd of people on it; in its centre was a burned-out tram, and the tramlines had fallen onto the bridge. The crowds were convinced that the lines were still live, and each person gingerly stepped over them, bringing progress almost to a halt. When they finally reached the other side of the bridge, they saw an old maternity hospital that had been transformed into a military one. It was on fire, and the staff were throwing wounded soldiers, often with missing limbs, down to the street. Those running past were ordered to stop and help, but they ignored the command.

Heinrich's group moved past buildings that were also still burning, but less intensely as they moved away from the city. Once they passed Heidingsfeld, they met a driver from the fire service who agreed to bring them to Reichenberg (approximately twenty miles away) where Heinrich's uncles lived. Reichenberg was full of refugees eager to tell their stories, but Heinrich only wanted sleep. The uncles divided the family between them; it was finally over.

21:20: Würzburg

The city was an inferno. In the Ursulinergasse, a few minutes from the central Domstrasse, one woman took the fateful decision to leave the cellar in time and ran with her two children for the safety of the river or the country. As she did, she lost her grip on them, and the crowd behind her crushed them.[11] Gusti Schmitt was a young girl fleeing the city with her parents. As she climbed out of her cellar into the street, she saw a woman run past holding a burning package; another man tried to wrest it from her and she screamed, 'It's my child!' A few blocks later, she passed the school turned military hospital. A wounded patient's bandages had caught fire; he threw himself through the window, ran down the street, and died.[12] As in countless other cities, split-second decisions meant the difference between life and death. A wounded soldier, Karl-Heinz Wirsing, decided to seek shelter in neither the Domstrasse nor his military hospital, which was behind the cathedral.[13] He instead took the far riskier route across the Main and was let into a shelter near the Marienberg as the bombs were falling. It saved his life: no one came out of the Domstrasse or the Paradeplatz shelters alive.

The fires themselves tore through the streets, consuming everything in their paths. In the centre, near the Domstrasse, almost all of the houses had collapsed, leaving only mounds of rubble and sand. Everywhere else, only the façades survived. Thirty-five churches, all of the museums and monuments, the Residence, Rathaus, and the Marienberg fortress were destroyed.

The destruction of more than a millennium of architectural and cultural history took just over fifteen minutes. It was little more than a footnote in the bomber war; on that night alone, five other towns were bombed.[14] The Bomber Command Night Raid Report devoted five lines to Würzburg's obliteration. It noted that the 'intention was to complete the destruction of the built-up area and associated industries and rail facilities', a task that was 'practically completed'.[15] The report failed to mention that the Americans had already destroyed the railway on 21 February and that there were no industries of significance in the city.

The day after the attack, Hans Heer learned that his mother and sister were safe. His aunt, however, was not: her two-storey house had collapsed over her cellar, trapping her and everyone else inside. Across the city, the task of clearing the bodies began.

26

DESTROYING TOKYO

The ninth of March 1945 began as a sunny and pleasant day in Tokyo, but from the late morning its inhabitants noticed the wind beginning to pick up.[1] By late afternoon, gusts were sweeping through the capital's crowded streets, and clouds began pushing in overhead. By the evening, Tokyo was engulfed by a storm.

Curtis LeMay ordered the first of his B-29s to take off at 17:36. The great aeroplanes departed from Guam, Tinian, and Saipan.[2] Within two hours, some 334 bombers were in the air, racing at an altitude of three to four thousand feet towards the Japanese capital.[3] When LeMay told his airmen that they were coming in at this altitude, rather than the usual thirty thousand feet above the flak, some considered mutiny.[4]

As the bombers approached the mainland, picket boats recorded the convoy's arrival and sent frantic messages to navy receivers on the coast.[5] The navy relayed the warnings to the army, but the messages never came through. Winds of sixty to eighty miles per hour swept across the Kanto Plain, knocking down army antennae and playing havoc with military radar.[6] Japanese fighter defences, poor at the best of times, were paralysed, and the main Japanese fighter force in the Kanto area, No. 10 Squadron, remained on the tarmac as the Americans prowled the skies overhead.[7] At 00:30, two reports – one from the coast-watchers, one from Tokyo's Tsukishima (an artificial island at the mouth of the Sumida river) – finally reached the Eastern Army Command operations room, and the Japanese army announced to the country a major raid on Tokyo.[8] By then, the Americans' bomb bays were almost open.

At just before 01:00, the B-29 pilots pulled up on their sticks and ascended to their bombing altitude – seven thousand feet on average.[9] Their target was a compact, densely populated set of residential and industrial neighbourhoods north and northeast of Tokyo's Ginza district, then and now the city's main shopping and tourist area. Between 85,000 and 135,000 people crowded into each square mile, and buildings covered 40 per cent to 50 per cent of its surface area (the average for a typical American city at the time was 10 per cent). American versions of pathfinders, inspired by their British colleagues, had attempted to mark the area, without much success, with a large X. At 01:00, the Americans opened their bomb bays.

Five-hundred-pound clusters containing thirty-eight M-69 incendiary bombs fell from the planes in tight formations. At approximately two thousand feet, the clusters broke open, and the individual M-69s – steel pipes with a hexagonal section three inches wide by twenty inches long – scattered onto the buildings below. Some crashed through the roofs of the flimsy houses, hit the floor with a thud, and within a few seconds began spraying walls, furniture, and people with gobs of gasoline gel.[10] The gel burned and melted the skin of people it stuck to, and anything that could burn caught fire. Other bombs landed on roofs and sprayed their gel, sending flames spreading across the tops of the houses and climbing down the outer walls. Following government orders that all citizens protect their houses, families tried to douse the fires with sand, buckets of water, and wet blankets, but it rarely worked.[11] When it did, new fires soon replaced old: flames leaped from neighbouring houses and set the home ablaze again.

Miwa Koshiba was living in one of those houses in Asakusa, then a mostly working-class district with a large combined

Buddhist-Shinto temple, one of the most beautiful in Tokyo, at its core.[12] Along with the Honjo ward just across the river, it was the most densely populated district in Tokyo and was home mostly to industrial workers.[13] Miwa was unusual among her neighbours: she was the daughter of a wealthy industrialist named Koshiba, a name her husband, as custom dictated, took when they married. She had five children, three of whom she had evacuated from Tokyo plus two girls – a four-year-old and a baby – who stayed with her in Tokyo because they were too young to be without their mother. Her elderly parents were also living with her. In a move she bitterly regretted later, she had her husband bring her six-year-old son back to Tokyo on 8 March.

At the sound of the first bombs, Miwa rushed her children to the garden, in which her husband, following government directives, had dug a simple air-raid shelter not unlike those found in London and other British cities during the Blitz.[14] Leaving them there, he carried Miwa's mother while she helped her father. They led them to a local school and found them a spot to rest. Miwa's husband stayed with them, and she dashed back to the house.

It was gone: the fires had already burned it to the ground. In the garden, the small air-raid shelter was aflame; it had become a death trap. Horrified, she grabbed a bucket and doused the shelter, tore back the cover, and wrenched her children out. They were wailing in terror, and her son's face was badly burned. But they were alive.

Miwa pulled them to the street. The fires were gaining in intensity. Although the term firestorm is often used, the word has – at least for those knowledgeable of the science of fires – a very particular meaning. As seen in Hamburg, a firestorm occurs when the flames become so intense that the drawing in of oxygen produces storm-like winds as they rush to feed the fire. Flames from other, less intense fires follow the winds through the streets and, when they converge on a central point, shoot upwards into the sky. Hamburg was the clearest and most deadly instance, followed by Dresden, Darmstadt, and (to a lesser degree) Kassel. There was no firestorm in Tokyo in March 1945; rather, natural winds drove LeMay's fires forward, setting house after house, street after street, ablaze.

As Miwa and her children stepped out into the street, the flames were consuming Tokyo. As in Hamburg, split-second decisions determined life or death.[15] Those who huddled in their so-called shelters died of burns and asphyxiation. Those running in the streets faced brutal winds and flying debris. Everything was a firestarter. Sparks landed on government-recommended padded hoods (ostensibly to protect one's head and shoulders from burning cinders), setting them and the wearer on fire.[16] Mothers wrapped their babies with soft padding to protect them, and carried them – as was the practice – on their backs. Sparks lit the padding on fire, and before the mothers could react, the flames consumed their children. The wind carried burning planks through the air, which randomly and viciously planted new sprouts of flames, as if Ares himself was hurling lightning and fire at Tokyo's hapless citizens.[17] People dashed through the streets only to run into a wall of flame; they would turn around in retreat, only to see that another fire had followed them. They tried left, then right, but there was no escape. The fires converged on all sides and incinerated them.

Those who did escape, like Miwa, moved towards what they hoped was the safety of the Sumida river, which flows through Tokyo. On one side of it lies Sumida Park, a strip of greenspace no more than one hundred metres wide.[18] The desperate denizens of the neighbourhood pushed into the park and towards the water's edge. Some dived in to escape the heat and to soothe their burns. Biting cold replaced the searing heat (the water was icy), and they slipped under the surface and drowned. Crowds rushed towards the middle of the bridges at either end of the park. As more and more people drove themselves in, the inevitable fight for shrinking space began. Seeking relief, people climbed over the railings and clung to the sides, the deep water one hundred metres below them. As the fires raged on, the bridge's superstructure began to heat up, eventually to an intolerable degree. Those hanging onto the sides let go, plunging into the water, while the crowds on the bridge pushed others off.[19] Almost all met their deaths in the river.[20] By morning, hundreds of bodies were piled up along the banks, and hundreds floated down the river, following the path that thousands – possibly tens of thousands – had taken the night before.

When Miwa and her children reached the park, her heart sank. She saw no point in joining the death traps that were the water's edges or the bridges, so she pushed across one of the latter and sought the only safety she could find: a sewer pipe that emptied into the river. Even there, the heat was overwhelming, and her baby stopped breathing. She revived him, he breathed for a while and then stopped again – three times in total. She faced a horrible choice: watch her children die from the heat, or cool them the only way she could, with sewage water. She chose the latter, using a rag to bathe her children in a toxic mix of rain, faeces, and urine.

In Honjo (today, part of Sumida), Hidezo Tsuchikura was at home with his two young children.[21] He was a working man who had survived the Great Earthquake of 1923, during which a building collapsed on him. Before the air raid started, his wife and a new-born baby had moved to a safer, outlying area. As the first incendiaries landed, Hidezo made a quick, wise decision: defending his house (as the government had ordered Tokyo's residents to do) or sheltering in the garden would both mean certain death. Instead, he took his children to the only secure building in the neighbourhood, the Futaba Grade School.[22] It was a large, reinforced concrete building, one of the few concrete buildings in the area (indeed, in all of Tokyo). Hidezo was among the first to arrive there, and he took his children to the basement, which the authorities had designated as an air-raid shelter.

They were not alone for long. As the fires spread through the neighbourhood, more and more people made their way to the school. The basement was filling quickly, and Hidezo thought of the 1923 earthquake. Terrified of being buried alive, he grabbed his children and dashed to the school's swimming pool, hoping it would provide refuge. It too was full of people, so he went to one of the classrooms on the third floor. But, like the basement, they too were soon overflowing with people. His daughter, perhaps having inherited her father's sixth sense, begged for them to leave. Over the protests and warnings of others, he relented and took his children out of the room.

Outside, the scattered fires that had caused Hidezo to flee became a great wave of flames rolling from the Sumida to the school. People ran down the street, screaming. Some dashed into the school, only to dash out again. Others exploded in flames like human torches. 'The whole spectacle,' Hidezo later remarked, 'with its blinding lights and thundering noise reminded me of paintings of purgatory – a real inferno out of the depths of hell itself.'[23]

As he came out of a stairwell onto the roof, luck was again on this very lucky man's side: there was a water tank on the otherwise barren roof. He and his children made a dash for it.[24] As they took shelter against its cool walls, sparks set his daughter alight. He patted her down but then heard his son screaming: he was now on fire. Hidezo plunged him into the tank, threw his daughter in next, and jumped in after them. They cooled themselves as the conflagration raged around them.

* * *

The next morning, Miwa was still in the sewer with her children.[25] She could no longer see: the hot winds had sealed her eyelids together, blinding her. Several hours passed before other refugees from the fires found her as they exited the sewer. They took her by the hand and led her to a shelter – she could later not remember where – at which she was given rice and a clean cloth to wash her face and eyes. Partially recovered, she took her children back towards the Sumida, attempting to cross back into Asakusa to find her parents. The first bridge she tried was the Kototoi, not far from the small, narrow park to which she and her children originally fled. The bridge was blocked: it was piled high with the bodies of those who had burned, suffocated, and been crushed.

She tried again to make the crossing later that day further upstream, and found the Hajima Bridge unobstructed. But again she could not cross: it was still searing hot, and she had lost her shoes in the fire. She retreated and dug around the corpses until she found shoes that would fit her. Then she, her daughter, her burned son, and her gasping baby crossed the bridge. No one took notice of their misery as there was nothing unusual about it on that Tokyo morning.

Moving through her old neighbourhood was tortuously difficult. A thick haze hung over the city, and streets were strewn with burned-out cars, bomb canisters, charred wood, stone, and bodies. In the districts further away from the air raid's aiming points, the dead were unrecognisable. Blackened bodies covered the streets. A small, charcoaled baby lay dead on its back with the mother a few inches away, her face pressed down as she died gasping for air.[26] The fires in many cases burned the flesh off their victims, leaving only skeletons.[27] Still more intense fires had transformed people into the shrunken lumps of charcoal found in Hamburg's streets almost two years earlier.[28] When the winds came, these latter victims disintegrated into the air, a scene that was almost a funerary ritual for those who had died so horribly.

After three days of her slow struggle, much of which involved finding food and water for her children and trying unsuccessfully to find ointments for her son's burns, Miwa found her parents. Miraculously, they were alive. But now her son was ill with a severe fever. They had to get out of Tokyo. After more struggle and much delay, Miwa, her parents, and her children boarded a packed train heading west that inched its way along tracks recently cleared of debris. They all seemed to be safe.

But it was not to be. Before they could reach Gifu hot springs, in the centre of Japan, far from Tokyo, and with moist air to heal their lungs, her elderly mother had a fatal heart attack. Then, having fought a fever for hours, her young son died in her arms.[29]

Three days earlier, on the morning of 10 March, Hidezo and his two children were still huddling in the water tank on the roof of Futaba School. As dawn broke, they climbed out and met another twelve or so people who had joined them on the roof. They pulled open the door that separated them from the floors below. Smoke billowed out. Below them, throughout the classrooms, in the swimming pool, and down the corridors through which they had passed a few hours earlier, everyone was dead. Fires had shattered the school's large windows, setting books, desks, and walls alight. Like many others, the government-recommended shelter was a death trap. 'The entire building,' he recalled,

> had become a huge oven three stories high. Every human being inside the school was literally boiled or boiled alive . . . . Dead bodies were everywhere in grisly heaps. None

of them appeared to be badly charred. They looked like
mannequins, some of them with a pinkish complexion.
But the swimming pool was the most horrible sight of all. It
was hideous. More than a thousand people, we estimated,
had jammed into the pool. The pool had been filled to the
brim [with water] when we first arrived. Now there wasn't
a drop . . . only the bodies of the adults and children who
had died.[30]

The great Tokyo raid, eclipsed in the public memory by the
horrors of the atomic bombings and Dresden, was the single most
devastating conventional raid in history. Approximately 100,000
people died in a single night – four times as many as the highest
(reliable) estimates for the Dresden attacks and higher still than
the immediate casualties of the atomic bombings in Hiroshima
and Nagasaki (that is, without including those who later died of
radiation poisoning and cancer). The winds did most of the work:
the bombers set the city's paper and wood buildings on fire, and
the storm carried the flames from house to house, street to street,
Tokyoite to Tokyoite.

Curtis LeMay was delighted with the results, and he immediately sent a report on them to Arnold.[31] 'The heart of the
city,' his diary notes, 'is completely gutted. It is the most devastating raid in the history of aerial warfare.'[32] LeMay quickly
followed up on the raid with similar ones. On 11 March, XXI
Bomber Command attacked Nagoya. LeMay hoped to expand
the conflagration by avoiding dropping bombs on areas that
were already burning, so he doubled the space between bomb
drops from 50 to 100 feet.[33] The effect was the opposite: fires
consequently remained isolated, and a better organised fire
department – aided by more firebreaks, fire-resistant buildings,
and adequate supplies – was able to keep them that way.[34] The

effect on production was minimal.[35] But so was the cost to the Americans: only one aeroplane was lost.

LeMay did not make the same mistake twice. On 13 March, he set his dogs on Osaka, bombing, as in Tokyo, in close concentrations. The only difference between these two raids was that LeMay armed his rear gunners for the Osaka attack and ordered them to take out Japanese searchlights. Heavy cloud cover foiled this plan, but it made little difference. Blind bombing destroyed eight square miles of the city, killed three thousand Japanese people, and cost the Americans only two bombers.[36]

Kobe was next. On 16 March, 325 B-29s dropped more than two thousand tons of bombs – another record – on a densely populated section of the city.[37] The incendiaries destroyed three square miles of the city, killed eight thousand people, and left 650,000 homeless.[38] The fifth and final raid was a return to Nagoya on 19 March. LeMay, having learned his lesson the first time, ordered a much more concentrated bombing. It did the job, burning out three square miles of the city.[39] A day after the attack, smoke from the fires remained so intense that photographing the extent of the damage was impossible.[40]

After the second Nagoya raid, LeMay had all but run out of incendiaries, and he paused his carpet-bombing campaign. In the UK, the equivalent would be the loss in ten days of half the surface area of London, Birmingham, Manchester, Leeds, Bradford, Liverpool, and Sheffield. Taking the German comparison, American air forces inflicted, at almost no cost to themselves, much more damage over five raids than that suffered by the most heavily bombed German cities. Overall, these few raids inflicted approximately 41 per cent of the *total* destruction meted out against German cities over the entire course of the war.[41] Arnold was deeply impressed and – like Harris before him – seduced by the image of an entire city being obliterated in a single air raid.[42]

* * *

In April, the Americans – partly due to a shortage of incendiaries, partly because old habits do die hard – returned to precision bombing, with daylight and night-time attacks on Japan's aircraft industry.[43] These raids, and above all daytime precision raids, all but knocked out two engine factories and scored direct hits on 70 per cent of the overall Japanese aircraft industry.[44] But this return to earlier ideals and strategies did not signify an end to area bombing. In mid-April, US air forces relaunched the incendiary campaign, destroying 240,000 structures and wiping out 22 square miles of Tokyo, Kawasaki, and Yokohama, in that order of devastation.[45] During the following month, the Americans dropped 15,500 tons of bombs on three major cities – Nagoya, Yokohama, and Tokyo – and 1,800 on secondary targets.[46] On the final incendiary raid on Tokyo, flames consumed the Imperial Palace. The Americans had not intended to destroy the Palace, and there has been some question about whether the bombing was accidental, but the debate seems misplaced: when you light a city on fire, it is futile to hope that you can control the direction of the flames.

As summer 1945 arrived, all pretences of pursuing anything resembling precision bombing had been abandoned. The Americans were deliberately and systematically burning out one Japanese city after another. In the month of May, the US air forces threw 71 per cent of their bombs at cities, compared to 6 per cent against airfields, 6 per cent against oil facilities, and 4 per cent against aircraft plants.[47] In June, B-29s pounded Osaka repeatedly, as well as Kobe. By the middle of the month, the Americans had destroyed 102 square miles of Japanese cities: half of Tokyo, more than half of Kobe, a third of Nagoya, and a quarter of Osaka.[48] The ratios, as well as the results, would have made Arthur Harris proud.

The costs of the American campaign, calculated in shattered buildings and destroyed acres of land, have been noted. The human costs were stunning: over three months, American bombs killed as many as 250,000 Japanese civilians – a figure well higher than the initial death toll after the atomic bombings.[49] The human costs to the Americans were very low, which in part explains the appeal of the strategy. Whereas tens of thousands of British, Commonwealth, and American airmen died over Europe, the figure over Japan was in the hundreds. Overall, 243 US airmen lost their lives. Exactly that many Americans had died during a single bombing raid on Berlin in 1943.

By the summer of 1944, Japan's empire was collapsing; the home islands were surrounded and blocked; its air defences were all but non-existent; the Americans were masters of its skies. An invasion could not be far off. The Japanese government, dominated by the military and steeped in a culture that valued conformism over all else, had to decide how to respond. It was a debate in which an unlikely figure would play the decisive role.

27

DOUBTS

On 6 March 1945, ten days before the destruction of Würzburg, Richard Rapier Stokes, a decorated First World War hero and devout Catholic, stood up in the House of Commons. He read from the *Manchester Guardian*: 'Tens of thousands who lived in Dresden are now burned under its ruins. Even an attempt at identification of the victims is hopeless. What happened on that evening of February 15? There were one million people in Dresden, including six hundred thousand bombed-out evacuees and refugees from the east. The raging fires which spread irresistibly in the narrow streets killed a great many from sheer lack of oxygen.' Stokes went on to quote from the 17 February dispatch of Associated Press reporter Howard Cowan: 'Allied Air Chiefs have made the long-awaited decision to adapt deliberate terror bombings of German populated centres as a ruthless expedient to hasten Hitler's doom. More raids such as those carried out recently by heavy bombers of the Anglo-American Air Forces on residential sections of Berlin, Dresden, Chemnitz and Kottbus are in store for the Germans for the avowed purpose of heaping more confusion on Nazi road and rail traffic and to sap German morale.'[1] Cowan's source was an 'off-the-record' SHAEF press briefing in Paris by C. M. Grierson, an RAF intelligence officer.[2] Grierson described air force plans to bomb large population centres and, afterwards, to block relief supplies.[3]

Grierson's statement, Stokes continued, was widely broadcast in America and in Germany but not in the United Kingdom.

'Is terror bombing,' Stokes demanded of the government, 'now part of our policy? If so, why was this declaration from S.H.A.E.F issued for publication and then suppressed? If it is not part of the policy, why was the statement handed out at all? And why is it that the British people are the only people who may not know what is done in their name? . . . I think we shall live to rue the day we have done this and that, in many ways, it will stand for all time as a blot upon our escutcheon.'[4]

About this time, Violet Bonham Carter, the daughter of First World War Prime Minister H. H. Asquith and graduate of a Dresden finishing school, marched up to 10 Downing Street and demanded to speak with Churchill. The young Churchill had been a Liberal cabinet minister under her father. She rounded on the prime minister, who quietly took it in, for the bombing of Dresden.[5]

While the storm was brewing, Harris continued his work. In March 1945, the month of Würzburg's destruction, Harris dropped sixty-seven thousand tons of bombs on Germany. It was the largest monthly tonnage ever dropped on the country, and only slightly less than the total dropped between 1939 and 1941.[6] All of the cities listed in Harris's 1 November appeal to Portal had been heavily bombed, and most were thoroughly destroyed. In the last weeks of the war, Harris returned to the Ruhr. Essen was blasted for the last time, and, on 12 March, eleven hundred RAF bombers dropped five thousand tons of bombs on Dortmund, wiping what was left of that city off the map. Four days later, it was Würzburg's turn. From 1 to 27 March, Harris area bombed thirteen cities with more than a thousand tons of bombs on each raid. During the same period, the Eighth Air Force dropped 40 per cent of its bombs on rail targets, 13 per cent on oil, and the rest on jet, vehicle, tank, and U-boat production. The Fifteenth Air Force dropped 60 per cent of its bombs on marshalling yards and 25 per cent on oil. March 1945 was thus the peak of the bombing offensive in Europe.

On 28 March 1945, Churchill penned a memorandum for General Ismay, his chief of staff. 'It seems to me,' wrote the prime minister,

> that the moment has come when the question of bombing
> of German cities simply for the sake of increasing the
> terror, though under other pretexts, should be reviewed.
> Otherwise we shall come into control of an utterly ruined
> land . . . . I am of the opinion that military objectives must
> henceforward be more strictly studied in our interests
> rather than that of the enemy.
>
> The Foreign Secretary has spoken to me on this subject,
> and I feel the need for more precise concentration upon
> military objectives such as oil and communications behind
> the battle-zone, rather than on mere acts of terror and
> wanton destruction, however impressive.[7]

The war was coming to an end, and Churchill-the-commander was giving way to Churchill-the-historian. The prime minister was capable of great emotion, and he did feel genuine regret over Dresden's destruction. The memo was nonetheless a calculated effort to distance himself from a bombing war that he had long, if somewhat erratically, supported.

And it infuriated Harris. Bottomley sent him the note the next morning. The allegations of terror were an 'insult to both the Air Ministry's bombing policy and to the way Bomber Command had executed it'. The destruction of German cities had fatally weakened the enemy, and only it was allowing the armies such an easy walk across Germany. Unless it could be clearly shown that bombing would neither shorten the war nor save Allied lives, it had to continue. Playing off Bismarck's line that Eastern Europe was 'not worth the bones of a Pomeranian grenadier', Harris wrote: 'I personally do not regard the whole of the remaining cities in

Germany as worth the bones of one British grenadier.'[8] Then, all guns blazing, Harris heaped contempt on those who were, possibly strategically, becoming sentimental about Dresden: 'The feeling, such as there is, over Dresden could be easily explained by a psychiatrist. It is connected with German bands and Dresden shepherdesses. Actually, Dresden was a mass of munitions works, an intact government centre, and a key transportation point to the east. It is now none of those things.'[9]

Harris's description of Dresden was hardly an accurate one, but he nonetheless had a point. Dresden was no different from dozens of other German cities that had been destroyed. It had dozens of small industries and – more importantly – it was part of a central rail system linked with Berlin and Leipzig.[10] A precision raid on the railyards would have been logical and consistent with the transportation plan.[11] But the raid was not a precision attack; it was an obliteration raid. And it echoed around the world not simply because of the city's exceptional baroque beauty ('Florence on the Elbe'), although that was certainly part of it. The destruction of Dresden was a window onto the broader area-bombing campaign. It brought home to people, in a way that dozens of euphemism-ridden official reports could not, what the RAF had been doing to Germany since Hamburg in 1943 and particularly since 1944. It was a raid like any other, not a 'raid too far', and for this reason it was the beginning of the end of Harris.

Harris's angry reply eventually harmed him more than Churchill, but in the short term, it did its job. Churchill withdrew the memo and issued a more anodyne version on 1 April:

It seems to me that the moment has come when the question of the so called 'area bombing' of German cities should be reviewed from the point of view of our own interests. If we come into control of an entirely ruined

land, there will be a great shortage of accommodation
for ourselves and our Allies; and we shall be unable to
get housing materials out of Germany for our own needs
. . . . We must see to it that our attacks do not do more to
harm ourselves in the long run than they do to the enemy's
immediate war effort. Pray let me have your views . . . .[12]

Ten days later, Harris was at the SHAEF conference. There, he
proposed another raid, this time on Potsdam. The seat of Frederick
the Great and home to fine architecture had made it to that point
in the war largely untouched. Under Harris's plan, bombing would
destroy the city's rail facilities and military barracks. Tedder
thought there wasn't much point; they weren't important enough
to justify even a precision raid. In addition, Soviet High Command,
which was closing in on Berlin, might have a view on the matter.
Tedder told Harris to clear it with the Chief of Air Staff.

On 12 April, Spaatz and Bottomley, after consulting Tedder,
issued Strategic Directive No. 4, the final one of the war. It placed
aid to the land campaign at the top, followed by oil, enemy communications, the Luftwaffe, and U-boats. The catch-all category
of 'important industrial areas' was not listed.

Two nights later, without consulting Portal, Harris ordered a
strike on central Potsdam. RAF bombers flattened portions of the
old city centre and killed as many as five thousand people.[13]

One hundred and twenty-five miles to the south, in Dresden, communications were still functioning. Despite the February raids,
Dresden's railway stations were still running. In the largest single
raid launched on the city (counting the two British raids in February
separately), the Americans attacked them. At a cost of four to five
hundred civilian lives, they took these targets out for good.[14]

THE LONG ROAD TO A
JAPANESE SURRENDER

On the morning of 18 March 1945, a diminutive man with a slight stoop stepped gingerly through the ruins of a shattered Tokyo accompanied by a small coterie of staff.[1] It was the 43-year-old emperor of Japan, Hirohito. That he was in Tokyo at all was note-worthy. The Japanese army had urged the emperor to join princes already cloistered in provincial palaces, in order to protect him but also to neutralise him politically.[2] He refused and steadfastly insisted on remaining in the centre of a capital that was turning to ash and dust all around him. Surveying the endless destruction, it should have been clear to the emperor that there was no hope for a Japanese victory.[3] The Americans had driven Japan's army from all but a handful of occupied territories,[4] destroyed its navy, surrounded the country in preparation for a naval blockade, and obliterated its cities. The war was lost.

The problem was that his military refused to see what should have been obvious to all. Japanese militarists believed that there was a strategic case for continuing the war. American tolerance for casualties, they maintained, was far lower than their own. If Japan were to marshal all remaining military and human resources for a final battle, it would impose such punishing losses on the Americans that the invaders would pause, allowing the Japanese government to negotiate a satisfactory peace. The pro-jected – and accepted – costs of testing that theory were enor-mous. From above, 5,350 planes, when not hidden under trees or camouflage nets, would launch suicide missions on American ships, including troop transports and landing barges, killing as many soldiers as possible.[5] From below, tiny suicide submarines armed with two torpedoes each would attack US vessels, while suicide frogmen would detonate explosives against the ships' hulls.[6] The Americans who survived would face broad columns of Japanese soldiers ready to fight viciously and to the death in order to stop the American advance; behind them, Japanese civilians stood ready to turn their wrecked cities into battlegrounds. The militarists were happy to see tens of millions of their fellow citizens die in the process.

This cadre's political power was formidable. Japan had been a military dictatorship since 1937. The country was run nominally by a cabinet headed by a prime minister, but the military could veto the prime minister's appointment and effectively exercised complete control. There had been sixteen prime ministers since the war, and each of them had every reason to tread carefully. In 1935, a lieutenant colonel, brandishing his sword, executed the director of the Military Affairs Bureau at his desk. And, in 1936, junior officers of the First Army Division launched a mutiny. They slaughtered the finance minister, the Lord Keeper of the Privy Seal (and former premier), and the inspector general of military education. Another three, including future Prime Minister Suzuki, survived, though just barely. When soldiers broke into his house on 26 February, he at first tried to temporise but eventually gave up: 'Kill me, then!' he shouted, and the troopers dutifully sprayed him with bullets.[7] Miraculously, the doctors saved him.

As the prime minister's power shrank, so did that of the Diet, which was often little more than a rubber stamp for decisions made by the military. The Privy Council, once a powerful group advising the throne, was consulted only after major decisions had already been made.[8] The Cabinet remained in theory the core of the Japanese government, but its role was passive rather than active: the military reported its decisions to the Cabinet which, in turn, ratified them.[9] The role and precise power of the emperor himself was a matter of much controversy (more on this below), but his formal role resembled that of a constitutional monarch in Westminster democracies: able to advise and nudge but otherwise unable to make any consequential decisions himself. At the same time, the monarch enjoyed such widespread and intense veneration that his every utterance carried – literally, as he was defined as one – the power of a god.

In the emperor's case, the truth, as so often, was somewhere in the middle. If the analogy of a constitutional monarchy implies too little power, that of a deity (though, again, it was no analogy for the Japanese) implies too much: the mystique of an emperor flowed partly from the fact that he was 'above politics'. Indeed, even in moments of intense national crisis, his advisers hesitated greatly before bothering Hirohito with such trivial matters as coups and attempted assassinations. This veneration of imperial authority laid the foundation for a theory of false consciousness: if the emperor did not support the army's position, he failed to understand his true preferences because treasonous advisers were providing him with false information and flawed arguments.

Beyond the army, there were two other loci of power. The first was another advisory group, the *jushin*, made up of seven senior statesmen – Hiranuma, Hirota, Wakatsuki, Okada, Konoe, Tojo, and the former Lord Keeper of the Privy Seal, Makino. The jushin advised the government on policy and appointments. Their influence was real, as demonstrated by their role in Tojo's downfall (though Tojo, once deposed, joined them as a former prime minister). But in early 1943, they were no springboard to peace. Three weeks before Tokyo's destruction, Hirohito consulted them. Amid falling bombs (air raids interrupted the meeting), all of these statesmen bar one urged continued prosecution of the war.[10] The only exception was Prince Konoe, who saw two threats to the imperial structure: an American invasion from without and a Communist revolution, with which he was rather obsessed, from within.[11] In a 14 February 1945 written report to the emperor, he made this case and urged Hirohito to purge the military of extremists and to sue for peace. The emperor demurred.

The second locus of power was the Supreme Council for the Direction of the War, an inner cabinet known as the 'Big Six', created by the previous prime minster, Koiso, on his July 1944 appointment.[12] The Council was broadly divided between a peace lobby and a war lobby, though it leaned towards the former in July 1945, thanks to its new titular head, Prime Minister Kantaro Suzuki. Suzuki, a hero of the Russo-Japanese War who, against all odds, led a charge against the Czarist fleet off Tsushima,[13] was in his seventy-eighth year. He had done everything he could to avoid becoming prime minister, nominating Prince Konoye (a dove) and resisting his own nomination until the Lord Keeper of the Privy Seal, Marquis Koichi Kido, invoked imperial authority to persuade him.[14] Modest, gentle, deaf in one ear (which, along with his tendency to doze off, caused him often to miss key points in cabinet debates), and paralysed by a fear of assassination, he made an unlikely Arthurian figure in Japan's hour of need.[15]

A less qualified, though by no means less morally compromised, member of the peace lobby was Foreign Minister Shigenori Togo. Togo enjoyed the double distinction of being the man who plunged Japan into war (albeit with reluctance) and then sought desperately to get the country out of it.[16] He was a man of a keen mind and intellectual bent and, like a few others in that category, found it difficult to conceal his contempt for those less cerebrally inclined. In a country in which niceties are respected with time-honoured thoroughness, he was aloof and had little time for sensitivities in personal interactions. Added to the mix was a dogmatic streak and venomous, eloquent attacks on those with whom he disagreed. They caused, as one observer put it, 'his friends much embarrassment and his enemies much pain'.[17] In a culture that emphasised consensus above all else, and in a government in which pressure against raising one's head above the parapet was overwhelming, Togo was the man for the moment.

Admiral Mitsumasa Yonai, an ardent critic of war with the United States and widely regarded as pro-American, was with Togo the second anchor of the peace lobby.[18] Strikingly handsome as a young man, a weakness for whisky and an officer's typically sedentary life had left him with a bulging red nose and sagging skin, with large pouches under his eyes.[19] His love of drink, however, reflected a love of life, and a warm smile quickly swept any first-impression apprehensions aside and attracted many people to this decent man. A favourite of the jushin, Koiso appointed him to the post of navy minister after Tojo's July 1944 downfall, and he acted, again with the jushin's strong support, as a sort of deputy prime minister, one intent on making peace. Although he shared nothing of Suzuki's wavering indecisiveness, he shared with the old man a target on his back: 'death,' writes author William Craig, 'lurked in the barracks, in the officer's club, [and] in the hearts of young men unable to comprehend defeat.'[20] He too had to be cautious and to move only when the moment was right.

Against Togo, Yonai, and Suzuki stood three military members – the other half of the Big Six. The most powerful among them was General Korechika Anami, minister of war and spokesperson for the army.[21] He was a stubborn man: he only entered the Imperial Japanese Army Academy on his fourth attempt, and this experience instilled in him a lifelong determination not to give up. But he was not a fanatic. In 1926, he was made an aide to Hirohito, and as such he became close with Marquis Kido, who later became

Lord Keeper of the Privy Seal and the emperor's closest and most influential adviser. Anami's desire to drive a middle path between the disputing factions in the Imperial Army, one he had pursued since the 1930s, made him acceptable to both the peace and war factions following the collapse of the Koiso government. A daily intake of five cups of sake aside, he was no bon vivant. He had a rather bland personality; his real passion was kendo. His interaction with younger officers was gentle to the point of being paternal. But on one issue his stubborn side asserted itself, and he would not be moved: there would be no surrender without one final battle. On this point, his obstinacy was Hitlerian.

At Anami's side stood his implacable chief of staff, General Yoshijiro Umezu. A product of the fanatical Kwantung Army, he – like Tojo – had been at the centre of the Japanese army's imperialist drive into China in the 1930s. His manner was gruff and his appearance stark; his shaven head and menacing eyes reminded his enemies of Benito Mussolini.[22] He was an easy man for the Allies to hate. Superficially, his attitude to war was more flexible than that of his boss: he understood the country was heading for defeat and wanted peace with 'honour', which meant substantially better terms than those that would be offered at Potsdam. In practice, this meant no peace at all.

The sixth member of the Council and the third member of the war lobby was Navy Chief of Staff Admiral Soemu Toyoda, a beefy man with a pockmarked face, a fiery sense of nationalism, and a legendary hatred of foreigners.[23] His appointment was the product of a spectacular lapse of judgement on Navy Minister Yonai's part. Perhaps allowing himself to be blinded by the common clan and home region the two men shared, Yonai thought that Toyoda would lean towards peace and nudge Umezu in the right direction. He could not have been more wrong. Although his navy rested at the bottom of the sea, a testament to the overwhelming power of the Americans, Toyoda threw his support fully behind the army. Worse still from Togo and Yonai's perspective, Toyoda was reasonable, eloquent, and persuasive, and he dissected his opponents' pacifist arguments point by point.[24] Yonai had not empowered an ally but, rather, created a great obstacle.

These six men, prodded and cajoled by the jushin, decided Japan's fate.

Potsdam and Moscow

From late June 1945, in its indefatigable fight against the facts, Tokyo looked to Moscow in the hope that Stalin could serve as an intermediary between Japan and the Western Allies. This was of course sadly deluded, but the sentiment was genuine enough at the time. On 30 June, Togo sent a proposal to Ambassador Sato in Moscow for 'firm and lasting relations of friendship' with the Soviets; Molotov, as Sato predicted, 'swirled to the tunes of diplomatic evasion'.[25] On 7 July, the emperor also raised the possibility of Soviet mediation.[26] Suzuki and Togo agreed that Prince Konoe, as a former prime minister, would be the best choice, and they sounded him out the next day.[27] On 12 July, Togo sent a note – duly intercepted by the Americans – to Sato in Moscow stating that the 'Emperor was greatly concerned over the daily increasing calamities and sacrifices faced by citizens of the various belligerent countries', that it was 'His Majesty's desire to see the swift determination of the war', and that Hirohito wished to send Prince Konoe as a special envoy to Moscow.[28] Thus, an unlikely ambassador – Konoe was paranoid in his fear of a Communist revolution in Japan – would try to reach an unlikely peacemaker: Stalin. Sato, the actual ambassador in Moscow, viewed these efforts as pointless and absurd, and he urged Tokyo to surrender unconditionally.[29] No one listened.

As Togo's message was travelling from Tokyo to Moscow, the president of the United States was travelling from Washington to Berlin. On 16 July, Truman toured the devastated capital by car. He felt no sense of triumph. On the contrary, shells of buildings and acres of rubble, the blackened and deformed trees, and the long, haggard faces of a thoroughly beaten people left him more depressed than he had been in a very long time.[30] 'I thought of Carthage, Baalbek, Jerusalem, Rome, Atlantis, Peking . . . [of] Rameses II . . . Sherman, Jenghiz Khan [sic],' he wrote in his diary. 'I hope for some sort of peace – but I fear that machines are ahead of morals by some centuries and when morals catch up there'll be no reason for any of it.'[31] The urban analogies were more apt than Truman realised: that day, at 13:29 Berlin time, as Truman was viewing the city, the Americans successfully tested the atomic bomb at Alamogordo Army Air Base in New Mexico. On the same day, Arnold gave Spaatz overall command of the US Army Strategic Air Forces in the Pacific – the same job he had in Europe – and Doolittle brought the Eighth Air Force to bases in the Philippines and Okinawa.[32] Precisely the same men who had opposed area bombing over Germany, always rhetorically and mostly (until the war's last months) in practice, were helping to pursue it with a vengeance over Japan.

The meetings of Truman, Stalin, and Churchill took place in Potsdam's Cecilienhof, the vast, neo-Tudor summer palace of Crown Prince Wilhelm of Prussia. In one of history's ironies, Potsdam, a garrison city and symbol of Prussian power, had escaped the war in much better shape than Berlin, the city of Jews, gays, workers, and artists. The conference work involved much recognition of facts on the ground. If Yalta, with its infamous 'spheres of influence' decision, anticipated and endorsed Europe as it would be, Potsdam accepted Europe as it was. With a few exceptions (northern Norway, Austria), the Soviet Union would colonise all the countries they had, in quick succession, liberated and then subjugated. Polish and Soviet troops were at the Oder and Neisse rivers, and Germany would lose all territories to the east of them. Poland itself lost land in the east when the Soviet Union retained most of the territory it had seized in September 1939 in its pact with Nazi Germany. Millions of Germans were trekking westwards as they fled the rampaging Soviet army, and the Polish and Czechoslovakian states were actively expelling millions more. In a bit of bureaucratic tidying up, the three leaders agreed on both the Oder-Neisse line as Germany's eastern border (supposedly temporary and subject to a final peace settlement, but in practice permanent) and to the 'orderly and humane' transfer of the Germans from Eastern Europe.[33] In the latter, they created an infrastructure that (although individuals involved did their level best) ensured that the expulsions would be neither orderly nor humane.[34]

The only forward-looking element in the Potsdam conference was the green-lighting of the atomic bomb. Truman received a full report on the bomb's destructive power on 21 July, and the next day, he agreed to make Hiroshima the first target. The intentions behind the bomb are subject to much conspiracy and myth-making: was it an act of revenge for Pearl Harbor, a grisly, mass medical experiment on human subjects, or an effort to intimidate the Soviet Union? The Americans' intensions were in fact more prosaic: they hoped that the shock of achieving with one plane and one bomb that which had required hundreds of bombers and thousands of bombs (over Germany from 1943 and Japan from 1945) would tilt the balance within the Japanese government in favour of surrender.[35] Stimson persuaded Truman to spare Kyoto – 'a shrine of Japanese art and culture' – but failed to persuade him to relax further the unconditional surrender requirement in order to send a stronger signal that the emperor would be spared.[36] Compared to Germany, the surrender requirement had already been relaxed, something for which the Americans rarely get credit: on 8 May, Truman included in his call for a Japanese surrender some reassurances regarding the emperor, and it was possible to read them into the Potsdam Declaration itself.[37] Any further step in this accommodationist direction would have faced not only Secretary of State James Byrnes's opposition but also that of the American public: only 7 per cent of Americans, according to Gallup, believed that the Japanese imperial system should be retained, and one-third thought Hirohito should stand trial as a war criminal.[38]

American moral agonising over the atomic bomb began only after it had been dropped. At Potsdam, there was a consensus among the US team – Byrnes, Stimson, Marshall, Leahy, Arnold, and Truman himself. American conventional bombers had destroyed city after city in Japan and deliberately killed hundreds of thousands of Japanese. The atomic bomb was an extension of, rather than a radical departure from, this strategy. Moreover, the US investment of two billion dollars towards developing the bomb made it unthinkable not to use it. Indeed, an understanding that the bomb, once developed, would be used was 'embedded in the shared understanding of Roosevelt and those directing the Manhattan project'.[39]

'Using' did not, however, necessitate dropping it on a major city. It was theoretically possible to use the bomb without killing anyone by exploding it, for instance, at sea. But that possibility had been considered and rejected months earlier. An interim committee of eight civilian officials, appointed by Stimson in May to advise him on the bomb, gave 'ten minutes' of consideration to using the first bomb in a casualty-free demonstration in order to concentrate Japanese minds; the second bomb would only be used on a Japanese city if the country's leaders still failed to surrender.[40] The committee rejected the proposal on various practical grounds, and it referenced the firebombing of the Japanese capital: '. . . would the bomb cause any greater loss of life than the fire raids that had burned out Tokyo?'[41] As in Berlin in February 1945, crossing one moral line makes it easier to cross another, and, in war, killing some civilians makes it easier to kill more. For his part, Truman was particularly haunted by the spectre of massive US casualties following an invasion, as well as by the reaction of the American people to them. '. . . how could a President . . . answer to the American people,' writes historian David McCullough, 'if when the war was over, after the bloodbath of an invasion of Japan, it became known that a weapon sufficient to end the war had been available by midsummer and was not used?'[42]

Some observers have attributed the bombing to baser motives – above all, anti-Asian bigotry.[43] To be sure, mercy and pity for the nation that had precipitated Pearl Harbor, the Bataan death march, the murder of POWs, and kamikaze attacks were in short supply in July 1945. There is also no doubt that the decision was taken against a backdrop of deep anti-Asian racism in the United States, expressed in, among other forms, harsh restrictions on Asian migration and the internment of Japanese Americans. It was a time in which many forms of prejudice – against Asian Americans, Jews, African Americans, and gay Americans – was far more intense than it is today, and this sentiment may have hardened the American heart further against pity towards Japanese civilians. But the fact of these sentiments does not prove that racism underpinned the decision, and the documentation on American decision-making in the lead-up to Hiroshima suggests strategic motivations. Similarly, strategic considerations overruled any racial preference the Americans had for north

Europeans. By the end of the war, Americans were deliberately killing large numbers of German civilians – often Germans with identical names and similar ancestries to the Americans themselves – with equanimity. Overall, the Allies killed more Germans than they did Japanese, and had the atomic bomb been available a year earlier, the first target would have been a German city.[44]

By late July, the pace of events was quickening. A day before the Potsdam Declaration, Emperor Hirohito decided definitively in favour of peace: he summoned Kido, expressed his opposition to the army proposal for a final battle, and urged him to help achieve peace with the Allies.[45] Peace, but not capitulation: had the emperor then ordered the government to surrender, all the horrors of the coming two weeks would have been spared.[46] But he did not. On 26 July, Byrnes and Truman released the Declaration:

> The time has come for Japan to decide whether she will continue to be controlled by those self-willed militaristic advisers whose unintelligent calculations have brought the Empire of Japan to the threshold of annihilation, or whether she will follow the path of reason . . . .
>
> We do not intend that the Japanese shall be enslaved as a race or destroyed as a nation, but stern justice shall be meted out to all war criminals, including those who have visited cruelties upon our prisoners. The Japanese Government shall remove all obstacles to the revival and strengthening of democratic tendencies among the Japanese people. Freedom of speech, of religion, and of thought, as well as respect for the fundamental human rights shall be established . . . .
>
> We call upon the government of Japan to proclaim now the unconditional surrender of all Japanese armed forces, and to provide proper and adequate assurances of their

good faith in such action. The alternative for Japan is prompt and utter destruction.

The response in Tokyo amounted to a shrug. As the Japanese had seen their cities obliterated on a single night by fleets of American bombers, and as the atomic bomb was unimaginable before Hiroshima, Tokyo presumably thought that the Americans were threatening more of the same. And more came. On 1 August, US bombers burned out 80 per cent of the city of Hachioji (twenty-three miles west of Tokyo), 65 per cent of Nagaoka (on the west coast of Honshu), 65 per cent of Mito (sixty miles northeast of Tokyo), and a staggering 99.5 per cent of Toyama (also on the west coast of Honshu).[47] In public, the army assured Japanese radio listeners that the Americans meant more firebombs (how this was reassuring to the residents of the country's razed cities was the Japanese army's secret). As the Americans had lied about not wanting to hurt civilians when they claimed that 'since bombs do not have eyes, we cannot tell where they will fall', they were, the army continued, lying about a more devastating attack.[48]

In private, the reaction was more complex, but barely so. Foreign Minister Togo, a dove, urged acceptance of the terms, and he made much of the semantic distinction between 'the unconditional surrender of Japan' and the 'unconditional surrender of Japanese forces'.[49] According to one source, he also argued that the American public, tired of the bloodshed, was clamouring for peace.[50] Such an argument would hardly sway the militarists, since putative American war exhaustion was exactly why they wished to carry on. In the event, the government responded with a semantic disaster. The Council begrudgingly agreed to a compromise in which they would 'ignore' the proclamation rather than publicly denouncing it.[51] The Japanese verb used was *mokusatsu*, meaning both (a) 'to remain wise in inactivity' and (b) 'to take no notice of; to treat with silent contempt'.[52] Prime Minister Suzuki most likely meant the former, but when – perhaps in another mental lapse – he suddenly declared, 'we will *mokusatsu* [the Potsdam Declaration]', at a press conference, journalists understood the latter. On 30 July 1945, Japanese newspapers defiantly reported that the government could not even be bothered to reject the Proclamation.[53]

Newspapers around the world republished the Japanese press's slanted interpretation of Suzuki's remarks.[54] Stimson was among the millions reading them. If the Potsdam Declaration was 'unworthy of public notice', he wrote after the war, then the United States 'could only proceed to demonstrate that the ultimatum had meant exactly what it said: . . . the inevitable and complete destruction of the Japanese armed forces and just as inevitably the utter destruction of the Japanese homeland.'[55] Perhaps more damningly, this silence in response to the declaration occurred against the backdrop of other words, namely communications between Togo and Ambassador Sato, intercepted by the Americans, which made it clear that (a) there was no consensus in the Supreme Council in favour of surrender even if the emperor were retained and (b) that all the Japanese were prepared to consider at this late date was a Soviet mediation to secure terms favourable to Japan and unacceptable to the Americans.[56] The die was cast.

On 6 August 1945, a lovely summer morning, at 08:15, a 'shattering flash of light, brighter than a thousand suns' engulfed Hiroshima.[57] The lucky, those close to the epicentre, were vaporised; all that was left of one man on a stone bridge was his shadow etched in the stone, one foot in the air and pulling a laden cart.[58] People located one mile or more away from that point had their skin stripped from their bodies, leaving them in agony, their pink muscles exposed.

The skin of others remained on their bodies but burned to a dark brown or black hue, and they died in agony – sometimes over minutes, sometimes over hours.[59] Men, women, and children threw themselves into whatever water they could find, flailing madly with swollen faces grimacing in pain. Burned and bloody children cried out for their mothers in vain desperation as they slowly died. People still further out from the point of impact appeared to have survived unscathed, but they were the walking dead. Within days, they too died, vomiting blood. Some of those who survived were left horribly deformed: horrendous burns, missing limbs, fingers fused together. A single bomb had taken the horrors of Hamburg, multiplied them with sheer force, and added the sickening and torturous effects of radiation poisoning. Dante could not have conjured up such a perfect image of hell.

The reaction in Tokyo to the greatest instance of destruction the world had seen was muted but evolving. The first response was confused and delusional. 'A small number of enemy B-29s,' a Japanese army communiqué noted on 7 August, 'penetrated into Hiroshima and dropped a small number of bombs', a new 'parachute . . . bomb and it appears to explode in the air'.[60] Only the army could see a silver lining in the atomic bomb, and it did: the Americans must be desperate to end the war to use such a weapon.[61]

The second reaction was silent and inert. On the same day as the communiqué, Togo reported Truman's comments on Hiroshima to the Cabinet: 'We have spent two billion dollars on the greatest scientific gamble in history – and won. [If the Japanese] do not now accept our terms they may expect a rain of ruin from the air, the like of which has never been seen on this earth . . . .'[62] In response, the government did nothing. 'The Army,' Togo wrote in his memoirs, 'obviously intended not to admit the nature of the atomic attack, but to minimise the effect of the bombing.'[63] This formulation implies that Togo himself was entirely in favour of unconditional surrender, but contemporary documents present a less clear picture. He told the Cabinet that the bombing was a 'serious violation of international law', the merits of which evidently the Japanese had belatedly discovered, and he recommended that Japan register a strong protest with the International Red Cross.[64] Togo also continued to press Sato on the prospects for Soviet intervention.[65] The Cabinet, in the end, did nothing.

The third reaction was inspired: Togo appealed directly to the emperor on the evening of 8 August, arguing that the atomic bomb meant that it was 'all the more imperative that we end the war'.[66] The emperor's reply has generated much controversy in the relevant historiography, and it has been cited to prove both (a) that the atomic bomb and *not* the Soviet Union's declaration of war on Japan led Tokyo to surrender and (b) that the Soviet Union's declaration of war and *not* the atomic bomb led Japan to surrender.

The difference of interpretation turns on whether Hirohito was urging Togo to reach out to Moscow or to Washington. He was doing neither. He in fact said: 'In order to obtain more favourable conditions, we should not miss a chance to terminate the war. We must consult [on the] terms ["*(joken wo) so-dan suru*"]; we should avoid the situation where we cannot come to an agreement.'[67] Historian Sadao Asada translated the relevant phrase – *(joken wo) so-dan suru* – as 'bargaining' and then asked the obvious question, 'with whom?'[68] Asada answered this question by putting words into the emperor's mouth – or, rather, brackets between the emperor's words: '[with the Allied powers]'.[69] Historian Tsuyoshi Hasegawa responded to this interpretation by pointing out that Tokyo was not bargaining with the Western Allies over anything on 8 August 1945, and that Japan's only bargaining partner was the Soviet Union.[70] Thus the brackets should rather read '[with the Soviet Union]'.[71] If 'consult' rather than 'bargain with' is the correct translation, then the debate collapses: the emperor wanted clarification on what the Declaration actually meant – above all, one can reasonably hypothesise, for the imperial structure that was his main concern and that of everyone else in the Supreme Council and Cabinet.

During all of these debates, before and after Hiroshima, the firebombing continued apace. Indeed, LeMay greatly feared that the atomic bomb would reduce, as it certainly did, the credit post-war observers would give to his area bombing campaign in defeating Japan. In the eleven days between the Potsdam Declaration and Hiroshima, over ten thousand Japanese died under American incendiary bombs. To much greater effect, LeMay also continued aerial attacks on shipping and railroads, a campaign that reached its climax from late June to August 1945. The Americans' bombing and mining campaigns resulted in the loss of 459,000 tons of shipping, a figure well above the losses (46,000 tons) due to submarines.[72] US bombers pursued the Japanese mercilessly. After mines had chased the Japanese from the East China Sea, the Americans began mining Korean ports and destroying Korean rail lines.[73] The effect was devastating. At the time, the seemingly endless bombing raids added to the impression that the atomic bombs reflected continuity in, although certainly an intensification of, the challenges facing Japan.

Early the next morning, government ministers awoke to a new challenge: the Soviet Union, despite the ongoing negotiations and despite the Soviet–Japanese Neutrality Pact, had declared war.[74] Within an hour of Molotov's declaration of war on 8 August at 23:00 Tokyo time, Soviet armies had punched through the Manchurian border.[75] Under the weight of this massive, well-planned, and well co-ordinated assault, Japanese troops, denuded by transfers to the homeland, fell back on all fronts.

News reached Tokyo within a few hours, first via a Soviet radio broadcast at 04:00.[76] At 05:00, the Cabinet Chief Secretary rushed to Suzuki's residence to report the Soviet declaration of war.[77] At 07:10, a call came through the Ministry of War: there was to be an emergency meeting of the Supreme Council.[78] At roughly the same time, Togo called senior Foreign Office officials to his home. Whatever lingering hopes he might have had were definitively gone. He and his officials agreed that the war had to be ended immediately, with only the preservation of the national policy – that is, the emperor – as a condition.[79] Togo then raced to Suzuki's home and urged him to surrender: 'Because the Soviets have now joined the war, I think it is necessary for us to decide to terminate the war quickly.'[80] He made the same argument to Navy Minister Yonai, likely an easy sell, and the emperor's younger brother, Prince Takamatsu.[81]

The emperor was next. At 09:55, Kido had the first of several meetings that day with Hirohito.[82] Hirohito was now more definitive. Against the backdrop of the Soviet invasion, the emperor urged Kido to speak with Suzuki about 'a plan to save the war situation'.[83] As if on cue, Suzuki arrived ten minutes later. Kido passed those views on to the prime minister: the war was to be ended immediately by accepting the Potsdam Declaration.[84] Suzuki agreed to emergency meetings of both the Supreme Council and Cabinet as well as consultations with the jushin.[85] At Suzuki's request, the Supreme Council convened at 10:30 on the morning of 9 August 1945. The emperor's intervention pushed the prime minister, at least temporarily, into the peace camp. Citing Hirohito's views, he opened the meeting with the following plea: 'I believe that we have no alternative but to accept the Potsdam Proclamation, and I would now like to hear your opinions.'[86] No one replied. At last, Yonai broke the silence. 'We're not,' he observed, 'going to accomplish anything unless we speak out. Do we accept the enemy ultimatum unconditionally? Do we propose conditions? If so, we had better discuss them here and now.'[87]

The words began to flow. For two hours, the councillors debated their situation. There was agreement on two points. First, the imperial structure had to be preserved.[88] Protecting Hirohito from abdication, much less the unimaginable horror of a war crimes trial, mattered more than anything: more than saving Japanese lives, Japanese cities, or Japan itself. For without the emperor, there was no Japan. Second, following the atomic bomb and the Soviet invasion, no one any longer demanded a blanket rejection of the Potsdam Declaration.[89]

Beyond this point, there was no consensus. Suzuki, Togo, and Yonai argued for accepting the Allied ultimatum with a single provision regarding the emperor. Anami, Umezu, and Toyoda insisted on conditions that amounted to conditional surrender: at most a skeleton occupation force outside Tokyo, demobilisation of Japanese troops overseen by Japanese officers, and trials of war criminals in Japan conducted by Japanese authorities (one could imagine the verdicts).[90] It was, as Pacific War Society historians noted two decades later, a repudiation of the very concepts of defeat and surrender.[91] It was also, following the example of German militarists at the end of the First World War, an effort to surrender formally while planting the seeds of the idea that the Japanese military had not really been defeated at all.[92] Togo challenged the militarists at every turn: the Americans would ignore their conditions and continue the war; there was no chance of a Japanese victory; and even if the Japanese landed successful blows on the first American assault on the homeland, a second and third would most assuredly come.[93] Even without the atomic bomb, Japan would be finished. But the minister of war would not be moved. Although he could (no longer) give assurances of ultimate victory, his men might drive the Americans back into the sea or, even if the Americans did establish bridgeheads, Japanese soldiers could inflict heavy losses on them.[94] His chiefs of staff fell dutifully in line, a triad of the delusional.[95]

By late morning, there was more dreadful news. Around 11:30, reports reached the council of a second atomic bomb dropped on Nagasaki.[96] The bomb missed the port and city centre, decimating instead the outlying working-class sectors and the city's Roman Catholic population. Shock waves, which unleashed greater intensity than those of Hiroshima but without the fires, flattened the rest of the city.[97] Nagasaki was, in the words of the Prefecture, 'a graveyard with not a tombstone standing', although the number of deaths was lower than Hiroshima and lower than intended.[98]

Yet the Council would not budge: the three-three split remained. The Supreme Council adjourned around 13:30. Suzuki then went directly to Kido and falsely reported that the Supreme Council had agreed to surrender on the militarists' terms: no occupation, self-disarmament, war crimes trials in Japan by the Japanese, and maintenance of the imperial structure.[99] Either he misunderstood, perhaps after dozing off again, or he decided to report the lowest-common-denominator position.[100] Kido agreed to present this conclusion to the emperor.[101] In either case, it was a terrible move, and others said so immediately. Prince Konoe urged the emperor's brother, Prince Takamatsu, to see that the Allies would regard such conditions as a refusal to surrender.[102] At 14:45, Takamatsu presented exactly this argument to Kido, and Kido reported his view to Hirohito at 15:10.[103] At 16:00, former Foreign Minister Mamoru Shigemitsu reinforced the same message once more: conditional acceptance of the Americans' terms would be tantamount to rejection.[104]

With the Supreme Council deadlocked, the matter went to the full Cabinet. The Ministers debated until 22:00, with Anami again leading the charge in favour of continuing the battle: 'Everyone understands the situation . . . but we must fight the war through to the end no matter how great the odds against us!' Even if the result were a final battle on Japanese soil, the country would, he concluded with cryptic mysticism, 'find life out of death'.[105] Togo argued for accepting the terms, but the interior minister added a new argument: surrender would lead to widespread civil disobedience, a coup, and political murder.[106] Although a weak majority supported acceptance of the Americans' terms, the unanimity requirement translated into another deadlock.[107] Togo and Suzuki knew they had one card to play.

Emperor Hirohito, who occupied the throne for sixty-two years, remains a figure of enduring and likely irresolvable controversy. The occupation of China, the attack on the United States, and the Pacific war, with all their horrors – the massacre of and enslavement of civilians, the use of gas warfare, medical experimentation on the Chinese, the beatings, torture, starvation, and bestial murder of POWs – all occurred on his watch. The Empire of Japan did not set out to destroy an entire people, but beyond that important exception, it behaved in Asia much as Nazi Germany did in Europe. The extent of the horror can be conveyed in the raw numbers and in the appalling stories of human misery. In the former, the Japanese Empire's actions resulted in 17,222,500 deaths, the majority (ten million, a conservative figure) in China.[108] In the latter, the Japanese reserved a particularly brutal fate for American airmen, eight of whom the Western Japan military command gave to medical professors at Kyushu Imperial University. Over three weeks, 'the Professors cut them up alive, in a dirty room with a tin table where students dissected corpses. They drained blood and replaced it with sea water. They cut out lungs, livers, and stomachs. They stopped blood flow in an artery near the heart, to see how long death took. They dug holes in a skull and stuck a knife into the living brain to see what would happen.'[109] Another fourteen thousand civilians – the majority Chinese, but also Soviets and Southeast Asians – suffered identical and similar horrors at the hands of Unit 731, a medical branch of the Imperial Army.[110] 'Asia under the Japanese,' concludes historian Gavan Daws, 'was a charnel house of atrocities.'[111]

During all of this, there is no record – for surely his defenders would have produced one – of the emperor issuing any formal protest, still less of any order to make it all stop. Hirohito's supporters argue that he could not protest, that the constitution gave him no power to do so, and they highlight subtler moves – literary references, silences – that suggested his displeasure with the war. They also emphasise the paradox of his position: supposedly divine, yet ever threatened by the prospect of a coup that would leave him effectively imprisoned or even deposed. The critics, in turn, pick up the last point and make it the basis of condemnation rather than comprehension: the emperor's interest was in himself and his throne; his apparently noble actions in the last hours of war reflected only a concern for himself and his institution, not his people; and his passive support for the Japanese war of conquest and extermination meant that he should have at the very least abdicated and quite possibly been prosecuted as a war criminal. Two recent books, both by credible scholars with extensive knowledge of Japanese sources, reach diametrically opposing conclusions on Hirohito and his role in the war.[112]

This debate will continue, but this much we know: on 9 August 1945, Hirohito decided the course of the war. As the Cabinet meeting floundered that day, Suzuki ended it by stating that he and Togo would report to the emperor.[113] The prime minister asked the foreign minister to report on the Council and Cabinet meetings, and Togo duly explained the deadlock.[114] Suzuki then asked Kido for an audience with the emperor. At 22:50, Kido formally asked for 'the convocation of a council in the imperial presence, and the participation of President Hiranuma of the Privy Council and myself in this gathering'.[115] This could only mean one thing, and the emperor knew it. He agreed.

At 23:50 on 9 August 1945, Emperor Hirohito, wearing a khaki-coloured general's uniform, quietly entered a semi-circular hall in the imperial shelter that was located fifty feet under the palace and protected by concrete walls thicker than twenty feet.[116] Suzuki distributed the Potsdam Declaration, 'proceeded to recount the day's events as though the emperor knew nothing of them', and gave the floor to Togo.[117] The foreign minister delivered a long report on the international situation, the exhaustion of the Japanese people, the obliteration of one hundred Japanese cities, the parlous state of industry and transport, the threat of more bombs, and the spectre of a Soviet invasion.[118] He argued in favour of surrender with one condition: the preservation of the emperor. Anami, Umezu, and Toyoda retorted with their now well-worn call for a final decisive battle.[119] Hiranuma threw his weight behind the peace lobby, arguing that the continuation of the war was more likely to lead to a domestic uprising than ending it.[120] The whole thing went on for two hours, until Suzuki – to everyone's great surprise – turned to Hirohito. 'I shall humbly present myself at the foot of the throne and I will ask that the august Imperial opinion close the debate with such a decision as may please his Majesty to take.'[121] The aged prime minister rose, unsteadily made his way to Hirohito and fell at his feet, arms stretched before the throne and head on the floor. Violent sobbing broke out. The emperor asked Suzuki to return to this seat. He replied, in language contrasting sharply with the prime minister's solemnity: 'Why not?'[122]

More sobs. Hirohito spoke: a continuation of the war would lead not only to the annihilation of the Japanese people. The country was no longer able to wage war, and it was doubtful that it could defend its shores. 'That it is unbearable for me,' he continued, 'to see my loyal troops disarmed goes without saying. It is equally unbearable that others who have rendered me devoted service should now be punished as instigators of the war. But the time has come to bear the unbearable. I give my sanction to the proposal to accept the Allied Proclamation on the basis outlined by the Foreign Minister.'[123] The emperor then rose and slowly left the room.

The words were a thunderbolt. The Council, from which discord and invective had flowed but a few moments ago, was silent. Not once in modern Japanese history had a prime minister asked the emperor to make a decision.[124] Suzuki then delivered the *coup de grâce*: 'His Majesty's decision,' argued the prime minister, 'should be made the decision of this conference as well.'[125] No one dared argue directly, but Anami was not finished yet: he demanded that Suzuki clarify whether he was prepared to continue the war if the one condition, maintaining the imperial structure, was refused.[126] Suzuki, 'in a low voice', stated that he was, and Yonai gave the same reply to the same question.[127]

But the matter could not quite rest there. Much more so than in Germany in May 1945, governance structures were at least formally intact in Japan in August. For the decision to take effect, the Cabinet needed to endorse it. There too, however, Hirohito's intervention had the same decisive effect. Debate on whether to surrender was over; the question was on how. Here again, there was a widespread consensus: the one condition on which there could not be compromise was maintenance of the imperial structure.[128] The fragile consensus in favour of surrender would never have held in either the Supreme Council or the Cabinet if members of either body believed that Hirohito would have to abdicate. With or without the emperor's support, the war to maintain the emperor would have continued.

At 04:00, two hours after Hirohito's intervention, Tokyo cabled dispatches to Switzerland and Sweden for subsequent transmission to the Allies. They read:

The Japanese government are ready to accept the
terms enumerated in the joint declaration which was
issued at Potsdam on July 26th, 1945, by the heads of the
Governments of the United States, Great Britain, and
China, and later subscribed to by the Soviet Government,
with the understanding that the said declaration does not
comprise any demand which prejudices the prerogatives of
His Majesty as a Sovereign Ruler.

Unconditional surrender, then, with a condition.

President Truman piled on the pressure. At 21:00 on 9 August,
Washington time, he gave a radio address about Potsdam and
Japan. He began with the utterly disingenuous claim that 'the first
atomic bomb was dropped on Hiroshima, a military base. That
was because we wished in this first attack to avoid, insofar as possible, the killing of civilians.' He ended with an equally disingenuous threat: 'We shall continue to use it until we completely destroy
Japan's power to make war. Only a Japanese surrender will stop
us.'[129] It was a bluff: the Americans had only one more bomb near
to ready, and it was destined not for Tokyo or any other Japanese
city but, rather, the beaches of Japan – the first strike in a US invasion.[130] We know this now; the Japanese did not.

* * *

The next morning, the Japanese cable arrived in Washington. A
few hours earlier, seventy B-29s bombed the Tokyo Arsenal, killing 232 people.[131] The cable's sentence on the emperor incited,
predictably, immediate controversy and reignited a longstanding debate between the 'China lobby' and the 'Japan lobby',
represented by Secretary of State James F. Byrnes and Stimson

respectively. Byrnes, who overall adopted a harsher and more punitive position than Stimson, thought the Japanese request objectionable in principle – unconditional surrender does not allow conditions – and utterly unrealistic given the weakness of the country's position.[132] 'I cannot understand,' he objected, 'why we should go further [in compromising] than we were willing to go at Potsdam when we had no atomic bomb, and Russia was not in the war.'[133] Against this, the generally understated Stimson saw the choice as one between accepting the Japanese condition and continuing the war at great cost in American lives – the avoidance of which was the essential justification for the horror of the atomic bombs.[134] 'Use of the Emperor,' he told Byrnes, 'must be made in order to save us from a score of bloody Iwo Jimas and Okinawas all over China and the New Netherlands [contemporary Indonesia].'[135] Under Secretary of State Joseph Grew, who had served as ambassador to Japan, also supported a flexible American response.[136] A compromise was worked out, and the reply read: 'From the moment of surrender the authority of the Emperor and the Japanese government to rule shall be subject to the Supreme Commander of the United States who will take such steps as he deems proper to effectuate the surrender terms.'[137] The next paragraph read: 'The Emperor and the Japanese High Command will be required to sign the surrender terms.' The penultimate paragraph stated that '. . . the ultimate form of government of Japan shall, in accordance with the Potsdam Declaration, be established by the freely expressed will of the Japanese people.'

Truman and his Cabinet approved the reply, and it was dispatched to London, Moscow, and Chungking for comment. The Chinese immediately signalled their approval. Moscow appealed for delay, and Molotov advocated for two supreme commanders – one American and one Soviet – to oversee Japan. London, and specifically Attlee, Bevin, and Churchill, argued that it was gratuitous and undiplomatic to force the emperor to sign the instrument of surrender and instead suggested that the note state, 'The Emperor shall authorise and ensure the signature by the government of Japan and the Japanese General Headquarters of the surrender terms.'[138] The Americans saw the point and accepted the British suggestion, but they viewed the Soviet move as brazen given the country's small contribution to victory over Japan. Harriman, by then ambassador to the Soviet Union, told Molotov that his proposal was 'absolutely inadmissible'. Moscow retreated, and the revised reply was sent to Japan. While waiting for Tokyo's response, Truman ordered a halt to the atomic bombing campaign but – to keep the pressure up – an intensification of firebombing.[139] The US air forces would, however, return to their roots. Spaatz, impressed with United States Strategic Bombing Survey research demonstrating that targeting oil and transportation, not cities, ruined German production, received and immediately issued an order making transportation, rail targets/bridges, aircraft industry, and munition storage, and only then cities, the main targets.[140] LeMay dutifully passed the orders on, but they came too late in the war to do anything to unhinge his reputation as a demonic wrecker of Japanese cities.

The Japanese Foreign Office picked up the American message, in Morse code, at 00:45 on 12 August 1945.[141] Everything turned on how the Japanese interpreted 'subject to the Supreme Commander of the United States' and 'government of Japan'. Here, Vice Minister of Foreign Affairs Shunichi Matsumoto played his cards well. Like his boss, Matsumoto had advocated acceptance of the Potsdam terms. He knew that if he passed the message on to the army and navy, they would interpret it as they wished to – as an assault on the emperor and a justification, indeed demand, for the continuation of the war. Matsumoto consulted the chief cabinet secretary, Hisatsune Sakomizu, on how to proceed. They decided on two translations. First, 'subject to' would be understood as 'controlled by' rather than 'obedient to'. Second, 'government' would be understood to exclude the emperor. They naturally had no idea if the Americans shared these understandings, but they were the minimum that was required to keep the fragile peace coalition together. Indeed, it was not then clear if even their generous interpretations would do that.

The two men presented, separately, their translations to Suzuki and Togo. The foreign minister was less than delighted with the American response, but he saw enough wiggle room to save the imperial structure. Rejection meant that it, and everything else, would be lost.

Others, perhaps unremarkably, did not agree. As word of the American response worked its way through the Japanese military establishment, the precarious consensus in favour of surrender began to unravel. Young, radical officers who wished to continue the war at all costs acted. Two of them burst into the rooms of Umezu and Toyoda and demanded rejection of the American terms with such ferocity that the two chiefs of staff requested, and secured, a meeting with the emperor, in order to convey the objections to the American note. Hirohito, unsure on whose behalf they were speaking, played for time, saying that he would make a decision once he had seen the American note himself. When Togo did present it at 23:00, the emperor quickly agreed that the government should accept it. He asked Togo to inform the prime minister of his views.

Suzuki, however, was at this point vacillating once again. Anami and the president of the privy council, Hiranuma, ganged up on the old man and soon convinced him that the note, if accepted, meant the end of the imperial structure. That the imperial family did not agree was, it seems, irrelevant: that day, the imperial princes and their families met at the palace to pledge their support to Hirohito's decision to end the war.

Anami and Hiranuma, with Suzuki on side, presented their case to an extraordinary session of the Cabinet. Togo exploded. He leaped to his feet, accused the three men of violating the imperial will, and denounced the continuation of the war as 'senseless'. Before anyone could reply, he left the room and phoned Matsumoto. The vice minister urged his boss to secure an adjournment of the meeting in order to avoid a vote. As Togo re-entered the room, Suzuki was saying that the Allied reply did not guarantee the imperial polity. Togo, regaining his composure, diplomatically replied that the prime minister's concerns deserved careful consideration but needed to be weighed against the fact that, unless Japan could win, there remained a strong case for suing for peace. 'I therefore propose,' he concluded, 'that the meeting be adjourned until the official communication from the Allies has been received.' The Cabinet rose. As soon as they left, Togo rounded on the prime minister. He told Suzuki that his attitude was unfathomable given that the emperor himself had endorsed surrender, and that if he did not return to the peace camp, Togo would ask Hirohito to order him to do so.

Matsumoto, meanwhile, decided to buy the peacemakers some time. Late on 12 August, he picked up the phone and called the Foreign Office's telegraph section and asked to speak with the duty officer. 'Watch for any Allied messages that come in this evening,' Matsumoto told him.[142] 'If they do, stamp them received as of tomorrow evening. Above all keep them secret.' His deception bought the peace faction some time, and Matsumoto went home feeling very pleased with himself. At 18:40, the duty officer in the telegraph office retrieved an incoming note from James Byrnes. The duty officer marked it as having arrived on the morning of 13 August at 07:40 – thirteen hours in the future – and filed it away. As he did, another message arrived from the Japanese ambassador to Sweden, Suemasa Okamoto:

THE AMERICANS ARE HAVING A HARD
TIME HARMONISING THE OPINIONS
OF THE ALLIES – RUSSIA AND CHINA
WANT THE EMPEROR OUT – GREAT
BRITAIN ADVOCATES THE TEMPORARY
RECOGNITION OF THE EMPEROR –
THE LONDON TIMES IS AGAINST THE
EMPEROR SYSTEM.

Togo meanwhile brought Suzuki into line by going through the emperor. The Foreign Minister spoke with Marquis Kido, and Kido in turn assured him that he would bring the prime minister around. At 21:30, Kido called Suzuki to his offices. 'If we do not accept the Allied position now,' Kido sternly told the prime minister, 'we will be sacrificing hundreds of thousands of innocent people to the continued ravages of war . . . . Furthermore it is His Majesty's wish that we advance on the basis of the views held by his Foreign Minister.'[143] The last line turned Suzuki. He moved firmly, and at last definitively, into Togo's camp.

The following morning, the Supreme Council met at 09:00 at what they believed to be an hour and twenty minutes after Byrne's reply reached Tokyo. It was a case of back to the future: the American reply had blown open old disagreements, and the militarists, led by Toyoda, accepted neither Togo's interpretation of 'subject to the Supreme Commander of the United States' nor the horrendous idea of the Japanese people determining their governance arrangements.[144] After three hours of debate, during which all the old arguments were rehearsed, the Supreme Council adjourned at noon. That day, B-29s dropped not bombs but leaflets with the text, in Japanese, of the government's conditional surrender offer and a copy of Byrnes's reply.[145] A chamberlain handed Kido a copy. The blood drained from his face; the news might provoke the dual nightmare of a civil *and* military uprising.[146]

That evening, the question of surrender went to the Cabinet. By 19:00, there was still no consensus. Twelve ministers favoured immediate acceptance of the American terms, and three opposed it. Anami repeated the arguments he made in the Supreme Council; the interior minister argued that the national [i.e. imperial] polity could not be preserved under foreign occupation; and the minister of justice argued that democracy was incompatible with that structure.[147] Suzuki, in presenting the case in favour of surrender, cited the Soviet invasion. As he told a navy officer who appealed for a two-day delay after the meeting, 'If we don't act now, the Russians will penetrate not only Manchuria and Korea but northern Japan as well. If that happens, our country is finished. We must act now, while our chief adversary is the United States.'[148] The example of Germany – the Soviets deep in the country, the capital sacked, and the country dismembered – weighed heavily on the consciences of the peace camp.

With the Council and Cabinet once again unable to reach agreement, Suzuki again looked to the man who was meant to be above politics: the emperor.

On 14 August, the shy, soft-spoken, 44-year-old Hirohito once again entered the small underground shelter. The Cabinet members, the Supreme Councillors, and a few other high government officials were there. 'I have listened carefully,' he told the ministers, 'to all the arguments opposing Japan's acceptance of the Allied reply as it stands. My own opinion, however, has not changed. I shall now restate it.'[149]

'I have examined the conditions prevailing in Japan and in the rest of the world, and I believe that a continuation of the war offers nothing but continued destruction. I have studied the terms of the Allied reply, and I have come to the conclusion that they represent a virtually complete acknowledgement of our position as we outlined it in the note dispatched a few days ago.'

The emperor paused. 'In short, I consider the reply to be acceptable.' He wiped his eyes, and then continued speaking:

Although some of you are apprehensive about the preservation of the national structure, I believe that the Allied reply is evidence of the good intentions of the enemy. The conviction and resolution of the Japanese people are, therefore, the most important consideration. That is why I favour acceptance of the reply.

I fully understand how difficult it will be for the officers and men of the Army and Navy to submit to being disarmed and to see their country occupied. I am aware also of the willingness of the people to sacrifice themselves for their nation and their Emperor. But I am not concerned with what may happen to me. I want to preserve the lives of my people. I do not want to see them subjected to further destruction. It is indeed hard for me to see my loyal soldiers disarmed and my faithful ministers punished as war criminals.

He continued with great effort:

If we continue the war, Japan will be altogether destroyed. Although some of you are of the opinion that we cannot

completely trust the Allies, I believe that an immediate
and peaceful end to the war is preferable to seeing Japan
annihilated. As things stand now, the nation still has a
chance to recover.

I am reminded of the anguish Emperor Meiji felt at
the time of the Triple Intervention. Like him, I must bear
the unbearable now and hope for the rehabilitation of the
country in the future . . . .

I cannot express the sorrow I feel as I think of all those
who were killed on the battlefield or in the homeland of
their bereaved families. I am filled with anxiety about the
future of those who have been injured or who have lost all
their property or their means of livelihood. I repeat, I will
do everything in my power to help.

Hirohito then made what was, for its time, an extraordinary
offer.

As the people of Japan are unaware of the present situation,
they will be deeply shocked when they hear of our decision.
If it is thought appropriate that I explain the matter to them
personally, I am willing to go before the microphone. The
troops, particularly, will be dismayed at our decision. The
War Minister and the Navy Minister may not find it easy
to persuade them to accept the decision. I am willing to go
wherever necessary to explain our action.

He ended with words, the power and force of which is impossible to convey retrospectively: 'I desire the Cabinet to prepare as
soon as possible an Imperial Rescript announcing the termination
of the war.' The emperor then rose and left the room.

The dam broke. Seasoned, cynical, and hard-bitten men broke

out in sobs. Some slipped from their chairs to floor and knelt, 'in sorrow and reverence'.[150]

Within three hours, Tokyo sent a cable to Japanese embassies in neutral Stockholm and Bern, which in turn sent it on to Washington, London, Moscow, and Chungking. This time it unconditionally accepted the Potsdam Declaration.[151]

There were two days between the emperor's appearance before Cabinet and the official Japanese surrender. During that time, Japan's fate turned on the behaviour of the military. Would it accept the emperor's decision or invoke the easy theory that his treacherous advisers had misled him? A cabal of young officers was seething in anger and determination to fight on, and they launched a coup. In a reversal of the situation in Germany in July 1944 (Colonel Claus von Stauffenberg was thirty-six, General Henning von Tresckow was forty-three), older officers were prepared to surrender while the younger ones wished to fight on. Led by a fanatical hothead major named Kenji Hatanaka, a small number of officers hoped to murder Kido and Suzuki, convince the army to mutiny, surround and 'protect' the emperor, take possession of a recording – made but not yet broadcast – in which he announced the surrender to the Japanese people, and instead broadcast their renewed commitment to battle. They murdered General Takeshi Mori, commander of the First Imperial Guards Division, and issued false orders, under Mori's name, to surround the Imperial Palace. They entered it and began terrorising imperial staff.[152] Quick-thinking chamberlains hid the recording of the imperial broadcast and claimed – despite in one case a severe beating – to know nothing of its whereabouts. But it was the minister of war whose inaction was decisive. Anami, despite his desire to see the war continue, would not disobey the emperor and refused to support the plot. Without his support, the coup collapsed. But it could easily have gone the other way, and the result turned on Anami's loyalty to Hirohito. The failure of the July 1944 coup against Hitler meant that the war went on for another nine months; the failure of the August 1945 coup against Suzuki and Kido prevented the war going on for another six months.[153]

At exactly noon on 15 August 1945, all across the country, people crowded around radio sets in private houses, studios, and shops that had survived the bombings. They were to listen to something the vast majority of them never imagined they would hear: the voice of the emperor. Hirohito spoke in slow, controlled tones, with a slightly hoarse voice. When it was over, the Japanese people were at once overwhelmed and confused, for Hirohito spoke an antiquated Japanese that was as close to Chinese as it was to everyday Japanese.[154] The population understood only when an official translated the emperor's words into the vernacular:

> The war situation has developed not necessarily to Japan's
> advantage [NB: a tortuous phrase designed to appease
> Anami and the army], while the general trends of the world
> have all turned against her interest. Moreover, the enemy
> has begun to employ a new and most cruel bomb, the power
> of which to do damage is indeed incalculable . . . . Should
> we continue to fight, it would not only result in an ultimate
> collapse and obliteration of the Japanese nation, but . . .
> [also] the total extinction of human civilisation . . . . This
> is the reason [NB: or perhaps 'These are the reasons', as
> Japanese does not distinguish the singular and the plural]
> why we have ordered the acceptance of the provisions of
> the Joint Declaration of the [Allied] Powers.

Robert Guillain, a French journalist who remained in captivity in Japan during the course of the war, observed people's reactions in a mountaintop village to which he had been transferred.

'When the announcer came on to explain the Emperor's speech, the people remained stiff and silent for a few moments more in the intensity of concentration. Then it was over. They had understood, and the sobbing broke out . . . . Something huge had just cracked: the proud dream of Greater Japan.'[155]

As eight years of conquest, torture, and murder came to an end, an eerie scene descended on Tokyo. Fires once again lit up the Tokyo sky, as officials furiously burned all documents in the courtyards of army headquarters, the imperial palace, and the ministries. Anami and Hatanaka killed themselves, and Generals Honjo (Hirohito's former aide-de-camp) and Tanaka (who helped put down the coup) followed them later, as did the father of the kamikaze attacks, Admiral Onishi. Lower-level army and navy officers also committed suicide, some of them within the imperial palace, facing the imperial house as they died.[156]

Sporadic fighting, suicides, and a few mutiny attempts marked the coming weeks, but it was over. On 1 September, the battleship *Missouri* – chosen by President Truman in a burst of local pride – glided into Tokyo Bay, off Yokohama, its men on the lookout for mines below and kamikazes above. But there were none. Over the course of the day, 260 ships filled the Bay. As in Germany in 1918, an army that had led the country to disaster tried to avoid anything to do with the formal surrender. 'The feeling of Japan's leaders,' wrote diplomat Mamoru Shigemitsu, to whom the job fell, 'was characteristic. They abhorred . . . the act of shouldering responsibility for the deed of surrender, and they did their best to avoid it. To sign the deed of surrender was . . . for a soldier or sailor virtual suicide.'[157] Wearing a top hat and leaning on a cane (he had lost a leg to a bomb attack), Shigemitsu signed the surrender for the government, followed by Umezu for the military. Just before they did, the man responsible for accepting the Japanese surrender, the Supreme Commander for the Allied Powers,

General Douglas MacArthur, rose to the occasion. He delivered a speech that deeply impressed the Japanese for its spirit of generosity towards the Americans' vanquished enemies: '[It is not] for us here to meet, representing as we do a majority of the people on earth, in a spirit of mistrust, malice, or hatred. But rather it is for us, both victors and vanquished, to rise to that higher dignity which alone befits the sacred purposes which we are about to serve, committing all our people unreservedly to faithful compliance.'[158] The more thoughtful among Japanese leaders knew that, had they won the war, their enemies could have expected neither such rhetoric nor the largely benevolent treatment that followed it.

AS THE LAST BOMBS FELL

On 15 March, 1945, a day before the raid on Würzburg, Richard Peck, Assistant Chief of Air Staff, wrote a memorandum to the Under Secretary of State: 'You will remember the great anxiety on the part of the C.-in-C. Bomber Command [Harris] that the public should be reminded at the time of the entry of our armies into the great German industrial cities that these have been devastated by Bomber Command.'

Two weeks later, on 30 March, an American GI named Tony Vaccaro crossed the Rhine at Wesel.[1] The city had been bombed so many times that it looked like the face of the moon; in the centre, not even the outline of the street plan remained. Vaccaro, like many GIs, was first awed, then dismayed.[2] He began taking photos, and his and many others were sent out of Germany. As they arrived in Britain, criticism grew.

The government was all too happy to forget the bombings. After the German surrender, Arthur Harris waited for his invitation to ceremonies marking Germany's surrender. None came, and on 12 May, he wrote to Portal in protest. The next day, Churchill gave a national broadcast celebrating the victory in Europe.[3] The prime minister spoke of the early days of the war, the Battle of Britain, the Blitz, the importance of Northern Ireland, the work of the Royal Navy and the Merchant Navy in the Battle of the Atlantic, the entry into the war of Russia, Japan, and the United States, the liberation of France, the defeat of the V-weapons campaigns, the invasion of the Continent, and the post-war world. With the exception of a vague reference to bomb 'shattered' Berlin, the bomber offensive got not a single mention.

Harris waited for some other recognition for his role in defeating Germany. It did not come. The British government excluded Bomber Command from the honours liberally handed out. It was denied a campaign medal. Clement Attlee, Churchill's successor as prime minister, thought little of Harris. He denied him a peerage (Harris alone among major British war leaders failed to secure one), and Churchill declined to intervene.[4] Harris was given no offer of further employment, and he departed for South Africa at the end of 1945, making no effort to hide his bitterness about how he and his men had been treated.[5]

Harris rushed his memoirs into print in 1947, but they did nothing to rescue his plummeting reputation. His inability to be anything but brutally honest damaged it further. He made no apologies for civilian deaths or cultural losses, claimed that bombing in fact only 'occasionally killed women and children', defended area bombing as 'comparatively humane', and suggested that if he had only had more bombers he would have single-handedly defeated the Germans.[6] The United Kingdom's most prestigious military institute refused to review Harris's book in its *Royal United Services Institution Journal*. Harris was finished. He spent the next eight years in South African obscurity, running a shipping company. He returned to England in 1953, retiring in Goring-on-Thames. He spoke little, and his neighbours knew nothing of his wartime activities. To the end, he retained the support and loyalty of his men.

On the German side, Speer and Göring were tried for war crimes at Nuremberg. Göring was sentenced to death by hanging, but – it is believed – an American guard gave him, deliberately or inadvertently, the cyanide with which he killed himself.[7] Erhard Milch was convicted of war crimes (against prisoners of war and slave labourers) and sentenced to life in prison. The Americans later reduced this to fifteen years, and he was released in 1954. He wrote a book on the Luftwaffe and made a living as an adviser to industry. Adolf Galland did rather better, enjoying a long career in aviation that began with lectures to the RAF on tactics.

Speer was sentenced to twenty years' imprisonment and was released in 1966. He spent most of the post-war period trying to justify his role in the Nazi regime, denying his knowledge of the worst Nazi crimes, and making a fortune in the process.[8] He was, for a time, the darling of the media circuit in both Britain and Germany. Only near the end of his life did he effectively admit to biographer Gitta Sereny that he knew, at the time, that the Jews of Europe were being murdered in their millions. Had he said so at Nuremberg, he would have been hanged.[9] Scholarship over the last fifteen years has made clear his enthusiastic support for National Socialism; his commitment to German victory until very late in the war; his intimate involvement in certain national socialist crimes (the dispossession of Jews and slave labour); and his thorough knowledge of all of them.[10]

Churchill lost the 1945 election to Attlee, but – ever the master of the historical record – managed to escape ignominy for carpet bombing. After ordering the destruction of Dresden, his strategic memo of 1 April 1945 is still cited as evidence of Churchill's opposition to bombing civilians.

On the other side of the Atlantic, Eaker, Arnold, and Spaatz fared much better. Eaker and Spaatz were promoted, retired with honours, and enjoyed successful post-war careers. President Truman personally signed a bill making Arnold the air force's only permanent general. Across the United States, roads, schools, airports, and bases bear these men's names. Curtis LeMay certainly received his share of post-war criticism, but most of it centred on the bombing of Vietnam rather than

Japan. LeMay feared that the atomic bombs would distract from the success of the firebombing campaign; what they in fact did was shift the debate about morality in warfare away from the American incineration campaign against Japanese cities and towards Hiroshima and Nagasaki. There is no American equivalent of British national soul searching over Hamburg and, above all, Dresden.

The aircrew who survived, against the odds, headed home. Lasting friendships between comrades – but also between former enemies – formed after the war. For only an airman – whether German, American, Canadian, or British – could understand what it really had been like. There were moments when this was clear even in pitched battle. After a bombing run, a German fighter was closing in on a B-17 from the 348th Squadron, 99th Bomb Group, machine-gun fire blasting at the bomber's wings and cockpit. Jules Horowitz, the pilot, reached for the flare gun in the ceiling of the cockpit to shoot at the fighter. Jules forgot to turn off the gun's safety, and the fighter simply missed. When the fighter saw Jules's hand in the air, from about forty feet, he thought he was waving; the German waved back.[11] After the war, the contact was more than fleeting. On the fiftieth anniversary of the October 1943 Schweinfurt raid, two Germans, Dr Helmut Katzenberger and Vomar Wilckens, attended the reunion in New Orleans of the Second Schweinfurt Memorial Association (SSMA) to give a presentation on the raid. In 1996, the SSMA members invited more of their former enemies to another reunion in Las Vegas. They included Georg Schaefer, who worked in a flak battery in Schweinfurt and whose grandfather founded one of the ball-bearing factories targeted in the attack. At the Americans' suggestion, a joint American–German war memorial was erected at the site of an air-raid shelter in Schweinfurt.

After the last bomb had fallen, the civilians set about rebuilding their lives. Elfriede Bock, Werner Wendland, and Ernst-Günther Haberland all stayed in Hamburg, with Werner and Ernst-Günther returning to their old neighbourhood. In Würzburg, Heinrich Giesecke, Hans Heer, and Heinrich Weppert also stayed in their hometown. Hans became a teacher, while Heinrich set up his own business. Herbert Oechsner took the English book he found in the rubble as a cue and left Germany, ending up in Australia. As late as the mid-2000s, he returned to Würzburg every summer.

In Japan, Miwa Koshiba, who struggled unsuccessfully to save her young son, stayed in Tokyo and prospered.[12] She went on to marry a successful industrialist, and in the 1980s she was running two large manufacturing companies herself. Until the end of her life, she remained traumatised by the Tokyo bombing, though oddly not by the fires but, rather, by the incorrect belief that LeMay's bombers machine-gunned Tokyoites as they fled. The B-29s had no guns, and no such machine-gunnings occurred, but, as no doubt often happens in intensely traumatic situations, a horrific false memory lodges in place of an equally horrific real one.[13]

In the United Kingdom, the initial euphoria of victory partially gave way to the cold realities of the post-war years. Rations and general austerity lasted into the 1950s, when the economy finally picked up and Britons enjoyed growth and rising standards of living, although both lagged behind Germany and the rest of northwestern Europe until the 1980s.[14] Some rebuilding began right away. Plans for reconstructing the House of Commons were drawn up in January 1945, but the task was not completed until October 1950. The Commonwealth provided the furniture for the new Chamber – Australia provided the Speaker's Chair; Canada, the table; and South Africa, the three clerks' chairs.[15] India and Pakistan gave the entrance doors. Over the next decade, other architectural wonders – Westminster Abbey, the Inns of Court, and the Temple Church – were restored to their former glory. The Queen's Hall, home of the Proms, was never rebuilt.

The story was a less happy one for many London neighbourhoods. The planning mania of the post-war years led local councils to flatten whole neighbourhoods and replace them with soulless public housing. Vast swathes of Elephant and Castle, Southwark, and other working-class neighbourhoods were blighted by cheap concrete tower blocks.

The story was similar outside London. Coventry was rebuilt along modernist lines. Today, its most beautiful structure is probably the burned-out cathedral, left untouched as a memorial to the war. In Birmingham, the result was worse still: the old core, with its solid public architecture, was torn out and replaced with freeways, tunnels, and towers.

For all of the destruction and all of the mistakes, England was too old and the bombing too limited for the character of the country to be radically changed. London is much more like its pre-war self than Berlin is, and the list of beautiful towns in England is long. As in Germany, however, the most untouched architecture is to be found outside the cities, in the towns and villages left alone by both bombers and planners.

For Germany, the task of rebuilding was mammoth, almost overwhelming. Many people thought the country could never recover; one of Germany's allies predicted that it would take a century.[16] Allied bombing had killed some 400,000 people.[17] Over sixty cities were destroyed and another hundred were damaged. Before the war, Germany had many dozens of Europe's finest cities; today, it has a handful. Well over a thousand churches and museums burned to the ground. The medieval centres of Frankfurt, Ulm, Aachen, Würzburg, Cologne, and Nuremberg were simply wiped off the face of the earth. A millennium of Europe's finest architecture and culture was gone. Twenty million books were turned to ash. The destruction often took no longer than an average coffee break.

The cities were nonetheless rebuilt, often at breakneck speed. Some – Frankfurt, Cologne, and Darmstadt – decided to embrace modernity. Others, often but not always the more conservative ones, rebuilt their cities according to original plans. Nuremberg was partially rebuilt in pre-war style, and its famous old city (Altstadt) was restored to at least some of its former glory. Munich also bears much resemblance to its old self. A few of Würzburg's most important buildings – the Rathaus, some of the churches, and above all, the palace – were restored, but the rest of the city clearly dates from the 1950s. It looks its best from the hills above, where the red rooftops evoke the pre-war city. In Hamburg, much of the old city – the narrowest lanes and tiny courtyards – is gone, but the administrative and commercial centre – around the Rathaus – was sensitively rebuilt, and the city declared the Cremon Island, with its red-brick merchant and storage houses, a preservation zone.[18] The St Nicholas Church – which was in the centre of the aiming point on 28 July 1943 – was left in ruins, a memorial to the horrors of war. For its part, Berlin was rebuilt at least twice. Both East and West Berlin embraced modernism in the early postwar years, with predictably dispiriting results. Unification gave Berlin a second chance, and thanks to the survival of more pre-war buildings in East Berlin (not through intention, but because the East Germans lacked the money to redevelop) and to a traditionalist city planner – Hans Stimmann – contemporary Berlin is both more attractive and more like old Berlin than its Cold War self. Other cities have recently followed suit, and private houses, public buildings, castles and, in some cases such as Frankfurt, entire old cores that have been gone for seventy-five years are being rebuilt.

If German cities are a shadow of their former selves, Japanese cities are unrecognisable. Pre-war Tokyo took inspiration from Europe, post-war Tokyo from America.[19] The result is a thoroughly modernist, chaotic city of glass and steel in which 'demolish and rebuild' is not merely one planning option among many but part of the city's DNA. The architecture is often striking, but it bears no relationship to the Tokyo that was. Temples were rebuilt, and few stone buildings – the Wako department store in Ginza, Asakusa Station – survived the firestorm, as did Golden Gai, now a clutch of tiny bars. The city's generally high-rise, glass-and-steel canvass is also punctuated by low-rise, crowded neighbourhoods mixing residence, shopping and entertainment, especially in the Shitamachi ('low town'), the former working-class neighbourhoods of Edo that, although often built with modern materials, follow and recall an older street plan.[20]

But with these and a few other exceptions, the overwhelming impression of the city is one of thrusting modernity. This result is partly a matter of building materials – wooden Tokyo burned far more thoroughly than stone Berlin – and partly indifference to heritage architecture.

On the level of collective memory, the Japanese have memorialised the Second World War far less than the Germans have, and Tokyo is no exception. The Yūshūkan, a private museum near the Yasukuni Shrine, is an apologetically nationalist and revisionist rendering of the war: Japanese conquests were wars of anti-colonial liberation. The Nanking massacre receives no mention except the suggestion that the battle was 'confused'. The Edo-Tokyo Museum, a municipal history museum, provides a far more neutral examination of the firebombings, although there is no mention, as one would expect in Germany, of Japan's own tactical bombing campaigns against Chinese cities. In the neighbourhoods that were at the centre of the destruction themselves, there is another private museum devoted to a scholarly examination of the Tokyo firebombing and a small monument in Sumida's Yokoamicho Park, near the Sumida river where so many died. As is the case in moral debates over bombing, the destruction of Hiroshima and Nagasaki have largely dislodged Tokyo from collective memory, Japanese and non-Japanese. Only a fraction of those who have heard about the bombing of Dresden, in which 25,000 died, know anything of Tokyo, where as many as 100,000 died.

CONCLUSION

By August 1945, the bombing wars were over. More than sixty cities in Germany and Japan had been destroyed.[1] In Germany, bombing had left 400,000 Germans and 83,000 Allied aircrew dead. The figures for Japan are equally horrifying – perhaps more so in that the deaths occurred during a greatly compressed period of time: some 330,000 people between March and July 1945.

From the moment the last bomb fell, the bombing campaign in Germany has been surrounded by controversy – always lively, sometimes hysterical. In Japan, by contrast, the atomic bombs have dominated debate on the morality of warfare, very much to the exclusion of the firebombings. But in both countries, two overlapping but not identical questions lie at the centre of debate: were the bombings justified, and did they work? Answering the first question depends on the answer to a third question: justified against which standard?

Some of the most sophisticated work on this question was undertaken by the moral theorist Michael Walzer. Walzer argued that targeting civilians, though generally unacceptable, is tolerable as an exceptional matter when: (a) there are no other alternatives, and (b) the country is facing the 'supreme emergency' of total extinction.[2] The theory has attracted many critics, but I take it as valid. Indeed, I endorse a looser, utilitarian standard: the deliberate killing of civilians by bombing is justified if it demonstrably shortens a war and thus saves lives (other lives, but lives) on both sides. Readers may or may not disagree with this looser standard, but it allows both the British area bombing and the American firebombing campaigns to be judged by an expansive standard that does not condemn them by definition.

The 'supreme emergency' standard justifies the area bombing of Germany – as Walzer intends it to – during the Blitz, and a utilitarian standard justifies the area bombing campaign over Germany – against Rostock, Lübeck, Cologne, and a few other cities – up to the middle of 1943. It does so because until then area bombing's effects were uncertain. After Hamburg, it was clear – and increasingly so – that area bombing was not delivering the goods. The RAF's switch from precision bombing to area bombing in 1942 was based on more than the fact that precision bombing was, this early in the war, difficult. It was instead based on the theory that area bombing would produce results. Before Hamburg, this was an untested theory; at Hamburg, the theory was fully tested. The raid achieved a level of destruction that was unmatched until then and only matched again in early 1944. The statistics were and are staggering: 40,385 buildings were obliterated, including 60 per cent of Hamburg's residential accommodation; 3,785 industrial plants were destroyed, as were 7,190 small businesses, two-thirds of the city's retail stores, 83 banks, 379 office buildings, 112 Nazi party offices, 13 public utility premises, 22 transport premises, 76 public offices, 80 military installations, 12 bridges, 24 hospitals, 277 schools, 58 churches, 77 cultural institutions (operas, cinemas), and one zoo. Perhaps most impressive were the human consequences: some 35,000 died, and between 900,000 and one million people fled the city.[3] The extent of death and destruction exceeded that of Dresden, where at most 25,000 people died. Little wonder that, figuratively speaking, champagne bottles were cracked open at High Wycombe.[4]

If any area raid was going to knock the Germans out of the war, it would have been Hamburg. There is no question that the bombing slowed the city down. By the end of 1943, 35 per cent of the city's workforce was not turning up for duty, and production was at 82 per cent of its pre-bombing level. The problem was that most of the workers who left Hamburg found jobs elsewhere (making Hamburg's loss some other city's gain and sparing the overall German economy). The US official history estimates that the production loss for Hamburg, which suffered the most devastating raid of the entire war, was 9 per cent of a month's production spread over eleven months following the attack.[5] The official British history arrived at the same conclusion: the area bombing of Hamburg 'had only an irritant effect on German production'.[6] The much smaller raids, late in the war, on Hamburg's transportation links with the Ruhr had a much greater effect on production. A return to the Ruhr in the summer of 1943 might have produced results. Instead, 'RAF bomber command exhausted itself in the perverse attempt to "win the war" by wrecking Berlin.'[7]

Area bombing – working 'on the principle that in order to destroy anything it was necessary to destroy everything'[8] – failed to deliver the results that Harris and other supporters promised. Given Britain's isolation during 1941–2, the spectre of a Nazi-dominated Europe, and the inability to bomb with any measure of precision, the choices were area bombing or nothing. But, as bombing became more intense and more destructive of lives and property, the argument against it became stronger with each passing day. This conclusion is not based on hindsight. In March 1943, the Committee of Operations Analysts (COA) issued a report concluding that it was 'better to cause a high degree of destruction in a few really essential industries or services than to cause a small degree of destruction in many industries'.[9] The COA recommended precision attacks on industries suffering bottlenecks: ball-bearings, propellers, tyres, and engines. It deferred a decision on oil until more information was available. A year later, on 21 June 1944, it called for direct attacks on the aircraft industry, oil, and ball-bearings.[10]

The oil and transportation raids, from the summer of 1944, starved German industry of resources and ground the movement of men and materiel to a halt. They were kept on the agenda by the Americans, pushed for heavily by Spaatz and Tedder, and opposed by Harris. They were only possible, as the Americans well knew, because of another type of precision bombing: the destruction of the Luftwaffe. Despite repeated pleas that Harris join the fight, the destruction of the Luftwaffe was an American achievement.[11] Over the course of the war, the bombing that damaged Germany most effectively was American.[12]

The Ruhr campaign presents an intriguing counterfactual. It was, like all post-Harris bombing, carpet bombing, but the dense concentration of industry meant that factories, railroads, and rolling stock would inevitably be destroyed in intensive, repeated area bombing campaigns. A sustained Ruhr campaign would have combined a precision campaign against steel, chemicals, and coal with a localised (but significant, given the complex rail nexus at the centre of the area) transportation plan. It is for this reason that the Battle of the Ruhr, at least towards its last stages, produced such impressive results, negating all of Speer's plans for a further increase in production.[13] Adam Tooze is surely right that, had Harris not got distracted by the pointless destruction of one German city after another, the repeated hammering of the Ruhr might have fatally undermined the German war effort. Instead, by turning to Berlin, 'the ongoing disaster that Speer and his cohorts expected in the summer of 1943 was put off for another year.'[14] As with all counterfactuals, we will never know, but both data and intuition suggest that this conclusion is tenable.

Subject to that counterfactual, another is worth considering: bombing's secondary effects. Bombing did not win the war directly

– as no one but its advocates said it would – but it had important indirect effects. The defence of the Reich against bombing forced a diversion of resources from the rest of Germany's war effort:

> By 1944, some two million soldiers and civilians were engaged in ground anti-aircraft defence. This was more than the total employed in the whole of the aircraft industry. A large quantity of war material was produced specifically for defence against bombing. Speer estimated that 30 per cent of total gun output and 20 per cent of heavy ammunition in 1944 was intended for anti-aircraft defences. Some 50 per cent of electro-technical production and 33 per cent of the optical industry was devoted to radar and signals equipment for anti-aircraft installations, starving the front of essential communications resources. In addition, material had to be diverted from new capital investments to satisfy the demands for repairs to damaged factories and communications.[15]

These secondary effects were not unknown to the bombers at the time; indeed, British propaganda emphasised them, as did Harris himself after the war.[16] The 'manpower' transfer is sometimes exaggerated: many of those manning the flak and searchlights were teenagers, who were of questionable effectiveness at the front (although that did not stop Hitler from sending 200,000 youngsters there), or women, who were not allowed to serve.[17] And some transfers came back to haunt the Allies: as the Allies entered Germany, flak guns were turned horizontally, sending their ammunition slicing through advancing troops.[18] There can be no doubt, though, that the task of defending Germany required massive amounts of resources that could not by definition be used elsewhere.

How important was this transfer? It clearly did not put a halt to German industrial production, which increased right up to September 1944, when it began to fall off sharply. True to form, Speer exaggerated his role in securing increased production. Speer's predecessor, Todt, had undertaken much of the early rationalisation of Germany industry (streamlining army production, bringing industrialists into decision-making, and establishing a committee structure to oversee weapons production), and Speer's later work built on these accomplishments.[19] But the important fact is that, despite the weight of the bombs, production continued to increase. There is a good case to be made that the incompetence of Göring and his associates, infighting across the Third Reich, the exclusion of industrialists from decision-making, outdated manufacturing techniques, and more prosaic forms of bureaucratic inefficiency, did more to disrupt production than any area bombing raid.[20]

Much has been made in the literature of yet another counterfactual: in the absence of bombing, industrial production might well have been higher still. Richard Overy, who popularised the argument, concludes that the transfer created a ceiling to German war production: '. . . the important consequence of bombing was not that it failed to stem the increase in arms production, but that it prevented the increase from being very considerably greater than it was.'[21]

It is an intriguing argument, but it is impossible to prove.[22] It is inherently difficult to explain why something wasn't rather than why it was. The argument also misses half the picture: we need to think of both the Allied and the German sides of the ledger. That is, we cannot ask how the war would have developed for the Germans if the planes, guns, fuel, and people employed for defence had been used on the front instead *without* asking how the war would have developed for the Allies if the planes, guns, fuel, and people they used to bomb Germany had been available for use over the Atlantic, in the Mediterranean, or in the Pacific. How would the war have developed if the huge resources expended on bombing had been spent on earlier, more intensive and more consistent attacks on transportation and oil or in the Battle of the Atlantic? In the latter, air power was decisive to victory.[23] Precision bombing destroyed submarines and component parts in harbours, reduced fuel supplies for naval factories (through attacks on synthetic oil plants), and denied the reconnaissance aircraft necessary to launch an effective war on Allied convoys (because the Germans were forced to replace fighters taken out by the Americans).[24] The result was that the German navy's great effort to revive its submarine campaign, which continued into 1945, became a huge diversion of scarce human and material resources producing too few submarines too late and above all without any air support.[25]

The comparative statistics on production make it clear that transfers were by no means one-sided and merely German. From 1940, Britain and America produced 130,620 bombers; Germany produced 17,498.[26] In 1944, when Allied bombing was at a peak, Britain and America had 3.54 million workers in the aircraft industry; in 1941, when bombing by Germany was at a peak, it had 1.85 million.[27] Germany spent large amounts of resources on radar and optical equipment in defending German cities; the Allies spent large amounts of money on radar and radar-jamming equipment in bombing them. The two clearest 'debits' against the Germans are absenteeism (which affects the bombed, not the bomber) and flak production. Taking the last, there is no flak without bombs: the large German output on flak has to be set against the large Allied output on bombs. And, as noted, flak guns could be pointed horizontally as well as vertically. Absenteeism, for its part, could be problematic, but as the US official history emphasises, it had little effect: absenteeism was highest among women (who generally were not directly involved in German industrial production); absentee workers found jobs in other German cities; and absentee workers were often replaced with forced labourers.[28] The definitive study of the German wartime economy observes that much of the increase in German war production, which continued right up to 1944, reflected in large measure the seemingly inexhaustible supply of slave labour on which Speer could draw.[29] That same study also notes that Soviet resistance to the German invaders forced Berlin to pay for a sharp increase in steel allocation to the army (for tanks, guns, shells, and bullets) through cuts to aeroplane production for the Luftwaffe.[30] In other words, instead of the bombing war depriving the German army of equipment in the east, the German war on the eastern front – and above all the dogged resistance of the Red Army – deprived the Luftwaffe of the equipment needed to defend Germany against the British.

The statistics in the previous paragraph do not fully compare like with like, and of course much bombing had nothing to do with cities. They can thus only provide a very rough picture. It is nonetheless one that gives us no reason to believe that the resource transfers needed to protect German cities were significantly greater in absolute terms than the resource transfers needed to bomb them. Indeed, as one of the clear reasons for Allied success in the bombing war was the ability, above all the American ability, to out-produce the Germans, it is likely that more Allied resources were expended on the bombing war. At the very least, resource transfers on both sides cancelled each other out.[31] It is certainly true that the larger American economy bore this transfer more easily than did the German one, but the Americans (as the Soviets would discover four decades later) could win any arms race they chose to enter.

More importantly, most, if not all, of the resource transfers created by bombing could have been created by precision bombing alone, with no recourse to area bombing. During the war itself, the Americans recognised and exploited the diversionary effects of precision bombing.[32] Intense, targeted precision bombing raids wreaked havoc with German industrial production, and defence of industrial targets was a mammoth task. A countrywide precision-bombing campaign of the sort achieved during the transportation plan would have required a massive, co-ordinated German defence. The Americans recognised this early on, as they tried to develop the capability to bomb aircraft industry in the Augsburg area. Doing so weakened the Luftwaffe and made 'the Germans split their defences, as well as their radar control, by compelling them to protect from attacks from the south *and* [the] north'.[33] At the same time, the effects of bombing Germany's resource base were even more detrimental for the fronts than the transferred men and material. For the air force, the shortage of liquid fuel became intolerable from September 1944 onwards, since as from that date the allocation was cut down to 30,000 tons a month, whereas the monthly requirements amounted to between 160,000 and 180,000 tons.[34] So far as the Army was concerned, the shortage of liquid fuel, which in this case was also due to supply difficulties, first became catastrophic at the time of the winter offensive of 16 December 1944, and this played a role in the rapid collapse of the German defensive front against the Soviet Vistula-Oder offensive in January 1945. There were approximately fifteen hundred tanks ready for action, but these lacked sufficient supplies and were consequently immobilised.[35] These were, of course, the oil raids that Portal urged and Harris ridiculed. After 1943, as precision improved, as daylight bombing became (thanks to fighter escorts) safer, and as area bombing failed to deliver on its promises, there was less and less reason to bomb German cities. Yet these were precisely the years during which the area bombing campaign reached its merciless climax.

Although city bombing has attracted most scholarly attention, it was only part of Bomber Command's war. Throughout
the conflict, Bomber Command devoted substantial resources
to mine-laying and to strategic attacks on ships, harbours,
transportation, and oil targets. In 1942, the year of the Rostock,
Lübeck, and Cologne raids, some 50 per cent of Bomber
Command's efforts went into naval targets.[36] Some of this precision bombing led to significant and morale-boosting precision
attacks – the maiming of the *Scharnhorst* and *Gneisenau* battle-
ships, and of course the dambusters raid – and at the end of the
war the attacks on oil did much to undermine the Nazi regime.
The August 1943 attacks on rocket production were successful:
they knocked production back and forced Speer to devote substantial resources to a gimmicky weapon that would never have
determined the course of the war.[37] Without these attacks, and
above all without the late 1944 attacks on oil, the war would
have lasted longer than it did and still more people would have
died. The problem is that all of these attacks were undertaken
only reluctantly, with less force, and less often than they could
have been. Over the course of the war, the Americans made 347
separate oil strikes; the British made 158 (including oil strikes
made in the early years of the war). As weather did not distin-
guish between Americans and Britons,[38] it is difficult to see how
Harris could have been doing, as he claimed, his best. The result
was many missed opportunities to attack the Ruhr, transportation, and oil targets.

Oil was the most important precision target. It was not, however, the only one. Attacks on transportation – railway stations,
bridges, roads – were complementary to the oil campaign in that
they further disrupted the movement of oil and made repairs to
damaged equipment more difficult. They also interfered with
the movement of coal and finished goods, destroying German

industry's supply lines. During 1945, the US Eighth Air Force dropped 50 per cent of its bombs on transportation targets; the figure for the RAF was 13 per cent.[39] There continues to be debate about whether attacks on oil or transportation did more to undermine the German economy; there can be no debate that these precision targets were far more important than cities.

And then there was the Luftwaffe, which the Americans alone destroyed. Had they not done so, no bombing war of any sort would have been possible. The great advantage of the American strategy was combining offence and defence into a single, mutually supportive strategy. The British had viewed the two as separate and competing.[40] Throughout the war Harris sought complete independence for Bomber Command and often expressed frustration at the constraints placed on him and his Command. Fighter Command and Bomber Command remained separate organisations, and they were jealous of each other's prestige and power.

Harris was in many ways an impressive commander, almost a great one. He was decisive and tenacious, and he generated complete loyalty from his men. He was one of them. He was a product of Bomber Command, defended it uncompromisingly, and gave the world the impression that more than anything else he loved his men. They affectionately referred to him as 'Butcher' Harris, because he killed them – as well as Germans – in their thousands. Harris equally affectionately called them 'my old lags'. The men loved him as much as he loved them. He accomplished this while doing nothing to court popularity. Sidney Thomas ('Tom') Wingham, wing commander with 102 Squadron, recalled a rare visit by Harris. The Polish airmen exploded in applause, table banging, and cheers when they saw Harris. The commander-in-chief did not smile; he looked directly at them and, saying nothing, nodded sharply, turned on his heels, and left the room.[41]

These characteristics allowed Harris to serve Bomber Command well. He was steadfast in his refusal to see the organisation folded into the other two main military wings; he fought tirelessly for more and better planes and for improved pay and conditions for his men; and he managed throughout the war to maintain morale among a group of volunteers whose chances of survival over a tour stood at around 50 per cent.

Harris was in many ways almost a revolutionary, and like many revolutionaries, his actions were driven by ideology as much as evidence. Harris's commitment to area bombing was total, and he was at best blind and at worst hostile to any facts challenging it. When area bombing did not work, and when intelligence reports suggested it could not work, Harris found himself backed into a corner. He could only respond by denying the evidence (hence his invectives against experts) and by calling for more bombing. As technological developments and industrial production made bombing more effective and more deadly, the result was ever more death and destruction. By the end of the war, Harris had made the complete obliteration of German cities the end goal. The bombing of German cities – originally adopted because all other options were impossible or unpalatable and because it promised to save lives – had become an end in itself, one that appeared to be something like indiscriminate slaughter.

After the war, Harris pointed out that area bombing, including the Dresden raid, had been ordered by others.[42] He certainly had a point. Harris was not behind the February 1942 directive initiating the era of carpet bombing. The initiative was drafted by the Directors of Bomber Operations and approved by the Cabinet. Harris, however, interpreted it in a manner that strayed from its authors' intentions. In his dispatches, published after the war, he gave the misleading impression that the phrase 'to focus attacks on the morale of the enemy civilian population and, in particular, on the industrial workers' was the unalterable foundation of the directive.[43] It was not. Air Staff saw the directive not as an immutable principle that would guide air force policy throughout the war regardless of circumstances. It was rather to be a *temporary* policy, justified by the lack of tactical alternatives, pursued until precision bombing was possible. As Air Commodore Bufton, Co-Director of Bomber Operations during Harris's tenure, put it: '[Harris's] interpretation was correct for the period immediately following the issue of the directive, but it does not, in my view, *as the person who drafted the directive originally*, embrace the whole intention of the Air Staff at that time. The intention was *always* to return to the bombing of precise targets as quickly as [the] tactical capabilities of the bomber force would permit.'[44] This is not retrospective memory. The directive itself makes clear that area bombing was to be a temporary expedient: once Gee was introduced, it should allow 'for effective attacks on *precise* targets'.[45] Harris of course never willingly returned to precise targets. He continued to destroy German cities, crossing a line through each city on a Ministry of Economic Warfare list, totalling 104 cities, as he did.[46]

Although Harris often complained that he faced constant interference, he enjoyed an inordinate degree of autonomy. Subject to loose and malleable official instructions, he chose in most cases what to bomb and how to bomb it. The Air Ministry would not know a target until a few hours before it was attacked, and Harris was no better at keeping his American allies informed in advance.[47] This sovereignty flowed in part from the nature of the RAF command structure. As Tedder argued in a 1931 RAF Staff College lecture, operational matters were left to the Commander-in-Chief.[48] The Chief of Air Staff – Portal's job – was weak and ambiguous; at best, he was a 'shadow commander', with all the status and trappings of office, but without the power.[49]

The same was true in the United States. Throughout the war, Arnold, with his usual lack of tact, urged Spaatz to be more blood-thirsty. In August 1944, he accused Doolittle of being 'afraid of the Hun'; a few months later, he implied that Spaatz and his men lacked 'a desire to kill Germans'.[50] Arnold could put immense pressure on Spaatz, and there were times – such as in the debate concerning Berlin in February 1945 – when the commander relented. But it was Spaatz who took the ultimate decisions.[51]

After Casablanca, the directives made city bombing the lowest priority (though they did allow it); Harris made it the first priority. POINTBLANK had left the door open to destroying cities, mainly to appease Harris, but the cities he selected for destruction had – almost brazenly – nothing to do with POINTBLANK. A September 1943 Air Ministry memorandum urging the bombing of Augsburg, Brunswick, Gotha, Kassel, and Leipzig as centres of the German aircraft industry expressed mystification over the fact that Harris was attacking Hamburg, Berlin, Nuremberg, and Mannheim.[52] A few months later, the Air Staff ordered Harris to leave Berlin and Germany's other big cities alone and to attack smaller cities with a high concentration of POINTBLANK-relevant industries.[53] He refused.

Harris dismissed, and did everything he could to block, the precision-bombing campaigns – against ball-bearings, oil, the Luftwaffe, and transportation – that did so much damage to the German war effort. These facts come out at many points in the history. What's striking about the Harris–Portal exchange in 1944 and 1945 is the accuracy of Portal's assertions (about the state of the German economy, about the shortage of oil, about the importance of destroying the Luftwaffe, about the need to overwhelm the choke points in German industry through repeated attacks, and about the complementary nature of oil and transportation attacks) and the inaccuracy of Harris's arguments (about oil's supposed irrelevance, about the time wasted on the Luftwaffe, about the role of city bombing in aiding the armies' advance on Europe, and about the problems caused by city bombing for the Germans). In a rare admission of failure, Harris conceded after the war that the oil campaign had been 'a complete success', but added: 'I still do not think it was reasonable, at the time, to expect that the campaign would succeed; what the Allied strategists did was to bet on an outsider, and it happened to win the race.'[54] And yet the supporters of the oil and transportation plans, in Britain and in America, based their conclusions on the work of the Committee of Operations Analysts, the Ministry of Economic Warfare, the Joint Intelligence Committee, and multiple intelligence reports. Throughout the war, Harris insisted on claims that proved to be wrong. He insisted that area bombing would force the Germans to capitulate; it didn't. He insisted that precision bombing wouldn't work; the Americans made it work. He insisted that going after the Luftwaffe was pointless; doing so made the bombing war possible. He insisted that oil, transportation, and ball-bearings were irrelevant; they were either decisive (oil, transport) or could have been (ball-bearings). Harris insisted on a strategy that failed and that cost hundreds of thousands of lives – British, American, and Canadian, as well as German.

But the matter cannot rest there. Harris's zeal placed him in a category of his own, but his support for area bombing certainly did not. Harris did not come up with the strategy, and he was not the first in the RAF to endorse it officially; Portal was. Under Portal's leadership, the Air Staff gave it support, seeing the killing of skilled workers as one of its chief advantages, throughout 1942 and, in a more qualified way, much of 1943.[55] In November 1942, Portal approvingly presented the Chiefs of Staff with the grisly prediction that eighteen months of bombing would kill 900,000 Germans, seriously maim another one million, destroy six million homes, and render twenty-five million people home-less.[56] All along the way, Harris had strong if erratic support from Churchill. Many other high-level officials were prepared to turn a blind eye, and the Air Ministry could be contradictory, if not disingenuous, on the issue. After Operation GOMORRAH, the Ministry's Director of Intelligence congratulated Harris on his use on incendiaries: '. . . the complete wipe-out of a residential area by fire is quite another and better conception: May it long continue!'[57] It is little surprise that Harris found it hard to take seriously the Ministry's protests a few months later when he spoke openly about the killing of German civilians as a matter of deliberate RAF policy. Finally, and most importantly, civilian control of the military remained intact throughout the war. Had the British government wished to stop Harris, it could have, with immediate effect. It was all too easy after the war to let Harris, whose stubborn refusal to express even a sliver of regret did him no favours, bear the full ignominy for a policy whose responsibil-ity was in fact widely shared.

Throughout the war, and after, American airmen overdrew the distinction between area bombing and precision bombing. In practice, the latter was often not very precise. Much precision bombing involved casualties, at times extensive ones, and in some cases – when there was extensive cloud cover – 'precision' bomb-ing was based on little more than a hope and a prayer. Until 1944, radar could help pilots find cities covered in cloud but not specific targets within cities. Because they weren't sure they would hit their targets in cloud cover, the Americans regularly used a high percentage of incendiaries (60 per cent incendiaries to 40 per cent high explosives during the 14 February 1945 raid on Dresden, a typical mix for a city raid) in the hope that a wider circle of destruction would take out the target.[58] An unknown number of civilians – but certainly one in the thousands – were killed that day. In the implementation of the transportation plan, bombing the railway station in the centre of the city inevitably meant destroying the area around it. If the city were small enough, bombing would destroy the entire town. And in several cases – over Münster in October 1943 and Berlin in February 1945 – the Americans area bombed intentionally. As noted earlier, excluding attacks on transportation targets, the Americans launched over the course of the war at least sixty-nine substantial raids (meaning more than a hundred bombers each), dropping almost sixty thousand tons of bombs on the centres of twenty-five German cities.[59] Some three-quarters of the American effort against German targets between 1943 and 1945 involved 'blind bombing' with H_2X radar.[60] American area bombing occurred in two broad waves – in the winter of 1943–4 and again in February 1945. For the calendar year 1944, Eighth Air Force statistical reports show that 43,611 tons of bombs fell on 'city areas'; the peak month was July, during which the Americans launched a series of blind-bombing raids on Munich.[61] The report of 8 May 1944 is not shy about targets: 'Berlin city area attacked . . . . Believed that the center of Berlin was well hit.'[62] As the Americans in effect area bombed, the British also precision bombed. Although Harris always opposed precision attacks, around half of RAF bombs fell on precision targets, often very effectively.

Whereas Harris made no bones about – or apologies for – how he conducted the bombing war, the Americans were less than honest about what they did. Near the end of his life, Spaatz looked back on the early February 1945 bombing of the German capital with regret. 'We never had as our target in Europe anything except a military target – except Berlin.'[63] This is not true, or only true in the most technical sense possible. After the February 1945 controversy over Dresden and Operation CLARION, the Eighth Air Force's statistical summary records not a single ton of bombs falling on German cities.[64] This result is wildly out of line with the previous report, and it is simply impossible given bombing inaccuracy under overcast conditions. The Americans were doctoring their records for posterity.

The difficulty in drawing clear and complete distinctions between American and British bombing does not mean that none can be drawn. The differences between American and British bombing narrowed, but they never disappeared.[65] The first point concerns precision bombing. It is at times argued that Bomber Command did not have the luxury of precision bombing by 1943.[66] This is not true. The dambusters raid showed that Bomber Command was capable of the most impressive precision – to within a few inches. It was rather that precision bombing of this sort remained weather-dependent and exacted a heavy toll – up to 20 per cent of a bombing force. Both factors meant that there could only be a limited number of such raids before there were no more bombers – or aircrew – to carry out the bombing. The question for both the Americans and the British was thus: is it better to lose more aircrew on a given raid but to bomb less overall? The Americans answered yes, accepting a casualty rate on a given raid of approximately double that of the British – 10 per cent – but bombing less.

The second point concerns intention. With notable lapses, going right back to the 1943 destruction of Münster, Spaatz tried until 1945 to avoid killing German civilians; Harris killed them deliberately and with equanimity. Even on the worst winter days in 1943 and 1944, when the Americans 'blind bombed' in the heaviest of clouds, they were trying to hit and destroy military targets. They just generally weren't that successful at it. Generally, but not invariably. After Harris's September 1944 obliteration raid on Darmstadt failed to reduce production (it was fully restored within a month), the Americans knocked the city's suburban industries out in December, with little loss of life or civilian property.[67] Another precision raid a few weeks later on Voss and Blohm's aircraft concern in Hamburg (the *Hamburger Flugzeugbau*) destroyed six aircraft on the runway and so enraged the Nazi élite that Walter Blohm was sentenced to six months in prison.[68]

For Harris, the whole point of bombing was to destroy cities, and technological developments were only useful insofar as they aided this eliminationist project. It is certainly reasonable to conclude, as historian Ronald Schaffer does, that by 1945 the United States had 'reverted from its selective bombing doctrine to the Douhetian principles of mass attack and terror'.[69] However, the German war was by then drawing to a close, and this late conversion to terror bombing, at precisely the moment when oil and transportation campaigns were having such a powerful effect, does not change the fact that for most of the war precision bombing against non-civilian targets was the American aim. As late as January 1945, Harris was bemoaning 'the fact that the U.S. bombers have taken no serious part in area attacks'.[70]

The numbers speak for themselves. Looking at the whole war, one German study opts for a conservative estimate of German casualties: 400,000.[71] Of these, it estimates that 75 per cent were killed by the RAF, 25 per cent by the US Air Forces. Another author concludes that the RAF killed hundreds of thousands, the Americans tens of thousands.[72] No one can know for certain, but the figures roughly track the official statistics. Over the course of the war, the RAF dropped 48 per cent of its bombs – some 500,000 tons of them – on heavily populated city centres. If Harris had had his way, the figure would have been a million tons. By contrast, the Eighth Air Force dropped somewhere between 6 and 13 per cent (the lower figure includes bombs aimed at cities; the higher those that hit them anyway).[73] From January 1942, 56 per cent of Bomber Command sorties targeted city centres.[74] If Bomber Command killed three civilians for every one killed by the US Air Forces, it is hard to credit the claim that there was little difference between the two.

By 1945, American tactics changed, first tentatively over Germany and then fully over Japan. Until January 1945, the Eaker/Doolittle/Hansell position dominated American policy. From then, American policy changes in both theatres, with the 6 January 1945 sacking of Hansell by Arnold serving as a useful marking point. From then, the Americans pursued with gusto a policy that they had hitherto been condemned as strategically pointless and a moral abomination. The 2 February raid on Berlin was a pure area attack. In Dresden, only a last-minute handover to the RAF prevented the Americans from launching the 13 February raid that destroyed the old city.

Curtis LeMay's incendiary campaign against Japanese cities began at roughly the same time – early 1945 – as the American switch to area bombing over Germany, so the two campaigns should be viewed as complementary rather than sequential. In six months, the US Air Forces, with few casualties, destroyed as many cities as the Combined Bomber Offensive had over Germany – sixty-four – and killed 330,000 people. Assuming, and it can as noted only be a rough estimate, that 25 per cent of the German death toll is attributable to American bombing, US forces killed almost exactly as many Japanese as the British did Germans. LeMay's raids had exactly the same eliminationist quality to them as Harris's. On 17–18 June 1945, his B-29s attacked four cities stretching roughly across the length of the southern half of Japan: Yokkaichi and Hamamatsu, near Nagoya, and Omuta and Kagoshima, on Kyushu. In a single night, the bombers destroyed three of the cities (44 per cent to 70 per cent of the urban area) and only Omuta, through luck rather than intention, escaped with light bombing.[75] Including these four, there were still 137 cities on the Americans' target list, and they were selected primarily according to their likelihood to burn and only secondarily for the existence of war industries.[76] The firebombings, moreover, had the full support of the air force leadership. Hap Arnold and Curtis LeMay were enthusiastic supporters of these exterminationist raids, and Spaatz threw his full support behind the campaign.

Given this, we have to ask the same questions of the US firebombing campaign that were asked of the RAF: was the campaign moral, and was it effective? As the latter determines for our purposes the former, the relevant questions concern the effect of firebombing on (a) production and (b) the surrender. Certainly, the US was not facing a supreme emergency in March 1945. The US had complete air superiority; had all but crippled Japan's navy; and had liberated Manila. It was clear that the Japanese would lose the war, but there was still much fighting ahead, and firebombing cities might have, in theory, shortened the war.

Whether it did or not is not an easy question to answer, since the Japanese destroyed every document they could get their hands on between the 15 August 1945 cessation of the war and the formal 2 September 1945 surrender to the Americans. For this reason, the US Strategic Bombing Survey had much less to work with than its German counterpart. It is nonetheless the best that we have.

As the survey notes, the American naval blockade played the decisive role in strangling Japanese steel, oil, coal, chemicals, aircraft, and naval production.[77] Precision bombing played a central role in that campaign. In the last twelve months of the war, the tonnage sunk by air attack increased to 1,379,000 gross registered tons or 50 per cent of the total sunk. Precision bombing was also decisive in reducing steel production through precision attacks on the Showa steel works, which led to a 28 per cent decline in pig iron, ingot, and rolled steel from Manchuria in 1944. Precision attacks on iron ore and coal shipments between Hokkaido and Honshu reduced coal movement by 40 per cent, leaving 700,000 tonnes of iron ore and 1.2 million tonnes of coal unshipped. Coal shortages in turn led to a 33 per cent drop in concrete production between 1943 and 1945. Precision bombing of nickel supplies and raids on the Japanese navy cut off nickel supplies in 1943. Along with submarine attacks, interference with Japanese transport from the Dutch East Indies reduced oil, gasoline, and diesel consumption by 50 per cent of their 1944 peaks. The mining of the Yangtze reduced movement of iron ore stockpiles in Manchuria from 374,000 tons in the January–June 1943 period to 37,000 in the six months leading up to December 1944. Finally, precision attacks on aircraft targets in November 1944 – the moment, it will be recalled, when Arnold was rapidly losing patience with Hansell – led to a 55 per cent fall in engine production and a 37 per cent fall in airframe production. These accomplishments were very significant, and the US Air Forces deserve full credit for them and the role they played in undermining the Japanese war machine. Firebombing contributed nothing, or almost nothing, to them.

As was true of the British case, city bombing was not entirely without its effects; indeed, it would be bizarre if the obliteration of over sixty cities had no effect at all on the Japanese war effort. The destruction of cities seriously disrupted local transportation and destroyed many vehicles (although vehicle production was already in sharp decline due to low steel supplies, a result of the war on Japanese shipping). It had a particularly concentrated effect on electrical and communications equipment for the armed services. Manufacturers depended on 60 per cent of their parts coming from urban subcontractors, and firebombing took these contractors out. Area bombing also greatly damaged textiles, another industry reliant on small-scale, urban production. The production of clothing was seriously disrupted: 18 per cent of the cotton industry's capacity was destroyed and along with it two billion square yards of cloth. Finally, firebombing led to sky-rocketing absenteeism. The labour force was all but driven out of Tokyo and Kobe-Osaka, with the strongest effects in electricity/ communications and construction. Some thirteen million people fled in March 1945 alone.

These effects were real, but they paled in comparison with the effects of the naval blockade, in which – again – the air power played a fundamental role. These relatively meagre achievements cannot justify the deaths of hundreds of thousands of civilians.

It could be reasonably pointed out that the effect of bombing on production was less relevant to Japan's surrender than one might think because wrecked production, whatever the causes, did *not* drive the Japanese to surrender. The question would then become centred on the role of the destruction of over sixty cities, the deaths of over 300,000 Japanese citizens, mostly civilians, and the ensuing mass exodus in tipping the government in favour of capitulation.

The answer is reasonably clear: firebombing played little, if any, role in driving the Japanese to surrender. Indeed, there is exactly *one* documented reference in the extensive debates within the Supreme Council, sitting in a torched and charred Tokyo, about surrender to the strategic bombing campaign: a suggestion by Suzuki on 9 August, in the presence of the emperor, that the Japanese people 'cannot withstand the air raids any longer'.[78] The prime minister had never said this before, and it is unclear whether he believed it or simply thought it might give an extra push to the momentum in favour of surrender. As we saw earlier, it was Hirohito's inter-vention with both the Cabinet and the Supreme Council that was decisive. Before he acted, neither the atomic bomb nor the Soviet invasion were enough to convince the hardliners to sue for peace. This is not to say that they were entirely ineffective: they likely emboldened the peace lobby, but that alone did not determine the course of the war. Only the emperor's order to accept the American terms, and then to accept the Americans' vague commitments on the imperial structure, forced the matter, and then only just; had Anami thrown his weight behind the coup, the war would almost certainly have continued.

Understanding what led the Japanese to surrender thus requires understanding what drove Hirohito. That will never be fully possible. The imperial archives, even assuming the relevant documents were not destroyed, are as likely to be opened as those of the Vatican. The protocol and mystique surrounding the Japanese emperor would never have allowed him, even if he wanted to, to tell the world what motivated him. All conclusions are thus tentative.

Subject to these qualifications, it is reasonable to conclude that while both the bombs and the Soviets motivated his decision to surrender, the invasion was by some measure the most decisive factor. The firebombings' effect was minimal. The emperor had watched every major city but three turn to ashes.[79] There were as many immediate deaths in Tokyo as there were at Hiroshima, and yet this slaughter did not compel him to speak. The atomic bombs certainly weighed on Hirohito – and he cited them in his speech to the Japanese people – but their effects on his decision should not be exaggerated. Whether the Americans could or would continue their atomic programme was a matter of speculation, and some Japanese officials expressed accurate doubts that the Americans could really sustain a large-scale atomic bombing campaign. More importantly, both the Americans *and* the Japanese thought of Hiroshima and Nagasaki as an extension of the firebombing campaign – only Curtis LeMay did not. Since previous firebombings did not force the Japanese to surrender, why would new, atomic ones – above all, as there was so little left to destroy?

The Soviet attack alone destroyed all hope of a Soviet mediation and a surrender that could be anything but conditional. Thanks to the German example, Hirohito and the Japanese government knew what a Soviet invasion meant: brutal occupation of half the country, division, and the almost certain end of the imperial system. Finally, there is the chronology: as Hirohito only acted after the Soviet invasion, it is fair to conclude that, although multiple other factors, including of course the atomic bomb, figured in his calculations, the invasion itself played the greatest role.

This in turn means that firebombing played a minor role. It had at most a belated influence on Hirohito, who cited the suffering of the Japanese people without specifying either atomic or conventional bombing. It had no effect on the Supreme Council or the Cabinet, which watched the obliteration of one Japanese city after another without moving closer to peace.

The last point leads to the inevitable counterfactuals. The first concerns the role of bombing in the event of an American invasion of Japan. Had such an invasion occurred, city bombing would likely have aided the army to a degree in that wrecked infrastructure and a modest effect on industrial production would have made a Japanese defence more challenging (although wrecked infrastructure also complicates an invasion, as it inhibits mobility and creates snipers' dens). Bombing's role would nonetheless have been very much subordinate to the sinking of Japan's navy, the blockade of the country, and the dropping of the third and final atomic bomb on the beaches of Japan. Although people continue to try to evade it,[80] the conclusion is inescapable: as was the case in Germany, area bombing's results cannot justify their immense cost in blood and treasure.

The limited effect of area bombing over both Germany and Japan, especially in relation to the tremendous human cost involved, raises a simple question: why did it continue, above all when, particularly over Germany, there were alternatives? As ever, several factors were at play. One factor might have been technological determinism: the bombers were built, bombers bomb, and therefore they bombed. The British heavy bombers in particular were built for area bombing. This argument, however, only takes us so far. RAF Bomber Command was capable by 1944, if not earlier, of a degree of precision that impressed even Harris; the B-29s were built with precision bombing in mind; and, as LeMay demonstrated, some simple changes altered the purpose and effect of the bombers. Another factor – and this likely played a larger role – was related to the bombers' dream: airmen on both sides of the war were desperate to show a role in the victory that justified a separate, and well-funded, post-war air force. This was particularly true of the United States, where the air force was part of the army until 1947. As the war drew closer to an end, this goal required more, not less bombing; and, despite their limited impact on the war itself, moments of intense destruction – Hamburg, Tokyo – signalled the enormity of air power. Finally, the nature of war and the passage of time helped seal the fate of Japanese cities. In all wars, scale and consequence defy control. War, once unleashed, acquires its own logic and momentum. The longer the war, the more likely it is that the conflict results in a wilful pursuit of bestial brutality that would have earlier horrified those committing it.

The last comment takes us to the difficult issue of morality in warfare. We can never forget who started the Second World War, how they started it, and what they did in an effort to win it. Germany and Japan launched unilateral wars that brought death, destruction, and suffering to tens of millions of people around the globe. The defeat of both countries was a necessity, and the Allies were right to mobilise all of their resources in achieving this goal. It was a geopolitical necessity, but also a moral necessity: the Second World War was, as Richard Overy notes, in an important sense, a moral war, and moral clarity aided in some unmeasurable but important way the Allied victory.[81] Moral clarity, however, has two sides to it: it gives the Allied war aims moral purpose, and it defines the limits within which those aims are pursued. In the light of the limited effect of area bombing on the course of the war, it is impossible to justify either the degree of death and destruction meted out by Harris, and tolerated (if intermittently) by Churchill, or the degree of death and destruction meted out by LeMay, and supported by Arnold and Spaatz.

Recognising this fact in no way tarnishes the Allies' victory or the honour of those who did what they could to ensure it. Judging area bombing is not the same thing as judging the young aircrew serving their country and following orders. The loss of some 83,000 of them, most of them still boys, is one of the great tragedies of the war. In the case of Germany, one often-overlooked element of the bombing war is the extent to which both Allied aircrew and German civilians had much in common: during a raid, they were both in a desperate struggle for survival. The need to defeat Germany and Japan, however, cannot provide a blanket justification for what in the end became in both countries a massacre. It cannot change the fact that area bombing was a moral and strategic failure. We cannot shy away from this conclusion out of a fear of giving succour to the far right or of offending American, British, Commonwealth, or Polish aircrew. On the contrary: the freedom to write and speak the truth is what they were fighting for.

NOTES

Preface

1 Randall Hansen, F*ire and Fury: The Allied Bombing of Germany,*
   1942–1945 (Toronto: Doubleday, 2008)
2 See my *Disobeying Hitler: German Resistance in the Last Year of World*
   War II (London: Faber & Faber, 2015), chapters 14, 15, and 17.

Chapter 1

1 Ernst-Günter Haberland related this story to me in Hamburg on 1
   August 2003.
2 In April, the police president published a 'Leaflet for All Households'
   instructing them to have at the ready a *Schutzraumgepäck* (an air-raid
   shelter bag) with washing, towels, drinks, money, family papers, and so
   on. Ernst-Günther's mother left this task rather late, but she got there
   in the end. 'Merkblatt für alle Haushaltungen', April 1943. Reproduced
   in Renate Hauschild-Thiessen, *Die Hamburger Katastrophe vom*
   Sommer 1943 in Augenzeugenberichten (Hamburg: Verlag Verein für
   Hamburgische Geschichte, 1993), p. 8.
3 The figure includes Hammerbrook, Rothenburgsort, St Georg, Hohenfelde,
   Hamm, Eilbek, and portions of Wandsbek and Barmbek. Hans Brunswig,
   Feuersturm über Hamburg: Die Luftangriffe auf Hamburg im Zweiten
   Weltkrieg und ihre Folgen (Stuttgart: Motorbuch Verlag, 2000), p. 243;
   Hauschild-Thiessen, *Die Hamburger Katastrophe*, p. 61.
4 Elfriede Bock's story is based on my interview with her in Hamburg on
   1 August 2003.
5 Overy, *Bombing War*, p. 334.
6 For the flightpath, see Martin Middlebrook, *The Battle of Hamburg: The*
   Firestorm Raid (London: Cassell & Co., 2002), p. 262.

7 Werner Wendland's story is based on a written report he gave to the author in August 2003.

8 There was no second warning. Brunswig, *Feuersturm über Hamburg*, p. 212.

9 The chief of the police ordered in early 1940 that breakthroughs be constructed in Hamburg cellars so that, in the event of fire, the residents could escape to the next building. Hamburg Staatsarchiv, I 16, 'Bestimmungen über Mauerdurchbrüche in bestehenden, unmittelbar benachbarten Gebäuden', 30 March 1940.

10 For photos of the early stages of this process, see Brunswig, *Feuersturm über Hamburg*, pp. 221–3.

11 Some did, others waited too long, and still others grew passive, accepting their fate. Ibid., p. 236.

12 See the report of a Hamburg waterworks engineer cited in Brunswig, *Feuersturm über Hamburg*, who saw some 400 bodies in a 150-foot (50-metre) stretch of the area at the corner of Ausschläger Weg and Süderstrasse. They had left an air-raid shelter in a school on the corner and died trying to reach the nearby canal. The engineer only lived to draft his report because he arrived after the worst of the flames had subsided and because he drove into a water-filled crater that protected him from the heat. Report cited ibid., pp. 228–9.

13 Report cited in ibid., p. 232.

14 Ibid., pp. 225–26.

15 Although it was southeast of the intended aiming point, the St Nicholas Church in the centre of Hamburg. Ibid., p. 212.

16 Hauschild-Thiessen, *Die Hamburger Katastrophe*, p. 7.

17 Ibid., p. 8.

18 Ibid., p. 7.

19 Brunswig, *Feuersturm über Hamburg*, p. 174. The party passed the costs of these defences onto the city of Hamburg.

20 The majority of the neighbourhood's buildings had been consumed by fire within thirty minutes of the first bombs landing. Ibid., p. 224.

21 Ibid., pp. 217, 225–6

22 Overy, *Bombing War*, p. 334.

23 See the photographs in the Hamburg Staatsarchiv, I 18 E, 'Todesopfer', undated. The bodies in the cellars of Hammerbrookstrasse, Hammer Deich, and Süderstrasse were burned to ash.

24 See and report of Hamm and Hohenfelde's fire services in Brunswig, *Feuersturm über Hamburg*, p. 225 and the photograph on p. 229.

25 Report of Luise Solmitz in Hauschild-Thiessen, *Die Hamburger Katastrophe*, p. 62. There is no reason to believe that her story was unique.

26 Report of a Hamburg water works engineer cited in Brunswig, *Feuersturm über Hamburg*, p. 229.

27 Matthias Gretzschel, 'Hamburg im Feuersturm', *Hamburger Abendblatt*, 19 July 2003.

28 Stories of people carrying charcoaled bodies circulated in post-war Germany and were often disbelieved, but the great number of people who claimed to have seen them suggests they were true. The heat was certainly so intense that it turned bodies to ash and charcoal (see Hamburg Staatsarchiv, I 18 E, 'Todesopfer', undated), and it is understandable, perhaps even to be expected, that trauma-mad parents would carry the remains of their children with them. For a brief discussion of such accounts, see W. G. Sebald, *On the Natural History of Destruction* (London: Hamish Hamilton, 2003), pp. 28–30.

29 See the calculations in note 42, chapter 13.

30 Hamburg Staatsarchiv, I 18 E, 'Todesopfer', undated, p. 1.

31 See Hansen, *Disobeying Hitler*, chapter 25.

32 Hauschild-Thiessen, *Die Hamburger Katastrophe*, p. 103.

33 There is some debate about whether he ordered the evacuation of women and children only or of everyone. The documents only mention women and children, whose return to the city was still forbidden by mid-August, but in any case, the photographs show men, women, and children fleeing. Hamburg Staatsarchiv, I 18 B, 'Evakuierungen', July/August 1943; I 18 G, 'Photo selection for July 1983 NDR documentary on Operation Gomorrha'; Hauschild-Thiessen, *Die Hamburger Katastrophe*, p. 103.

34 Hamburg Staatsarchiv, I 18 C, 'Versorgung der Bevölkerung', 7, undated but likely early August 1943.

Chapter 2

1 The next two paragraphs come from Hansen, *Disobeying Hitler*, p. 3.

2 On the Polish air force, see Gerhard L. Weinberg, *A World at Arms: A Global History of World War II*, second ed. (Cambridge: Cambridge University Press, 2005), p. 51.

3 Quotation and statistics ibid., p. 57.

4 Statistics from Richard C. Lukas, *The Forgotten Holocaust: The Poles under German Occupation 1933–1944* (Lexington: Kentucky University Press, 1986), p. 3, drawing on Polish sources.

5 Overy, *Bombing War*, p. 62.

6 Chaim Kaplan, *Scroll of Agony: The Warsaw Diary of Chaim A. Kaplan* (New York: Macmillan, 1965), p. 29.

7 Ibid., pp. 62–4.

8 For the calculations, and the difficulties inherent in making them, see ibid., pp. 63–4.

9 Ibid., p. 65.

10 Ibid.

11 Story and quotation from Philip Ziegler, *London at War 1939–1945* (Toronto: Knopf, 1995), p. 113.

12 Roy Porter, *London: A Social History* (London: Hamish Hamilton, 1994), p. 338. Also see Dietmar Süß, *Death from the Skies: How the British and Germans Survived Bombing in World War II* (Oxford: Oxford University Press, 2014), p. 305. Londoners sought refuge in the Underground as soon as the bombing began. On 7 September, the first day and night of heavy bombing, several thousand people bought Underground tickets and stayed after closing. Overy, *Bombing War*, p. 148.

13 Overy, *Bombing War*, p. 148.

14 Stories from Philip Ziegler, *London at War* (London: Pimlico, 2002), pp. 113–17.

15 Peter Ackroyd, *London: The Biography* (London: Vintage, 2001), p. 740.

16 Richard Overy, *The Battle of Britain* (London: Penguin, 2000), p. 83.

17 Ibid., p. 79.

18 See Overy, *Bombing War*, pp. 82–9.

19 Overy, *Battle of Britain*, p. 79.

20 Ibid., p. 79.

21 Overy, *Bombing War*, p. 85.

22 Keith Lowe, *Inferno. The Devastation of Hamburg*, 1943. (London: Viking, 2007), p. 57.

23 Ibid.

24 'A good time,' a Warden of an Oxford college remarked to me sixty years later, 'to buy a house.' 'A risky one,' I replied.

25 Porter, *London*, p. 339.

26 Peter Hennessy, *Never Again: Britain 1945–1951* (London: Vintage, 1993), p. 35.

27 On this, see Richard Overy, *The Air War 1939–1945* (Washington: Potomac Books, 2005), pp. 32–3.

28 Overy, *Air War*, p. 34.

29 Richard Overy, *Why the Allies Won* (London: Pimlico, 1996), 133; Porter, *London*, pp. 340–1.

30 Ibid., p. 133.

31 Overy, *Bombing War*, p. 241.

32 Ibid., p. 238. For a discussion of the Hague Rules, and an argument that they applied for the entirety of the Second World War, see Stephen Garrett, *Ethics and Airpower in World War II: The British Bombing of German Cities* (New York: Palgrave Macmillan, 1993).

33 Overy, *Bombing War*, p. 239.'

34 Ibid., pp. 238–9.

35 Ibid., p. 242. A few aircrew, struggling against the cold, dropped the bundles without cutting them, making them a potentially lethal weapon.

36 Denis Richards, *Portal of Hungerford: The Life of Marshal of the Air Force Viscount Portal of Hungerford* (London: Heinemann, 1977), p. 122.

37 As Air Member for Personnel, in charge of appointments, promotions, postings, discipline, and awards.

38 Overy, *Bombing War*, pp. 238–9.

39 Max Hastings, *Bomber Command* (London: Pan Books, 1999), pp. 65–6.

40 Ibid., p. 65.

41 Details ibid., pp. 71–2.

42 Details ibid., p. 74.

43 Richard Overy, *The Bombing War: Europe 1939–1945* (London: Allen Unwin, 2013)

44 Ibid.

45 Ibid.

46 Details from Martin Middlebrook, *The Bomber Command War Diaries: An Operational Reference Book 1939–1945* (Barnsley: Pen & Sword, 2014), p. 111.

47 Overy, *The Bombing War*, p. 251.

48 Quoted in Richards, Portal of Hungerford, p. 163.

49 Hastings, *Bomber Command*, 95. Quotations from this page.

50 Quoted in ibid., p. 98.

51 Quoted in ibid., p. 97.

52 Ibid., p. 109.

53 On this, see Sir Arthur Harris, *Bomber Offensive* (Barnsley: Frontline Books, 1998), pp. 52–3.

54 Portal papers, file 2, Development and Employment of the Heavy Bomber Force, memorandum from Portal to Churchill, 22 September 1941 (sent to Churchill on 25 September 25).

55 Portal papers, file 2, minute from Portal to Churchill, 25 September 1941.

56 Portal papers, file 2, personal minute from Churchill to Portal, 27 September 1941.

57 Quoted in Richards, *Portal of Hungerford*, pp. 189–90.

58 Roy Jenkins, *Churchill* (London: Pan Books, 2001), p. 741.

59 Quoted in Richards, *Portal of Hungerford*, pp. 189–90.

Chapter 3

1 Arthur Harris's own *Bomber Offensive* is the main source, along with his biography by Henry Probert, for this section.

2 Henry Probert, *Bomber Harris: His Life and Times* (London: Greenhill Books, 2001), pp. 30–1.

3 See Harris, *Bomber Offensive*, p. 16.

4 Probert, *Bomber Harris*, p. 34.

5 Harris, *Bomber Offensive*, p. 16.

6 Probert, *Bomber Harris*, p. 36.

7 Harris, *Bomber Offensive*, pp. 16–17.

8 Probert, *Bomber Harris*, p. 40.

9 I owe this turn of phrase to Frederick Taylor.

10 Tami Davis Biddle, *Rhetoric and Reality in Air Warfare: The Evolution of British and American Ideas about Strategic Bombing, 1914–1945*. Princeton: Princeton University Press, 2002, chapter two.

11 Probert, *Bomber Harris*, pp. 47–55.

12 Harris, *Bomber Offensive*, pp. 22–3.

13 Ibid.

14 Probert, *Bomber Harris*, pp. 58–9.

15 Harris, *Bomber Offensive*, p. 25.

16 Quoted in Probert, *Bomber Harris*, p. 60.

17 Probert, *Bomber Harris*, p. 60. Although the Italian theorist General Giulio Douhet is often cited as the intellectual father of area bombing (more on this below), there is little evidence that he was widely read in Britain before the 1930s. Biddle, *Rhetoric and Reality*, p. 107.

18 Ibid., p. 61.

19 Probert, *Bomber Harris*, p. 64.

20 Ibid., p. 77.

21 Harris, *Bomber Offensive*, p. 28.

22 Ibid., p. 31.

23 Ibid., p. 10.

24 Ibid.

25 Ibid., p. 11.

26 Ibid.

27 Probert, *Bomber Harris*, p. 86.

28 Ibid., p. 109.

29 This paragraph is taken from Harris, *Bomber Offensive*, p. 49.

30 Ibid., p. 51.

31 Ibid.

32 Quoted in Probert, *Bomber Harris*, p. 110.

33 Harris, *Bomber Offensive*, pp. 51–2.

34 Gerard J. De Groot, *Liberal Crusader: The Life of Sir Archibald Sinclair* (London: Hurst & Co., 1993), p. 186.

35 Probert, *Bomber Harris*, p. 122.

36 Ibid., p. 123. On Sinclair's (complex) support for Harris, see De Groot, *Liberal Crusader*, pp. 186–7.

37 Probert, *Bomber Harris*, p. 123.

38 De Groot, *Liberal Crusader*, p. 186.

39 Hastings, *Bomber Command*, p. 134.

40 Quoted in John Colville, *The Fringes of Power* (New York: W. W. Norton, 1985), p. 311.

41 Hastings, *Bomber Command*, p. 133.

42 The whole interview is included in the 1942 propaganda film, 'On the Chin!' Available at: https://www.youtube.com/watch?v=to4djmDqJRI. The film was made on the eve of the thousand-bomber raid on Cologne, discussed below.

43 Maurice Cowling, *The Impact of Hitler: British Politics and British Policy, 1933–1940* (Cambridge: Cambridge University Press, 1975), p. 215.

44 Parliamentary Debates (Commons), 25 February 1942. Available at: https://api.parliament.uk/historic-hansard/commons/1942/feb/25/war-situation.

Chapter 4

1 Story from Thomas M. Coffey, *Hap: The Story of the U.S. Air Force and the Man who Built It, General Henry H. 'Hap' Arnold* (New York: Viking Press, 1982), pp. 1–2.

2 Details on Ferson ibid., p. 265.

3 Ibid.

4 Richard G. Davis, *Hap: Henry H. Arnold, Military Aviator* (Washington, DC: Air Force History and Museum Program, 1997), p. 2.

5 Coffey, *Hap,* p. 40.

6 Ibid., pp. 42–8.

7 See ibid., pp. 61–3 for details.

8 Ibid., p. 92.

9 Ibid., pp. 86–7.

10 Ronald Schaffer, *Wings of Judgment: American Bombing in World War II* (New York: Oxford University Press, 1985), p. 12.

11 Wayne Thompson, *Air Leadership: Proceedings of a Conference at Bolling Air Force Base, April 13–14, 1984.* Available at: https://permanent.access.gpo.gov/airforcehistory/www.airforcehistory.hq.af.mil/Publications/fulltext/air_leadership.pdf

12 Richard G. Davis, 'Spaatz', *Air Force Magazine* (December 2000), 66–73, 68.

13 Ibid., p. 69.

14 Ibid.

15 Story from James Parton, *'Air Force Spoken Here': General Ira Eaker and the Command of the Air.* (Bethesda, MD: Adler & Adler 1986), pp. 28–9.

16 Ibid., p. 30.

17 Ibid., pp. 17–20.

18 Ibid. Now Southeastern Oklahoma State University. Alice H. Songe, *American Colleges and Universities: A Dictionary of Name Changes* (Metuchen, NJ: Scarecrow Press, 1978), p. 190.

19 I owe this imagery to Milan Kundera's *The Unbearable Lightness of Being.*

20 Quoted in Richard B. Frank, *Downfall: The End of the Imperial Japanese Empire* (New York: Penguin, 1999), p. 39.

21 Donald L. Miller, *Masters of the Air: America's Bomber Boys who Fought the Air War against Nazi Germany* (New York: Simon and Schuster, 2006), p. 31.

22 Alfred F. Hurley, *Billy Mitchell: Crusader for Air Power* (Bloomington: Indiana University Press, 1975), pp. 2–3; Miller, *Masters of the Air*, p. 31; Douglas C. Waller, *A Question of Loyalty: Gen. Billy Mitchell and the Court Martial that Gripped the Nation* (New York: HarperCollins, 2004), p. 9.

23 Waller, *Question of Loyalty*, p. 6.

24 Hurley, *Billy Mitchell*, pp. 36, 75–7. Mitchell never specifically credited Douhet with his ideas, but the two men seem to have met. In addition, Douhet's ideas were presented to Mitchell by an Italian air attaché in Washington in the early 1920s. Also see Waller, *Question of Loyalty*, p. 251.

25 Giulio Douhet, *The Command of the Air* (Washington, DC: Air Force History and Museums Program, 1998), p. 196.

26 Ibid., p. 189.

27 Ibid., p. 190.

28 See the discussion ibid., pp. 28–33.

29 Schaffer, *Wings of Judgment*, p. 25.

30 Quoted in Waller, *Question of Loyalty*, p. 20; also see Hurley, *Billy Mitchell*, p. 101.

31 Miller, *Masters of the Air*, p. 37; Waller, *Question of Loyalty*, pp. 172–5, 195–6.

32 Waller, *Question of Loyalty*, p. 333–7.

33 Ibid., pp. 341–3. The man, George Crawford, was eventually extradited, his alibi was challenged by several witnesses, and he changed his plea to guilty.

34 Carl Spaatz papers, box I: 136, interview with James Parton by Captain H. S. Stackpole, 28 November 1943.

35 Major Craig R. Edkins, *Anonymous Warrior: The Contributions of Harold L. George to Strategic Air Power* (Montgomery, AL: Air University, 1997).

36 Including Laurence Kuter (who taught bombardment strategy and was known for his sharp mind and brilliant sense of humour), Kenneth Walker (an intense, methodological student of strategic bombing), and Haywood S. Hansell (a southern engineer and fighter pilot with a deeply reflective and analytical mind). Schaffer, *Wings of Judgment*, p. 32.

37 Carl Spaatz papers, box I: 135, interview with Brigadier General H. S. Hansell by Dr Bruce C. Hopper, 5 October 1943.

38 Miller, *Masters of the Air*, p. 39.

39 Hurley, *Billy Mitchell*, p. 128.

40 Spaatz papers, box I: 135, interview with Brigadier General H. S. Hansell by Dr Bruce C. Hopper, 5 October 1943.

41 Miller, *Masters of the Air*, p. 39.

42 Spaatz papers, box I: 135, interview with Brigadier General O. A. Anderson, 10 November 1944, pp. 19–20.

43 Overy, *Bombing War*, p. 356.

44 Quoted ibid., pp. 356–7.

45 Haywood S. Hansell, *The Strategic Air War against Germany and Japan: A Memoir* (Washington, DC: Office of Air Force History, United States Air Force, 1986), p. 13.

46 On this, see John Keegan, 'We wanted beady-eyed guys just absolutely holding the course', *Smithsonian Magazine* 14, no. 5 (1993).

Chapter 5

1 Conrad Black, *Franklin Delano Roosevelt: Champion of Freedom* (New York: Public Affairs, 2003), p. 466.

2 Quoted in Coffey, *Hap,* p. 466.

3 Quoted in Miller, *Masters of the Air*, p. 45.

4 See Godfrey Hodgson, *The Colonel: The Life and Wars of Henry Stimson, 1867–1950* (New York: Knopf, 1990).

5 Ibid., 43; Schaffer, *Wings of Judgment*, pp. 5–6.

6 Henry L. Stimson, *The Military Needs of the United States: Report of the Committee on National Affairs of the Republican Club of the City of New York* (New York: Republican Club of the City of New York, 15 February 1915).

7 Quoted in Schaffer, *Wings of Judgment*, p. 15.

8 Quoted in Coffey, *Hap,* p. 232.

9 Quoted ibid., p. 233.

10 Spaatz papers, box I: 135, interview with Brigadier General H. S. Hansell by Dr Bruce C. Hopper, 5 October 1943. Remaining details in this paragraph from ibid.

11 Thomas R. Searle, '"It Made a Lot of Sense to Kill Skilled Workers": The Firebombing of Tokyo in March 1945', *Journal of Military History* 66, no. 1 (2002), pp. 103–33, 105.

12 Quoted in Richard G. Davis, *Carl A. Spaatz and the Air War in Europe* (Washington, DC: The Smithsonian Institution, 1992), p. 41.

13 Ibid., chapter 2.

14 Quotations from Coffey, *Hap*, pp. 227–8.

15 Quoted ibid., p. 228.

16 Ibid. The estimate was a reasonable one: air intelligence estimated (with some conjecture) that the output of British combat aircraft fell from a peak of 1,100 in July 1940 to 550 in April 1941. Overy, *Bombing War*, p. 113.

17 Coffey, *Hap*, 230. Beaverbrook has been quoted as saying 'overrun' and 'run over' by the Germans. "Run down' seems to capture the sense, as in chased, caught, and crushed as one would be by a horse.

18 Coffey, *Hap*, p. 231.

19 Overy, *Bombing War*, p. 261.

20 Quoted in Coffey, *Hap*, p. 234.

21 Ibid.

22 Miller, *Masters of the Air*, p. 61.

23 Quoted in Coffey, *Hap*, pp. 251–2; Parton, *'Air Force Spoken Here'*, p. 128.

24 Parton, *'Air Force Spoken Here'*, p. 129.

25 Ibid., p. 130.

26 Quoted ibid.

27 Overy, *Bombing War*, p. 310.

28 Or, as Overy puts it, a 'marriage of convenience'. Ibid., p. 308.

29 'A farewell to the non-flying fortress', *Daily Telegraph*, 18 August 2001. I am grateful to the current owner of Springfield for showing me around the house and pointing this detail out to me.

30 Details in this paragraph from Parton, *'Air Force Spoken Here'*, p. 134.

31 Ibid., p. 141.

32 Ibid.

33 Ibid., p. 142.

34 For the details, see ibid., p. 143.

Chapter 6

1 Statistic from Robin Neillands, *The Bomber War: Arthur Harris and the Allied Bomber Offensive, 1939–1945* (London: John Murray, 2001), p. 110.

2 Details from Harris, *Bomber Offensive*, p. 91.

3 Ibid.

4 1,000- and 4,000-pound bombs. Neillands, *Bomber War*, pp. 111–12.

5 Ibid.

6 Quoted in Hastings, *Bomber Command*, p. 147.

7 On this, see ibid., p. 146.

8 Harris papers, BUFT 3/27, letter from Harris to VCAS, 29 April 1942.

9 Jörg Friedrich, *The Fire: The Bombing of Germany 1940–1945* (New York: Columbia University Press, 2006), pp. 70–1.

10 Lutz Wilde, *Bomber gegen Lübeck: Eine Dokumentation der Zerstörungen in Lübecks Altstadt beim Luftangriff im März 1942* (Lübeck: Verlag Schmidt-Römhild, 1999), p. 13 [consulted in Archiv der Hansestadt Lübeck, L II 2995].

11 Hans-Günter Feldhaus, *Nun zu guterletzt* (Lübeck: Druckerei Wulf, 2003), p. 104.

12 Details on timing from Archiv der Hansestadt Lübeck, Materialsammlung zum Luftangriff 1942 – Flakuntergruppe Lübeck 1-6, file 6, 'Erfahrungsbericht über den Grossangriff auf Lübeck in der Nacht vom 28. zum 29. 3. 1942'. The author, the division commander for Flakabteilung 161, Major Schreiber (later Landessuperintendant in Lübeck), noted the new strategy: 'Der Grossangriff auf Lübeck scheint in dieser Art erstmalig in Deutschland geflogen zu sein, und zwar hinsichtlich massierten Einsatzes kriegserfahrener Piloten auf ein räumlich eng begrenztes Ziel mittelalterlicher Bauart nach genau festgelegtem Angriffsplan mit geschicktester Taktik und rücksichtlosen Einsatz. Der Gegner versuchte im Anflug zu täuschen.' ('The major attack on Lubeck seemed to be the first such one carried out in this manner in Germany, [by] amassing experienced combat pilots on a geographically narrow target of medieval structures with a precisely defined attack plan, sophisticated tactics, and ruthless execution. The enemy sought to throw us off [its strategy] as it approached.')

13 Archiv der Hansestadt Lübeck, Materialsammlung zum Luftangriff 1942 – Flakuntergruppe Lübeck 8–22, 17, 'Batterie Chronik der 2. Schwere Flak Abt. 161', p. 52.

14 Details from report by Renate Brockmüller, Lübeck, undated (spring 2007).

15 Details from Wilde, *Bomber gegen Lübeck*, pp. 15–16.

16 Ibid., p. 15.

17 Hans Schönherr, *Lübeck – Aufbau aus dem Chaos* (Lübeck: Verlag Lübecker Nachrichten, 1962), p. 9.

18 Jörg Friedrich, *Der Brand. Deutschland im Bombenkrieg 1940–1945* (Munich: Ullstein Heyne, 2002) [German version of *The Fire*, cited above]. For photos of the interior of St Mary's following the bombing, see Archiv der Hansestadt Lübeck, HS 1192, 'Aufnahmen über

Zerstörungen durch den Luftangriff auf Lübeck in der Nacht zum 29. März 1942'.

19 Friedrich, *The Fire*, p. 71

20 Archiv der Hansestadt Lübeck, Materialsammlung zum Luftangriff 1942 – Flakuntergruppe Lübeck 1-6, file 6, ,Erfahrungsbericht über den Grossangriff auf Lübeck in der Nacht vom 28. zum 29. 3. 1942'.

21 Ibid.

22 Middlebrook, *Bomber Command War Diaries*, p. 251.

23 Hastings, *Bomber Command*, p. 150.

24 Ibid.

25 Quotations in this and following two sentences from Archiv der Hansestadt Lübeck, 'Britischer Luftüberfall auf Lübeck' (collected newspaper clippings), including articles entitled 'Lübeck's Flak kämpfte wie Helden', 'Lübecks Herzen stärker als Englands Bomben', 'Schnelle Hilfe auf allen Gebieten', 'Sie sind gefallen wie Soldaten in der Schlacht', 'Ein neues Lübeck wird erstehen', 'Lübeck wird wieder sein altes Gesicht erhalten', and 'Wie Lübeck die Nacht zum Palmsonntag erlebte'.

26 Archiv der Hansestadt Lübeck, eyewitness report by Günther Becker, 30 May 1942.

27 Friedrich, *The Fire*, p. 71.

28 Jenkins, *Churchill*, 478. The turn of phrase is Jenkins's.

29 *Sir John Wheeler-Bennett and Anthony Nicholls, The Semblance of Peace: The Political Settlement after the Second World War (New York: W. W. Norton & Co., 1974), p. 179.*

30 Adrian Fort, *Prof: The Life and Times of Frederick Lindemann* (London: Jonathan Cape, 2003), pp. 43–5.

31 The rest of the paragraph is based on ibid., pp. 58–61.

32 For a more detailed discussion, see William Farren and George P. Thomson, 'Frederick Alexander Lindemann, Viscount Cherwell. 1886–1957', *Biographical Memoirs of Fellows of the Royal Society* 4 (1958), pp. 45–71.

33 Cherwell Papers, Nuffield College, Oxford, A 14/f4, letter to Lindemann, 2 November 1932.

34 A rumour reinforced by his own occasional antisemitic remarks. On this, and the rumour itself, see Fort, *Prof*, p. 3.

35 In response to a note from Cherwell to Churchill on air defence measures, Harris wrote to Portal in 1940 that 'our work is made no easier by the continual necessity of leaving it in order to answer the naïve

queries of outside busybodies who peddle second-hand information in the guise of esoteric knowledge . . .' Quoted in Probert, *Bomber Harris*, p. 109.

36 Roy F. Harrod, *The Prof: A Personal Memoir of Lord Cherwell* (London: Macmillan, 1959), p. 74. Emphasis in the original.

37 Fort, *Prof*, pp. 246–8.

38 Ibid., p. 247.

39 Ibid.

40 Portal papers, file 2, memorandum from Cherwell to Churchill, 30 March 1942.

41 Quoted in Hastings, *Bomber Command*, p. 128.

42 Quote from Max Hastings, *Finest Years: Churchill as Warlord, 1940–45* (London: HarperPress, 2009), p. 148.

43 The details of Churchill's routine come from Richard Hough, *Winston and Clementine: The Triumphs and Tragedies of the Churchills* (London: Bantam Books, 1990), p. 449–50.

44 The Oxford psephologist, David Butler, recounted to a seminar – in autumn of 1994 or 1995, I believe – an interview with Churchill, who lay in bed, a brandy in hand. He asked the young Butler his age, and then used his fingers to calculate the difference between the young don and Napoleon at the peak of his career. Finally arriving at the sum, he told Butler that he had better get on with it.

45 Jenkins, *Churchill*, p. 774.

46 See Hastings, *Bomber Command*, pp. 129–32.

47 Spaatz papers, box I: 136, interview with Sir Henry Tizard by Maj. James Lawrence, 15 November 1944.

48 Quoted in Hastings, *Bomber Command*, p. 130.

49 Tizard's comments on the Battle of the Atlantic were prescient. See the conclusion of this book.

50 Quoted in Hastings, *Bomber Command*, p. 130.

51 Solly Zuckerman, *From Apes to Warlords* (London: Hamish Hamilton, 1978), pp. 139–46 [Zuckerman's autobiography].

52 Quoted in Maurice W. Kirby, *Operational Research in War and Peace – The British Experience from the 1930s to 1970* (London: Imperial College Press, 2003), p. 141.

53 Both quoted in Hastings, pp. 130–1.

Chapter 7

1 Quotations and two previous paragraphs taken from Parton, '*Air Force Spoken Here*', p. 148.
2 Ibid.
3 Ibid., p. 158.
4 Friedrich, *Der Brand*, pp. 183–4; Hans-Werner Bohl, Bodo Keipke, and Karsten Schröder (eds.), *Bomben auf Rostock* (Rostock: Konrad Reich Verlag, 1995); Middlebrook, *Bomber Command War Diaries*, p. 261.
5 Harris, *Bomber Offensive*, p. 108.
6 George Axelsson, 'Bomb Toll Goes Up', *New York Times*, 5 May 1942.
7 Ibid., p. 150.
8 Harris, *Bomber Offensive*, p. 109.
9 Ibid.
10 Neillands, *Bomber War*, p. 120.
11 Hastings, *Bomber Command*, p. 150.
12 Interview with Jack Pragnell, Walton Heath Way, 18 May 2005.
13 Middlebrook, *Bomber Command War Diaries*, p. 270.
14 George Axelsson, 'Bomb Toll Goes Up'.
15 Eric Taylor, *Operation Millennium. 'Bomber' Harris's Raid on Cologne, May 1942* (London: Robert Hale, 1987), p. 45.
16 Middlebrook, *Bomber Command War Diaries*, p. 270.
17 Quoted in Taylor, *Operation Millennium*, pp. 46–67.
18 Charles Messenger, *Cologne: The First 1000-Bomber Raid* (London: Ian Allan Ltd., 1982), p. 40.
19 Ibid.
20 Ibid.

Chapter 8

1 Details on Leeming from Taylor, *Operation Millennium*, pp. 83–7.
2 Ibid., p. 85.
3 Ibid., p. 83.
4 Ibid., p. 84.
5 Ibid., p. 86.
6 Ibid., p. 87.
7 Story related by Hastings, *Bomber Command*, pp. 151–2.

8 Story related by John Sweetman, *Bomber Crew: Taking on the Reich* (London: Little, Brown, 2004), pp. 80–1.

9 Gertrud Türk, 'Kriegserlebnisse im Agnesviertel', sent to the author in April 2004. Freischlader was her maiden name.

10 '*Wenn sich Sekunde an Sekunde, Minute an Minute reihen, die wie eine Ewigkeit erscheinen, wächst die Angst ins Unermeßliche.*'

11 Middlebrook, *Bomber Command War Diaries*, p. 272.

12 Friedrich, *The Fire*, p. 73.

13 Middlebrook, *Bomber Command War Diaries*, p. 272.

14 Quotations from Parton, '*Air Force Spoken Here*', p. 160.

15 Ibid.

16 Miller, *Masters of the Air*, p. 58.

17 Quoted ibid.

Chapter 9

1 Richard Overy, *Goering: The 'Iron Man'* (London: Routledge, 1984), p. 232.

2 Ibid., p. 234.

3 Quoted ibid.

4 Ibid., pp. 232–4.

5 Quoted ibid., p. 236.

6 Overy, *Iron Man*, p. 25.

7 Ibid.

8 Werner Maser, *Hermann Göring: Hitlers janusköpfiger Paladin* (Berlin: Quintessenz Verlag, 2000), pp. 253–60.

9 Richard Overy, *Goering: Hitler's Iron Knight* (London: I. B. Taurus, 2012), p. xi.

10 Overy, *Iron Man*, p. 128.

11 Ernst Udet, head of Luftwaffe procurement, killed himself in November 1941; Hans Jeschonnek, chief of staff, did the same in August 1943.

12 Overy, *Iron Knight*, p. 4.

13 Ibid., p. 5.

14 Ibid., pp. 5–6.

15 Stefan Martens, *Hermann Göring – 'Erster Paladin des Führers' und 'Zweiter Mann im Reich'* (Paderborn: Schöningh, 1985), p. 16.

16 Ibid., pp. 7–8.

17 Ibid., chapters 2 and 3.

18 Ibid., p. 181.

19 Maser, *Hermann Göring*, p. 377.

20 Overy, *Iron Man*, p. 189.

21 Ibid.

22 Numerous English-speaking accounts claim that this was an antisemitic slur. It is not. *Meier* is rather a very common surname in Germany, suggesting utter banality. There is no English equivalent of the phrase, but 'if you believe that, I have a bridge to sell you' captures the sense.

23 Middlebrook, *Bomber Command War Diaries*, pp. 247–78.

24 Matthias Schmidt, *Albert Speer – Das Ende eines Mythos* (Bern: Scherz Verlag, 1982), p. 36.

25 National Socialists gravitated towards Tessenow, but the architect, according to another student, was utterly indifferent to his students' politics, whether they were far left or far right. Werner Durth, *Deutsche Architekten: Biographische Verflechtungen 1900–1970* (Stuttgart: Krämer, 2001), p. 60.

26 Magnus Brechtken, *Albert Speer: eine deutsche Karriere* (Munich: Pantheon, 2018), p. 29.

27 His style is different, but future generations may wonder the same of those enthralled by Donald Trump's rambling, incoherent speeches.

28 Brechtken, *Albert Speer*, p. 32.

29 Schmidt, *Albert Speer*, p. 43.

30 Brechtken, *Albert Speer*, p. 35.

31 Sven Felix Kellerhoff, 'Der erfolgreichste Manipulator des Dritten Reiches', *Die Welt*, 31 May 2017. Available at: https://www.welt.de/geschichte/zweiter-weltkrieg/article165100739/Der-erfolgreichste-Manipulator-des-Dritten-Reiches.html.

32 Brechtken, *Albert Speer*, p. 36.

33 Albert Speer, *Inside the Third Reich* (London: Phoenix, 1995), p. 54.

34 Joachim Fest, *Speer: The Final Verdict* (London: Weidenfeld & Nicolson, 2001), p. 30; Speer, *Inside the Third Reich*, p. 56.

35 Brechtken, *Albert Speer*, p. 40.

36 Ibid.

37 Details in this paragraph ibid., pp. 45–6.

38 Albert Speer, *Erinnerungen* (Munich: Propyläen, 2003), p. 41.

39 Brechtken, *Albert Speer*, p. 48.

40 Ibid., p. 49. Even Speer's sharpest critics have accepted Speer's claims of sole or primary authorship for Nuremberg and, later, the Olympic Games (as did, it must be said, the 2008 version of *Fire and Fury*). See,

for instance, Adam Tooze, *The Wages of Destruction: The Making and Breaking of the Nazi War Economy* (New York: Viking, 2006), p. 553.

41 Brechtken, *Albert Speer*, p. 49.

42 Ibid.

43 On this, and the debate, see ibid., pp. 50–1.

44 Speer, *Erinnerungen*, p. 46.

45 Brechtken, *Albert Speer*, p. 52.

46 Ibid.; André Deschan, *Im Schatten von Albert Speer: Der Architekt Rudolf Walters* (Berlin: Gebr. Mann Verlag, 2016), p. 79.

47 Brechtken, *Albert Speer*, p. 57.

48 Dan Van Der Vat, *Der gute Nazi* (Berlin: Henschel, 1997), pp. 78–80.

49 Brechtken, *Albert Speer*, p. 60.

50 Ibid., p. 67.

51 Speer, *Erinnerungen*, 76; Brechtken, *Albert Speer*, pp. 67–8.

52 Brechtken, *Albert Speer*, p. 72.

53 On Speer's 'reluctance', see Tooze, *Wages of Destruction*, p. 552.

54 Brechtken, *Albert Speer*, p. 73.

55 Ibid., p. 81; Léon Krier, *Albert Speer: Architecture 1932–1942* (New York: Monacelli Press, 2013), p. 45.

56 Gernot Schaulinski, 'Baustelle Zeichentisch – Der Beginn der Neugestaltung Berlins', in Paul Spies and Gernot Schaulinski (eds). *Berlin 1937: Im Schatten von morgen* (Berlin: Stiftung Stadtmuseum Berlin, in co-operation with the Stiftung Neue Synagoge Berlin – Centrum Judaicum, 2017), pp. 114–15.

57 Susanne Willems, *Der entsiedelte Jude: Albert Speers Wohnungsmarktpolitik für den Hauptstadtbau* (Berlin: Edition Hentrich, 2000), p. 25.

58 See Bundesarchiv (BArch) Berlin, R 2/25496. These included long discussions about costs of acquiring buildings, challenges in relocating existing ministries, and leases that had years to run on them.

59 Willems, *Der entsiedelte Jude*, pp. 72–3.

60 Ibid.

61 Martin Gilbert, *The Holocaust: The Jewish Tragedy* (London: Fontana Press, 1986), p. 69.

62 Ibid., pp. 69–70.

63 Ibid., p. 69.

64 Willems, *Der entsiedelte Jude*, p. 81

65 Ibid., p. 87.

66 Schaulinski, 'Baustelle Zeichentisch', p. 116.

67 Willems, *Der entsiedelte Jude*, p. 11.
68 Schaulinski, 'Baustelle Zeichentisch', p. 116.
69 Willems, *Der entsiedelte Jude*, p. 15.
70 Brechtken, *Albert Speer*, 81; Willems, *Der entsiedelte Jude*, p. 23.
71 Ian Kershaw, *Hitler: 1936–1945. Nemesis* (London: Penguin, 2000), p. 502.
72 Fest, *Final Verdict*, p. 128.
73 Brechtken, *Albert Speer*, p. 156.
74 Weinberg, *World at Arms*, p. 274.
75 Ibid.; Christian Hartmann, 'Verbrecherischer Krieg – verbrecherische Wehrmacht? Überlegungen zur Struktur des deutschen Ostheeres 1941–1944', *Vierteljahreshefte für Zeitgeschichte* 52, no. 1 (2004), pp. 5–6.
76 Brechtken, *Albert Speer*, p. 156. Generals Fromm and Thomas shared the same view. Tooze, *Wages of Destruction*, pp. 553–4.
77 Brechtken, *Albert Speer*, p. 155.
78 Speer, *Inside the Third Reich*, p. 274.
79 Van Der Vat, *Der gute Nazi*, pp. 155–6.
80 Brechtken, *Albert Speer*, p. 157 n5.
81 Speer, *Inside the Third Reich*, p. 276.
82 Willems, *Der entsiedelte Jude*, p. 40.
83 Brechtken, *Albert Speer*, p. 158.
84 In February 1942, Speer had full authority over the equipment needs of the army and ammunition production across all services. This amounted to about 45 per cent, which consumed around one-sixth of all industrial production. In June 1943, the navy would be incorporated into his sphere of control, and in spring 1944, the Luftwaffe would follow. Tooze, *Wages of Destruction*, pp. 558–9.

Chapter 10

1 Quoted in Parton, '*Air Force Spoken Here*', p. 215.
2 Winston Churchill. *Memoirs of the Second World War: An Abridgement of the Six Volumes of the Second World War* (Boston: Houghton Mifflin, 1959), p. 667.
3 William Averell Harriman and Elie Abel, *Special Envoy to Churchill and Stalin, 1941–1946* (New York: Random House, 1975), p. 180.
4 Details in this paragraph from Robert Murphy, *Diplomat among Warriors* (Garden City, NY: Doubleday, 1964), p. 165.

5 Ibid.

6 Harriman and Abel, *Special Envoy*, p. 181.

7 Alex Danchev and Daniel Todman, eds., *War Diaries, 1939–1945: The Diaries of Field Marshal Lord Alanbrooke* (Berkeley: University of California Press, 2001), 350; Churchill, *Memoirs*, p. 667.

8 Julian Jackson, *A Certain Idea of France: The Life of Charles de Gaulle* (London: Allen Lane, 2018), pp. 210–11.

9 Churchill, *Memoirs of the Second World* War, p. 667.

10 Murphy, *Diplomat among Warriors*, p. 165.

11 Warren F. Kimball, *Forged in War: Roosevelt, Churchill, and the Second World War* (New York, William Morrow & Co., 1997), p. 184. According to Kimball, the average was closer to 01:00.

12 Quoted in Hastings, *Bomber Command*, p. 184.

13 Weinberg, *World at Arms*, pp. 380–1.

14 UKNA, 14/3507, letter from Harris to the Prime Minister, 17 June 1942.

15 Quotations from Parton, '*Air Force Spoken Here*', p. 218.

16 Ibid.

17 Details in this paragraph from Spaatz papers, box I: 136, interview with James Parton by Captain H. S. Stackpole, 28 November 1943.

18 Parton, '*Air Force Spoken Here*' p. 221.

19 Quotations and previous paragraph from Parton, '*Air Force Spoken Here*', p. 220.

20 Ibid., p. 222.

21 Ibid. UK sources indicate that, before the meeting, Churchill's staff had already convinced him to allow the USAAF to attempt daylight bombing. Sir Charles Webster and Noble Frankland, *The Strategic Air Offensive against Germany 1939–1945*, 1:360–3. As Searle points out, this only means that Eaker and the USAAF convinced the staff and the staff convinced Churchill. Searle, 'It Made a Lot of Sense', p. 107.

22 Murphy, *Diplomat among Warriors*, p. 167.

23 Ibid.

24 Meredith Hindley, *Destination Casablanca: Exile, Espionage, and the Battle for North Africa in World War II* (New York: Public Affairs, 2017), p. 357.

25 Ibid.; Murphy, *Diplomat among Warriors*, p. 167.

26 Danchev and Todman, *War Diaries of Alanbrooke*, pp. 358–63; Hindley, *Destination Casablanca*, pp. 357–65.

27 Murphy, *Diplomat among Warriors*, p. 168.

28 Ibid.
29 Churchill, *Memoirs*, p. 674.
30 Ibid.
31 UKNA, AIR 19/189, 'Combined Chiefs of Staff: the Bomber Offensive from the United Kingdom', 21 January 1943.
32 US Department of State, Office of the Historian, Memorandum of the Combined Chiefs of Staff, Casablanca, 21 January 1943. Available at: https://history.state.gov/historicaldocuments/frus1941-43/d412.
33 Hastings, *Bomber Command*, pp. 184–5.
34 J. Alwyn Phillips, *The Valley of the Shadow of Death* (New Malden: Air Research Publications, 1992).
35 Webster and Frankland, *Strategic Air Offensive*, 2:22.
36 Harris, *Bomber Offensive*, p. 144.
37 Martin Gilbert, *Winston S. Churchill: Road to Victory 1941–1945* (Hillsdale, MI: Hillsdale College Press, 1986), pp. 19–20.
38 See UKNA AIR 20/4832, letter from Bufton to ACAS (Ops), 27 May 1943, in which Bufton suggests that Harris be reminded that 'only a proportion of the night bombing effort can be employed effectively' against Luftwaffe targets.

Chapter 11

1 Franz-Josef Brüggemeier, *Leben vor Ort: Ruhrbergleute und Ruhrbergbau 1889–1919,* Munich: C. H. Beck, 1984), p. 42
2 Ibid. pp. 48–9.
3 Lynn Abrams, 'Zur Entwicklung einer kommerziellen Arbeiterkultur im Ruhrgebiet (1850–1914)' in Dagmar Kift (ed.), *Kirmes, Kneipe, Kino: Arbeiterkultur im Ruhrgebiet zwischen Kommerz und Kontrolle* (Paderborn: Schöningh, 1992), pp. 41–7.
4 Tooze, *Wages of Destruction*, pp. 597–8.
5 Harris, *Bomber Offensive*, p. 144.
6 Police report, 'Der Angriff', sent to the author by H. Pavis, April 2007.
7 'Die Nacht als Essen unterging', *NRZ: Zeitung für Essen*, 6 March 1993.
8 Middlebrook, *Bomber Command War Diaries*, p. 366.
9 Tooze, *Wages of Destruction*, p. 597.
10 Middlebrook, *Bomber Command War Diaries*, p. 388.
11 And as such are well known. This account draws mostly on Neillands, *Bomber War*, chapter 10.

12 Quoted in Probert, *Bomber Harris*, p. 254. Harris later denied making this statement, but it certainly sounds like him.

13 Ibid.

14 Ibid.

15 Overy, *Bombing War*, p. 324.

16 Neillands, *Bomber War*, p. 232.

17 Ibid.

18 Hopgood's story told at 'A Dambuster's Daughter'. Available at http://www.bombercommandmuseum.ca

19 Neillands, *Bomber War*, p. 232.

20 Overy, *Bombing War*, p. 324.

21 Spencer Dunmore, *Above and Beyond: The Canadians' War in the Air, 1939–45* (Toronto: McClelland & Stewart, 1996), p. 258.

22 Another theory holds that friendly fire killed Gibson: '"Friendly fire" claim over Dambuster Guy Gibson's death', *BBC News*, 12 October 2011. Available at: https://www.bbc.com/news/uk-england-lincolnshire-15258690. Filmmakers claimed that a British veteran, wracked by guilt, confessed to shooting Gibson's plane down. There has been no verification of the theory, and how he could have known it was Gibson's plane is unclear.

23 The 'Baby Blitz', Operation Steinbock, was six months away. It involved revenge attacks on London, Bristol, Hull, and smaller English cities, killing some 1,500 Britons, but it cost the Germans more in lost aircraft and increasingly scarce airmen.

24 'How The Times Reported the Dambusters Raid', available at: https://www.thetimes.co.uk/article/how-the-times-reported-the-dambusters-raid-lgxr6wvxr

25 Speer, *Inside the Third Reich*, p. 384. Speer's claims here are corroborated by BArch Berlin, R3/1737, 18 March 1943, p. 34.

26 Overy, *Bombing War*, p. 325.

27 Tooze, *Wages of Destruction*, p. 597.

28 Seven thousand from the Atlantic Wall according to Speer, *Inside the Third Reich*, p. 385. We have documentary evidence of his 'return in May, June and July to energise the emergency response and to rally the workforce with well-advertised displays of personal bravery'. Tooze, *Wages of Destruction*, p. 598. For the documents, see BArch Berlin R 3/1738, 11 June 1943, pp. 83–5. More on this below.

29 Speer, *Inside the Third Reich*, p. 385.

30 Ibid.

31 Tooze, *Wages of Destruction*, p. 597.

32 Overy, *Bombing War*, p. 325.

33 Middlebrook, *Bomber Command War Diaries*, pp. 390–1.

34 Ibid., p. 395.

35 Ibid., p. 394.

36 UKNA, AIR 19/189, letter from Portal to Churchill, 15 October 1943.

37 Details in this paragraph from Middlebrook, *Bomber Command War Diaries*, pp. 396–401.

38 Neillands, *Bomber War*, p. 222. Calculated at 1,000 aircraft seven aircrew per plane.

39 Quoted in Probert, *Bomber Harris*, p. 254.

40 UKNA, AIR 8/1109, Joint Intelligence Committee, 'Effects of Bombing Offensive on German War Effort', 22 July 1943; AIR 20/476, Air Ministry DOI, 'Effects of Air raids on Labour and Production', 17 August 1943; O. Lawrence (MEW) to Morely (BOPs I), 6 September 1943; note from Lawrence to Bufton, 24 October 1943.

41 Overy, *Bombing War*, p. 326.

42 Tooze, *Wages of Destruction*, p. 598.

43 Ibid.

44 Overy, *Bombing War*, p. 322.

45 Speer, *Inside the Third Reich*, p. 383.

46 Probert, *Bomber Harris*, p. 339.

47 On this, see Harris, *Bomber Harris*, pp. 176–7.

48 UKNA, 14/3507, letter from Harris to the Prime Minister, 17 June 1942.

49 In Europe, it was the second largest after London, but the claim was always a bit of a fudge: its defined urban area is nineteen times larger than compact Paris. If a similar portion of Île de France is included, Paris was and is much larger than Berlin.

50 Overy, *Bombing War*, p. 304; The Churchill Archives Centre, Churchill College, Cambridge, CHAR 20/87, letter from Churchill to the Secretary of State for Air, 17 August 1942.

Chapter 12

1 Friedrich, *The Fire*, p. 25.

2 Fort, *Prof*, p. 28.

3 William S. Farren and R. V. Jones, 'Henry Thomas Tizard. 1885–1959', *Biographical Memoirs of Fellows of the Royal Society*, 7 (1961): pp. 313–48, 331.

4 Ibid., pp. 329–30.

5 Friedrich, *The Fire*, pp. 25–6.

6 Farren and Jones, 'Tizard', p. 333.

7 Friedrich, *The Fire*, pp. 25–6.

8 R. V. Jones, *Most Secret War* (London: Hamish Hamilton, 1978), pp. 290–291.

9 Ibid.,p. 291.

10 Ibid.

11 Hastings, *Bomber Command*, p. 129.

12 Ibid., p. 205.

13 RAF Archives, H 35. Memo from Arthur Harris on 'Window', 13 May 1942; Harris, *Bomber Offensive,* p. 143.

14 Hastings, *Bomber Command*, p. 205. Overy says 15 July; see notes 125 and 126 on page 741.

15 Brunswig, *Feuersturm über Hamburg*, p. 194.

16 Ibid.

Chapter *13*

1 The details in this paragraph are taken from Keith Lowe, *Inferno: The Devastation of Hamburg, 1943* (London: Viking, 2007), 78–80. The weather that day was lovely. See https://www.metoffice.gov.uk/binaries/content/assets/mohippo/pdf/d/k/jul1943.pdf.

2 Quoted in Lowe, *Inferno*, p. 79.

3 Ibid., pp. 80–1.

4 Quoted ibid., pp. 82–3.

5 Ibid., p. 83.

6 Ibid., p. 86.

7 There were 791 bombers in total: 347 Lancasters, 246 Halifaxes, 125 Stirlings, and 73 Wellingtons. Brunswig, *Feuersturm über Hamburg*, p. 193; Hauschild-Thiessen, *Die Hamburger Katastrophe*, p. 13.

8 Lowe, *Inferno*, p. 93.

9 Ibid.

10 For the biographical details, see 'Kammhuber, Josef (1896–1986)' in David T. Zabecki (ed.), *Germany at War: 400 Years of Military History* (Santa Barbara, CA: ABC-CLIO, 2014), p. 683.

11 Overy, *Bombing War*, p. 275.

12 Ibid., p. 323.

13 Friedrich, *The Fire*, p. 30; Overy, *Bombing War*, p. 275.

14 Friedrich, *The Fire*, p. 30.

15 Ibid.; Overy, *Bombing War*, p. 275.

16 Friedrich, *The Fire*, p. 30.

17 Details in this paragraph from Friedrich, *The Fire*, p. 31.

18 Lowe, *Inferno*, pp. 92, 94.

19 Brunswig, *Feuerstürm über Hamburg*, p. 194.

20 The quotation is a supposition on my part. According to Lowe, *Inferno*,
    94, Schwabedissen 'demanded to know what was going on'. Given the cir-
    cumstances, and that Germans are generally not given to understatement,
    this was likely the mildest interpretation of what he might have said.

21 Lowe, *Inferno*, p. 94.

22 Quoted ibid., p. 95.

23 Middlebrook, *Battle of Hamburg*, p. 135.

24 UKNA (24/25 July 1943). Bomber Command Night Raid Report no.
    383. AIR 14/3410. London, pp. 398–400.

25 'Heute vor 60 Jahren in Hamburgs Zeitungen', *Hamburger Abendblatt*,
    22 July 2003, p. 12.

26 Middlebrook, *The Battle of Hamburg*, p. 137.

27 728 of 791 dispatched. TNA (24/25 July 1943). Bomber Command Night
    Raid Report no. 383. AIR 14/3410. London, pp.398–400.

28 Kevin Wilson, *Bomber Boys: The Ruhr, the Dambusters, and Bloody
    Berlin* (London: Cassell, 2005), p. 259.

29 Norman Longmate, *The Bombers: The RAF Offensive against Germ*any
    (London: Hutchinson, 1983), pp. 265–6.

30 Overy, *Bombing War*, p. 327; Private papers of Winston Churchill,
    Churchill College, Cambridge ("Churchill papers'), BUFT 3/27 (i), 'The
    Employment of H.E. Bombs in Incendiary Attack', 18 November 1942.
    The Air Ministry's work on obliterating cities by fire had begun at least
    a month earlier: BUFT 3/27, 'Air Attack by Fire', 17 October 1941.

31 Overy, *Bombing War*, p. 327.

32 Churchill papers, BUFT 3/27 (i), 'Employment of H.E. Bombs'.

33 Ibid.; Overy, *Bombing War*, p. 326.

34 Lowe, *Inferno*, p. 97.

35 With the exception of the fourth and sixth waves.

36 Staatsarchiv Hamburg (undated). Dr. Zaps, Oberst der
    Feuerschutzpolisei, 'Bericht über die Erfahrungen des FE-Dienstes bei
    den Luftangriffen auf Hamburg in der Zeit vom 24.7.–3.8.1943'. 333–3 I
    Feuerwehr I. Hamburg.

37 Brunswig, *Feuersturm überHamburg,* p. 201; Hauschild-Thiessen, *Die Hamburger Katastrophe*, p. 16.

38 Overy, *Bombing War*, p. 333.

39 Staatsarchiv Hamburg (undated). Zaps Bericht.

40 Brunswig, *Feuersturm über Hamburg,* pp. 204–5.

41 Ibid., p. 206; Longmate, *The Bombers*, p. 266.

42 Middlebrook, *Bomber Command War Diaries*, p. 412. There is a great deal of debate on the exact German death toll in the Battle of Hamburg. Overy, *Bombing War*, p. 34, citing several German sources (not all of which agree on the figure), estimates 37,000, down from earlier estimates of more than 40,000. However, his separate figures for the 24–5 and 27–8 July raids – 10,289 and 18,474, respectively – leave over 8,000 unaccounted for. Moreover, the casualty rate for the 24–5 July raid is well above most estimates, that of 28–9 July well below. I take 37,000 as the total, rely on Middlebrook for the smaller raids (1,500 on 24–5 July, 370 on 29–30 July and 57 on 2–3 August), and thus arrive at a figure of 35,143 for the night of the firestorm.

43 Middlebrook, *Battle of Hamburg*, p. 141.

Chapter 14

1 BArch Koblenz, N 1318/2, Rudolf Walters, 'Chronik', (February 1942), Bl. 16, 12.

2 Ibid., Bl. 16-18, Zit. B. 18. Cited in Brechtken, *Albert Speer*, p. 160.

3 Brechtken, *Albert Speer*, p. 160.

4 Ibid., p. 161.

5 Ibid.

6 Ibid.

7 Ibid.

8 Ibid.

9 Fest, *Final Verdict*, p. 138.

10 Ibid.

11 Brechtken, *Albert Speer*, p. 161.

12 Tooze, *Wages of Destruction*, p. 559.

13 Ibid.

14 Speer, *Inside the Third Reich*, p. 389.

15 Adapted from ibid.

16 Brechtken, *Albert Speer*, p. 48.

17 Staatsarchiv Hamburg (undated), Zaps Bericht.

18 Remaining details in this paragraph from Lowe, *Inferno*, pp. 303–4.

19 Dietmar Süß, *Tod aus der Luft: Kriegsgesellschaft und Luftkrieg in Deutschland und England* (Munich: Siedler, 2011), p. 412.

20 See the interview with Jochen Arndt in Clara Glynn, *The Hidden Jews of Berlin* 20:16, 1999, https://www.youtube.com/watch?v=V3_MIAEdAYg.

21 Tooze, *Wages of Destruction*, p. 554.

22 Alfred C. Mierzejewski, *The Collapse of the German War Economy, 1944–1945* (Chapel Hill: University of North Carolina Press, 1988), chapter 1.

23 Tooze, *Wages of Destruction*, p. 555.

24 Ibid., p. 556.

25 For the details, see Brechtken, *Albert Speer*, pp. 208–13.

26 Tooze, *Wages of Destruction*, p. 556. On the propaganda effort, which made a supposed 'armaments miracle' 'one more Triumph of the Will', see pages 553–5.

27 Tooze, *Wages of Destruction*, p. 556.

28 Details on the Schweinfurt-Regensburg raids taken from Martin Middlebrook, *The Schweinfurt-Regensburg Mission: The American Raids on 12 August 1943* (London: Allen Lane, 1983), pp. 65–67.

29 Martin Middlebrook, *The Berlin Raids: RAF Bomber Command Winter 1943–44* (London: Cassel, 2001), pp. 6–7.

30 Middlebrook, *Schweinfurt-Regensburg Mission*, p. 76.

31 Quoted in Schaffer, *Wings of Judgment*, p. 68.

32 UKNA, AIR 19/189, letter to Portal, 25 September 1943.

33 Schaffer, *Wings of Judgment*, p. 18.

34 Curtis LeMay (with MacKinlay Kantor), *Mission with LeMay: My Story* (New York: Doubleday, 1965), p. 425.

35 Middlebrook, *Schweinfurt-Regensburg Mission*, pp. 76–7.

36 Middlebrook, *Schweinfurt-Regensburg Mission*, p. 80.

37 Schaffer, *Wings of Judgment*, p. 66.

38 Spaatz papers, box I: 136, interview with Colonel Curtis LeMay by Dr. Bruce C. Hopper, 7 September 1943, p. 21.

39 Quoted in Middlebrook, *Schweinfurt-Regensburg Mission*, p. 174.

40 Middlebrook, *Schweinfurt-Regensburg Mission*, p. 184.

41 Interview with Wilbur Klint, 24 August 2007. Two of the eight RAF squadrons providing escort support were Polish. Middlebrook, *Schweinfurt-Regensburg Mission*, p. 184.

42 Interview with Wilbur Klint.

43 Ibid.

44 Middlebrook, *Schweinfurt-Regensburg Mission*, p. 198.

45 Ibid., p. 201.

46 Ibid., pp. 221–2.

47 Hanson W. Baldwin, 'Air Power: What it Can – and Cannot – Do', *New York Times Magazine*, 26 March 1944.

48 Overy, *Bombing War*, p. 340.

49 Tooze, *Wages of Destruction*, p. 604. Tooze attributes the suicide to Hamburg, raids that had occurred two weeks earlier.

50 Parton (1986), '*Air Force Spoken Here*', p. 311.

51 UKNA, AIR 19/189, 'Most Secret. Increased importance of Schweinfurt as an Objective for RAF Bomber Command', 12 December 1943, and letter from Bottomley to Harris, 17 December 1943.

52 UKNA, AIR 19/189, letter from Bottomley to Harris, 23 December 1943.

53 Portal papers, letter from Harris to Portal, 18 January 1945.

54 UKNA, AIR 19/189, letter from Harris to Bottomley, 28 December 1943.

55 He had been doing so since 1942. See UKNA AIR 14/3507, letter from Harris to the Prime Minister, 2 May 1942. It is a response to Churchill's questions on (a) why he bombed Augsburg and (b) why he did not bomb Schweinfurt.

56 Wilson, *Bomber Boys*, p. 312.

57 Overy, *Bombing War*, p. 342; Martin Middlebrook, *The Peenemünde Raid: The Night of 17–18 August 1943* (London: Pen & Sword, 2000), p. 220.

58 Brechtken, *Albert Speer*, p. 216.

59 German Historical Institute, 'Forced Labour for the "Final Victory"', 2011. https://www.ghi-dc.org/events-conferences/event-history/exhibitions/forced-labor-for-the-final-victory-mittelbau-dora-concentration-camp-1943-1945.html.

60 Brechtken, *Albert Speer*, p. 216. Speer himself visited Mittelwerk in December 1943 and saw at first hand the conditions. He was unmoved by them. See ibid., p. 225.

61 Ibid., p. 216.

62 Tooze, *Wages of Destruction*, p. 623.

63 Jens-Christian Wagner, 'Mittelbau-Dora – Stammlager', in Wolfgang Benz and Barbara Distel (eds.), *Der Ort des Terrors: Geschichte der nationalsozialistischen Konzentrationslager* (Munich: C. H. Beck, 2008), pp. 230–1.

64 Tooze, *Wages of Destruction*, p. 623.

65 Dwight D. Eisenhower, *Crusade in Europe* (Baltimore: Johns Hopkins

University Press, 1948), p. 260; Middlebrook, *Peenemünde Raid*, p. 220. Speer, with the support slave labour provided by Himmler, took the lead on moving production underground. Brechtken, *Albert Speer*, p. 215.

66 Overy, *Bombing War*, p. 343. In response to claims in the July briefing about Schweinfurt's importance, Harris scribbled in the margin, 'sez you!' Overy cites the following primary documents: UKNA, AIR 8 14/783, letter from Portal to Harris, 7 October 1943, enclosed Air Staff Memorandum on 'The Extent to which the Eighth U.S.A.A.F. and Bomber Command have been able to implement the G.A.F. Plan'; and RAFM, Harris papers, H47, Norman Bottomley, 'Special Brief for the Schweinfurt Operation', 25 July 1943; and letter from Bottomley to Harris, 20 December 1943.

67 Overy, *Bombing War*, p. 342.

68 Albert Speer, *Inside the Third Reich,* p. 391.

69 Ibid., p. 390.

70 Overy, *Bombing War*, pp. 340–1.

71 Quoted in Coffey, *Hap*, p. 321.

72 Ibid.

73 Danchev and Todman, *War Diaries of Alanbrooke*, p. 441; Parton, *Air Force Spoken Here*, p. 303.

74 Details and quotations in this section from Parton, *Air Force Spoken Here*, pp. 303–5. The original text, as was the style at the time, is written in third-person past tense. I have put it into the present for ease of reading.

75 Emphasis added.

76 Details from Parton, *Air Force Spoken Here*, pp. 305–6.

77 Ibid., p. 306.

78 Coffey, *Hap*, p. 322.

79 Parton, *Air Force Spoken Here*, p. 313.

80 Quoted in Coffey, *Hap*, p. 322.

81 Quoted in Ian L. Hawkins, *The Munster Raid: Before and After* (Trumbull, CT: FNP Military Division, 1999), p. 72.

82 Quotations and story ibid., pp. 74–5.

83 Interview with Wilbur Klint, 24 August 2007.

84 Ira Eaker papers, box I: 17, 'Text of Cable – Eaker to Arnold', 15 October 1943.

85 Ibid.

86 Speer, *Inside the Third Reich*, p. 391.

87 Ibid.

88 UKNA, AIR 19/189, 'Most Secret. Increased importance of
Schweinfurt', 12 December 1943; letter from Bottomley to Harris, 17
December 1943: 'It is suggested that a night area attack on Schweinfurt
be made by the main force of Bomber Command . . . A successful attack
would undoubtedly justify great efforts to secure destruction of this
target, and would constitute a major contribution to the success of the
Combined Bomber Offensive Plan.'

89 Ira Eaker papers, 'Text of Cable – Eaker to Arnold', 15 October 1943.

90 Speer, *Inside the Third Reich,* p. 391.

91 TNA, AIR 19/189, 'Most Secret. Increased importance of Schweinfurt',
12 December 1943; letter from Bottomley to Harris, 17 December 1943.

Chapter 15

1 Details from Middlebrook, *Berlin Raids*, pp. 8–9.

2 Ibid., p. 8

3 Ibid., p. 7.

4 Ibid.

5 Ibid., pp. 8–9.

6 Stories and quotations ibid., pp. 53–5.

7 Ibid., p. 55.

8 Kevin Hornibrook's story is found ibid., pp. 58–60.

9 Ibid, p. 58.

10 Interview with Werner Schenk, 24 August 2007.

11 Rolf-Dieter Müller, *Der Bombenkrieg 1939–1945* (Berlin: Ch. Links
Verlag, 2004), p. 167.

12 Ibid.

13 Interview with Günther Ackerhans, 13 July 2007.

14 Details from the diary of Hans-Werner Mihan, portions of which he
provided to the author.

15 Peter Spoden's story and quotations from Middlebrook, *Berlin Raids*,
pp. 51–3.

16 Reported in secondary accounts as Grunewalddamm 69, but there is no
such street in Berlin, there is no evidence available that indicates such
a street existed during the war. Kurfürstendamm, however, leads to
Grunewald, and number 69 is a typical block of purpose-built flats from
the Wilhelminian period.

17 'Wild Sow' or 'Wild Pig' is the better translation as the German for boar

is *der Eber*, but Wild Boar is widely used within the secondary literature.
18 Neillands, *Bomber War*, p. 239.
19 Middlebrook, *Berlin Raids*, p. 16.
20 Ibid.
21 Neillands, *Bomber War*, p. 239.
22 Middlebrook, *Berlin Raids*, pp. 16–17.
23 The V-1 and V-2 rockets were the result of an argument among Third Reich leaders about how to use the Luftwaffe. Erhard Milch favoured from late 1942 a full concentration on air defences against Allied bombing; Hitler, with Göring's sycophantic support, wanted the Luftwaffe to remain an offensive weapon. Hitler's victory, which led to the ineffective Baby Blitz as well as the V-1 and V-2 raids, did much good for the Allied cause. Overy, *Iron Knight*, pp. 193–5.
24 Portal papers, letter from Harris to Churchill, 3 November 1943.
25 Middlebrook, *Bomber Command War Diaries*, p. 440; Overy, *Bombing War*, p. 342. Kassel is a small city, so 5,600 deaths represented a higher percentage of the urban population than the Hamburg death toll.
26 Overy, *Bombing War*, p. 342.
27 Letter from Harris to the Prime Minister, 3 November 1943.
28 Middlebrook, *Berlin Raids*, p. 307 (bombing statistics) and p. 321 (civilian casualties).
29 Longmate, *The Bombers*, p. 288.
30 Sebastian Cox, 'Introduction', in Arthur Harris, *Despatch on War Operations 23rd February, 1942 to 8th May, 1945* (London: Frank Cass, 1995), p. xxi.
31 UKNA, AIR 19/189, letter from W. A. Coryton, ACAS (Ops) to Portal, 5 November 1943.
32 Neillands, *Bomber War*, p. 290.
33 Middlebrook, *Bomber Command War Diaries*, p. 477.
34 Ibid., pp. 482–3.
35 Hastings, *Bomber Command*, p. 257.
36 Longmate, *The Bombers*, p. 293.
37 Middlebrook, *Bomber Command War Diaries*, p. 487.
38 Longmate, *The Bombers*, p. 298.
39 Hastings, *Bomber Command*, p. 268.
40 See Neillands, *Bomber War*, p. 301.

Chapter 16

1 'Bomb Damage at Essen', *The Times*, 21 March 1942, p. 3.
2 Quoted in *The Times*, 'Bomb Havoc in Germany. Sir A. Sinclair's Forecast: Ruthless Attacks', 24 August 1942, p. 2. Similarly, after Cripps's 25 February 1942 speech, Sinclair told a Bristol audience that the 'one force which can and will strike hard blows this year and at the very heart of Germany is the Royal Air Force . . . . [When the weather improves,] Bomber Command will be ready to carry into Germany destruction on a greater scale than your own beautiful city suffered a year ago.' UKNA, AIR 8/619, 'We must take Germany by the Throat – and Start in 1942', 28 February 1942.
3 'R.A.F. Targets in Germany. Comparison of Bombing Damage', *Times*, 1 January 1943, p. 8.
4 'Effects of Bombing Inside Germany. New Propaganda Note', *Times*, 21 June 1943, p. 3.
5 'U-Boat Yard Blazes Night and Day', *Daily Sketch*, March 30, 1942.
6 'Hamburg Smoke at 24,000 feet. Fires Seen 200 Miles Away', *Times*, 29 July 1943.
7 UKNA, AIR 19/189, letter from William Cantaur to Sinclair, 9 July 1943.
8 UKNA, AIR 19/189, letter from Sinclair to the Archbishop of Canterbury, 19 July 1943.
9 UKNA, AIR 20/4191, note from Richard Peck to U.S. of S. (L), 17 June 1944.
10 UKNA, AIR 20/4191, note to A.C.A.S (G), 2 May 1944.
11 UKNA, AIR 20/4191, Bombing Restriction Committee, 'Stop Bombing Civilians!' (1943), p. 5.
12 Schaffer, *Wings of Judgment*, p. 69.
13 Ibid.
14 Jana Flemming, 'Der Bombenkrieg im Meinungsbuild der britischen Öffentlichkeit 1940–1944' in Bernd Heidenreich and Sönke Neitzel (eds.), *Der Bombenkrieg und seine Opfer* (Wiesbaden: Hessische Landeszentrale für politische Bildung, 2004), 21.
15 Ibid.
16 The Air Ministry noted the trend. On 28 January 1944, Richard Peck, assistant chief of Air Staff, noted the 'volume of sympathy for German "civilians" affected by our air attacks is tending to increase'. UKNA AIR 20/4191, letter from Peck to U.S. of S. (L) [likely Robert A. Lovett], 28 January 1944.

17 See, for instance, UKNA, AIR 20/4191, Bombing Restriction Committee, 'Stop Bombing Civilians!' (1943), p. 5.

18 Air Commodore Howard-Williams, '74,000 tons of Bombs on Nazis in 100 days', *Daily Telegraph*, 21 October 1943. Copied from UKNA, AIR 2/7852.

19 UKNA, AIR 2/7852, letter from Arthur Harris to the Under Secretary of State, Air Ministry, 25 October 1943.

20 Ibid.

21 UKNA, AIR 19/189, letter from A.W. Street to Portal, 28 October 1943.

22 UKNA, AIR 2/7852, Minute from the Deputy Chief of the Air Staff, Norman Bottomley to Richard Peck, 5 November 1943.

23 UKNA, AIR 2/7852, letter from A.W. Street to Arthur Harris, 15 December 1943.

24 Emphasis in the original.

25 UKNA, AIR 2/7852, letter from Harris to the Under Secretary of State, Air Ministry, 23 December 1943.

26 Ibid.

27 UKNA, AIR 8/1161, 'Joint Report by Ministry of Economic Warfare and Air Intelligence on Effects of Bomber Offensive', 4 November 1943. Also see 'Joint Intelligence Sub-Committee: Effects of Bombing on German War Effort', 12 November 1943.

28 See UKNA, AIR 8/1167.

29 UKNA, AIR 2/7852, letter from Air Ministry to Harris, undated.

Chapter 17

1 Quoted in Davis, *Carl A. Spaatz*, pp. 299–300. Spaatz had viewed Luftwaffe fighters as the greatest threat since at least September 1944, before the Schweinfurt raid. Carl Spaatz papers, box 50, file on 'Aircraft Development – Jet Propellers', letter from Arnold to Spaatz, 21 September 1944.

2 Spaatz papers, box I: 135, Major General Orvill Anderson, Chief, Strategic Bombing Survey, interviewed by Historical Section, USSTAF, 22 August 1945, p. 9.

3 Ira Eaker papers, box I: 17, 'Text of Cable – Eaker to Arnold', 15 October 1943.

4 Miller, *Masters of the Air*, p. 247.

NOTES

5 Spaatz papers, box I: 137, 'Jockey Committee: Its History and Functions', undated.

6 UKNA, AIR 19/189, letter from Portal to ACAS (Ops), 10 June 1943.

7 UKNA, AIR 19/189, letter from A.W. Street to Portal, 31 October 1943.

8 Miller, *Masters of the Air*, p. 254.

9 Davis, *Carl A. Spaatz*, p. 303.

10 Details on Leigh-Mallory found ibid., pp. 310–12.

11 Quoted ibid., p. 318. On that night, the RAF dropped 2,642 tons of bombs on Berlin, killing 320 people. Neillands, *Bomber War*, p. 290.

12 See clippings in Spaatz papers, box I: 75.

13 Quoted in Davis, *Carl A. Spaatz*, p. 318.

14 Miller, *Masters of the Air*, p. 257.

15 Ibid.

16 On this, see ibid., p. 321.

17 Kirk liked eccentric schemes. He once secured $3,000 from the City of San Diego to study means of mechanically extracting rain from passing clouds. The city council was, however, reminded of a 1915 experience in which it paid a rainmaker, Charles Hatfield, to help the city with a particularly severe drought. Hatfield constructed a twenty-foot tower, poured a rain-making brew into pans, and set the fluid on fire. Seventeen inches of rain fell in the following five days, and thirty overall in January 1916. Floodwaters and landslides swept away homes, roads, railroad tracks, and telephone lines, and supplies had to be ferried into San Diego. Hatfield was never paid. Fearing another Hatfield deluge, the council backed out of its deal with Kirk. On Hatfield, see Christopher Klein, 'When San Diego Hired a Rainmaker a Century Ago, It Poured', *JSTOR Daily* (12 December 2015). On Kirk, see Jack Scheffler Innis, *San Diego Legends: The Events, People, and Places that Made History* (San Diego: Sun Belt Publications, 2004), p. 102.

18 Davis, *Carl A. Spaatz*, p. 257.

19 Spaatz papers, box I: 169, 'Materiel behind the "Big Week"', 25 April 1944.

20 Spaatz papers, box I: 153, Notes on the Weather Aspects of Strategic Air Force Operations during the Period 20–25 February, 1944; 'Heavy Rain, Hail, and Snow Storm Lashes City, Crippling Power Service', *Los Angeles Times*, 21 February 1944.

21 Details from Davis, *Carl A. Spaatz*, p. 260.

22 Miller, *Masters of the Air*, p. 256.

23 Ibid., p. 260.

– 471 –

24 Quoted in Davis, *Carl A. Spaatz*, p. 323.

25 Tooze, *Wages of Destruction*, p. 626.

26 Spaatz papers, box I: 169, 'The Big Week'.

27 Davis, *Carl A. Spaatz*, p. 323.

28 UKNA, AIR 14/739A, letter from Norman Bottomley to Arthur Harris, 19 January 1944. For the memorandum, see the 'Secret Telegram to Washington', 29 January 1944.

29 UKNA, AIR 14/739A, letters from Harris to Bottomley, 21 and 22 January 1944 and 'Attacks delivered against German towns associated with G.A.F. production', 4 June 1943.

30 Carl Spaatz papers, box I: 144, 'Operations of the R.A.F./February 20th-25th inclusive', undated; Middlebrook, *Bomber Command War Diaries*, pp. 473–6.

31 Miller, *Masters of the Air*, p. 271.

32 Quoted ibid., p. 272.

33 Jeffrey Ethell and Alfred Price, *Target Berlin. Mission 250: 6 March 1944* (London: Jane's Information Group, 1981), p. 95.

34 Statistics on lost bombers and destroyed German fighters from Overy, *Bombing War*, p. 371.

35 Ibid. Miller, *Masters of the Air*, p. 273, suggests a larger figure of sixty-six fighters, which seems too high.

36 This quotation and details in the following two paragraphs from Miller, *Masters of the Air*, pp. 274–5.

37 Gunners used foraged armour plates as 'eunuch protectors'.

38 Overy, *Bombing War*, 373. Statistics from January to June.

39 Ibid.

Chapter 18

1 Royal Air Force Museum, *The Liberation of Northwest Europe* (London: Royal Air Force Museum Archives), I:142.

2 Ibid., p. 145.

3 Ibid., p. 142.

4 Ibid., p. 147.

5 A view that had not changed in over fifteen years: 'the Air Force,' he said in the late 1920s, 'does not aim to win wars by itself – nor do any of the other services.' Royal Air Force Museum, Tedder papers, B 270, Lecture on 'Air Power', 2 February 1928.

NOTES

6 Davis, *Carl A. Spaatz*, p. 347

7 Quoted ibid., p. 349.

8 Details of the meeting found ibid., pp. 350–3.

9 Quoted ibid., p. 350.

10 Ibid.

11 UKNA, AIR 41/66, RAF Narrative, 'The Liberation of Northwest Europe,' I:154.

12 Quoted in Probert, *Bomber Harris*, pp. 291–2.

13 Spaatz papers, telegram from Spaatz to Cabell, 17 March 1944.

14 Quoted in Probert, *Bomber Harris*, p. 291.

15 Middlebrook, *The Bomber Command War Diaries*, p. 479.

16 Probert, *Bomber Harris*, p. 291.

17 Davis, *Carl A. Spaatz*, p. 353.

18 Spaatz papers, box I: 136, Interview of General Carl Spaatz by Dr Bruce C. Hopper, Historian USSTAF, 20 May 1945, pp. 14–15.

19 Quoted in Davis, *Carl A. Spaatz*, p. 353.

20 Ibid., p. 354.

21 In the first quarter of 1944, synthetic oil plants near coal deposits in the Ruhr, Silesia, and around Leipzig produced over half of Germany's total fuel supplies. Miller, *Masters of the Air*, p. 313.

22 Parton, *'Air Force Spoken Here'*, p. 385.

23 Davis, *Carl A. Spaatz*, p. 386.

24 Davis, 'Spaatz', *Air Force Magazine*, p. 72.

25 UKNA, AIR 8/1229, letter from the Chief of Staffs to Churchill, undated.

26 UKNA, AIR 8/1229, extract from Minute to the Prime Minister from the Chief of the Air Staff, 19 January 1944.

27 UKNA, AIR 8/1229, War Cabinet. Chiefs of Staff Committee, 'Operation Crossbow. Report by the Vice Chiefs of Staff', 8 December 1943.

28 'Army and Navy: Silence is Golden', *Time*, 19 June 1944.

29 Overy, *Bombing War*, p. 371.

30 Adolf Galland, *The First and the Last: The Rise and Fall of the German Fighter Forces, 1938-1945* (London: Methuen & Co., 1955), p. 280.

31 Davis, *Carl A. Spaatz and the Air War in Europe*, p. 396.

32 Overy, *Bombing War*, p. 371. German reports claimed 73 bombers (see Galland, *First and Last*, p. 280), but it was common for defending fighters to overstate 'kills'.

33 Overy, *Bombing War*, p. 371.

34 Speer, *Inside the Third Reich*, p. 468.

35 Quoted in Brechtken, *Albert Speer*, p. 257. The original source is Lutz
    Graf von Krosigk, *Es geschah in Deutschland: Menschenbilder unseres
    Jahrhunderts* (Tübingen: Rainer Wunderlich Verlag, 1951), pp. 300–5.

36 Boog, *Bomber Offensive*, p. 849.

37 Davis, *Carl A. Spaatz*, p. 398.

38 Ibid.

39 Quoted in Miller, *Masters of the Air*, p. 290.

40 Wesley Frank Craven and James Lea Cate, *The Army Air Forces in
    World War II. Volume 3: Argument to V-E Day* (Chicago: University of
    Chicago Press, 1951), p. 178.

41 Overy, *Bombing War*, p. 371.

42 Last two quotations from Galland, *First and Last*, p. 279.

43 Fest, *Speer*, p. 219.

44 Miller, *Masters of the Air*, p. 272. By November, Speer reported that these
    attacks had sealed off the Ruhr. Tooze, *Wages of Destruction*, pp. 650–1.

45 Russell F. Weigley, *Eisenhower's Lieutenants: The Campaign of France
    and Germany 1944-1945* (Bloomington: Indiana University Press, 1981),
    p. 24.

46 Quoted in Galland, *First and Last*, p. 289.

47 Mierzejewski, *Collapse of the German War Economy*, p. 185.

Chapter 19

1 Quoted in Davis, *Carl A. Spaatz*, p. 399.

2 Webster and Frankland, *Strategic Air Offensive* (London: HMSO, 1961),
   3:47.

3 F. H. Hinsley, *British Intelligence in the Second World War*, (London:
   HMSO, 1979) vol. 3, part 2, pp. 502–3.

4 Details from Webster and Frankland, *Strategic Air Offensive*, 3:47.

5 Ibid.

6 Figures from Max Hastings, *Armageddon. The Battle for Germany
   1944–45*. (London: Macmillan, 2004), pp. 348–9.

7 Both quoted in Davis, *Carl A. Spaatz*, p. 442.

8 UKNA, War Cabinet. Joint Intelligence Sub-Committee. 'Effects of the
   Bombing Offensive on the German War Effort'. Report by the Joint
   Intelligence Committee (JIC [44] 241), 13 June 1944.

9 Details from Robert L. Beir, *Roosevelt and the Holocaust* (New Jersey:
   Barricade, 2006), p. 246.

10 Martin Gilbert, *Auschwitz and the Allies* (New York: Hold, Rinehart, and Winston, 1981), p. 190.

11 Jewish Virtual Library, *The Holocaust: The Vrba-Wetzler Report (Auschwitz Protocols) (April 25–27, 1944)*. https://www.jewishvirtuallibrary.org/the-vrba-wetzler-report-auschwitz-protocols.

12 Kastner negotiated with the Nazis to allow, in exchange for payment, 1,687 Jews to escape by train to Switzerland. One of them was Peter Munk, who over sixty years later endowed the Munk School of Global Affairs and Public Policy, where I teach. See Nina Munk, preface to Erno Munkácsi, *How it Happened: Documenting the Jewish Tragedy of Hungarian Jewry* (Montreal: McGill-Queen's University Press, 2018).

13 Gilbert, *Auschwitz and the Allies*, p. 232; David S. Wyman, *The Abandonment of the Jews: America and the Holocaust, 1941–1945* (New York: The Free Press, 1984), p. 290.

14 David S. Wyman, 'Why Auschwitz was never Bombed', *Commentary* 65, no. 5 (1978): pp. 37–46, 38; Gilbert, *Auschwitz and the Allies*, p. 232.

15 Gilbert, *Auschwitz and the Allies*, p. 233.

16 Quoted in Beir, *Roosevelt and the Holocaust*, pp. 247–8.

17 Wyman, *Abandonment of the* Jews, p. 290.

18 Gilbert, *Auschwitz and the Allies*, p. 238.

19 Ibid., p. 339.

20 From early that year, the SS expressed fears that the Allies were targeting concentration camps and that such attacks would allow prisoners to escape. BArch Berlin, NS 19/1542, letter to Oswald Pöhl and Richard Glücks, 1943 (unclear month and date, but possibly February). The Allies were not.

21 Richard G. Davis, *Bombing the European Axis Powers: A Historical Digest of the Combined Bomber Offensive, 1939–1945* (Alabama: Air University Press, 2006), pp. 407–8.

22 Ibid., p. 406.

23 Miller, *Masters of the Air*, p. 323.

24 Davis, *Bombing the European Axis Powers*, p. 403.

25 Jewish Virtual Library, *Franklin Delano Roosevelt Administration: Statement on Holocaust Victims and Justice*, 24 March 1944. Available at: https://www.jewishvirtuallibrary.org/roosevelt-statement-on-holocaust-victims-and-justice

26 Davis, *Bombing the European Axis Powers*, p. 398.

27 Details in this paragraph from Gilbert, *Auschwitz and the Allies*, chapter 28.

28 Ibid., p. 270.

29 Ibid., p. 272. Italics in original.

30 Ibid., p. 279.

31 Ibid., p. 285.

32 Quoted in Beir, *Roosevelt and the Holocaust*, p. 248.

33 Ibid., p. 251.

34 Ibid.

35 Gilbert, *Auschwitz and the Allies*, p. 301.

36 Ibid., p. 309.

37 Wyman, *Abandonment of the Jews*, p. 300.

38 Gilbert, *Auschwitz and the Allies*, p. 303.

39 Wyman, *Abandonment of the Jews*, p. 300.

40 Miller, *Masters of the Air*, p. 327.

41 Ibid.

42 Letter from Shalom Lindenbaum to Martin Gilbert, 13 June 1980, quoted in Gilbert, *Auschwitz and the Allies*, p. 311.

43 Tooze, *Wages of Destruction*, p. 631.

44 UKNA, 14/3507, Letter from Harris to the Prime Minister, 17 June 1942.

45 UKNA, AIR 8/1229, Flying Bomb Statement by the Prime Minister, undated. See also AIR 8/1229, 'Attack on German Civilian Morale', 1 August 1944.

46 UKNA, PREM 3/4/2, minute from Portal to Churchill, 20 June 1944.

47 UKNA, AIR 8/1229, minute VCAS 1803, VCAS to CAS, subj: Crossbow, 2 July 1944.

48 UKNA, AIR 8/1229, War Cabinet. Chiefs of Staff Committee. '"Crossbow": Question of Retaliation', 5 July 1944.

49 UKNA, AIR 19/189, letter to CAS, 29 December 1943.

50 UKNA, AIR 8/1229, minute VCAS 1803, VCAS to CAS, subj: Crossbow, 2 July 1944.

51 Ibid.

52 UKNA, AIR 8/1229, 'Bombing of German towns in Retaliation for Flying Bomb Attacks: Appendix A', 1 July 1944.

53 Ibid.

54 Ibid.

55 UKNA, AIR 8/1229, minute VCAS 1803, VCAS to CAS, subj: Crossbow, 2 July 1944.

56 UKNA, AIR 8/1229, '"Crossbow" – the question of retaliation', 4 July 1944.

57 It is possible, but impossible to prove, that his reading of the Auschwitz

Protocols may have influenced his belligerent attitude. I owe this point to Richard Davis.

58 Davis, *Carl A. Spaatz*, p. 433.

59 UKNA, AIR 8/1229, note from Portal to Deputy Chief of Air Staff, 5 July 1944; AIR 8/1229, '"Crossbow" – the question of retaliation', 4 July 1944.

60 UKNA, AIR 8/1229, War Cabinet. Chiefs of Staff Committee. '"Crossbow": Question of Retaliation', 5 July 1944.

61 UKNA, AIR 8/1229, '"Crossbow" – the question of retaliation', 3 July 1944.

62 UKNA, AIR 20/4831, 'Operation Thunderclap', undated.

63 Schaffer, *Wings of Judgment*, p. 75.

64 Ibid., p. 76.

65 Quotations ibid.

66 Davis, *Carl A. Spaatz*, p. 438.

67 Details in this paragraph from Webster and Frankland, *Strategic Air Offensive*, 3:50.

68 UKNA, AIR 14/739a, note from Churchill to Sinclair, 13 July 1944; Harris, 'Memorandum: Attack of Flying Bomb and Rocket Installations in Enemy Occupied Territory', 18 July 1944.

69 Harris, 'Memorandum', ibid.

70 Andreas Förschler, *Unser Stuttgart geht unter: die Bombenangriffe im Juli und September 1944* (Wiesenthal: Wartberg, 2004), pp. 25–36.

71 Middlebrook, *Bomber Command War Diaries*, p. 549.

72 UKNA, AIR 8/1229, War Cabinet. Chiefs of Staff Committee. 'An Attack on German Civilian Morale', memorandum by the Chief of Air Staff, 1 August 1944. See also UKNA, AIR 20/4831, 'Attack on German Civilian Morale', 17 July 1944.

73 UKNA, AIR 20/4831, COS (44) 650 (O), 'Attack on German Civilian Morale', 2 August 1944.

74 Carl Spaatz Papers, box I: 146, D.B. Ops., '"Operation Thunderclap": Attack on German Morale', 20 August 1944.

75 UKNA, AIR 20/4831, 'Operation Thunderclap', undated. These projected figures are very close to the eventual death toll in the March 1945 destruction of Tokyo.

76 UKNA, AIR 8/1229, 'Attack on German Civilian Morale', 1 August 1944, emphasis in the original.

77 Ibid.

78 UKNA, AIR 20/4831, draft D.B., Ops comments on 'Attack on the German Government Machine', outline plan by Joint Planning Staff J.P (44)203(O). Revised preliminary draft, 15 August 1944.

79 Max Hastings, *Bomber Command*, p. 301.
80 Carl Spaatz papers, box I: 146, Robert A. McLure, 'Operation "Thunderclap"', 16 September 1944.
81 Ibid.
82 Miller, *Masters of the Air*, p. 412.
83 Spaatz papers, box I: 153, letter from Maj. General L. S. Kuter to Maj. General Frederick L. Anderson, 15 August 1944.
84 Spaatz papers, ibid.
85 Spaatz papers, box I: 135. Interview with Brigadier Gen. Cabell, 9 July 1944.
86 Quoted in Schaffer, *Wings of Judgment*, p. 83.
87 Spaatz papers, diary, box I: 15, letter from Spaatz to Arnold, 21 August 1944.
88 Schaffer, *Wings of Judgment*, pp. 61–2.
89 Spaatz papers, box I: 135, memorandum from Arnold to General F. L. Anderson, 12 September 1944.
90 Spaatz papers, box I: 153, C.P. Cabell, 'Attacks for Demoralisation of the German People', 26 June 1944.
91 Spaatz papers, box I: 153, 'Plan for Systematically Attacking Morale within Germany', 18 September 1944.
92 UKNA, AIR 8/1229, minute from the Prime Minister to the Chiefs of Staff, 23 August 1944.
93 Ibid.
94 Spaatz papers, diary, box I: 15, 'Daily Summary of Intelligence', 18 August 1944.
95 Webster and Frankland, *Strategic Air Offensive*, 3:50.
96 Davis, *Carl A. Spaatz*, pp. 434–5.
97 Spaatz papers, subject file 1929–1945, memo from Anderson to director of operations, 21 July 1944.
98 Davis, *Carl A. Spaatz*, p. 435.
99 Spaatz papers, subject file 1929–1945, memo from Anderson to director of operations, 21 July 1944.
100 Searle, 'It Made a Lot of Sense', p. 108.
101 Overy, *Bombing War*, p. 347.
102 Details from Walter Gilbert's journal, sent to the author by his granddaughter, Michelle L. Gilbert, 13 September 2007.
103 Davis, *Carl A. Spaatz*, p. 443.

Chapter 20

1 Searle, 'It Made a Lot of Sense', p. 109.
2 Miller, *Masters of the Air*, p. 365.
3 Quoted ibid., pp. 364–5.
4 Davis, *Carl A. Spaatz*, p. 569.
5 Quoted in Miller, *Masters of the Air*, p. 365.
6 Overy, *Bombing War*, p. 347.
7 Neillands, *Bomber War*, p. 338.
8 Details on the bombing from Peter Engels, 'Darmstadts Zerstörung aus der Luft', in Bernd Heidenreich and Sönke Neitzel (eds.), *Der Bombenkrieg und seine Opfer* (Wiesbaden: Hessische Landeszentrale für politische Bildung, 2004), pp. 47–57. Also see Hastings, *Bomber Command*, chapter 13.
9 Middlebrook, *Bomber Command War Diaries*, pp. 580–1. On the internees, see Hastings, *Bomber Command*, p. 318.
10 Quoted in Engels, 'Darmstadts Zerstörung', pp. 47–57.
11 Miller, *Masters of the Air*, p. 439.
12 Neillands, *Bomber War*, p. 338.
13 Figures here from Middlebrook, *The Bomber Command War Diaries*, pp. 582–4.
14 Davis, *Bombing the European Axis Powers*, p. 424.
15 UKNA, AIR 14/3507, letter from Harris to Churchill, 30 September 1944. See also UKNA, AIR 20/4832, 'Weekly GAF Priority Signal', 31 August 1944 and 'A Counter Air Force Program for the Period from now until the German Collapse', [US Embassy], 24 October 1944.
16 Davis, *Bombing the European Axis Powers*, p. 437.
17 Middlebrook, *Bomber Command War Diaries*, p. 602.
18 Ibid.
19 Figures from Davis, *Bombing the European Axis Powers*, pp. 424–5.
20 Davis, *Bombing the European Axis Powers*, p. 425.
21 Quoted ibid., p. 446.
22 Portal papers, Harris correspondence 1944, No. 32, letter from Harris to Portal, 1 November 1944.
23 Biddle, *Rhetoric and Reality*, p. 248.
24 Spaatz papers, diary, letter from Spaatz to Arnold, 5 November 1944. Quoted in Davis, *Carl A. Spaatz*, p. 519.
25 UKNA, AIR 20/4832, memorandum by Wing Commander DS Allen, 26 October 1944.

26 Details in the next two paragraphs from Davis, *Carl A. Spaatz*, p. 521.

27 Quoted ibid., p. 522.

28 Middlebrook, *Bomber Command War Diaries*, p. 612.

29 Ibid., p. 613.

30 Portal papers, letter from Portal to Harris, 6 November 1944.

31 Stadtarchiv Solingen, *Solingen im Bombenhagel: 4. und 5. November 1944* (Wiesental: Wartberg Verlag, 2003).

32 Portal papers, letter from Harris to Portal, 6 November 1944.

33 Middlebrook, *Bomber Command War Diaries*, p. 583, Neillands, *Bomber War*, pp. 326–7.

34 Middlebrook, *Bomber Command War Diaries*, pp. 614-617.

35 Portal papers, letter from Portal to Harris, 12 November 1944.

36 Portal papers, letter from Portal to Harris, 6 November 1944.

37 Emphasis in the original.

38 'Designating' in the original, likely a typo.

39 Portal papers, letter from Harris to Portal, 24 November 1944.

40 Ulrich P. Ecker, *Freiburg 1944–1994: Zerstörung und Wiederaufbau* (Freiburg: Stadarchiv, 1994).

41 Gerd R. Ueberschär, 'Freiburgs letzte Kriegstage bis zur Besetzung durch die französische Armee am 21 April 1945', in Thomas Schnabel and Gerd R. Ueberschär, *Endlich Frieden! Das Kriegsende in Freiburg 1945* (Freiburg i. Br.: Schillinger Verlag, 1985), p. 9. Ecker, *Freiburg*, cites 3,000 deaths. With a few exceptions, it is wisest to opt for the lowest death toll estimates in bombing raids. Middlebrook, *Bomber Command War Diaries*, p. 623, puts the figure at 2,088.

42 Figures from Davis, *Bombing the European Axis Powers*, p. 467.

43 Hubert Bläsi and Christhard Schrenk, *Leben und Sterben einer Stadt* (Heilbronn: Stadtarchiv Heilbronn, 1995), p. 85.

44 Middlebrook, *Bomber Command War Diaries*, p. 627.

45 Details from Erich Lacker and Manfred Koch, *Zielort Karlsruhe: Die Luftangriffe im Zweiten Weltkrieg*, Karlsruhe city archives series, (Karlsruhe: Badenia Verlag, 1996).

46 Middlebrook, *Bomber Command War Diaries*, pp. 589–90. For the February attack, see page 658.

47 Portal papers, letter from Portal to Harris, 6 December 1944.

Chapter 21

1 The paragraphs on the Ardennes offensive draw on Hansen, *Disobeying Hitler*, pp. 170–6.
2 John Powell, ed., *Magill's Guide to Military History*, (Pasadena: Salem Press, Inc., 2001), p. 238.
3 R. V. Gersdorff, 'The Ardennes Offensive', n.d., USAMHI, D 379.F6713. The accent mark on Liége flipped to Liège in 1946.
4 Ibid.
5 David Jordan and Andrew Wiest, *Atlas des Zweiten Weltkriegs: vom Polenfeldzug bis zur Schlacht um Berlin* (Vienna: Tosa, 2005), p. 166.
6 Kershaw, *Hitler: Nemesis*, p. 742.
7 Ibid.
8 Weinberg, *World at Arms*, p. 766.
9 Gersdorff, 'Ardennes Offensive'.
10 UKNA, HW 1/3378, TOO 0745, West Europe, 12 December 1944.
11 Kershaw, *Hitler: Nemesis*, p. 742.
12 Davis, *Carl A. Spaatz*, p. 532.
13 Ibid.
14 Probert, *Bomber Harris*, p. 314.
15 Fest, *Final Verdict*, p. 239.
16 Miller, *Masters of the Air*, pp. 372–3.
17 Conrad Black, *Roosevelt: Champion of Freedom*, p. 1032.
18 Hastings, *Armageddon*, p. 236.
19 Miller, *Masters of the Air*, p. 372.
20 Kershaw, *Hitler: Nemesis*, p. 744.
21 Ibid.
22 Miller, *Masters of the Air*, p. 372.
23 Quotations ibid., p. 373.
24 Galland, *First and Last*, p. 243.
25 Miller, *Masters of the Air*, p. 374.
26 Galland, *First and Last*, p. 243.
27 Spaatz papers, box I: 135, 'Combined Intelligence Objectives Sub-Committee: Interrogation of Albert Speer – Former Minister for Armaments and War Production', pp. 5, 14. Emphasis in the original.
28 Hastings, *Armageddon*, pp. 269–72.
29 Portal papers, 'letter from Harris to Portal, 12 December 1944.
30 Middlebrook, *Bomber Command War Diaries*, p. 633.
31 Portal papers, letter from Portal to Harris, 22 December 1944.

32 Portal papers, letter from Harris to Portal, 28 December 1944.

Chapter 22

1 Middlebrook, *Bomber Command War Diaries*, p. 649.
2 Portal papers, letter from Portal to Harris, 8 January 1945.
3 Friedrich, *The Fire*, p. 306. Alfred Heidelmayer gives a higher, and probably exaggerated, figure of sixteen thousand. See Heidelmayer, 'Magdeburg 1945: Zwischen Zerstörung und Kriegsende – in Bericht', in Matthias Puhle (ed.), *Dann färbte sich der Himmel blutrot . . .* (Magdeburg: Grafisches Zentrum, Calbe, 1995) [exhibition in the Museum for Cultural History, Magdeburg, January–May 1995].
4 Portal papers, letter from Harris to Portal, 18 January 1945. On 9 January probably before receiving Portal's 8 January letter (it addresses none of the points Portal raised), Harris sent him a letter concerning the shortage of high explosives. See Portal papers, letter from Harris to Portal, 9 January 9, 1945; for the reply, see letter from Portal to Harris, 27 January 1945.
5 Emphasis in the original.
6 Emphasis in the original.
7 Portal papers, letter from Portal to Harris, 20 January 1945.
8 Max Hastings, *Armageddon*, p. 352.
9 BArch Berlin, R 3102/2969, report by Albert Speer on German industrial production, pp. 12–23.
10 Ibid., p. 21.
11 Ibid., pp. 12–23.
12 Remaining details in this paragraph found ibid., pp. 1–6.

Chapter 23

1 Quoted in Miller, *Masters of the Air*, p. 424.
2 Quotations and story found ibid., pp. 424–5.
3 On the last, see Erik Smit et al., *3. Februar 1945: die Zerstörung Kreuzbergs aus der Luft* (Berlin: Kunstamt Kreuzberg, 1995).
4 Miller, *Masters of the Air*, p. 425.
5 Hans-Georg von Studnitz, *While Berlin Burns: The Diary of Hans-George von Studnitz, 1943–1945* (London: Weidenfeld and Nicolson,

1963), pp. 241–2. 'Bespatters' is used in the text; I have corrected for grammatical accuracy.

6 John Briol, *Dead Engine Kids: World War II Diary of John J. Briol, B-17 Ball Turret Gunner* (Rapid City, SD: Silver Wings Aviation, 1993), p. 181.

7 Quoted in Miller, *Masters of the Air*, p. 427.

8 Ibid., p. 425.

9 Ibid., p. 427.

10 UKNA, AIR 41, 'The RAF in the Bombing Offensive against Germany' (official narrative), 6:198.

11 Ibid.

12 Miller, *Masters of the Air*, p. 413.

13 UKNA, AIR 41, 'The RAF' (official narrative), 6:198–9.

14 Webster and Frankland, *Strategic Air Offensive*, 3:100.

15 UKNA, AIR 41, 'The RAF' (official narrative), 6:199; Webster and Frankland, *Strategic Air Offensive*, 3:100.

16 Webster and Frankland, *Strategic Air Offensive*, 3:101.

17 Quoted in Dudley Saward, *'Bomber' Harris: The Story of Marshal of the Royal Air Force Sir Arthur Harris* (London: Cassell, 1984), p. 283.

18 Quotations from Frederick Taylor, *Dresden: Tuesday, 13 February 1945* (London: Bloomsbury, 2004), p. 185–6.

19 Quoted in Miller, *Masters of the Air*, p. 415.

20 On this, see Spaatz papers ibid., p. 416.

21 Davis, *Bombing the European Axis Powers*, p. 493.

22 Spaatz papers, box I: 40, telegram from Doolittle to Spaatz, 30 January 1945.

23 Miller, *Masters of the Air*, p. 416.

24 Ibid. Remaining quotations and paraphrasing in this paragraph found ibid., p. 419.

25 Spaatz papers, box I: 41, telegram from Doolittle to Spaatz, 2 February 1945.

26 Spaatz papers ibid. Spaatz's handwritten note about the telephone conversation can be found at the bottom of the telegram.

27 Studnitz, *While Berlin Burns*, p. 243.

28 Miller, *Masters of the Air*, p. 411

29 Details of the raid found in Taylor, *Dresden*, chapters 19–22.

30 There is some debate on this point. Taylor, *Dresden*, p. 318, produces a 25 February 1945 report from the 1st Bombardment Division's commander as well as oral history indicating the centre of Dresden as the target. Spaatz

claimed after the war, and historian Richard G. Davis argues, that it was a typical US raid, with marshalling yards as the main target. [See Davis, *Carl A. Spaatz*, p. 564]. Davis argues that the percentage of incendiaries was 30 per cent ('high but not unusual'); Taylor, p. 319, claims 40 per cent. On the basis of the 25 February report, I have opted for Taylor's interpretation.

31 Taylor, *Dresden*, p. 332.

32 UKNA, AIR41, 'The RAF', (official narrative), 6:225.

33 Ibid.

34 Quoted ibid. and in Davis, *Bombing the European Axis Powers*, p. 511.

35 UKNA, AIR41, 'The RAF', (official narrative), 6:225.

36 Middlebrook, *Bomber Command War Diaries*, p. 673.

37 Ibid.

38 Spaatz papers, box I: 170, 'General Plan for Maximum Effort Attack against Transportation Objectives', 17 December 1944.

39 Miller, *Masters of the Air*, p. 441.

40 Spaatz papers, box I: 170, 'General Plan', 17 December 1944.

41 Miller, *Masters of the Air*, pp. 441–2.

42 Quoted ibid. And in Schaffer, *Wings of Judgment*, p. 92.

43 Spaatz papers, box I: 40, telegram from Eaker to Spaatz, 22 February 1945.

44 Spaatz papers, box I: 40, telegram from F. L. Anderson to Spaatz, 22 February 1945.

45 Davis, *Carl A. Spaatz*, p. 575.

46 Spaatz papers, box I: 170, Headquarters, United States Strategic Air Forces in Europe, Office of the Director of Intelligence, 'Study of Results Achieved by Operation Clarion', undated; Davis, *Carl A. Spaatz*, p. 572.

47 Miller, *Masters of the Air*, p. 442.

48 McDonald quotations from Hoover Institution Archives, Stanford University, Frederick Anderson collection, box 50, fol. 2, letter from McDonald to Anderson, 21 February 1945. Quoted in Miller, *Masters of the Air*, pp. 444–5.

49 Miller, *Masters of the Air*, p. 445.

50 Ibid.

51 Davis, *Carl A. Spaatz*, p. 572.

52 See ibid. and, for the full list of targets, the Eighth Air Force Historical Society, *WWII 8th AAF Combat Chronology: January 1945 through August 1945*, https://www.8thafhs.org/combat1945.htm.

53 Davis, *Carl A. Spaatz*, p. 565.

54 Ibid., p. 568.

Chapter 24

1 Kenneth P. Werrell, *Blankets of Fire: U.S. Bombers over Japan during World War II* (Washington: Smithsonian Institution Press, 1996), p. 39. Photographs taken at the time show an eerie resemblance to firebombed cities of the Second World War. See British Pathé, 'Scenes of Japan's Earthquake Disaster' (1923), https://www.youtube.com/watch?v=mfYXgUjo1gA.

2 William L. Mitchell, 'Strategical Aspect of the Pacific Problem', quoted in Mark A. Clodfelter, 'Molding Air Power Convictions: Development and Legacy of William Mitchell's Strategic Thought', in Phillip S. Meilinger (ed.), *The Paths of Heaven: The Evolution of Air Power Theory* (Alabama: Air University Press, 1997), p. 92.

3 Quoted in Frank, *Downfall*, p. 48.

4 Hugh Byas, 'Most of All Japan Fears an Air Attack', *New York Times*, 4 August 1935.

5 Bonner Fellers, 'The Psychology of the Japanese Soldier', paper presented at the Command and General Staff School, 1934–1935, HRA 142.041-1.Quoted in Werrell, *Blankets of Fire*, p. 39.

6 E. Bartlett Kerr, *Flames over Tokyo: The U.S. Army Air Forces' Incendiary Campaign against Japan, 1944–1945* (New York, D. I. Fine, 1991), pp. 28–9.

7 Claire Lee Chennault and Robert B. Hotz, *Way of a Fighter: The Memoirs of Claire Lee Chennault* (New York: Putnam, 1949), p. 97; Michael S. Sherry, *Rise of American Air Power: The Creation of Armageddon* (New Haven: Yale University Press, 1989), pp. 101–2.

8 Werrell, *Blankets of Fire*, p. 52.

9 Ibid., p. 50.

10 Biddle, *Rhetoric and Reality*, p. 265; Conrad C. Crane, *Bombs, Cities and Civilians: American Airpower Strategy in World War II* (Lawrence: University of Kansas Press, 1993), p. 127.

11 Mark Clodfelter, *Beneficial Bombing: The Progressive Foundations of American Air Power, 1917–1945* (Lincoln: University of Nebraska Press, 2010), p. 202.

12 Air War Plans Division, discussed in chapter 5.

13 Werrell, *Blankets of Fire*, p. 87.

14 Clodfelter, *Beneficial Bombing*, p. 198.

15 Werrell, *Blankets of Fire*, p. 88.

16 Ibid.

17 Coldfelter, *Beneficial Bombing*, pp. 199–200.

18 Werrell, *Blankets of Fire*, p. 89.

19 Quoted in Maj. Gen Gurney, *Journey of the Giants* (New York: USAF Book Support Program, 2012), pp. 78–80.

20 Donald P. Miller, *The Story of World War II* (New York: Simon and Schuster, 2001), p. 442.

21 Clodfelter, *Beneficial Bombing*, p. 199.

22 Miller, *Story of World War II*, p. 442.

23 Clodfelter, *Beneficial Bombing*, p. 200.

24 On this, see my comments in chapter 4.

25 See LeMay, *Mission with LeMay*, p. 425.

26 Ibid., p. 322. Robert McNamara, then head of a statistical control unit for XX Bomber Command, gives LeMay full credit for the insight. 'Lesson 4', *The Fog of War*, directed by Errol Morris (2003; New York: Sony Pictures Classics).

27 Miller, *Story of World War II*, p. 443.

28 Kerr, *Flames over Tokyo*, p. 91.

29 Hansell had too much information on US tactics and capabilities, so he was not allowed to lead the mission.

30 Clodfelter, *Beneficial Bombing*, pp. 205–6.

31 Kerr, *Flames over Tokyo*, p. 101.

32 Clodfelter, *Beneficial Bombing*, p. 206.

33 Miller, *Story of World War II*, p. 445.

34 Kerr, *Flames over Tokyo*, p. 102.

35 Quoted in Miller, *Story of World War II*, p. 445.

36 For the details, see Kerr, *Flames over Tokyo*, pp. 108–18.

37 Ibid., pp. 110–11.

38 Kerr, *Flames over Tokyo*, p. 119.

39 Clodfelter, *Beneficial Bombing*, pp. 211–12.

40 Kerr, *Flames over Tokyo*, p. 125; William W. Ralph, 'Improvised Destruction: Arnold, LeMay, and the Firebombing of Japan', *War in History* 13, no. 4 (2006): pp. 495–522, 506.

41 Miller, *Story of World War II,* p. 443.

42 Kerr, *Flames over Tokyo*, p. 125.

43 Kerr, *Flames over Tokyo*, pp. 128–32.

44 The raid did do substantial damage, though, to the Japanese air force, which put up an unusually strong defence.

45 Werrell, *Blankets of Fire*, p. 155.

Chapter 25

1 Details of raids from UKNA, AIR41, 'The RAF' (official narrative),
   VI:225–6.
2 UKNA, AIR 19/189, letter from Harris to Bottomley, 28 December 1943.
3 Middlebrook, *Bomber Command War Diaries*, p. 676.
4 Ibid., p. 678.
5 Heinrich Giesecke's story comes from a report given by him to the author.
6 Dieter W. Rockenmaier, *Als vom Himmel Feuer fiel: so starb das alte
   Würzburg* (Würzburg: Fränkische Gesellschaftsdruckerei, 1995).
7 Middlebrook, *Bomber Command War Diaries*, p. 682.
8 A loose translation of '*Starker Kampfverband im Anflug auf unsere Stadt.
   Luftschutzmässiges Verhalten ist dringend erforderlich!*'
9 Herbert Oechsner heard two stories about his mother's fate. This version
   was told to him at the time by someone at the clinic, possibly an orderly.
   Decades later, he met the daughter of a woman who was at the scene,
   and she claimed that his mother was among the bodies. Herbert, who
   changed his name to the anglicised 'Osner' after the war, regards her
   account as somewhat unreliable, and, given the difficulty in recognising
   the bodies at the time, the woman may have mistaken someone else for
   his mother.
10 Heinrich did not specify which shelter. There was an air-raid shelter
   in the Mergentheimer Strasse on the side of the Old Main Bridge to
   which Heinrich and his family fled. It is, however, a ten-minute walk
   south of the bridge. There may have been a shelter in or around the
   Saalgasse, to which the Old Main Bridge directly leads, or Heinrich
   may have found a private cellar. On the Mergentheimer Strasse shelter,
   see Max Domarus, *Der Untergang des alten Würzburg im Luftkrieg
   gegen die deutschen Großstädte* (Gerolzhofen: Franz Teutsch, 1969),
   pp. 34–5.
11 Fritz Bauer, *Würzburg im Feuerofen* (Würzburg: Echter Verlag, 1985),
   p. 20.
12 Klaus M. Höynck and Eberhard Schellenberger, *16. März 1945:
   Erinnerungen an Würzburgs Schicksalstag und das Ende des Krieges*
   (Würzburg: Bayerischer Rundfunk, 2005), p. 26.
13 The next four sentences are based on a report by Karl-Heinz Wirsing,
   mailed to the author on 17 June 2005.
14 Christoph Kucklick. *Feuersturm: der Bombenkrieg gegen Deutschland*
   (Hamburg: Ellert & Richter, 2003).

15 UKNA, AIR 14/3412, Bomber Command Night Raid Report No. 867 (16/17 March 1945).

Chapter 26

1 Robert Guillain, *I Saw Tokyo Burning: An Eyewitness Narrative from Pearl Harbor to Hiroshima* (London: John Murray, 1981), p. 181.
2 David Rees, *The Defeat of Japan* (Westport, CT: Praeger, 1997), p. 107.
3 Werrell, *Blankets of Fire*, p. 161.
4 Richard Rhodes, *The Making of the Atomic Bomb* (New York: Simon & Schuster, 1998), p. 597.
5 Hoito Edoin, *The Night Tokyo Burned* (New York: St Martin's Press, 1987), p. 59.
6 Ibid., p. 58.
7 The Americans estimated the Japanese fighting force over central Japan and eastern Honshu to be just over 2,400. See Hoyt S. Vandenberg papers, 'Japanese Air Forces', undated.
8 Edoin, *The Night Tokyo Burned*, p. 59.
9 Details in this paragraph from Werrell, *Blankets of Fire*, p. 161.
10 Kerr, *Flames over Tokyo*, p. 190.
11 Ibid.
12 This portion of Miwa Koshiba's story found in Edoin, *The Night Tokyo Burned*, pp. 60–1.
13 Kerr, *Flames over Tokyo*, 105.
14 On the development of Tokyo's wholly inadequate fire defences, see Kerr, *Flames over Tokyo*, pp. 105–8.
15 Ibid., p. 191.
16 Guillain, *I Saw Tokyo Burning*, p. 185. The hoods are visible in *The Fog of War*, dir. Errol Morris, cited above, at 32:30.
17 Guillain, *I Saw Tokyo Burning*, pp. 184–5.
18 Kerr, *Flames over Tokyo*, p. 193.
19 Ibid.
20 One source says that a 'fireball' consumed them, but it is more likely that their deaths were caused by smoke inhalation, exhaustion, trampling, and in some cases, drowning due to an inability to swim. Francis Pike, *Hirohito's War: The Pacific War, 1941–1945* (London: Bloomsbury, 2015), p. 1026.
21 Hidezo's story is taken from Kerr, *Flames over Tokyo*, pp. 195–8.

22 Kerr states that the building had three storeys. The current, concrete building on the site has five.

23 Quoted in Kenneth D. Rose, *Myth and the Greatest Generation: A Social History of Americans in World War II* (New York: Routledge, 2008), p. 27.

24 Hidezo's story is also told in Pike, *Hirohito's War*, p. 1026.

25 This portion of Miwa's story comes from Edoin, *The Night Tokyo Burned*, pp. 79–81.

26 For the documentary evidence, see *The Collection of Tokyo Air Raid Photographs* (Tokyo: The Centre of the Tokyo Air Raids and War Damage), p. 256.

27 *The Collection of Tokyo Air Raid Photographs*, p. 255.

28 Ibid., p. 254.

29 Edoin, *The Night Tokyo Burned*, p. 81.

30 Quoted in Frank, *Downfall*, p. 13.

31 LeMay papers, box II, III 1A/1, Official Correspondence with General Arnold, letters from LeMay to Arnold, 10 March 1945 and 11 March 1945.

32 Ibid., 3/II (F), daily diary, 11 March 1945.

33 Werrell, *Blankets of Fire*, pp. 163–4.

34 Werrell, *Blankets of Fire*, p. 164; LeMay papers, 3/II (F), daily diary, 12 August 1945.

35 Wesley Frank Craven and James Lea Cate, eds., *The Army Air Forces in World War II. Volume 5: The Pacific – Matterhorn to Nagasaki June 1944 to August 1945* (Chicago: The University of Chicago Press), p. 618.

36 Werrell, *Blankets of Fire*, p. 165; Craven and Cate, *Army Air Forces in World War II*, 5:620.

37 LeMay papers, 3/II (F), daily diary, 16 March 1945.

38 Werrell, *Blankets of Fire*, 165. Because they had run out of M-69s, the main bomb on the three raids, the US air forces used clusters of four-pound M-50 incendiaries (for the first time), 500-pound M-76 incendiaries (also for the first time), and many more of the 100-pound M-47 incendiaries. They also dropped nineteen tons of 500-pound cluster bombs that dispersed at 3,000 feet, targeted at fighters.

39 Ibid.

40 LeMay papers, 3/II (F), daily diary, 20 March 1945.

41 Werrell, *Blankets of Fire*, p. 167.

42 LeMay papers, III 1A/1, Official Correspondence with General Arnold, letter from Arnold to LeMay, 21 March 1945.

43 LeMay papers, BII, III 1A/1, Official Correspondence with General Arnold, letter from LeMay to Arnold, 5 April 1945.

44 Werrell, *Blankets of Fire*, p. 180.

45 LeMay papers, B 12, Lauris Norstad, 'Twentieth Air Force Participation in Operation ICEBERG', 17 April 1945; Werrell, *Blankets of Fire*, p. 181.

46 Werrell, *Blankets of Fire*, p. 188.

47 Ibid., p. 189.

48 Ibid., p. 193.

49 Casualty figures in this paragraph from Martin Gilbert, *The Second World War: A Complete History* (New York: Henry Holt & Co., 1989), p. 649.

Chapter 27

1 Parliamentary Debates (Commons), 6 March 1945, vol. 408, https://api.parliament.uk/historic-hansard/sittings/1945/mar/06.

2 Schaffer, *Wings of Judgment*, p. 99.

3 UKNA, AIR41, 'The RAF' (official narrative), VI:202.

4 Parliamentary Debates (Commons), 6 March 1945, vol. 408, https://api.parliament.uk/historic-hansard/sittings/1945/mar/06.

5 Story found in Taylor, *Dresden*, p. 364.

6 Ibid., p. 373.

7 UKNA, CAB 121/3, 'Bombing Policy in Europe', 28 March 1945.

8 Quoted in Probert, *Bomber Harris*, p. 322.

9 Ibid.

10 See Taylor, *Dresden*, chapter 13.

11 See Miller, *Masters of the Air*, p. 436.

12 Quoted in Hastings, *Bomber Command*, p. 344.

13 Middlebrook, *Bomber Command War Diaries*, p. 696.

14 Taylor, *Dresden*, pp. 380–1.

Chapter 28

1 Koichi Kido, *The Diary of Marquis Kido, 1931–45* (Frederick, MD: University Publications of America, 1984), p. 410.

2 Guillain, *I Saw Tokyo Burning*, p. 219.

3 There is scholarly debate on the emperor's position at this stage in the war. Edward Behr claims that he knew the war was lost. Behr, *Hirohito: Behind the Myth* (London: Hamish Hamilton, 1989), p. 343. The French journalist, Robert Guillain, drawing on post-war interviews, agrees. Guillain, *I Saw Tokyo Burning*, p. 219. Herbert Bix, citing Grand Chamberlain Hisanori Fujita, argues that the emperor, still delusional about possibilities for Soviet mediation, wanted to fight on. Herbert P. Bix, *Hirohito and the Making of Modern Japan* (New York: HarperCollins, 2000), pp. 489–90. It is most likely that Hirohito had serious doubts about war but remained committed to it, at least until a decisive victory shifted the balance of power in any negotiations with the Allies. He did not give up on this illusion until the defeat at Okinawa in June 1945. On t§his see Frank, *Downfall*, pp. 95–9.

4 Okinawa was still to be taken.

5 Frank, *Downfall*, pp. 186–7. William Craig, *The Fall of Japan* (New York: Dial Press, 1967), pp. 42–3 cites a lower figure of 5,225.

6 Both weapons are on display at the Yushukan, a right-wing, revisionist private military history museum located near Tokyo's Yasukuni shrine.

7 Guillain, *I Saw Tokyo Burning*, p. 202.

8 Craig, *Fall of Japan*, p. 105.

9 Togo Shigenori, *The Cause of Japan* (New York: Simon & Schuster, 1956), p. 276.

10 Bix, *Hirohito*, p. 487; Robert J. C. Butow, *Japan's Decision to Surrender* (Stanford: Stanford University Press, 1954), p. 46. Craig, *Fall of Japan*, p. 106.

11 Details on Prince Konoe from Bix, *Hirohito*, p. 489 and Butow, *Japan's Decision*, pp. 47–50.

12 Butow, *Japan's Decision*, p. 37.

13 Craig, *Fall of Japan*, p. 106.

14 Butow, *Japan's Decision*, p. 63.

15 Craig, *Fall of Japan*, p. 106.

16 See Robert J. C. Butow, *Tojo and the Coming of the War* (Princeton: Princeton University Press, 1961), chapter 11.

17 Craig, *Fall of Japan*, p. 107.

18 Guillain, *I Saw Tokyo Burning*, p. 217.

19 Craig, *Fall of Japan*, p. 106.

20 Ibid., p. 108.

21 The discussion of Anami's traits is based on Craig, *Fall of Japan*, p. 110.

22 Craig, *The Fall of Japan*, p. 110.

23 Ibid.

24 Ibid., p. 111.

25 Frank, *Downfall*, p. 221.

26 Togo, *Cause of Japan*, p. 302. Hirohito had secured agreement in principle for such a move from the Supreme Council on 22 June. Butow, *Japan's Decision*, pp. 118–20; Frank, *Downfall*, p. 102.

27 Togo, *Cause of Japan*, p. 302.

28 Richardson Dougall et al. (eds.), *Foreign Relations of the United States: Diplomatic Papers, Conference of Berlin (Potsdam), 1945* (Washington: GPO, 1960), I: 876 Available at: https://history.state.gov/historicaldocuments/frus1945Berlinv01.

29 Weinberg, *World at Arms*, p. 886; Frank, *Downfall*, pp. 225–6.

30 David McCullough, *Truman* (New York: Simon & Schuster), p. 415.

31 Ibid., quoting Truman's diary entry from 16 July 1945.

32 Frank, *Downfall*, p. 153.

33 Weinberg, *World at Arms*, pp. 838–9.

34 See R. M. Douglas, *Orderly and Humane: The Expulsion of the Germans after the Second World War* (New Haven: Yale University Press, 2013).

35 Weinberg, *World at Arms*, p. 889.

36 McCullough, *Truman*, p. 436. See also Frank, *Downfall*, chapter 14. Stimson had toured the city in the summer of 1926. 'It may be' writes his biographer, 'that Henry Stimson was the most important visitor Kyoto ever had.' What steeled Stimson in particular against the bombing was the advice of a cousin, Henry Loomis, who told Stimson over dinner of the glories of Japanese art, above all in Kyoto, knowledge which the young Loomis had acquired during undergraduate courses at Harvard. Contrary to the claims of conservatives, the humanities can certainly be policy relevant. Hodgson, *The Colonel*, p. 18 (quotation) and pp. 323–4 (Loomis).

37 Weinberg, *World at Arms*, pp. 887–8. For the full text of the 8 May call, see *The Public Papers of the President of the United States: Harry S. Truman 1945* (Washington: GPO, 1961), pp. 43–8.

38 McCullough, *Truman*, p. 436.

39 Frank, *Downfall*, p. 257.

40 Kennedy, *Freedom from Fear: The American People in Depression and War, 1929–1945* (New York: Oxford University Press, 1999), p. 840; Hodgson, *The Colonel*, p. 13.

41 Quoted in Kennedy, *Freedom from Fear*, p. 840.

42 McCullough, *Truman*, p. 439. Estimates on US casualties varied

between services and methods of calculations, and Truman was never given a clear picture. Indeed, some of the highest figures were deliberately kept from him by Marshall, who wanted to see Japan defeated by invasion and occupation. See Frank, *Downfall*, chapter 9.

43 Ronald Takaki, *Hiroshima: Why America Dropped the Atomic Bomb* (New York: Back Bay Books, 1996).

44 Weinberg, *World at Arms*, p. 884. Likely Berlin.

45 *Diary of Marquis Kido*, pp. 441–2.

46 See Frank, *Downfall*, chapter 14 for a strong argument. Magic intercepts showed the Americans that the Japanese government was interested in ending the war but far from accepting unconditional surrender even with the maintenance of the imperial structure.

47 Frank, *Downfall*, p. 154.

48 Spaatz papers, box 120, Japanese Home Broadcasts, 3 August 1945.

49 Pacific War Research Society (PWS), *Japan's Longest Day* (Tokyo: Kodansha International, 1968), p. 14.

50 Yukiko Koshiro, *Imperial Eclipse: Japan's Strategic Thinking about Continental Asia before 1945* (Ithaca: Cornell University Press, 2013), p. 227.

51 Butow, *Japan's Decision*, p. 145.

52 PWS, *Japan's Longest Day*, p. 17.

53 Butow, *Japan's Decision*, p. 148; PWS, *Japan's Longest Day*, p. 18.

54 Frank, *Downfall*, p. 234.

55 Henry Stimson, 'The Decision to Use the Atomic Bomb', *Daily Telegraph*, 14 February 1947. Extracts available at: http://www.nationalarchives.gov.uk/education/heroesvillains/transcript/g5cs2s3t.htm.

56 See the review of communications in Frank, *Downfall*, chapter 14, especially pp. 235–9.

57 Quotation and details from Guillain, *I Saw Tokyo Burning*, p. 234.

58 Frank, *Downfall*, p. 263

59 Ibid., p. 265.

60 Spaatz papers, box 120, Japanese Home Broadcasts, 6–7 August.

61 Ibid. It took a full day for this inaccurate claim to be corrected. Butow, *Japan's Decision*, pp. 150–1.

62 Quoted in PWS, *Japan's Longest Day*, p. 21.

63 Togo, *Cause of Japan*, p. 315.

64 Koshiro, *Imperial Eclipse*, p. 236.

65 Tsuyoshi Hasegawa, *Racing the Enemy: Stalin, Truman, and the Surrender of Japan* (Cambridge, MA: Belknap Press, 2005), pp. 184–5.

66 *Diary of Marquis Kido*, p. 443; Togo, *Cause of Japan*, p. 315.

67 I owe this translation to Asako Masubuchi, a PhD student in the Department of History, University of Toronto.

68 Sadao Asada, 'The Shock of the Atomic Bomb and Japan's Decision to Surrender: A Reconsideration', *Pacific Historical Review* 67, no. 4 (1998), pp. 477–512, 488.

69 Ibid.

70 Tsuyoshi Hasegawa, 'The Atomic Bombs and the Soviet Invasion: What Drove Japan's Decision to Surrender?' *Asia-Pacific Journal* 5, no. 8 (2007), pp. 1–31.

71 Ibid., p. 5.

72 Frank, *Downfall*, p. 156.

73 Ibid.

74 The prospect of a war with both the Soviet Union and the United States had haunted Kido, who since 1941 was convinced that such a war was unwinnable. *Diary of Marquis Kido*, 7 August 1941, p. 300.

75 Koshiro, *Imperial Eclipse*, p. 237.

76 Frank, *Downfall*, p. 288.

77 Noriko Kawamura, *Emperor Hirohito and the Pacific War* (Seattle: University of Washington Press, 2015), p. 163.

78 Koshiro, *Imperial Eclipse*, p. 237.

79 Frank, *Downfall*, p. 289; Koshiro, *Imperial Decline*, p. 238.

80 Quoted in Frank, *Downfall*, p. 289.

81 Ibid.

82 They met six times between 09:55 and 11:37, for a total of one hour and fifty minutes. Butow, *Japan's Decision to Surrender*, p. 159 n56.

83 *Diary of Marquis Kido*, p. 443.

84 PWS, *Japan's Longest Day*, p. 22; *Diary of Marquis Kido*, p. 444; Herbert Bix's critical biography of Hirohito makes no mention of these meetings, though the source material in their favour is strong.

85 *Diary of Marquis Kido*, p. 444; PWS, *Japan's Longest Day*, p. 24.

86 PWS, *Japan's Longest Day*, p. 24.

87 Quotations found ibid. For a different wording but the same content, see Butow, *Japan's Decision*, p. 160.

88 Togo, *Cause of Japan*, p. 317.

89 Ibid.

90 Butow, *Japan's Decision*, p. 161; Rees, *Defeat of Japan*, p. 164.

91 PWS, *Japan's Longest Day*, p. 25.

92 The infamous 'stab in the back' myth. Butow, *Japan's Decision*, p. 161.

93 Butow, *Japan's Decision*, pp. 162–3.

94 Togo, *Cause of Japan*, p. 318.

95 Butow, *Japan's Decision*, p. 161.

96 Kawamwura, *Emperor Hirohito*, p. 164.

97 Guillain, *I Saw Tokyo Burning*, p. 252.

98 Quoted in Butow, *Japan's Decision*, p. 159.

99 *Diary of Marquis Kido*, p. 444.

100 Frank, *Downfall*, p. 291.

101 Kawamura, *Emperor Hirohito*, p. 165.

102 Frank, *Downfall*, p. 291.

103 *Diary of Marquis Kido*, p. 444.

104 Butow, *Japan's Decision*, p. 159 n56; Mamoru Shigemitsu, *Japan and Her Destiny* (London: Hutchinson, 1958), p. 360.

105 Togo, *Cause of Japan*, p. 319.

106 Ibid., pp. 318–19; PWS, *Japan's Longest Day*, p. 28.

107 Butow, *Japan's Decision*, p. 165.

108 Robert P. Newman, *Truman and the Hiroshima Cult* (East Lansing: Michigan State University Press, 1995), pp. 134–9 (over 17 million, including perhaps, oddly, 1.5 million who died in the Bengal famine, a British responsibility). Historian Gerhard Weinberg concludes that 15 million is a 'reasonable approximation' (*World at Arms*, p. 894).

109 Gavan Daws, *Prisoners of the Japanese: POWs of World War II in the Pacific* (New York: William Morrow and Co., 1994), pp. 321–2. The story is corroborated by Toshio Tono, a first-year medical student in 1945 who broke the story in his 1979 book, *Disgrace*. At the age of 89, he insisted on publicising the atrocities on the seventieth anniversary of Japan's defeat. Justin McCurry, 'Japan Revisits Its Darkest Moments Where American POWs Became Human Experiments', *Guardian*, 13 August 2015. Also in 2015, professors at the university's school of medicine persuaded the university to add a section on the vivisections to the university's medical history museum. 'New Kyushu Museum Breaks Taboo with POW Vivisection Display', *Japan Times*, 4 April 2015.

110 Justin McCurry, 'Unit 731: Japan Discloses Details of Notorious Chemical Warfare Division', *Guardian*, 17 April 2018.

111 Daws, *Prisoners of the Japanese*, p. 363.

112 See Bix, *Hirohito*, and Kawamura, *Emperor Hirohito*.

113 Togo, *Cause of Japan*, p. 319.

114 Ibid.; PWS, *Japan's Longest Day*, pp. 34–5.

115 *Diary of Marquis Kido*, p. 444.

116 Guillain, *I Saw Tokyo Burning*, p. 253.

117 Frank, *Downfall*, p. 293.

118 Guillain, *I Saw Tokyo Burning*, p. 254.

119 Frank, *Downfall*, p. 293.

120 Ibid., p. 294.

121 Guillain, *I Saw Tokyo Burning*, p. 255.

122 Ibid. Frank presents a slightly different version of these events. In his version, Hiranuma first asks the emperor to speak, followed by Suzuki. *Downfall*, pp. 294–5.

123 Quotations from PWS, *Japan's Longest Day*, pp. 34–5 and Frank, *Downfall*, pp. 295–6.

124 PWS, *Japan's Longest Day*, p. 34.

125 Ibid., p. 35.

126 Frank, *Downfall*, p. 296.

127 Ibid.

128 Historian Yukiko Koshiro suggests that the willingness to fight on was no longer shared by the Japanese people. See Koshiro, *Imperial Eclipse*, p. 235. The source, however, is one journal – of Colonel Tanemura Sako of the Army War Operations Plans Division – and the conclusion is suppositional: 'no households' were hoisting the Japanese flag on 30 July 1945, the anniversary of Emperor Meiji's passing, which meant they regarded the national policy – the *kokutai* – as irrelevant. This assertion strains credibility.

129 Harry Truman, 'Radio Report to the American People on the Potsdam Conference', 9 August 1945, 22:00. *Public Papers of Harry S. Truman, 1945–1953*, Harry S. Truman Presidential Library & Museum, https://www.trumanlibrary.org/publicpapers/?pid=104.

130 Weinberg, *World at Arms*, p. 889.

131 Frank, *Downfall*, p. 298.

132 Stimson objected to LeMay's firebombing campaign and expressed moral qualms about the atomic bomb; Byrnes had none. Hodgson, *The Colonel*, p. 325.

133 Tsuyoshi Hasegawa, *Racing the Enemy*, p. 220.

134 Frank, *Downfall*, p. 301.

135 Quotations from Kennedy, *Freedom from Fear*, p. 851; Frank, *Downfall*, p. 301.

136 Weinberg, *World at Arms*, p. 890.

137 John P. Glennon et al. (eds.), *Foreign Relations of the United States: Diplomatic Papers, 1945, The British Commonwealth, The Far East,*

Volume VI, Office of the Historian, letter from James F. Byrnes to the Secretary of State to the Swiss Chargé (Grässli), 11 August 1945, https://history.state.gov/historicaldocuments/frus1945v06/d412.

138 Quoted in PWS, *Japan's Longest Day*, p. 43.

139 Weinberg, *World at Arms*, p. 891.

140 Frank, *Downfall*, p. 304.

141 Details in the next five paragraphs from PWS, *Japan's Longest Day*, pp. 44–50.

142 Quotations from Craig, *Fall of Japan*, p. 152.

143 Ibid., p. 153.

144 PWS, *Japan's Longest Day*, p. 53.

145 Frank, *Downfall*, p. 314.

146 Ibid.

147 PWS, *Japan's Longest Day*, p. 73.

148 Ibid.

149 Hirohito's speech was neither transcribed nor recorded. Hiroshi Shimomura, Director of the Cabinet's Information Bureau, reconstructed it from memory after the war, and Suzuki edited the document. PWS, *Japan's Longest Day*, p. 330 n5. The speech is reproduced in full at pp. 81–3.

150 PWS, *Japan's Longest Day*, p. 83.

151 Guillain, *I Saw Tokyo Burning*, 261.

152 Behr, *Hirohito,* p. 369.

153 I owe this comparison to Gerhard Weinberg. On the Tokyo coup, see *World at Arms*, p. 891.

154 Behr, *Hirohito*, p. 377.

155 Guillain, *I Saw Toyko Burning*, p. 269.

156 Behr, *Hirohito*, p. 378.

157 Shigemitsu, *Japan and Her Destiny*, p. 372.

158 Quoted in Hastings, *The Battle for Japan*, p. 586.

Chapter 29

1 Tony Vaccaro, *Entering Germany 1944–1949* (Cologne: Taschen, 2001).

2 On this, see Hastings, *Bomber Command*, p. 346.

3 Available at: https://winstonchurchill.org/resources/speeches/1941-1945-war-leader/end-of-the-war-in-europe/. The date was the fifth anniversary of his first speech in the Commons – the 'blood, toil, tears, and sweat' speech – as prime minister.

4 A. J. P. Taylor, *English History: 1914-1945* (Oxford: Oxford University Press, 1992), p. 592.

5 See Hastings, *Bomber Command*, pp. 346–7.

6 Harris, *Bomber Offensive*, pp. 176–7. Harris's suggestion is implied by the oft-quoted comments by Albert Speer on the immediate aftermath of Hamburg.

7 See Telford Taylor, *The Anatomy of the Nuremberg Trials: A Personal Memoir* (New York: Alfred A. Knopf, 1992), p. 623, naming US Army Lieutenant Jack G. ('Tex') Wheelis. See also the interview with US Army Private Herbert Lee Stivers in Catherine Elsworth, 'I Gave Göring His Poison Pill, Says American', *Daily Telegraph*, 8 February 2005 (naming himself).

8 See Brechtken, *Albert Speer*, part 5 (1966–1981).

9 Sereny, *Albert Speer*, p. 708. Also see Volker Ullrich, 'Speers Erfindung', *Die Zeit*, 4 May 2005.

10 Brechtken, *Albert Speer*, part 5.

11 Jules Horowtiz, *My Air War. North Africa–Italy* (unpublished diary). I am grateful to Mr Horowitz for sending this to me.

12 Details from Edoin, *The Night Tokyo Burned*, p. 81.

13 Some Dresdeners were convinced, against all evidence, that the Allies machine-gunned them in the streets.

14 See Tony Judt, *Post-war: A History of Europe since 1945* (New York: Penguin Press, 2005), pp. 354–9.

15 Gavin Mortimer, *The Longest Night: The Bombing of London on May 10, 1941* (New York: Berkeley Caliber, 2005), p. 320.

16 UKNA, HW/1 3744, 'Report from Japanese Minister Berne to Minister for Foreign Affairs, Tokyo', 27 April 1945.

17 The University of Exeter project on bombing in Europe from 1940 to 1945 estimates that 410,000 civilians were killed in the air raids. See 'The Bombing of Germany 1940-1945' on the project website, 'Bombing, States and Peoples in Western Europe, 1940–1945', https://humanities.exeter.ac.uk/history/research/centres/warstateandsociety/projects/bombing/germany/. The estimate is notably lower than earlier ones. In 1962, the West German Ministry of Displaced Persons, Refugees and War Victims arrived at a death toll of 593,000, including: 410,000 resident German civilians, 32,000 foreign civilians or prisoners of war, 23,000 members of the German army or police, and 128,000 German refugees from the eastern territories. Gunnar Heinsohn, *Lexikon der Völkermorde* (Reinbek bei Hamburg: Rowohlt, 1998), p. 115. We will

never know with certainty, but caution and conservatism in estimated deaths by bombing is advisable as many original, high estimates have been revised downwards.

18 Jeffry M. Diefendorf, 'War and Reconstruction in Germany and Japan', in Carola Hein et al. (eds.), *Rebuilding Urban Japan after 1945* (Houndmills: Palgrave, 2003), pp. 223–4. Ibid., pp. 226–7.

19 Takashi Hirai, 'The Heart of Tokyo: Today's Reality and Tomorrow's Vision', in Gideon S. Golany et al. (eds.), *Japanese Urban Environment* (New York: Pergamon, 1998), p. 26.

20 Ibid., pp. 26–7. Roughly equivalent to London's East End. As in the East End, *Shitamachi* has powerful cultural connotations and street credibility, not unlike Cockney. My thanks to Mark Manger for his help on this section.

Chapter 30

1 Fully 215 Japanese cities suffered some form of bomb damage, although this figure includes light damage and damage resulting from precision attacks. Carola Hein, 'Rebuilding Japanese Cities after 1945', in Hein et al., *Rebuilding Urban Japan*, p. 1.

2 Michael Walzer, *Just and Unjust Wars: A Moral Argument with Historical Allusions*, 5th ed. (New York: Basic Books, 2015), chapter 16.

3 Brunswig, *Feuersturm über Hamburg*, p. 295.

4 On Harris's reaction, see Overy, *Bombing War*, p. 336.

5 'The Economic Effects of the Air Offensive against German Cities' in *The United States Strategic Bombing Survey* (New York: Garland Publishing, 1976), p. 9.

6 Quoted in Lowe, *Inferno*, p. 298.

7 Tooze, *Wages of Destruction*, p. 625.

8 Webster and Frankland, *Strategic Air Offensive*, III:44.

9 Spaatz papers, box I: 146, COA Memorandum for Lt. General Arnold, 8 March 1943.

10 Spaatz papers, box I: 145, Revision of Basic Study, 'Report of the Committee of Operations Analysts, 8 March 1943', 21 June 1944.

11 See for instance UKNA, AIR 19/189, letter from A.W. Street to Portal, 31 October 1943 and minute from Chief of Air Staff, 7 February 1944.

12 This historical conclusion is confirmed by quantitative studies that examine all instances of airpower from 1917 to 1990. See Michael

Horowitz and Dan Reiter, 'When Does Aerial Bombing Work? Quantitative Empirical Tests, 1917–1999', *Journal of Conflict Resolution* 45, no. 2 (2001): 147–73. The authors conclude that 'punishment strategies' (including the area bombing of civilians) are ineffective because they do not undermine support for the regime (indeed, they often increase it); that air power is less likely to succeed when the bombers demanded regime change (as they obviously did during the Second World War); and that democracies are no more or less likely to be coerced than authoritarian regimes. Area bombing, in other words, did not work before, during, or after the Second World War.

13 Tooze, *Wages of Destruction*, p. 598.

14 Ibid., p. 602.

15 Overy, *Air War*, p. 122.

16 Harris, *Despatch on War Operations*, pp. 33–8; Biddle, *Rhetoric and Reality*, p. 282.

17 Torsten Schaar and Beate Behrens, *Von der Schulbank in den Krieg: Mecklenburgische Schüler und Lehrlinge als Luftwaffen- und Marinehelfer, 1943–1945* (Rostock: Neuer Hochschulschriftenverlag, 1999).

18 Weigley, *Eisenhower's Lieutenants*, p. 694.

19 Overy, *Iron Knight*, pp. 148–9.

20 For the details, see Overy, *Iron Knight*, chapter 6.

21 Overy, *Air War*, p. 123.

22 The president of Focke-Wulf, the aircraft manufacturer, thought the transfers of fighters from the eastern front to defend German cities was not 'in any sense decisive'. Spaatz papers, box I: 135: U.S. Strategic Bombing Survey, APO 413, Interview with Dr Kurt Tank, President, Focke-Wulf Aircraft Co., 19 May 1945.

23 Tooze, *Wages of Destruction*, p. 613.

24 Weinberg, *World at Arms*, p. 772. On the technical details of Mark XXI U-boat, 'arguably the world's first true submarine', see Tooze, *Wages of Destruction*, p. 613.

25 Weinberg, *World at Arms*, p. 773; Tooze, *Wages of Destruction*, p. 616.

26 Overy, *Air War*, p. 120.

27 Ibid., p. 171.

28 'Economic Effects of the Air Offensive against German Cities', *United States Strategic Bombing Survey*, pp. 8–12.

29 Tooze, *Wages of Destruction*, p. 567.

30 Ibid., p. 569.

31 The Allies' great material advantages *vis-à-vis* Germany made defeat far more likely than not. See Tooze, *Wages of Destruction*.

32 Ira Eaker papers, box I: 17, 'The American Bombing Report: the United States Air Force Strikes Hard in Europe', 4 September 1943. See also memo from Alfred R. Maxwell, Director of Operations, 18 February 1945.

33 Spaatz papers, box I: 136, interview of Robert A. Lovett by Dr Bruce C. Hopper, 7 June 1945.

34 Galland, *First and Last*, p. 281.

35 Spaatz papers, box I: 135, 'Combined Intelligence Objectives Sub-Committee: Interrogation of Albert Speer – Former Minister for Armaments and War Production', p. 10.

36 UKNA, AIR 20/4229, 'Note on the Role and Work of Bomber Command', 28 June 1942.

37 Tooze, *Wages of Destruction*, pp. 621–2.

38 Although there might have been more cloud cover by day than by night. A more detailed study of historical weather reports would be needed to establish or refute this point.

39 UKNA, AIR 10/3866, *The Strategic Air War against Germany 1939–1945*, report of the British Bombing Survey Unit (1949), pp. 58–60.

40 Harris's view was neither unique nor new. As Tedder put it in the late 1920s: 'As the bombers used for the offensive are not readily interchangeable with the fighters used for the defence, and in fact cannot be efficiently used for defensive purposes, the demand for a stronger defence cannot be immediately met unless there are fighters available to be drawn from other theatres of war. Ultimately to strengthen the defences one must weaken the offence, and in such a way that it cannot quickly and easily be strengthened again. We can only increase the number of fighters by devoting a greater part of our available resources to the construction and manning of fighters in place of bombers.' Tedder papers, B 270, Lecture on 'Air Power', 6th lecture, 2 February 1928.

41 Interview with RAF pilot Sidney 'Tom' Wingham, Bury St Edmunds, 5 May 2003.

42 Harris, *Bomber Offensive*, p. 242.

43 Sebastian Cox, 'Introduction', in Harris, *Despatch on War Operations*, p. xii.

44 Quoted ibid., p. xii. Emphasis added. See also Webster and Frankland, *Strategic Air Offensive*, appendix 8, document xxii, 4:144.

45 UKNA, directive, Air Vice-Marshal Bottomley to Air Marshal JEA

Baldwin, London, 23 February 1942. Emphasis added.

46 Overy, *Bombing War*, p. 310.

47 UKNA, AIR 19/189, letter from A. W. Street to Churchill, 28 October 1943.

48 Tedder papers, B 270, lecture on 'RAF Staff Organisation', RAF Staff College, 9th lecture, 15 June 1931.

49 Ibid.

50 Spaatz papers, box I: 136, letter from Arnold to Doolittle, 2 August 1944 and letter from Arnold to Spaatz, 14 August 1944.

51 Crane, *Bombs, Cities and Civilians*, pp. 6–7.

52 UKNA, AIR 20/438, 'German Cities Closely Related to GAF Fighter Assembly Plants', 14 September 1943.

53 See UKNA, AIR 19/189, letter from Bottomley to Harris, 23 December 1943 (quoted above). See also Davis, *Bombing the European Axis Powers*, p. 275.

54 Harris, *Bomber Offensive*, p. 220.

55 UKNA, AIR 20/4832, 'Memorandum on Extent to which the Eight USAAF and Bomber command have been able to implement the GAF Plan and on further measures for its execution', 7 October 1943. In the same document, however, Air Staff complained that Hamburg and Berlin, which Harris was bombing, had little to do with the German Air Force and suggested that precision bombing again be attempted. See UKNA AIR 20/4832, 'Note: the Bomber Offensive', 30 September 1943.

56 Overy, *Bombing War*, p. 310.

57 Eaker, committed to a very different strategy, joined in the praise, although his words were cryptic enough to be something less than effusive: when Robert Lovett wrote to him stating that 'the pasting Hamburg got must have been terrific', Eaker replied that the raids indeed had 'a tremendous effect'. Both sets of quotations from Overy, *Bombing War*, p. 336.

58 Miller, *Masters of the Air*, p. 438.

59 Searle, 'It Made a Lot of Sense to Kill Skilled Workers', p. 108.

60 Overy, *Bombing War*, p. 347.

61 Davis, *Carl A. Spaatz*, p. 569.

62 Ibid.

63 Quoted Miller, *Masters of the Air*, p. 420.

64 Davis, *Carl A. Spaatz*, p. 569.

65 Miller, *Masters of the Air*, p. 420.

66 Lowe, *Inferno*, p. 333.

67 Miller, *Masters of the Air*, p. 439.

68 Tooze, *Wages of Destruction*, p. 618. Blohm's family used their connections in Berlin to have the sentence overturned.

69 Schaffer, *Wings of Judgment*, p. 103.

70 Portal papers, letter from Harris to Portal, 18 January 1945.

71 Helmut Schnatz, 'Die Zerstörung der deutschen Städte und die Opfer', in Heidenreich and Neitzel (eds.), *Der Bombenkrieg und seine Opfer*, pp. 30–46.

72 Davis, *Bombing the European Axis Powers*, p. 575.

73 *Strategic Air War Against Germany: Report of the British Bombing Survey Unit*, pp. 58–60.

74 Davis, *Bombing the European Axis Powers*, p. 571.

75 Frank, *Downfall*, p. 150–1.

76 Ibid.

77 Statistics and other details in the following two paragraphs from United States Strategic Bombing Survey (USSBS), *The Effects of Strategic Bombing on Japan's War Economy* (Washington: GPO), pp. 45–55.

78 Frank, *Downfall*, p. 294.

79 The three cities were Sapporo, Kyoto, and Nara. Ishida Yorifusa, 'Japanese Cities and Planning in the Reconstruction Period: 1945–55', in Hein et al., *Rebuilding Urban Japan*, pp. 17–49, 18.

80 See Pike, *Hirohito's War*, p. 1039.

81 Overy, *Why the Allies Won*, pp. 285–6.

BIBLIOGRAPHY

1. Interviews & eyewitness reports

Alfred Abels, DFC (RAF 102 Squadron)
Günther Ackerhans (Berlin)
Karl Heinz-Alfeis (Hamburg)
Ruth Arloth (Lübeck)
Egon Asmus (Lübeck)
Wolfgang Bardorf (Berlin)
Günther Becker (Lübeck)
Else Birth (Essen)
Irmgard Blomberg (Wuppertal)
Gerhard Böhmer (Berlin)
Auguste Brandt (Mülheim an der Ruhr)
Elke Brandt (Mülheim an der Ruhr)
Renate Brockmüller (Mülheim an der Ruhr)
Udo Bungert (Mülheim an der Ruhr)
Anneliese Burger (Essen)
Detlev Burghardt (Dresden)
Sybilla Cappius (Essen)
Oktavia Christ (Hamburg)
John B. Daniels (450th Bomb Group, Fifteenth Air Force)
Robert A. Davis (450th Bomb Group, Fifteenth Air Force)
Rita Deichmann (Lübeck)
Asmus Egon (Lübeck)
Gottfried Elfes (Krefeld)
Johann Engels (Essen)
Kurt-Rolf Engels (Wuppertal)
Gertrud Everding (Hamburg)
Erich Felgenhauer (Würzburg)
Franz Ferring (Würzburg)
Roland Flade (Würzburg)

Helmut Försch (Würzburg)

Heinrich Giesecke (Würzburg)

Walter F. Gilbert (450th Bomb Group, Fifteenth Air Force)

Walter Grave (Essen/Dresden)

Ernst-Günther Haberland (Hamburg)

Edith Hahn (Hamburg)

Christel Hansen (Mönkhagen)

Hans Heer (Würzburg)

Frau Heissing (Essen)

Rolf Hering (Lübeck)

Gertraud Hermann (Lübeck)

Emmie Heuser (Sprockhövel)

Gerhard Hickmann (Mülheim an der Ruhr)

Horst Hirche (anti-aircraft auxiliary, Berlin)

Hildegard Högner (Essen)

Volker Holtmann (Lübeck)

Martin Honecker (Würzburg)

Paul Huben (Mülheim an der Ruhr)

Ursula Huben (Mülheim an der Ruhr)

Harry Hughes, DFC, DFM (RAF 102 Squadron)

Hedi Irle (Essen)

Hermann-Josef Baum (Düsseldorf)

Marlies Jung (Krefeld)

Wolfgang Kämmerling (Krefeld)

Ernst Kahlbaü (Berlin)

Elly Kammermeier (Würzburg)

Christel Kausen (Lübeck)

Ruth Klaus (Essen)

Hans-Georg Kleine-Limberg (Essen)

Hildegard Klemm (Dresden)

Wilbur Klint (303rd Bomb Group, Eighth Air Force)

Peter Koch (Würzburg)

Frau Koglin (Berlin/Potsdam)

Heinz Kretzer (Würzburg)

Christal Krausen (Lübeck)

Gisela Kretzschmar (Mülheim an der Ruhr)

Volker Kuhlwein (Hamburg)

Gisela Kundt (Essen)

Manfred Kunze (Bad Oeynhausen)

Friedrich van Laak (Dinslaken)

Gerhard Lange (Hamburg)

Friedhelm Ludwig (Essen)

Carmen Lyken (Krefeld)

Stefan Mehren (Berlin)

Julia Meseck (Essen)

Theo Michell (forced labourer, Würzburg)

Hans-Werner Mihan (Potsdam)

Alwine Mismahl (Essen)

Ursula Mohnke (Berlin)

Ursula Müller (Essen)

Karl-Heinz Nissen (Lübeck)

Herbert Osner [formerly Oechsner] (Würzburg)

Hans Pauels (Aachen)

Hermann Paus (Essen)

Herr Pfeil (Wuppertal)

Hildegard Plum (Düsseldorf)

Stefan Pick (Cologne)

Jack Pragnell (RAF 102 Squadron)

Wilfried Reichert (Essen)

Robert Reichlin (son of Matthew A. Reichlin, US 15th Air Force)

Ellen Reinhart (Essen)

Christa Renken (Hamburg)

Marianne Richter (Würzburg)

Horst Riewer (Mülheim an der Ruhr)

Maria Rotermund (Wülfrath)

Horst Rübenkamp (Mülheim an der Ruhr)

Eleonore Rudolph (Hamburg)

Werner Schenk (Berlin)

Fritz Schleede (Hamburg)

Gusti Schmitt (Würzburg)

Ruth Schomaker (Essen)

Lisa Schomberg (Hamburg)

Gerda Schroeder (Wuppertal)

Otti Schultz (Cologne)

Anita Schwarte (Essen)

Kurt Segering (Essen)

Elfriede Sindel (Hamburg)

Hans Smits (Krefeld)

Anne-Gerd Smola (Mülheim an der Ruhr)
Edith Stampe (Hamburg)
Sigrid Strauss (Lübeck)
Hilde Stringer (Essen)
Gertrud Türk (Cologne)
Rudolf Vetter (anti-aircraft auxiliary, Berlin)
Beke Wagner (Hamburg)
Heino Weiss (Lübeck)
Helmut Wender (Essen)
Werner Wendland (Würzburg)
Heinrich Weppert (Würzburg)
Paul Werner (Essen)
Hannelore Will (Essen)
Richard Wilson (RAF 102 Squadron)
Sidney 'Tom' Wingham (RAF 102 Squadron)
Karl-Heinz Wirsing (Würzburg)
Gerde Woldeit (Essen)
Gertrud Zimner (Essen)
Paul Zsigmond (Mülheim an der Ruhr)

Archives (cited documents)

United Kingdom

Christ Church, Oxford
The Private Papers of Sir Charles Portal

Churchill College, Cambridge
Sydney Bufton papers
Winston Churchill papers

Nuffield College, Oxford
Lord Cherwell papers

The National Archives, Kew
AIR 2
AIR 8
AIR 14

AIR 19
AIR 20
AIR 25
AIR 40
AIR 41
CAB 121
PREM 3

The Royal Air Force Museum, London
Sir Arthur Tedder papers
Sir Arthur Harris papers

Germany

Historical Archives of the City of Cologne
Police reports, 1939–1945

Federal archives of Germany (Bundesarchiv), Koblenz
Photo collection

Hamburg state archives
Private papers of the Krogmann family
Police reports, 1943
Fire Brigade reports, 1943

Lübeck city archive
Materialsammlung zum Luftangriff 1942
HS 1192, 'Aufnahmen über Zerstörungen durch den Luftangriff auf Lübeck in der nacht zum 29. März 1942'
Collected newspaper clippings, March 1942 raid

Würzburg city archive
Berichte über die Angriffe im Raum Würzburg
Newspaper collections on the 16 March 1945 raid

United States

Library of Congress manuscripts collection, Washington DC

BIBLIOGRAPHY

Henry H. Arnold papers
James Doolittle papers
Ira Eaker papers
Curtis LeMay papers
Carl Spaatz papers

INDEX

fighters, Japanese, 334, 348
fighters, US
   diversionary tactics, 275
   P-38s, 223
   P-47s, 169, 223, 226–227
   P-51s, 223, 227
   strategy, 219, 220, 223
fire protection
   Germany, 18–19, 98, 267–268, 286,
     319, 349
   Japan, 349, 351, 356
'firestorm,' meaning of, 350–351
First Army Division, 366
First World War, 2, 42–43, 53, 54, 56,
   59, 80, 102
Fischer, Fritz, 2
flak guns. *see also* anti-aircraft defences
   Aalborg, 34
   Augsburg, 194–195
   Berlin, 187–189, 225, 226
   Cologne, 97
   Essen, 129
   Frankfurt, 236
   Hamburg, 157
   Japan, 334
   Lübeck, 76, 78
   manned by teenagers, 415
   oil infrastructure, 262, 266
   port towns, 96
   Ruhr valley, 132
   Schweinfurt, 181
   used on advancing troops, 415
Fort, Adrian, 5
France. *see also specific towns/cities*
   British bombing, 75, 96
Frankfurt (Germany), 103, 118, 195,
   266, 408
Freeman, Wilfrid, 46
Freiburg (Germany), 251, 286
Freisler, Roland, 318
Friedrichshafen (Germany), 138
Fritzsche, Hans, 198
Funk, Walther, 113–114

Galland, Adolf, 227, 236, 238, 295, 404
Gee apparatus, 74–75, 423

Gelsenkirchen (Germany), 129, 277,
   278, 279–280, 282
George, Harold L., 59–60
Gerhart, John, 180
German Labour Front, 113
Germans, expulsion from Eastern
   European countries, 373
Germany. *see also specific towns/cities*
   air force. *see Luftwaffe*
   aircraft production, 102–103, 139,
     163, 178, 179, 219, 417, 418
   anti-aircraft defences. *see under*
     anti-aircraft defences
   armaments production, 164–165,
     173, 181, 182
   armed forces. *see Wehrmacht*
   Berlin Olympics (1936), 107
   bombing casualties (overall esti-
     mates), 499n17
   chemical industry, 163
   declares war on US, 111
   fire protection, 18–19, 98, 267–268,
     286, 319, 349
   industrial production, 173, 416–417
   invades Netherlands, 28
   invades Poland, 27–28
   invades Soviet Union, 113
   military coup, 398, 399
   military hospitals, 340, 345
   morale. *see under* morale
   new borders, 373
   Night of Broken Glass
     (*Kristallnacht*), 101, 109, 337
   Night of the Long Knives, 101
   post-war reconstruction, 408
   Reichstag fire, 101
   shipbuilding industry, 164
   slave labour, 101, 173, 340, 404, 417
   steel production, 138–139, 164
Gibson, Guy, 131–132, 133, 134
Giesecke, Heinrich, 337, 341–342
Gilbert, Walter, 262
Giraud, Henri, 117, 119
Glasgow (Scotland), 31
Goebbels, Joseph. *see also SA*
   (*Sturmabteilung*)